Cast in Deathless Bronze

First Lieutenant Andrew Summers Rowan.

Cast in Deathless Bronze

Andrew Rowan, the Spanish-American War, and the Origins of American Empire

Donald Tunnicliff Rice

WEST VIRGINIA UNIVERSITY PRESS
MORGANTOWN 2016

Copyright 2016 West Virginia University Press
All rights reserved
First edition published 2016 by West Virginia University Press
Printed in the United States of America

24 23 22 21 20 19 18 17 16   1 2 3 4 5 6 7 8 9

ISBN:
cloth   978-1-943665-42-6
paper   978-1-943665-43-3
epub   978-1-943665-44-0
pdf   978-1-943665-45-7

Library of Congress Cataloging-in-Publication Data
is available from the Library of Congress

Cover design by Than Saffel / WVU Press.
Cover illustration by Stanley M. Arthurs.

To Sean and Seth

By the Eternal! there is a man whose form should be cast in deathless bronze and the statue placed in every college of the land. . . . The world cries out for such: he is needed and needed badly—the man who can carry a message to Garcia.

—Elbert Hubbard, "A Message to Garcia"

CONTENTS

PREFACE

In 1992 in a used-book store in Mount Vernon, Ohio, I paid a dollar for a copy of "A Message to Garcia," an essay written ninety-three years earlier by a flamboyant entrepreneur named Elbert Hubbard. I was familiar with the title and had a vague idea what it stood for—the importance of completing one's assigned task—but I'd never taken the time to read it. When I glanced through this particular copy I found two news clippings. The headline of the first read, "Message to Garcia Delivered Thirty Years Ago Today." It recounted a dangerous spying mission to Cuba taken in 1898 by First Lieutenant Andrew S. Rowan, who carried "an urgent message from President McKinley to General Garcia [who was] commanding the Cuban insurgents opposed to Spanish rule." The second clipping was Rowan's obituary, published on January 12, 1943, and it too discussed the mission, which at that point had occurred nearly forty-five years earlier. I'd like to think the person who bought this 1907 edition of the pamphlet was the same person who, years later, clipped and saved the two articles.

The inclusion of the clippings convinced me that the pamphlet, though chipped and discolored, was worth owning. When I got around to reading it, I was appalled. Hubbard was a horrible writer, on the one hand intellectually pretentious and on the other exhibiting a sneering and disdainful view of American workers. How the "preachment" (as Hubbard called his essay) could have achieved such a wide circulation was a mystery to me.

Andrew Rowan, by contrast, intrigued me, and I wanted to know more about the man. He would be, I concluded, a great biographical subject for a kids' book. At the time that's as far as I took the idea. During the next dozen years other projects intervened, but one day in an idle moment I decided to take another look at Rowan. The further I delved into his life, the more I realized that hardly a word written about him by Hubbard was true; furthermore, almost nothing written about

Rowan by anyone else was true. He was, it turned out, not a good subject for a kids' book after all but an excellent candidate for a full-length biography. From his days as a young boy during the Civil War to his death as an old man during World War II, Rowan seemed to have been everywhere and met everyone. Yet, as extraordinary as his story was, it was also representative of army officers of his day. In 1881 he traveled from the United States Military Academy at West Point to the American West to perform standard garrison duties, eventually participating in the little-known preparations for an anticipated invasion of the United States by Great Britain. This was his entrée into the world of intelligence gathering, and the experience was pivotal in his being chosen to travel to Cuba.

Most Americans know very little about the Spanish-American War (1898) other than that the battleship USS *Maine* blew up in Havana's harbor, that Commodore George Dewey said, "You may fire when you are ready, Gridley," and that Teddy Roosevelt charged up San Juan Hill. They know even less about the Philippine War (1899–1902), and nothing at all about the Moro Campaigns (1902–13). Andrew Summers Rowan as first lieutenant, captain, and major in the U.S. Army risked his life in all three conflicts. After his first tour in the Philippines he was a working cog in the machinery that transformed the army into a force capable of engaging in global war.

Hubbard's essay turned Rowan into a celebrity, so well known that even his daughter's antics were reported in the press. The mission he undertook in 1898 inspired three movies (only two of which were produced), hundreds of newspaper stories, and scores of magazine articles. People stopped him on the street and asked for his autograph. After his death he continued to be celebrated with public honors and bronze tablets. Yet most of what was said and written about Rowan was little more than a repetition of Elbert Hubbard's fanciful interpretation of his Cuban adventure.

I found Rowan to be an ideal companion as I toured the American military establishment of his time, examining the people and events surrounding his life. For over six years he provided me with an excuse to travel to Cuba, Guatemala, the Philippines, and many American cities as I visited pertinent sites and searched through libraries and archival holdings. It was an illuminating journey, and eventually I even came to understand how Hubbard's badly written essay managed to become and to remain an inspiring, if fading, piece of Americana.

And who, exactly, was the mysterious García? In the many retellings of Rowan's adventure, the emphasis is always placed on the messenger. The recipient, Calixto García Íñiguez, an intriguing character in his own right and a national hero in Cuba, receives scant attention. In this account I rectify that.

Any moment in history is better than any previous moment for engaging in research, if for no other reason than that one can build on an ever-increasing amount of scholarship by others. I'd long had an interest in the Spanish-American War and, more by chance than design, had read a number of relevant books on the subject. During the course of my writing, these works were supplemented by dozens more—some old, some newly published. Much of the material regarding Rowan's military exploits I found in the treasure houses of the National Archives and Records Administration in Washington, D.C., and College Park, Maryland, where I copied many hundreds of documents.

And although one has to be wary of anything found on the Internet, that vast reticulation led to important sources that would otherwise have gone undetected. It was through the Internet, for example, that I happened on the nine boxes and seven scrapbooks containing the Andrew Summers Rowan Papers in the Hoover Institution Library and Archives at Stanford University. The Internet also took me down dozens of trails that led nowhere; as a tool, it grows more useful and more frustrating with each passing day.

Introduction

After the explosion of the USS *Maine* in Havana's harbor on February 15, 1898, war between the United States and Spain was, as Secretary of War Russell Alger put it, "regarded by the country at large as inevitable."[1] President William McKinley and the *Maine's* captain Charles Sigsbee cautioned that judgment should be withheld about what—or perhaps more to the point, who—caused the explosion, but popular opinion, enthusiastically abetted by most newspapers, immediately settled blame on Spain.

Reporter Murat Halstead gave a more sober analysis of what had probably happened, noting that "the *Maine's* boiler-room and the magazines for the ten-inch guns and the coal bunkers, were much crowded—only a steel wall a quarter of an inch thick between the magazine and the boiler-room." Making the point that it was probably an accident, Halstead went on to note that similar incidents had occurred on other ships, and that it should be no surprise if the "Spaniards should be acquitted of the execution of a horrible plot."[2]

Few Americans were convinced of Spain's innocence, and the course of history was sealed when a naval court of inquiry concluded that a submarine mine caused the explosion. The court was unable to obtain evidence that could place the responsibility on any person or persons, but in the eyes of the Americans the matter was settled.[3] "Remember the *Maine*" was to be the battle cry in the war with Spain.

Spain was already fighting insurgent forces led by General Calixto García Íñiguez in Oriente Province, Cuba. Anticipating a U.S. invasion of the island, the War Department dispatched a forty-year-old army lieutenant, Andrew Summers Rowan, on April 8, 1898, to determine what kind of support an invading U.S. Army could expect from García's rebels.[4] It was a mission Rowan would accomplish to great acclaim.

Americans had long coveted Cuba. John Quincy Adams and Henry Clay were two of many who felt the island should be annexed by the United States. Others felt strongly that Cuba should be independent. The problem was slavery. If Cuba gained independence, its slaves would be free, and this, as Daniel Webster pointed out in 1845, would mark the end of slavery in the United States. To forestall this and, equally important, to add slave territory to the Union, members of the administration of President Franklin Pierce used Spain's improper boarding of an American ship as an excuse to obtain the island by direct purchase. In 1854 they concocted a document, popularly named the Ostend Manifesto, which stated that if Spain refused to sell Cuba, the United States would "be justified in wresting it away."[5] Henry Cabot Lodge referred to it as "a barefaced argument for conquest."[6] Spain yielded to the extortion by apologizing for the boarding incident and paying an indemnity.[7] Previous to this there were regularly occurring insurrections in Cuba, some aided by Americans. In 1851 a boatload of adventurers set sail from New Orleans to foment a revolt they hoped would lead to Cuba's becoming America's newest slave state. The islanders failed to respond as expected, and the invading force was easily defeated, resulting in the first deaths of Americans attempting to take Cuba from Spain. In the late 1850s thoughts of annexation faded as Southerners tried to keep what slave states they already had.

Cuban-American activity, however, continued. Gun running—or filibustering, as it was then called—increased greatly during a protracted ten-year insurgency that began in 1868.[8] One incident resulted in the deaths of fifty-three Americans. The administration of President Ulysses S. Grant protested strongly, even hinting at war, should appropriate action not be taken by the Spanish government. Eventually Spain agreed to release the survivors, pay indemnities to the victims' families, and punish the officer who ordered the executions.

Interest in Cuba waned somewhat during the following years, particularly after the insurgents signed a peace treaty with Spain in 1878, but many among the thousands of Cuban exiles in the United States remained active, forming revolutionary *juntas*, accumulating money, and making plans for *Cuba libre*.[9] In April 1895, the aging general Máximo Gómez, the military leader during a previous insurrection, stepped ashore to once again command the rebel Cuban forces.[10]

Over the next few months, the propaganda machine was slowly cranked up to full effect. Between Spanish censorship on the one hand, and exaggerated reports and pure fiction on the other, it was impossible to learn the truth about Cuba in most newspapers. In October 1895 William Randolph Hearst bought the *New York Evening Journal*; and as the *Evening Journal* and the *New York World* battled for circulation, the truth became even more elusive. Among the vivid accounts of battles that never took place there were descriptions of murder and torture that never happened, and reports of machete-wielding Cuban Amazons that never existed.[11] For the most part the American public savored the diet of bombast and outright lies it was being fed.

Not that Spain wasn't deserving of nearly all the condemnation it received. For centuries the Spanish had a reputation for cruelty among indigenous peoples in the Americas. In his book *Incredible Voyage*, Tristan Jones repeats a Guarani legend concerning a treacherous young warrior who asks a medicine woman to turn him into a jaguar so he might be even more treacherous. This she does, and he enjoys terrorizing the forest until the day he is outwitted by a fox. He then asks her to be turned into a fox, and he enjoys killing small creatures until the day a snake slithers from his grasp. Then he asks to become a snake, which he remains until he is stung by a wasp. He returns to the medicine woman and asks to be made into a creature more ferocious than a jaguar, more cunning than a fox, more deceitful than a snake, and more vicious than a wasp. The witch turns him into a Spaniard.[12]

Like every imperial nation before and after, Spain engaged in whatever ruthless action it deemed necessary to maintain its stolen property. As Halstead wrote, "It has seemed that in proportion as the Spanish have lost their colonies their passion for Cuba grew, until latterly Spain has seemed to live and die for the island."[13] In early 1896 General Valeriano Weyler—"the Butcher" as the American press called him—was assigned the task of putting down the rebellion. At a time when physiognomy was all the rage, writers tried to outdo one another in describing Weyler's evil visage. Here is a choice example written by the newspaper correspondent Elbert Rappleye:

> Black eyes, black hair, black beard, dark, exceedingly dark complexion, a plain black attire, black shoes, black tie, a very dirty shirt and soiled standing collar, with no jewelry, and not a relief from the aspect of darkness anywhere on his person.... [H]is eyes far apart, bright, alert, and striking, took me in at a glance. His face seemed to run to chin, his lower jaw protruding far beyond any ordinary indication of firmness, persistence, or willpower. His nose is aquiline, bloodless, and obtrusive. Inferior physically, unsoldierly in bearing, exhibiting no trace of refined sensibilities, nor pleasure in the gentle associations that others live for, he is nevertheless, the embodiment of mental acuteness, crafty, unscrupulous, fearless, and of indomitable perseverance.[14]

One of Weyler's harsher policies was to gather the entire rural population of the four western provinces into concentration camps. His soldiers then killed their livestock and burned crops and buildings.[15] Thousands of *reconcentrados* died of starvation and disease. Conditions were so severe that McKinley asked for permission to send food and medicine. In December 1897 he anonymously subscribed $5,000 to the relief fund that financed the aid.[16]

Redfield Proctor was a well-connected and respected Republican senator from Vermont and former secretary of war under Benjamin Harrison.[17] For some time he had sympathized with the Cuban revolutionaries, and in early 1898 he considered traveling to the island to see for himself what was going on. In the company of Clara Barton, Proctor made three excursions to outlying areas. On his return he was pressed to speak to the full Senate regarding what he had observed.[18]

He read from a written account on March 17, 1898, speaking in his usual dry tones in clear, expository language. After explaining how and why he'd gone to Cuba, he said,

It is not peace, it is not war. It is desolation and distress, misery and starvation. . . . There are no domestic animals or crops on the rich fields and pastures except such as are under guard in the immediate vicinity of the towns. In other words, the Spanish hold in [the] four western provinces just what their army sits on. Every man, woman and child, and every domestic animal, wherever their columns have reached, is under guard and within so-called fortifications. . . .

Their huts are about ten to fifteen feet in size, and for want of spaces are usually crowded together very closely. They have no floor but the ground, no furniture, and, after a year's wear, but little clothing except such stray substitutes as they can extemporize; and with large families, or more than one, in this little space, the commonest sanitary provisions are impossible. Conditions are unmentionable in this respect. Torn from their homes, with foul earth, foul air, foul water, and foul food or none, what wonder that one-half have died and that one-quarter of the living are so diseased that they cannot be saved? A form of dropsy is a common disorder resulting from these conditions. Little children are still walking about with arms and chests terribly emaciated, eyes swollen, and abdomen bloated to three times the natural size. The physicians say these cases are hopeless. . . . I went to Cuba with a strong conviction that the picture had been overdrawn; that a few cases of starvation and suffering had inspired and stimulated the press correspondents, and that they had given free play to a strong, natural and highly cultivated imagination. . . . Before starting out I received through the mail a leaflet published by the *Christian Herald*, with cuts of some of the sick and starving *reconcentrados*, and took it with me, thinking these must be rare specimens, put up to make the worst possible showing. I saw plenty as bad and worse; many that should not be photographed and shown.[19]

He went on to give what was probably a clearer picture of the economic, social, and military conditions of the island than any of his fellow senators had heard or read up to that point.

While Proctor was in Cuba seeing the results of Weyler's reconcentration, Hearst's *Journal* was describing Weyler for its readers: "There is nothing to prevent his carnal, animal brain from running riot with itself in inventing tortures and infamies of bloody debauchery."[20] Those who considered this to be a rant had their minds changed by Proctor's speech, which was widely quoted. In fact, the speech was at the time—and still today—considered the final nudge that pushed the United States into war with Spain.[21] There were a few who were not moved by Proctor's speech—in particular, Representative Thomas Brackett Reed, the powerful leader of the House who was strongly opposed to war. Without having to mention that Proctor had gotten rich quarrying Vermont marble, an enterprise he still controlled, Reed noted that a war "will make a large market for gravestones."[22]

In spite of Hearst's alleged cable to Frederic Remington in Havana—"You furnish the pictures and I'll furnish the war"—he and his fellow yellow journalists did not cause the war.[23] They did, however, help create an atmosphere that permitted the realpolitik of the era to prevail.[24] Spain had long ceased to be among the ranking nations of the world, and the remnants of its empire were, in effect, up for grabs.[25] It was not in the interest of the United States to have Spain supplanted in the Caribbean by a stronger European power; sooner or later a canal was going to be built across the Isthmus of Panama, and whoever controlled the Caribbean was going to control traffic through the canal. There had been "canal fever" for some years; even though the French attempt in 1889 had failed, Americans were sure they could complete the task once they set their minds to it.

Germany was considered a strong contender for Spain's Caribbean holdings, particularly in light of Chancellor Bernard von Bülow's speech to the Reichstag in which he said, "We do not wish to put anyone into the shade, but we demand a place for ourselves in the sun."[26] There was only so much sun to go around, and an increased amount for Germany would surely dim other countries' shares. Other governments watched with disquietude as Admiral Alfred von Tirpitz built up the German Navy.[27] Estimates of Germany's military organization—regulars and reserves—that could be put on a war footing at that time was 9 percent of its total population, or a formidable 4,700,000 men.[28] A German presence in Latin America could not be tolerated. As Theodore Roosevelt noted, "with Germany, under the Kaiser, we may at any time have trouble if she seeks to acquire territory in South America."[29] Ironically, Kaiser Wilhelm II was strongly influenced in his expansionist thinking, as was Roosevelt, by American navy captain Alfred Thayer Mahan. Mahan argued in his 1890 book *The Influence of Sea Power on History* that a nation's security depended on its naval strength; that sea power at that time could be supported only by distant coaling ports; and that once the flag was planted in foreign colonies, trade and prosperity would follow.[30] Wilhelm wrote, "I am just now not reading but devouring Captain Mahan's book; and am trying to learn it by heart. . . . It is on board all my ships and constantly quoted by my Captains and Officers."[31]

As much as he bought into Mahan's arguments, Wilhelm had no interest in the Caribbean—other island groups, yes, but not the Antilles.[32] Unaware of his lack of interest in Cuba, military and political leaders in the United States believed preventive measures were necessary; they wanted to make sure that the Caribbean would be free not only of Europeans but of Cuban dominance. There were many in and out of government who were uncomfortable with the possibility that the Cuban revolution might succeed. They did not want Cubans ruling their own nation, because such a development would probably not be in the best interests of American businessmen or wealthy Cubans. And as William J. Calhoun, a judge appointed by McKinley to survey the Cuban situation, pointed out, there was always the danger of black domination of an independent Cuba.[33] The Cuban newspaper *El Pais* offered another explanation, charging that because Liberia failed to attract American blacks in large numbers, the United States wanted to acquire Cuba as a site for their relocation.[34] For many reasons, but chiefly because of the expansionists who were eager to increase America's territorial influence in the world, the United States headed inexorably for war with Spain.

And so, on April 8, 1898, fifteen days before the United States officially declared war on Spain, Lieutenant Andrew S. Rowan was dispatched to Cuba to learn what he could about the Spanish troops, the Cuban revolutionary army that had been fighting the Spanish, and the lay of the land.

CHAPTER 1

"It Is Meritorious to Be a Boy at West Point"

Cannons fired, bombs burst, and rockets glared. The scene lacked only Francis Scott Key to describe it. It was a few minutes after midnight on January 1, 1880, and the cadets at the United States Military Academy at West Point were celebrating the new year in a noisy and unauthorized fashion. A barrage from the thirty-two-pound cannons on Trophy Square was accompanied by the firing of rockets and Roman candles from the barracks windows. When senior officers tried to stop the pandemonium, they discovered all the doors to the barracks were locked, making it impossible to enter in order to put an end to the pyrotechnic eruptions. This was no spontaneous skylarking, but a carefully planned and executed maneuver under the command of fourth-year cadets, perhaps inspired in part by their course that year, Practical Pyrotechny.[1] It was both cocking a snoot at the academy's discipline and a perfect example of the effectiveness of that discipline. An investigation was later carried out, but little came of it. One has to suspect that the superintendent, Major General John Schofield, had to admire such a carefully planned military campaign in which there were no casualties.[2]

When Andrew Summers Rowan entered the academy in 1877, three years before the riotous New Year's Eve celebration, it was in its seventy-fifth year of existence. Except for those occasions when they were being studied under the magnifying glasses of the Board of Visitors, Rowan and the other cadets acted like all young college men of their time; otherwise, how was one to account for the 9,099 demerits the fifty-four men of Rowan's class of 1881 accumulated in their last two years at the academy? Rowan, with 142 demerits, had fewer than the average of 168.5.[3] In a fictional account of West Point set at the very time of Rowan's enrollment there, Williston Fish, a classmate, discusses the conflict between the outer soldier and the inner boy, noting, "It is meritorious to be a boy at West Point, which is a school of hard studies, hard drills, and hard traditions of control where generation after generation maintains all sorts of far-fetched hardships. It is the military idea that the good soldier must be miserable. He is given a heavy helmet, useless against rain or shine, a stiff stock, a position like that of a clothing-house dummy, and marched stiff-footed down the corridors of time, looking neither left nor right."[4] There was a nineteenth-century innocence to many of their recreations. In a later memoir, Fish recalled a fall day when he, Rowan, and two other cadets went a-nutting, of all things, and Rowan stood amid the autumnal splendor reciting a poem or speech—a scene unimaginable a hundred years later.[5]

Rowan, a West Virginian and the son of a respected politician, fit in well with this company of young men. Fish went so far as to write that the other cadets "loved Rowan very much. From the beginning he was called Corp and it was a title of great honor and affection. I suppose he was first called Corp by some nick-name genius in our class, because he stood up so straight and trim, and seemed in a modest way to be equal to all occasions. As he was." Fish gives this picture of Rowan:

> He was 5′ 7-1/2″; of light weight, perhaps 130 pounds; trim, boyish. He was not round and cylindrical as some are, but he was wide at the shoulders, and thence going tapering down. I do not think he was particularly muscular or that he cared for athletic sports. His face was not so far from round, but with great character and individuality, so that never have we seen anyone like Rowan. His eyes were blue, his forehead rather high, just high enough for symmetry, and perhaps his most pronounced feature was his Roman nose, maybe like that of Cervantes. His hair was brown.[6]

The new cadets, not a particularly sophisticated lot, were earnest young men whose lives were going to be changed irrevocably by their experiences at West Point. During Rowan's second year, a writer described the entering class as a "crowd of raw-boned, green, gaping specimens of young humanity." They may have entered raw-boned, but those who survived the four years were considered to be officers and gentlemen, and this may account for the mistaken impression of elitism. As one contemporary observer put it, "If honesty and truthfulness be 'aristocratic,' West Point is very aristocratic."[7] The academy's setting also lent an air of elitism. Summer mansions, those gilded lilies of the last quarter of the nineteenth century, overlooked the Hudson River in the vicinity of the academy, and a summer visitor in 1878 noted that the cadets gave balls to which they issued invitations to guests at nearby Cozzens' Hotel, owned by Mrs. Pierpont Morgan, "a favorite resort of wealthy and exclusive New-Yorkers."[8] This would explain the extraordinary charges totaling $995.40 against the cadets' accounts in 1877 for dancing lessons.[9]

On active duty in the U.S. Army, West Pointers were exemplars of proper behavior, no doubt a result of their training at the academy. In a study examining the military careers of all 2,826 graduates through 1878, only thirty-eight had been dismissed from the service for misconduct—drunkenness, neglect of duty, misapplication of funds, cowardice (one), and a dozen other examples of unbecoming behavior.[10] Few other professions can demonstrate such a level of probity.

Even though Rowan didn't quite shine at West Point, he applied himself with sufficient diligence to graduate forty-second out of a class of fifty-four. In his fourth year he ranked forty-fourth in engineering, forty-second in law, fiftieth in Spanish, thirty-ninth in ordinance and gunnery, and twentieth in discipline (knowledge of rules and regulations of conduct).[11]

Upon graduation he returned to his home in West Virginia, where he was mailed his commission as a second lieutenant in the army. On July 4, 1881, he swore and signed his oath of office before the clerk of the circuit court of Monroe County. This being a holiday, he must have made special arrangements in order for the clerk to be available. He mailed his oath to the office of the adjutant general of the army that same day.[12]

As a newly minted second lieutenant, Rowan had few options. After the Civil War the million-man army was eventually reduced to 25,000, occasionally reaching 28,000. Of that number, 2,100 or so were commissioned officers. Hundreds of Civil War officers stayed on, many of them having attained high rank during the war—ranks in many cases they were forced to relinquish in order to escape being returned to civilian life. George Armstrong Custer, for example, was a major general at the end of the war but a lieutenant colonel ten years later at Little Bighorn.[13] And of these officers, many grew old and often useless and did not always welcome the fresh young faces from the military academy. It was the practice at the time for promotions to first lieutenant and captain to occur only within a regiment. If old-timers stayed put, so did those beneath them. Sometimes only a calamity could provide opportunities for advancement, as when Custer was killed at the Battle of Little Bighorn in 1876, along with fifteen other officers, thereby creating opportunities for promotion in the Seventh Cavalry.[14]

By the time Rowan entered active service, the army wasn't particularly busy. Reconstruction duties in the South were virtually over, and in the West the army's chief duty seems to have been chasing trespassers off Indian and government lands, far from any population centers.[15] As Archibald Forbes, a well-known British war correspondent of the period, noted regarding the apparent absence of a standing army in the United States, "Of no nation which maintains a standing army are the troops so little *en evidence* as are those of the United States. . . . I had spent a whole winter in the United States, and traveled over two-thirds of them; but I could not remember that during that time I had seen a corporal's guard of the regular army. . . . By far the larger proportion of the American army is on service westward of the Missouri River." He pointed out that the military prison at Fort Leavenworth held five hundred prisoners—2 percent of the entire army—and that 90 percent of those imprisoned were being punished for desertion. It must be said that these accounted for only those few deserters who had been caught.[16] In the first three years of Rowan's commission, an average 3,664 enlisted men deserted each year—16 percent of the enlisted personnel.[17]

Many causes were suggested: "too much manual labor; deficiency and lack of variety in food; desire to obtain higher wages; unhealthiness of station; indebtedness to the Government for outfits issued upon enlistment; intemperance and dissolution."[18] In addition to recruiters doing a poor job of screening out misfits, soldiers were treated poorly by the very system that should have given them support. Their uniforms were totally unsuited for the task, and issued with no consideration to size; the soldiers themselves had to pay the cost of alteration, a charge that was taken from their meager pay. The woolen shirts were too warm for summer, too cold for winter, and in any event quickly wore out. The stiff and uncomfortable regulation shoes were held together with brass screws that added to the discomfort and conducted heat and cold. No matter where they were stationed—in New Mexico or the Dakota Territory—the clothing didn't vary. Those spending winters in the North had no overcoats, and those spending summers in the South wore unsuitable headgear. In nearly every category that one can imagine, the men were deprived of the most ordinary creature comforts: the food was terrible, and the diet not balanced; living quarters were shoddily built, infested with vermin, and without plumbing; medical and dental care was provided by incompetent and poorly trained hospital stewards; there were no provisions for recreation; and, particularly in the West, garrison life was tedious, lonely, and boring. On top of everything else, enlisted men were mistreated by noncommissioned and commissioned officers alike.[19] The wonder is that the desertion rate wasn't closer to 100 percent. Another discouraging factor for long-term enlistment was the lack of opportunity for advancement. In 1881, Rowan was one of sixty newly commissioned second lieutenants. Of those, fifty-two were military academy graduates, seven were civilian appointees, and one was promoted out of the ranks.[20]

Adding to the desertion rate were the many men who used the army for their own purposes: to secure transportation out West or to obtain temporary living quarters. And in the days before Social Security numbers and fingerprints, some saw the army as a door they could enter and exit at will, reenlisting and deserting whenever it suited them. General Oliver O. Howard, who was commander of the Department of the Platte in 1883,[21] gained some undeserved notoriety when he was understood to recommend that deserters be branded with a hot iron.

He had intended, he later explained, to recommend that convicted deserters be marked indelibly, as with a discreet tattoo, so they might be prevented from reenlisting.[22]

This is the military world into which Rowan was plunged, but it was at a time when a sincere reform movement was finally taking hold. One small but significant change that year was providing isolated army posts with kerosene lamps instead of candles. It must be remembered that civilians in the 1880s were enjoying not only gaslight but also electric lights. One writer called the provision of kerosene lamps the "most memorable fact" of the year for the troops. "The change from the *régime* of candles to that of coal-oil lamps means a difference in comfort, in a home-like halo for garrison quarters, and even in morality, such as can hardly be imagined by dwellers under gas and the electric light." General Montgomery C. Meigs noted that with just this tiny improvement in their lives the men could "spend more time in rational amusement and less time at the suttler's store, at the grog shops, and in the guard-house."[23] Meigs was quartermaster general in 1881 and, in that capacity, had been equipping and supplying the army for nearly fifteen years.[24] It's a pity he hadn't used his powerful position to correct this defect much earlier.

CHAPTER 2

Becoming an Intelligence Officer

First assignments for cadets graduated from the United States Military Academy at West Point were determined in part by class rank, the most desirable being that of the engineers. There followed, in order of preference, the artillery, cavalry, and infantry branches.[1] Considering Rowan's rank of forty-two out of fifty-four in his class, there was little doubt as to which branch he would become connected. His first assignment was with the Fifteenth Infantry Regiment at Fort Bliss, near El Paso in the westernmost corner of Texas.[2] After buying his uniforms and other necessary items, and after visiting with his family, Rowan set out;[3] fortunately, the Southern Pacific Railroad had been extended to El Paso earlier that year. It was here on September 26, 1881, that Andrew S. Rowan assumed his first duties as a second lieutenant in the U.S. Army. For the next few years he was bounced from one post to another, eventually being stationed at Fort Pembina in the far northeast corner of what was to became North Dakota.

A look at a map of nineteenth-century army forts shows a surprising two hundred or so dots scattered throughout the West.[4] The government was continuously being asked for more and more posts as settlers advanced the frontier in all directions. Rather than have numerous small posts, the War Department would have preferred larger garrisons, and fewer of them. Charles M. Conrad, secretary of war under President Franklin Pierce,[5] told Congress that having a multiplicity of small posts was a "more than doubtful policy." It was not only unreasonably expensive and inefficient, but the dispersion of the forces invited aggression.[6] Yet the pressure of the settlers overcame the inclinations of the War Department. Although the ostensible purpose of the army's presence was to control the Indians, many officers believed this was merely an excuse for stationing soldiers in order to provide a source of income for the white settlers. Some officers felt their purpose was to protect the Indians from the more predatory whites, rather than vice versa. At times, "Indian scares" were generated by speculators, ranchers, and farmers who urged the government to establish permanent garrisons in their neighborhoods. In a frontier economy operating on barter and promissory notes, any hard cash was welcome, and the soldiers were paid in gold (and later, silver). But it wasn't merely the miserable pay of a hundred enlisted men they sought. True, saloons and houses of prostitution, called "hog farms," quickly sprang up, but the real value in having a military post nearby was the lucrative business it gave to the contractors who constructed and supplied the forts. Enormous amounts were spent on materials, labor, and transportation. The hard labor was often provided by the soldiers themselves, who earned pennies a day, while the skilled, good-paying jobs went to civilians. And once the posts were built, provisioning them with food, fuel, horses, and other supplies became an ongoing enterprise that created many fortunes.[7] There were cases when a settlement's population increased to the point where Indian raids were quite unlikely; citizens then urged the government to move the troops to the new frontier where danger still existed. This was not necessarily an expression of the locals' concern for distant pioneers. Army reservations were extensive; they needed land to provide vegetables for the soldiers, hay for their horses, and woodlots for fuel. When troops moved out, they left substantial buildings and many acres of land behind, usually in choice locations. Speculators and settlers quickly moved in.[8]

The town of Pembina, about a mile south of the forty-ninth parallel that forms the border between the United States and Canada, began as a fur trading post in 1797.[9] To the consternation of the locals, the fort was situated on the Red River, twenty-nine miles from the village, but in a place best suited to the army's purposes. There was good land for vegetable gardens, pasturage, and hay. Nearby was an excellent woodlot. In all, the reservation extended over three square miles. It was a typical fort of the period and had 220-by-386-foot parade grounds with a flagpole in the center, bordered on three sides by frame buildings.

On the south side were four two-story officers' quarters. Each had a parlor, sitting room, dining room, and kitchen on the ground floor. Upstairs were two large bedrooms and one small bedroom. Across the way were the enlisted men's barracks. These were two long buildings with eight-foot-wide porches extending their lengths. Each barracks was divided by plastered walls into four squad rooms and two orderly rooms. At the west end of the grounds were the hospital and a storehouse. Other buildings beyond these included two kitchens, a bakery, a guardhouse, stables (with fifty-six stalls), and a magazine (the only building constructed of brick). In appearance the fort was quite as boring as one would expect. The original plans called for the buildings to be surrounded by a log palisade, but period photos and drawings don't show one. In spite of what we see in the movies, most forts were not surrounded by stockades because warring Indians simply weren't inclined to attack armed soldiers on their home turf.[10]

The officer corps was so small in those days that Rowan and his former classmates inevitably ran into one another. In the early summer of 1887, Williston Fish took a small company of recruits from Fort Snelling in Minnesota to Pembina. This was his and Rowan's first sighting of one another since their graduation six years earlier. With Fish and company taking advantage of the opportunity to stay a few days, he and Rowan spent much of their time reminiscing about the "files [cadets] and bringing all of West Point . . . back around us again." One evening at retreat, the fort's commanding officer read a long and tedious order. A first lieutenant later "sneered at the order in healthy subaltern fashion" and went on to refer to the officer as "the man of war."[11] This reference to Falstaff was particularly appropriate considering the size of the "K.O."[12] Rowan then admitted that during the reading of the order he had said to himself, "leave thy vain bibble babble" (the fool's words to Malvolio in *Twelfth Night*). Shakespearean allusions under these circumstances were not as unlikely as one might first suppose. As Fish reported, "Pembina . . . was a little, quiet, two-or-three-company post, situated . . . in the midst of an illimitable plain. Even in summer time it was all by itself except for the mail, and in the winter the mail was cut off. Corp told me that in the winter they read Shakespeare a great deal—that is a few of them. He was all full of

Shakespeare—for it was only June and the long, deep northern winter was just over." And as Fish noted on other occasions, Rowan had a good memory for literary pieces and, with only the slightest encouragement, would launch into a recitation. Fish thoroughly enjoyed his short visit and remarked that Rowan's appearance was little changed from their days at West Point. One thing was different: "At Pembina he had an infinity of time to be himself."[13]

Fort Pembina was, in fact, a two-company post at the time Fish visited, with enlisted men and officers divided between Companies B and I. Rowan was in Company I, sometimes serving as its commander. With so few commissioned officers having to fill a specified number of positions, they wore various hats. Rowan's officially designated role was post topographical officer, but—depending on who had been transferred out or was enjoying a leave of absence—he also served as post adjutant, acting signal officer, acting assistant quartermaster, post treasurer, superintendent of post schools, and range officer.[14] He wasn't quite as multicommissioned as Gilbert and Sullivan's Pooh-Bah, but at times approached it.

Daily life at a frontier post followed a prescribed routine, from the 5:30 A.M. reveille to taps being played anywhere from 8:15 to 9:45 P.M., depending on the season of the year. The officers probably relished their additional duties as a way of passing the time. Between the daily rituals the enlisted men performed whatever work was necessary to maintain life. Much of this involved keeping nature at bay, cleaning, disinfecting, and hauling garbage. They tended the vegetable gardens and cut wood for heat—until, at Fort Pembina, they eventually denuded the banks of the Red River, following which the fort purchased wood for fuel. In winter they cut ice on the river, storing it for use as water during the summer months. And until 1887, when a water main was built from the river, soldiers hauled barrels of water by wagon to the fort, where it was stored in cisterns—not a favorite job. As the writer Captain Charles King noted in one of his authentically drawn army novels set on the frontier, "Our truest heroes are those who bear with equanimity the heat and burden of the long monotonous round of garrison life with its petty tyrannies, exactions, exasperations, and bear them without break or murmur."[15] The climate didn't help. Once in early May, Rowan wrote, "The weather is becoming most uncomfortably hot and if I hate anything worse than a Dakota winter, it is a Dakota summer."[16]

To break the tedium, troops sometimes went on maneuvers, traveling up to twenty miles into the countryside for a night or two where they practiced their tent pitching, field cooking, and other bivouacking skills. At times the post commander might have his men assist the local authorities to deal with rowdies and criminals.

There was also limited social life. Soldiers could and did visit the saloons in Pembina and also drank alcoholic beverages, often to excess, on the post. Life for the local citizens in such an isolated area was not all that exciting, and they joined with the soldiers in having parties and balls. Such fraternization sometimes resulted in marriages, though there were never enough single women to satisfy the need. Then there were religious services, music classes, sports, and the Emerson Encyclic Literary Society. Yet none of this slowed down a fairly high rate of desertion.[17]

Although there were actions against Indians in the Dakota Territory during the late 1880s,[18] and the last major battle at Wounded Knee wouldn't occur until December 1890,[19] no guns were ever fired in anger by those stationed at Fort Pembina.[20] Any such experiences for Rowan occurred during other postings. He told of one occasion in which he participated in a summer-long campaign that was considered a great success. Accordingly, the grateful merchants in a nearby town put on a grand banquet for the officers. Though the haughty commanding officer thought it presumptuous of merchants to make such an offer, in light of the fort's public position he reluctantly decided that the soldiers had no choice but to attend. The merchants laid out an abundant spread of food and drink in the soldiers' honor, and the thirsty military men tossed down glass after glass during an evening of endless speeches by their hosts. Finally it was time for the major to make an answering address, and much to the delight of his junior officers, he made a drunken ass out of himself.

Because there were few confrontations with Indians during this period in the West, the principal job of post surgeons was treating illnesses.[21] Fort Pembina saw few serious problems—the occasional case of scarlet fever, diphtheria, smallpox, and the like, but no epidemics. These were easy enough to prevent, because at first news of any such problems in the area the surgeon quarantined the post.[22] And because there was no better medical facility for many hundreds of miles to which a patient might be transferred, the ambulance wagon was used more for recreational than medical purposes. A favorite ambulance jaunt for Rowan was across the border into Winnipeg to buy reasonably priced English-made clothes that were easily smuggled back without having to pay duty; he took one such trip with his old pal, Williston Fish. And it must have been in Winnipeg that he bought a pair of patent leather shoes. While these might seem impractical in a Dakota winter he made the decision, he said, after more study than "a man generally gives to choosing a wife." They were cheaper than ordinary leather shoes, he noted, because they didn't require the cost and effort involved in polishing.[23] In 1887 he actually made the fateful decision to choose a wife.

To understand the circuitous route by which Rowan met and married Miss Ida M. Symns, one has to go back to his birth on April 23, 1857, in Monroe County, West Virginia. Andrew was the first of three children born to John and Virginia Rowan. He was followed by a sister, Elizabeth Virginia (b. 1859) known as Betty, and a brother, John (b. 1862). As happened far too often in that period, his mother died shortly after delivering John.

A little more than two years later, in June 1864, his father married Sue Tiffany, a Confederate widow. As a result of the marriage, young Andrew and his two siblings acquired a younger stepsister, Mary Ann Tiffany, who was known as Nannie. Nannie later provided a rare description of Andrew as a boy, noting that

> he stands out in my childish memory as a lordly and awful being, who somehow hypnotized us younger ones into doing his will. We would roam the woods gathering berries or chestnuts—my stepsister Betty and I, and several pick ninnies—and when we came home with our pailful, Andrew would offer to divide them for us.

His way of dividing was to say: "Here's one for Nannie and one for me; one for Betty and one for me"—and so on till he took half of all we had gathered. I don't know why we let him do it![24]

Rowan's future in-laws, Andrew and Elizabeth Symns, both natives of Monroe County, had a connection with Nannie. Andrew Symns, known universally as A. B., had traveled west in 1853 to seek his fortune. After establishing himself in the grocery business in Doniphan, Kansas, he returned to Monroe County to marry his childhood sweetheart, Elizabeth. In time he moved the business to Atchison, Kansas, and became one of the largest wholesale grocers in the West.

Elizabeth happened to be an aunt of Rowan's stepsister Nannie on her father's side. Eighteen years after accompanying A. B. to Kansas, she went back to West Virginia for a visit. While there she took a liking to her young niece, who was the same age as her daughter Ida, and invited her to visit them in Kansas for a few months. There was no problem with Nannie's getting away; John Rowan had taken her and Betty out of school the previous year. As far as he could see, the two teenage girls were interested only in boys, and there was no point wasting money on an education.

Nannie loved Kansas. People came there with no known past and thus were solely judged by the way they acted when they arrived. There was no snobbery concerning social status, and a shopgirl could be as respectable as the banker's daughter. Furthermore, Kansans weren't persnickety about such innocent diversions as playing the piano on Sunday or carrying your knitting when you went visiting. Near the end of her stay, Nannie met the Aldersons, another transplanted West Virginia family. She was not impressed with their son, Walt, a handsome and irrepressible young man who'd run away to Texas to be a cowboy at age thirteen, but she ended up marrying him a few years later, and the couple left for Montana to start a cattle ranch.[25]

It may have been Nannie who made the suggestion that Rowan visit her aunt's family in Atchison, or it might have been Elizabeth Symns who extended the invitation after learning that the nice young man she'd met in West Virginia ten years earlier was now an army lieutenant stationed some six hundred miles almost due north. It's even possible the invitation was extended by A. B. himself, who was a friend and exact contemporary of John Rowan. By the late 1880s, A. B. had some thirty salesmen traveling throughout the West, and there is a good possibility that Fort Pembina was one of his accounts.[26] Traversing the distance between the two cities wouldn't be difficult. The town of St. Vincent, Minnesota, across the Red River from Pembina, was a railroad center where the Canadian Pacific joined a branch of the St. Paul and Pacific, and this line could be ridden to Minneapolis. From there train travel was possible in every direction. Rowan was granted a one-month leave of absence in August 1886, and this is when he first traveled to Atchison, where he met A. B.'s daughter Ida.[27]

They must have gotten along famously, because eight months later Mr. and Mrs. Symns issued wedding invitations.[28] The couple was married at 5:00 on the evening of April 12, 1887, in the First Presbyterian Church of Atchison. It was, according to "experienced wedding-goers, . . . a 'pretty wedding,'" the church having been tastefully decorated with roses and lilies of the valley by Miss Symns's young lady friends. The organist, one Professor Heck who came up from Topeka for the occasion, was considered to have played the wedding march with "great brilliancy." Among the crowd inside the church occupying reserved pews were the Friday Afternoon Club and the Sunday school class of which Miss Symns had been the teacher. Rowan chose to wear civilian clothes, no doubt smuggled into the country from Winnipeg, and the bride wore a dark blue traveling suit. Immediately after the ceremony, they were driven to the Union depot where they departed on a honeymoon trip to Chicago. From there they would travel to Pembina.[29] Andrew was a few days short of being thirty; Ida was twenty-four.

Life for the couple apparently passed routinely enough, and the following November Ida returned home for a two-month visit with her family. During her trip back to Pembina, a severe winter storm in northern Minnesota left a huge snowdrift that blocked the tracks for two days. The wait was particularly boring for Ida as the only woman passenger. It was made worse by a shortage of food and the fact that she had but one book to read. It was a cookbook she'd purchased in St. Paul, and she feared to read it lest it make her hungrier still.[30]

Rowan soldiered on in dreary Fort Pembina, his life now enlivened by Ida's presence. Yet it was during her first absence from him that—perhaps because he was bored, or saw an opportunity for advancement, or simply felt a sense of duty—he took his first step on the road to becoming a famous international spy.

Although seldom remembered today, there was a period in the last third of the nineteenth century when a great deal of animosity existed between the United States and Great Britain; to some there appeared a real potential for armed conflict. In answer to those who thought that the two nations couldn't possibly engage in war, an army captain writing in the *Journal of the Military Service Institution of the United States* pointed out that "we are not any more nearly related to England now, than we were in 1776 or 1812, and . . . there are still questions between us which are very far from settlement."[31]

The situation began to have an edge in the early 1860s when a newly built screw steamer, identified only as *290*, left Liverpool on a trial run and never returned. It sailed instead for a rendezvous off the Azores where its new captain, the Confederate officer Ralph Semmes, took command. Delivered by a separate ship were guns, ammunition, and fuel. Down went the British Union Jack and up went the Stars and Bars. The renamed CSS *Alabama*, with Semmes and his crew of foreign sailors (save some officers, there was not a Southerner among them[32]), terrorized Yankee shipping for more than two years until it was sunk by the USS *Kearsage* outside the three-mile limit off Cherbourg, France. A souvenir pictorial plate was issued to celebrate the sinking, and its caption clearly showed where Unionists placed the blame: "The rebel pirate *Alabama*, built in an English yard of English oak, armed with English guns, manned by an English crew, and sunk in the English Channel."[33]

The CSS *Alabama* and its English-built sister ships, the *Shenandoah* and the *Florida*, were responsible for the loss of millions of dollars in U.S. shipping. The United States held Great Britain responsible for having violated the laws of neutrality and demanded $19,021,000 in damages. Without admitting any wrongdoing, "Her Majesty's Government, in order to evince its desire of strengthening the friendly relations between the two countries," agreed to submit the claims to arbitration.[34] The following year the arbitration board awarded the United States $15,500,000 in gold.[35]

This wasn't the first, nor the last, of late nineteenth-century tensions between the two countries—especially as regarded Canada. In fact, it was the fear of being annexed forcefully or otherwise by the United States that caused delegates from the British North American provinces to hold the initial conference in 1864 that eventually led to their legal confederation in 1867. The North American Act passed by the British Parliament became operational on July 1 of that year and is still celebrated today as Dominion Day.[36]

Dozens of other issues, large and small, contributed to the ill will: fishing and sealing rights, border disputes, navigation questions, import duties, trade regulations, infected cattle, migration, belligerent Indians, railroad traffic, extradition of fugitives, copyright laws—the list goes on and on.[37] As issues were resolved, new ones arose.[38] The seriousness of these accumulated disagreements has to be understood to make sense of the great attention paid by the U.S. military to the northern border.

Partly in response to this situation, Adjutant General Richard C. Drum established what would later come to be known as the Military Information Division (MID),[39] its primary mission being to gather information about Canada. In a confidential memo, he directed commanders of military posts near the border to select officers known for their "tact and ability" to reconnoiter Canadian territory in order to compile an accurate military map of the region.[40]

Rowan, who at this time was fulfilling the role of post topographical officer at Fort Pembina,[41] was quick to volunteer for reconnaissance service in Canada. As proof of his suitability, his "Battle-fields of the Canadian North-west Territories" had recently been published as the lead article in the highly regarded *Journal of the Military Service Institution of the United States*. In it he described the geography, flora, lines of communication, and history of "Manitoba and the North-west Territories [which] begins at the east near Lake of the Woods and extends west and north-west to the Rocky Mountains" and gave a detailed analysis of the

Riel Rebellion and the conduct of the Canadian forces.[42] There is no doubt this had been read and referenced by staff members of the MID.

Rowan made a modest proposal: he would travel to Winnipeg, a trip quite familiar to him, "with a view to making a map of the lines of communication in the vicinity of this station," which was to say Fort Pembina. This is exactly the sort of information the MID was seeking. In order for a British invasion to be effective, troops would have to be moved across Canada, principally by rail, making descriptions of transportation and communication facilities vital to a proper U.S. defense. Additionally, for U.S. troops to operate effectively they would need detailed topographical information including identification of landmarks. Although Rowan's proposal was right in line with what Drum wanted, his commander, Captain C. I. McKibbin, didn't like the idea of sending an active-duty officer to spy on a foreign country. To satisfy his sense of propriety, he gave Rowan a leave of absence so that he might fulfill the mission on his own. Rowan and a fellow officer, Lieutenant E. S. Chapin, did exactly as Rowan had proposed and completed a map that they sent on to the MID.[43] Two years later the higher-ups in the MID, still obsessed with information gathering in Canada, assigned Rowan to conduct detailed reconnaissance along the entire Canadian Pacific line. Though officially stationed at Fort Pembina and acting on verbal orders from his post commander,[44] Rowan spent the better part of the summer traveling the length of the railroad.[45] He included snapshots, lithographs, postcards, and commercially prepared maps—the sort of collection that would barely qualify for a middle school student's report 125 years later.[46]

Not caring to stay on alone in Pembina, Ida traveled to Atchison to be with her parents, who were planning a two-week trip to Baltimore, Washington, D.C., and Mr. Symns's old home in Virginia. In November Rowan visited them in Atchison while on his way to Washington, where Ida would eventually join him in December.[47] He had been officially transferred to the Adjutant General's Office and assigned to the MID (though still listed in the Fort Pembina reports as being on temporary assignment).

In 1890 Rowan went back to Canada, this time to investigate the area around Sault Sainte Marie. Afterward, in a letter through an assistant, the secretary of war expressed to him "his appreciation of the energy, tact and ability which you displayed in the work recently performed . . . and he desires to recognize officially the fact that this work was begun voluntarily on your part, and that the plan adopted was of your proposing."[48] This was no light praise.

Throughout the year the Rowans' domestic life was disrupted numerous times as he was sent on various assignments, but in April and again in November they were able to spend some quiet time in Atchison. On November 28, 1890, eight years out of West Point, Rowan was promoted to first lieutenant and reassigned to the Ninth Infantry Regiment.[49] The lengthy passage of time before his first promotion was not a reflection of his soldierly worth. Although many reforms had been enacted in the 1880s, the army was still notoriously slow when it came to promoting officers.[50] In July 1891 Rowan was transferred once again, this time to the Nineteenth Infantry Regiment, and was sent to Central America to serve as a barometric hypsometrist (a measurer of elevations) and assistant astronomer with the Intercontinental Railway Commission. The trip to Atchison the previous April had resulted in a happy event for the entire family: a daughter, Elizabeth Symns Rowan, was born on January 13, 1891, and in March, Rowan managed to secure a few days' leave to travel to Atchison to see his new daughter.[51]

In May 1888, Congress authorized a conference at which would be considered, among other things, "direct communication" between the countries of North and South America and the encouragement of "such reciprocal commercial relations as will be beneficial to all and [will] secure more extensive markets for the products for each of said countries." In this context, "communication" referred to physical movement as opposed to an exchange of information. Delegates representing eighteen countries composed the Committee on Railway Communication, whose report was adopted by the conference in February 1889. It was decided that an international commission of engineers would scout out possible routes, determine their length, and estimate costs.[52]

Rowan was assigned to Corps Number One (of three), which was to survey a line from the western boundary of Mexico, through Guatemala,

El Salvador, Honduras, Nicaragua, and Costa Rica, and then through the Isthmus of Panama into Colombia, where it was scheduled to meet Corps Number Two on its way north. Together they were to take notes on the general topography, geological formations, nature of the soil, climatic conditions, character of agricultural and other industries, population, materials available for railway construction, and everything else they deemed important in connection with the proposed railway.[53]

There were eight in their party—the leader, Lieutenant Montgomery M. Macomb; six assistants, including Rowan; and a military surgeon. Their departure on April 20, 1891, was a pleasant occasion, as Macomb later reported: "The day of sailing was bright and spring-like, and at 1.36 P.M. the old Pacific Mail steamship *Colón* . . . swung out into the stream with everyone in good spirits and confident of success."[54] Eight days later they arrived at Colón in Limón Bay, Panama. The SS *Colón* made this journey regularly, and a dozen years earlier had delivered a delegation from New York to join Ferdinand de Lesseps on his initial tour of the isthmus, during which he became certain he could build a sea-level canal connecting the Atlantic and Pacific Oceans. A few weeks later Lesseps himself was aboard the *Colón* sailing for New York, where he received a hero's welcome. It wouldn't be until February 4, 1889, that the Compagnie Universelle Canal Interocéanique went belly up, the canal project a disastrous failure. When Macomb and his party arrived, the full extent of the financial scandal accompanying the collapse was still to emerge.[55]

From Colón the party traveled by railway and ship to Guatemala City, then the richest and most important of the Central American capitals. It had excellent schools, a four-hundred-bed hospital, hotels, and tradesmen selling virtually everything one could want. Macomb reported "that the linguistic accomplishments of most of those we met were more extensive than is common with us." In spite of its cosmopolitan air, the lack of a proper water supply (and as a result, no proper sewage system) kept the city from being the Paris of Central America, as it was referred to by some residents. Guatemala City would become unrecognizable to nineteenth-century visitors after being leveled by an earthquake in 1917.

After acquiring the necessary papers, horses to ride, and pack animals, the group set forth. As can be imagined, the load was considerable. They had sixty-some scientific instruments—among them sextants, chronometers, barometers, thermometers, psychrometers (to measure humidity), many engineering reference books, and a full field drafting office, including a large drawing table, instruments, different kinds of paper, and a typewriter. In addition they had a fourteen-foot tent, five nine-foot wall tents, two six-foot wall tents, and all the necessary furnishings. Other supplies included three rifles, a shotgun, five revolvers, hand excavating and chopping tools, a complete assortment of medical supplies, photographic equipment, and a year's worth of canned fruits, vegetables, and meat specially purchased from Park and Tilford of New York, well-known provisioners of fancy foods. It was expected they would supplement their food supplies along the way.

During the course of their travels in southwest Guatemala, Macomb and his party made notes on everything: timber, ancient artifacts, birds, animals, and insects, many of the latter being particularly bothersome. There were pesky bees that didn't sting, but numerous ants and gnats that did; ticks, mites, and jiggers that burrowed under the skin; and tarantulas and scorpions that infested tents and clothing. These creatures contributed to the general unhealthy atmosphere of the *tierra caliente*. For the most part, the members of the little band were mercifully spared the worst diseases, but one by one, various members of the party succumbed to the environment. Lieutenant S. M. Foote, one of the assistants, injured his eyes; another was stricken with tonsillitis and malaria; then Rowan asked to be relieved, according to Macomb, due to his not being able to "prosecute the work to advantage in the hot, moist climate of the lowlands." As soon as Macomb received notice that a replacement was on the way, he reluctantly relieved Rowan from duty effective May 16.[56] Rowan spent many days traveling from Guatemala to Atchison, staying there only a short time before leaving on the evening of June 20 to rejoin the MID in Washington.[57] The reports of the surveys and explorations made by the three corps were duly prepared and published between 1895 and 1898, but in spite of occasional renewed interest through the years, an intercontinental railway existed only in the reports; it has never been possible to travel

Figure 1. Andrew Rowan posing in 1891 with Corps No. 1 of the Intercontinental Railway Commission at Primavera, Guatemala. National Archives and Records Administration.

continuously by train from the United States through Central and South America.[58] The expedition did, however, provide Rowan with considerable experience as a trained observer, increasing his value to the MID.

For the first three years of its existence, the MID had been plodding along with the help of clerks borrowed from the Military Reservation System to which it was attached. The data they collected and sorted were gathered randomly by officers in the field. In September 1888, Congress finally got around to providing for "the pay of a clerk attendant on the collection and classification of military information from abroad" and authorized funds to detail officers for this purpose. In

March 1889, the first attachés were stationed in London and Berlin for the express purpose of reporting to the secretary of war on any matters that might be of military interest. During the following month the MID was established as a distinct entity supervised by the adjutant general of the army. Three clerks and a messenger occupied a single room in the State, War, and Navy Building, and they indexed and filed information provided by the attachés, who were eventually stationed in additional European capitals.

In March 1892, the MID was reorganized once again. For the first time its duties were specifically stated,[59] including the "collection and classification of military information of our own and foreign countries, especially with respect to armed, reserved, and available strength; natural and artificial means of communication (rivers, canals, highways, and railroads); the manufacture of arms, ammunition, and other war materials; supplies of food, horses, draught animals, &c." It was expected to be more proactive than in the past by preparing "instructions for the guidance of officers of the Army serving or traveling abroad" and by issuing "military maps, monographs, books, papers, and other publications." Furthermore, it was to interpret the relevance of collected data through the "study and preparation of plans for the mobilization and transportation of militia and volunteers and their disbandment, and for the concentration of the military forces of the United States at the various strategic points on or near the frontiers of the country."[60] The War Department still hadn't given up on a war along the Canadian border. This preoccupation was not a bad thing. Without doing any particular harm, spying on Canada provided training opportunities for future, more useful projects.

After his return from Central America, Rowan was stationed in Detroit, where he was occupied mapping hundreds of square miles along the Canadian border using a newly developed system. Maps were divided into sections one degree of latitude by one degree of longitude. Using existing maps, officers prepared "skeleton" maps for each section, and then traveled the actual ground to confirm or disprove the maps' reliability. The men photographed, sketched, and measured as they went along, creating new and highly accurate maps that varied considerably from what had been available. Rowan returned to the border repeatedly over the next two years, and eventually he and his fellow topographical officers mapped 10,886 square miles.[61]

In the midst of this work he campaigned to be assigned to a staff position as assistant quartermaster that would involve a promotion to captain. Testimonials were a necessity for such a move, and Rowan asked many friends and former superior officers to help out. They were apparently happy to comply. His former commander at Fort Pembina, C. I. McKibbin, now wrote from Fort Missoula in Montana, "Your habit of close study in the line of your chosen profession found you well equipped when you were selected by the War Department for special work, and I have reason to believe you made an enviable record in the performance of that duty. Aside from my strong personal friendship, I sincerely hope, in the interests of the service, you may be tendered a position in one of the Staff Corps." Another superior, Lieutenant Colonel H. A. Theaker, referred to Rowan as "an exceptionally good officer of fine ability and rare scientific attainments and exceedingly well qualified for staff duty." Retired colonel G. M. Brayton, under whom Rowan had served, noted that he performed his duties "with credit to himself and the service"; a businessman in Pagosa Springs, Colorado, one of Rowan's many military postings, "most cheerfully" recommended him; and a group of "Citizens and frontiersmen," also of Pagosa Springs, knew him to have been a "faithfull and efficent officer, kind and courteous alike to Citizens and Soldiers."[62] This was a good try, but not a success. Rowan's excellent work in Guatemala and on the Canadian border did get him appointed head of the MID map section in Washington, but the position came with no promotion.

Over the next few years Andrew, Ida, and little Elizabeth made any number of trips back and forth between Washington and Atchison, often being separated for months at a time.

By the time Rowan rejoined the MID in June 1893,[63] a special section had been created to concentrate on Hawaii and Latin America.[64] Since he had spent over a year in Central America, it made sense for him to take an interest in Latin American matters. In an officer's individual report to the adjutant general in March 1892, Rowan claimed a speaking and reading knowledge of Spanish, which would be of great benefit, though his student days at West Point tend to contradict this evaluation: during his final year at the academy, he placed fiftieth out of fifty-four cadets studying Spanish.[65]

As the officer in charge of the Map Section, Rowan worked on a large map of Cuba and, notwithstanding the fact that he had never been there, contributed substantially to a book titled *The Island of Cuba* published by Henry Holt and Company in 1896. His coauthor was M. M. Ramsey, professor of Spanish at the Columbian University (after 1904, George Washington University) in Washington, D.C. According to Ramsey, the two men had come into contact with one another "in connection with the discharge of official duties, to make some investigations relative to Cuba and its relations to the United States." Marathon Montrose Ramsey, who preferred to use the initials M. M., was the author of a popular Spanish textbook also published by Holt, and he had been hired as a specialist by the MID. In their search for information in the Library of Congress, Rowan and Ramsey discovered that only six works on Cuba had been published in the United States between 1870 and 1889 and one between 1890 and 1895; they also found that not even a single book on Cuba had been published in Great Britain or Ireland during this period. In 1896, responding to the growing interest in Cuba, there had been a spate of books, pamphlets, and articles, but they had a common failing—they were strongly biased in one direction or another. It was Rowan and Ramsey's stated object to "gain correct information and not to dress up a tale of woe or defend a party, [and in so doing] they . . . endeavored to divest themselves of passion and prejudice, and to present the truth as nearly as they could find it." Rowan, having current data at his fingertips, provided a detailed physical description of the island plus short discussions of agricultural products and transportation systems. Ramsey contributed two sections, one being a general history and the other an analysis of Cuba's political, social, and financial state.[66] That they succeeded to a respectable degree is demonstrated by the book's favorable reception. A reviewer for the *New York Times* wrote, "'This volume is opportune, and in the present connection as to the belligerent rights of the Cubans, Lieut. Rowan's and Prof. Ramsey's facts relative to the Island must be considered authoritative. The account of Cuban conditions is clearly given, as well as their entire history, and in addition the points of international law are carefully presented."[67] But the book didn't fare quite so well—or at least Ramsey's share didn't—in a review in the *American Historical Review*, which noted, "The historical portions, with which alone we have to do, are plainly the work of an amateur, and are far from presenting an adequate account of the history of the colony." The review went on to note, however, that "the narrative is clear and intelligible, and the temper is eminently fair in respect to recent events and present conditions,—so fair as to constitute a recommendation of the book outweighing much of its slightness and insufficiency."[68]

The book sold well enough to justify a second edition in 1897, and in Great Britain a third revised edition was published in 1898 by Gray and Bird. Holt printed a leaflet that Rowan and Ramsey dutifully included in correspondence with others and a poster that they distributed to bookshops in the Washington, D.C., area. Notably, among the many Cuban officers mentioned in the book, there isn't a word about Calixto García Íñiguez.

In March 1897 the MID was assigned a new chief—Major Arthur L. Wagner,[69] an assistant adjutant general and one of the more influential officers in the army at that time.[70] Like Rowan, Wagner had graduated near the bottom of his class at West Point—in his case, forty out of forty-five—with an astounding 189 demerits in his fourth year alone. Yet in his case, the demerits indicated the independent mind of an ambitious, hardworking reformer within the army. Unlike many of his other fellow officers, Wagner saw the army as a force to wage war rather than one of social change, and to that end he used his recognized intellect to turn it into a professional service that could successfully apply the lessons of the past to situations not yet encountered. For some years he was an instructor at the United States Infantry and Cavalry School at Fort Leavenworth, Kansas, and had authored a number of important articles and books on military science.[71] One work, *The Service of Security and Information*, was the first American book ever written on tactical intelligence and was adopted as a textbook at West Point. The secretary of war noted that Wagner's "previous studies had specially fitted him for this work."[72] In his book Wagner explained the two kinds of information necessary for a military commander:

1. That relating to geography, topography, and resources of the theatre of operations.
2. That which relates to the strength and composition of the enemy's forces, and their position, movements, and morale.[73]

With the possibility of a war with Spain, the MID was allotted three rooms instead of one, and officers worked night and day to collect data on Cuba.[74] The War, Navy, and State Departments had been receiving a steady supply of information since the renewal of the Cuban revolt in 1895. Businessmen, travelers, American volunteers fighting with the Cubans, and Cuban refugees all shared their observations.[75]

If it came to a war with Spain, the initial military confrontations would almost certainly occur in Cuba and Puerto Rico. In spite of a slew of reports coming in, very little of the situational information was currently known regarding enemy forces and the likely battlefields in which that war would take place. Hard facts were needed in order to design a campaign. As Wagner pointed out in his book, the approach to a particular military situation "depends upon so many different considerations that no definite rule on the subject can be prescribed."[76] Before generals could make decisions, they needed up-to-date information regarding the "morale and efficiency of the opposing forces and the military situation generally," information that could be provided only by trained military observers.

At this point much was known about Havana and its environs, but for the rest of the island the military had to rely on Spanish sources and reports from newspaper correspondents, which Wagner was certain were "colored so that they reflect the policy of their respective newspapers rather than the real condition of affairs."[77] For him there was but one possible solution: he would send people to Cuba and Puerto Rico to gather as much information as possible. But the adjutant general, Henry Clark Corbin, wouldn't hear of it; he considered it unethical for military officers to engage in clandestine peacetime espionage.[78] If this sounds naive, bear in mind that as late as 1929, Secretary of State Henry L. Stimson infamously closed the MID's code-breaking bureau and justified his action by writing, "Gentlemen do not read each other's mail."

Wagner tried again in December 1897. This time he pointed out some historical precedents for having third-party military officers survey areas controlled by opposing combatants. He noted that during the Civil War, Prince Napoleon, Lord Wolesley (then Lieutenant Colonel Garnet Wolesley), and the British colonel Arthur Lyon Freemantle visited both the Union and Confederate Armies. And to forestall any further ethical objections, Wagner recommended that the officers be volunteers and receive an unpaid leave of absence while pursuing their missions. He readily admitted there would be a "certain amount of danger involved," and though he claimed he personally knew "at least a dozen well qualified officers who would be glad to undertake the detail, . . . I should prefer to have [it assigned] to an officer now on duty in the Military Information Division." He was referring to his friend and colleague, Andrew Rowan.[79]

Two events occurred that caused the decision to be made in favor of the mission. First there was the notorious letter written by the Spanish minister in Washington, Dupuy de Lôme. The letter, sent to José Canalejas, a Spanish editor and politician, was stolen from him in Havana and eventually made its way, on February 8, 1898, onto the front page of William Randolph Hearst's *New York Evening Journal*. In the letter, Dupuy de Lôme said that President William McKinley was "weak and a bidder for the admiration of the crowd, besides being a would-be politician who tries to leave a door open behind himself while keeping on good terms with the jingoes of his party."[80] His calling McKinley weak was no worse than Theodore Roosevelt, then assistant secretary of the navy, saying he had "the backbone of a chocolate eclair"; similarly, Republican Party leader Joe Cannon observed that McKinley kept his ear so close to the ground that it was full of grasshoppers.[81] While such sentiments were perfectly acceptable coming from fellow politicians, few Americans cared to have their president so characterized by a high official in a foreign government with whom relations were already strained. Negotiations had been going on between the two countries for some time regarding the treatment of the Cubans and the possibility of their achieving autonomy. Spain had made a number of concessions and promises of further accommodations, but Dupuy de Lôme's letter showed this was all a farce. As Henry

Cabot Lodge wrote the following year, "the letter revealed the utter hollowness of all the Spanish professions, and showed that the negotiations in regard to autonomy and commercial relations were only intended to amuse and deceive the United States."[82]

The second event that helped forward the decision to send a spy into Cuba was, of course, the explosion of the *Maine* a week after the publication of the letter. Three weeks after the explosion, Congress passed, without a dissenting vote, a bill allocating $50 million "for the National defense and for each and every purpose connected therewith to be expended at the discretion of the President." The idea was to impress the Spanish government with the preparedness of the United States to back its words with deeds. The Spaniards were not merely impressed. According to Stewart Lyndon Woodford, the U.S. ambassador to Spain, they were "stunned."[83] Fifty million dollars was a huge amount of money in 1898, and for the United States simply to appropriate it from surplus funds was quite unimaginable in a country as strapped as Spain.[84] Secretary of War Russell Alger wrote that the appropriation "roused the enthusiasm of the people, fusing all shades of opinion into one patriotic thought."[85] And there was the rub.

The peacetime army at this point had approximately 2,140 officers and 26,000 enlisted men and had long been in need of reorganization. A bill to reform and provide for the expansion of the army when necessary was introduced in early March 1898 by John A. T. Hull, the chairman of the House Committee on Military Affairs. The problem with the Hull bill was that it didn't take into account the national guardsmen, who considered themselves superior beings to regular army officers and enlisted men. They wanted their share of the glory and were easily capable, through their elected representatives, of thwarting any War Department plans that excluded them. And it wasn't just the guardsmen. Volunteer companies, battalions, and even regiments sprang into being around the country, each group more eager than the next to go to war. Instead of an army capable of being expanded to 104,000, a number considered quite adequate by the professionals, the total was eventually increased to 275,000. Yet even this didn't satisfy the desire of American men to wear the uniform. Alger claimed it was "safe to say that a million men offered themselves. . . . It was the apotheosis of patriotism."[86]

What was to be done with all these patriots? The War Department was in no position to process, train, and equip a quarter of a million new soldiers. One problem was the wording of what became known as the Fifty Million Bill. The money was authorized only for "national defense," not to pay for an invading army to leave the country. The War Department, as Alger later pointed out, "had been able to do nothing in the way of accumulating material for offensive war."[87]

McKinley still hoped that war could be avoided. For this to happen, Spain would have to drastically revise its policies and genuinely assist the Cubans to achieve full self-government.[88] In the meantime, preparations for war continued. As early as 1894, students at the Naval War College in Newport, Rhode Island, had devised tactical plans for a sea war with Spain.[89] When it came to land battles, Major General Nelson A. Miles, commanding general of the army, had no plans for a massive invasion with tens of thousands of guardsmen and newly enlisted volunteers. Better, he thought, to attack the Spanish at vulnerable points with smaller units of experienced regulars. This would involve collaborating with the insurgents and providing them weapons, supplies, and technical advisers.[90] In order for this to occur, though, he needed up-to-the-minute information from the rebel forces in Cuba. At long last, President McKinley and Secretary of War Alger authorized Wagner to send his spies south.[91]

On April 8, 1898, Wagner asked Rowan to join him for lunch at the Army and Navy Club.[92] Wagner was known as something of a card, so when he asked Rowan during lunch if he knew when the next boat was leaving for Jamaica, Rowan suspected a joke in the works. Dutiful officer that he was, though, he quickly did some checking, probably in the newspapers at the front desk, which in those days printed such information. He learned that one of the vessels of the British Atlas line, the SS *Adirondack*, was leaving New York for Kingston the next day. He reported this to Wagner, who asked if he could be on board. Still thinking it was a joke, Rowan said he could. It was then that Wagner told him of his mission.[93]

Years later Rowan retold the story during an interview with the *San Francisco Chronicle*:

It had been decided to send an officer to Eastern Cuba, in case of war, to ascertain the military conditions existing in that region which was likely to become the theater of war, and that I had been selected for the job.

Major Wagner's instructions to me were delivered orally and were, in brief, to proceed to Kingston, Jamaica, by the first available transportation, and there make arrangements to get into Cuba upon receipt of a cipher cablegram to that effect. Once in Cuba I was to bring the military data up to date and conduct myself in accordance with my surroundings. I was authorized to attach myself to any body of the Insurgents operating in the field if the Cuban commander might so elect. I was to carry no papers other than such as might serve to identify me with the American Consul-General at Kingston, and through him with the Cuban Junta.[94]

Rowan left Washington by train at one minute after midnight on April 9, arriving in time to be on board the *Adirondack* when it left New York at noon.[95] Not wanting to draw attention, he kept pretty much to himself, but by doing so achieved the opposite effect: "I held myself aloof from the other passengers and learned only from a traveling companion, an electrical engineer, what was going on. He conveyed to me the cheerful information that because of my keeping away from them and giving no one any information as to my business, a bunch of convivial spirits conferred on me the title of 'the bunco steerer.'" This doesn't quite make sense; a "bunco steerer" was one who led unsuspecting souls into a con game or some other dangerous circumstances, an occupation that would necessarily involve person-to-person communication. Perhaps in order to explain his aloof behavior they jokingly determined that his game was to sit back and wait for an opportunity to strike.

Rowan didn't mention in the article that his traveling companion, E. C. Wescott, was also his roommate. This being Wescott's first sea voyage, and not knowing anyone else aboard, he'd thought it prudent to secure a private stateroom so that he would feel safe while sleeping. After depositing his bag in the room, he went on deck to look out at the receding shoreline. When at last he returned to the room, he was surprised to find a total stranger—Andrew Rowan—lying on the couch. Rowan explained that he'd walked into the wrong stateroom by mistake and then said to Wescott, "if you don't mind, I will share it with you."

Having seen Wescott's bag when entering, Rowan would have known at once the room was occupied and should have shut the door and gone looking for his own stateroom. But instead, he stayed. This was a scary mission on which he'd embarked, and perhaps he wanted some company. Or he also might have thought that if Spanish spies discovered the nature of his trip to Jamaica he would be less likely to be murdered in his sleep if he were sharing a stateroom. Whatever the reason, Wescott was taken with Rowan's manner and agreed to his staying—though he did exercise his proprietary right to the bottom bunk. As part of his cover, Rowan assumed a totally antijingoistic position vis-à-vis a potential war with Spain, going so far as to suggest to Wescott that the United States was afraid of such an encounter.[96]

During his second day at sea, the United States moved a step closer to declaring war when McKinley sent a message to Congress asking to be empowered to stop the hostilities in Cuba and to establish a government "capable of maintaining order and observing its international obligations." There was applause following the reading of the sentence, "In the name of humanity, in the name of civilization, in behalf of endangered American interests which give us the right and duty to speak and to act, the war in Cuba must stop."[97] Having been incommunicado since leaving New York, Rowan was totally in the dark regarding the state of hostilities between Spain and the United States. He was, therefore, understandably nervous when the ship entered Cuban waters as it passed around the eastern end of the island.

I had but one incriminating paper, a letter from the State Department to officials in Jamaica saying that I was what I might represent myself to be. But if war had been declared before the Adirondack entered Cuban waters she would have been liable to search by Spain, under the rules of international law. As I was contraband and the bearer of contraband I could have been seized as a prisoner of war and taken aboard any Spanish ship, while the British boat, after compliance with specified preliminaries, could have been sunk, despite the fact that she left a peaceful port under a neutral flag, bound for a neutral port, prior to a declaration of war. Recalling this state of affairs, I hid this paper in the life preserver in my stateroom and it was with great relief I saw the cape astern.[98]

What Rowan failed to disclose, perhaps having forgotten or perhaps wanting to increase the dramatic effect, was that he had been provided with a cover story and carried papers designating him as a military attaché bound for Santiago, Chile. The main purpose of the bogus assignment was to explain his presence should war with Spain break out while he was in Jamaica, a neutral country. The official orders, signed by Adjutant General Henry C. Corbin, were dated March 30, 1898, eight days before Wagner had given him the assignment. References to this assignment in his military records have caused many writers to assume incorrectly that Rowan actually went to Santiago.

At this point Rowan still didn't know if he would ultimately be sent to Cuba or Puerto Rico.[99] In either event, his mission would be the same: to stay in the area and send back regular dispatches regarding both the Spanish and insurgent forces—distribution, numbers, equipment, and character of officers—along with topographical information and sanitary conditions.[100]

Rowan disembarked at Kingston on April 14, checked into the Myrtle Bank Hotel, and then spent two fruitless days attempting to connect with junta members.[101] On April 16 he visited the U.S. consul, Louis A. Dent, showed his papers from the secretary of state, and explained his mission, requesting that he be put in communication with responsible parties who could land him in Cuba or Puerto Rico. Dent, an apparently hardworking and conscientious man, immediately called in junta-connected Cubans including José Francisco Pérez, the Jamaican agent of the Cuban Revolutionary Party.[102] Dent informed them of the mission but, for safety's sake, introduced Rowan as a State Department employee rather than a commissioned officer in the army.

The junta members were at first reluctant to offer any help because, according to Dent, "they had orders from Palma to suspend all operations." This was Tomás Estrada Palma, the New York delegate of the Cuban Revolutionary Party and coordinator of such junta activities.[103] Before things could continue, this matter would have to be resolved. That same day in a coded cable to Assistant Secretary of State William Day regarding other matters, Dent appended the line, "Advise War Department Rowan here."

A day or so after the initial meeting with the junta members, Rowan and Dent were passing through the lobby of Rowan's hotel, where a group of would-be war correspondents were spending their time awaiting any tidbit of news that might come their way. One of their number, an Associated Press reporter named Elmer Roberts, said to his colleagues, "I wonder who Mr. Dent's friend is? He looks like he might be an Army Officer who has come down here to go to Santiago." This was not a lucky guess on Roberts's part; having observed Rowan's meeting with Dent and the junta members, he had inquired about Rowan by cable and learned that he was an army officer. Considering the state of affairs, it was easy enough to reach the conclusion that Rowan was planning a trip to Cuba to gather intelligence. At the time Dent reacted calmly enough, later writing that he "met the remark with the reply that he was not so far as I knew; but was a traveling gentleman who had brought to me letters of introduction."[104]

In spite of their demeanor in public, Dent and Rowan were seriously worried. If news leaked out, not only would the mission be jeopardized but also Rowan's life. They decided they had no choice but to tell Roberts enough of the truth to dissuade him from speaking or writing any further on the matter, and this they did the next day. The understanding, according to Dent, was that Roberts would be told only that Rowan was indeed an army officer on a secret mission, and "if his identity were disclosed it would not only destroy the plans of his Government but would, in all probability, endanger his life. Subsequently, however, Mr. Rowan went further, and intimated to Mr. Roberts that he might go to Cuba, and Mr. Roberts said that he wanted to be in on an expedition of that kind." For whatever reason, Rowan agreed and, to Dent's discomfort, became very friendly with Roberts. For Roberts to be included in such an adventure would be a journalistic coup, and he no doubt used whatever persuasive skills he had to guarantee such inclusion. A cynic might suggest that Rowan found the idea of having his mission covered by his own personal correspondent very appealing, but a more generous interpretation of his motives would be that he merely wanted to have a fellow American along—one whom he would describe to Wagner as being "made of the right sort of stuff" to share the danger.[105] It was, after all, a daunting mission. According to Rowan, but never mentioned by Dent, Roberts had "letters from the New York junta to General García, and [his going] would save two trips and afford mutual protection if the correspondent and [I] proceeded together."[106]

Congress, in the meantime, was busily debating its response to McKinley's message. One of the major sticking points concerned postwar Cuba—was it to be annexed by the United States or allowed to become an independent republic? Finally, on April 19, a resolution generally referred to as the Teller Amendment was passed. First, it declared that "the people of the Island of Cuba are, and of right ought to be, free and independent"; second, it demanded that Spain quit the island immediately; third, it empowered McKinley to do whatever might be necessary to assure the first two points; and fourth, it disclaimed "any disposition or intention to exercise sovereignty, jurisdiction, or control" over Cuba.[107] On April 20, while Rowan was still cooling his heels in Kingston, McKinley signed the resolution. Spain was given until noon on April 23 to comply with the ultimatum. The day following the signing of the resolution, April 21, Wagner sent Rowan a coded cablegram ordering him not to go to Puerto Rico but to join García as soon as possible. Wagner also said that the Kingston junta would probably be notified that very day.[108]

The junta had to be notified that Estrada Palma okayed its participation, and this required Russell Alger's personal intervention with the New York junta. There was one important stipulation: the United States had to pay the junta for Rowan's passage, which, according to Estrada Palma, would cost over two hundred dollars.[109] The point of the transfer of funds from the War Department was to demonstrate the existence of a Cuban government; the Cubans were still fearful that the

United States was planning to install a government of its own. Once these details were worked out, an officer in the Liberation Army—a Spaniard named Comandante Gervasio Savio who made regular trips between Jamaica and Cuba transporting mail and passengers—agreed to carry Rowan.[110] Unfortunately the trip would have to be made in an open boat sailing under a tropical sun. This had been assumed previously, and Dent tried to procure the services of a small steam trawler to carry Rowan within four miles of the coast, at which point he and his guides would board a smaller boat to carry them to shore. But because of the difficulties involved in having to work through a third party, this plan fell through.[111]

On April 21, 1898, Rowan received his orders. That same day the junta members, having received the go-ahead from Estrada Palma, informed Dent that arrangements to take Rowan to Cuba were scheduled for April 23, and Dent so notified the War Department. Roberts, still not certain of being included, tried to make his own arrangements with the junta. They said they would take him along only with Dent's permission. Dent had a long conversation with Rowan regarding the advisability of Roberts's accompanying him. Rowan admitted then that he had given Roberts additional details on his mission and thus felt honor-bound to take him along. It was obvious to Dent that Roberts knew even more than he did, and he was unwilling to assume the responsibility for including the correspondent in the journey. This caused Rowan to threaten to abandon the mission. Rather than yield to this threat, Dent cabled the War Department on April 22, noting that Rowan "is insisting upon being accompanied by Associated Press correspondent here. Shall I permit? The expedition awaits my order to start." The answer couldn't be more clear: "Rowan expedition may go. Correspondent must not go."[112]

When informed of this, Rowan became obstinate, so Dent appealed privately to Roberts to drop his insistence on going. By now it had turned into an issue among all three men, and hard words were exchanged. Then a second telegram arrived, this one from Secretary of State William R. Day: "It is desired Lieutenant Rowan should be allowed to go at his own risk. No correspondent or any other person should go or be cognizant of his going." Dent informed Rowan of this latest message, and Rowan said he would let Dent know the following day if he intended to complete his mission.[113] Rowan returned to his hotel and wrote a letter to Wagner, laying all the blame for the confusion on Dent. It was Dent, he claimed, who brought Roberts into their confidence and who "explained everything to him"—meaning, apparently, the details of the mission. Dent had more than once denied any knowledge of the mission other than that Rowan was to meet with García. "Mr. Roberts," Rowan went on, "at once gave the fullest support and assistance and asked for a chance to go along. Relying on my general instructions I assented and from that time we have worked together to the common end." He didn't explain exactly what support and assistance Roberts could possibly have provided. Again he mentioned Roberts's New York junta letters to García, but Pérez's refusal to include Roberts without Dent's permission makes the existence of the letters questionable. At the end of the letter to Wagner, which wouldn't arrive in Washington for two or three days, Rowan wrote that he would probably be sending a cable that same day.[114]

The next morning, April 23, Pérez told Dent he would meet with Rowan at 3:00 that afternoon to begin the journey. Around midday, as planned, Rowan came into the consulate and Dent told him of the arrangements. Rowan said he had cabled the War Department, intimating that he was still trying to get the decision regarding Roberts reversed.

The hour for the meeting with Pérez was drawing close, so Dent asked Rowan what he would do if he received no reply before that time. Rowan said in that case it would be the War Department's responsibility if he didn't leave that day. Had he, Dent asked, informed the War Department of the importance of a timely answer? Rowan admitted he had not. The two men went round and round, and the upshot was that Rowan asked Dent to withdraw from the negotiations and that he would make the trip under his own responsibility. Pérez was called in and told of the new understanding. At first he objected, stating that the entire project was undertaken because Dent had requested it, but he finally agreed, and the mission continued as planned. Dent then sent a cable to Secretary Day informing him that the expedition was to start but that he had withdrawn his connection to it. "Junta after much reluctance, and only because their arrangements had been made, have agreed to take Rowan on his responsibility, representing the War Department."[115]

And so it was that on April 23, 1898, the day that Spain declared war on the United States and, coincidentally, that Rowan celebrated his forty-first birthday, he set out—without Elmer Roberts—for Cuba. "At noon . . . I placed myself in the hands of unknown friends [in a building on East Queen Street]. Three hours later a four-seated carriage, drawn by two small Jamaica horses, was driven rapidly up to the door. The moment I entered, the negro driver leaned forward, plying his whip, and we whirled furiously through the narrow streets and out the Spanish Town road." They were joined by another carriage four miles outside the city and continued at this pace until 10:00 P.M., finally slowing down for an hour until stopping for food at a small farmhouse. "During all this time no one had spoken a word to me and I had presumed to ask no questions." After rum was served all around, he was introduced to Gervasio Savio, the guide who would actually take him to Cuba. Rowan thought his "fierce, drooping mustache" made him look like a Caribbean pirate.[116]

Rowan and his companions continued their journey, traveling northwest and eventually arriving at St. Ann's Bay on Jamaica's northern coast.[117] About fifty yards offshore they sighted a small fishing smack, *El Mambi*,[118] named for the term used popularly for the Cuban rebel soldiers. After an exchange of signals, a sailor waded ashore and carried Rowan on his shoulders through the surf to the boat. At around midnight the five or six men in the party set sail for Cuba, one hundred miles away. Rowan later commented, "About three o'clock in the morning, I crawled under the seat among the ballast bowlders and went to sleep. When I awakened, the sun was shining hotly over the gunwale. The Cubans showed their white teeth with a 'Buenos dias, Meester Rowan,' and we began another day of converting time into distance."[119]

Their biggest fear at this point was meeting up with one of the Spanish *lanchas* guarding the coast. If they were caught, they would all be executed—Rowan as a spy, and the Cubans, because they were delivering a quantity of antiquated small arms, as filibusters.[120] According to

Figure 2. A map of Rowan's itinerary created to accompany his account in *McClure's* magazine of his journey to Cuba. *McClure's.*

Rowan, Savio "had figured out the time-table of the *lanchas* very closely," and they avoided meeting up with any. By 4:00 the next afternoon they saw the mountainous Cuban coast, but Savio preferred bobbing along in the offing until late at night with just a small jib to keep them on course. They needed to gain a tide that would take them over a reef barrier paralleling the shore. It was after midnight on April 24 when a long roller carried them into a quiet bay at a place called Gran Rincón.[121] There they spent another night in the boat.

While they were sleeping, the American Asiatic Squadron under the command of Commodore George Dewey lay anchored in Mirs Bay on the coast of China. The squadron was there, essentially, at the behest of then assistant secretary of the navy Theodore Roosevelt. In 1897, through the influence of his good friend and mentor Senator Henry Cabot Lodge, Roosevelt was appointed to the post in spite of the misgivings of many in the McKinley administration, including navy secretary John Long and McKinley himself. In a review of his friend Alfred Mahan's book, written seven years before his appointment, Roosevelt foretold what his attitude would be as assistant secretary of the navy and later as president. "Our ships should be the best of their kind,—this is the first desideratum, but, in addition, there should be plenty of them. We need a large navy, composed not merely of cruisers, but containing also a full proportion of powerful battle-ships, able to meet those of any other nation. It is not economy—it is niggardly and foolish short-sightedness—to cramp our naval expenditures, while squandering money left and right on everything else, from pensions to public buildings."[122] As the assistant secretary, Roosevelt used his influence to have George Dewey appointed commander of the Asiatic Squadron.[123] Taking advantage of Long's absence from the office on February 25, 1898, Roosevelt, as acting secretary of the navy, sent a message to Dewey: "Order the squadron . . . to Hong Kong. Keep full of coal. In the event of declaration of war Spain, your duty will be to see that the Spanish squadron does not leave the Asiatic coast, and then offensive operations in Philippine Islands." Dewey did all that was necessary to fulfill the order. This involved overhauling the ships, acquiring provisions, purchasing coal, and drilling the crews. They were waiting in Mirs Bay, fully prepared for battle, when orders arrived from Secretary Long on April 25: "War has commenced between the United States and Spain. Commence operations particularly against the Spanish fleet. You must capture vessels or destroy. Use utmost endeavor."[124] Rather than leaving immediately, Dewey awaited the arrival of Oscar F. Williams, the American consul from Manila, who he hoped would have current information regarding the defenses.

The next morning, in Cuba, the scene brought out the poet in Rowan. In a later account of the mission he wrote, "Above, the sun was rising gloriously behind El Turquino—the highest peak in all Cuba—and below, near the shore, rose a riotous wall of tangled grape, mangrove, and cactus, defended from the sea by a sandy rampart against which the water broke in long, lapping swells. In all probability I never shall look on a scene of more entrancing beauty." The poet then yielded to the soldier as he noted this was no place to land an invading army. It was a timely thought; later in the day Congress would pass a declaration—a few cut-and-dried legalisms, a mere 141 words—formalizing a course of action that would profoundly change millions of lives.

Rowan again rode piggyback, this time to the shore. He later expressed surprise that he was met by Cuban soldiers who he thought appeared to know he would be arriving.[125] They couldn't have known. There wouldn't have been time enough, nor would there have been any point in sailing to Cuba and back to deliver this information. Savio made the trip often, delivering mail, medicine, and men, and no doubt it was he who was expected. At any rate, Rowan became the first American soldier to cross enemy lines after the declaration of war.[126] And, dressed as he was in a "suit adapted to tropic temperatures and jungle topography" that had been tailor-made for him in Jamaica, he also became the first American officer in history to wear khaki in a combat zone.[127]

Rowan reported the group's being led by a "half naked Cuban lad" with bullet scars across his chest. According to a Cuban account, the patrol was under the command of Cavalry Lieutenant Eugenio L. Fernández Barrot, aide-de-camp of General Salvador Hernández Rios, chief of the region through which they were to pass. Fernández Barrot, who had studied in the United States, was able to speak to Rowan in English.[128] They plunged into the jungle and, six miles from the coast, reached the foothills of the Sierra Maestra Mountains. As Rowan later noted,

We had a practical lesson of the Cuban method of feeding an army. At convenient points along the path stood little thatched sheds, each with a smoldering camp-fire just in front. An aged Cuban man, or a woman with little naked children, stood guard. As the ragged soldiers pass along, the hungry ones rake sweet potatoes from the ashes, shuck off the skins, and eat them while they march. There is never a failure in the supply, never a time when the desperately poor wives and old fathers and little children in the hills cannot raise and roast enough potatoes to feed these ragged fighters for a desperate cause.[129]

They quenched their thirst with water from green coconuts. The next day, as they traveled further into the island, Rowan's superiors in Washington were promoting him to captain.[130]

At some point the group acquired saddle-galled horses that were, apparently, as dedicated to the revolution as their riders and "bore [their condition] with as little complaint as the Cuban soldier bears his hunger." During the entire trip they saw no Spaniards, but once they came upon a mule train carrying ammunition to García.[131]

On the morning of April 27, his third day in Cuba, Rowan and his guides began climbing into the mountains, and it was here that he got his best view of what an invading army would encounter: "great rounded peaks covered to the top with jungles of verdure." The following day they began their descent, and Rowan realized the difficulties an army would have during the coming rainy season when the streambeds would become rushing torrents. That night they stopped at a place called Jibaru, and Rowan offered his first real complaint about Cuban culture: "Here we partook of a meal which introduced several dishes new to me, and all poorly suited to my appetite. The remains of a beef newly killed, its dismembered parts hanging from the joists and dripping blood on the earth floor, made me affect an air of unconcern I did not feel." The next morning they met up with General Hernández Rios. Rowan joined him and several hundred cavalry heading for El Chino: "Here for the first time I found a field for the cavalry and artillery, although the intersecting watercourses, with their fringe of jungle, would still leave to the infantry the brunt of battle. [Cuba] is the land *par excellence* for infantry. This let us not forget."[132] It's too bad he couldn't have conveyed that information to Roosevelt, who on that very day was ordering two horses on which he planned to ride as a lieutenant-colonel with the First U.S. Volunteer Cavalry (the Rough Riders)—not that Roosevelt would have paid any attention to Rowan's advice anyway.[133]

At El Chino, Rowan was turned over to "a coal black negro, Dionisio López, a lieutenant in the Cuban army." He could, Rowan wrote, "trace a course through this trackless forest, through the tangled growth, as fast as he could ride. His skill with a machete was amazing. He carved a way for us through the jungle. Networks of vines fell before his steady strokes right and left; closed spaces became openings; the man appeared tireless."[134] As the day was ending, the small party approached Buey Arriba, "the best and most beautiful camp" Rowan ever made in Cuba.

On the other side of the world, the sun's first rays were lighting the sky over Manila Bay.[135] Commodore George Dewey was standing on the bridge of his flagship USS *Olympia* with Captain Charles Gridley. The American squadron, comprising one gunboat and five cruisers, had entered the bay a few hours earlier. Waiting for them, like a group of sitting ducks, was the Spanish squadron under the command of Admiral Patricio Montojo—two cruisers and five gunboats. At 5:40 A.M. Dewey uttered his immortal line, "You may fire when you are ready, Gridley." When the firing ended seven hours later, three of the Spanish ships were sunk and 161 Spaniards had died; another 210 were wounded; Dewey's ships suffered minor damage and his captains reported six men slightly wounded. Though hardly a clash of armadas, it was a historically important victory, though perhaps one somewhat undeserving of the patriotic proud mania that followed. The ships in the American fleet, after all, were younger (at an average age of nine years, compared to fourteen for the Spanish) and therefore more technically advanced; the American ships were larger (averaging 3,183 tons, compared with 1,670 tons), which means they carried more armoring and more firepower. The *Olympia* and the *Baltimore* each had four eight-inch guns capable of firing 250-pound projectiles with a muzzle velocity of 2,080 feet per second; the Spanish had nothing that compared with those. In all, the Americans had forty-seven large guns and fifty-six smaller rapid-fire guns; the Spanish, thirty-one and forty-nine, respectively.[136] It was an uneven match—but that, after all, is what success in war is all about.

Dewey validated Roosevelt's machinations to have him command the Asiatic Squadron when he performed all the preparatory actions necessary to support his victory. He speedily but methodically improvised a base, overhauled his ships and their machinery, drilled his crews, and acquired two supply ships, coal, provisions, and general stores so that when his orders arrived he was ready to go.[137] A few days after the battle, when Dewey's official dispatches reached Washington, he was promoted to the rank of rear admiral.[138] And many newborn boys were named Dewey.[139]

As the sun traveled farther west the day of the battle, a new day—May 1—was dawning in Cuba. Rowan was about to achieve his objective: a meeting with General Calixto García in the town of Bayamo.

CHAPTER 3

"A Most Perilous Undertaking"

Bayamo, Cuba, is fifty miles southwest of Holguín,[1] the town in which General Calixto García Íñiguez had been born fifty-nine years earlier. But the route he traveled between the occasion of his birth and that of meeting Rowan was long and circuitous. García was born, so the story went, as a troop of soldiers passed by in the street. "Is this boy to be a soldier," his mother asked, "who is born hearing the sounds of drums and marching soldiers?"[2] He came by his revolutionary ardor honestly enough: his grandfather, Calixto García Izquierdo, was jailed years earlier after calling for constitutional freedom for all Cubans, citizens and slaves alike.[3]

As a young man, Calixto García went to Havana to work in an uncle's law office; rather than finishing his studies and becoming a lawyer, he returned to Holguín to manage his family's holdings.[4] Among the landowning class in Cuba, there was inevitably talk of annexation to the United States, especially in the eastern part of the island where farms were smaller, family-run operations and where there were more people of color, both free and enslaved. Spain effectively squelched the movement by threatening to emancipate the slaves, a situation that would immediately make Cuba an unattractive acquisition to Southern annexationists from the United States. Following President Abraham Lincoln's Emancipation Proclamation in 1863, the Spanish threat no longer had any force. Slavery, though still practiced in Cuba, was doomed to fade away because people of all classes viewed it as a trap for both slave and master. As an alternative to slave labor, there was an increasing number of indentured Chinese who provided a much better return on investment since there was no lifetime commitment.

In cities throughout eastern Cuba, *juntas revolucionarias* were being organized by local Masonic lodges. The goal of these essentially white juntas was armed revolt, but they knew that without the support of the black slaves they would never succeed. And they knew they would not have that support if their fight for independence did not include equal independence for the slaves. Uncomfortable as this notion was for many white property owners, they realized they had no choice—yet they kept postponing the day of the actual insurrection.[5] When they intercepted a telegram from the Spanish captain general calling for the arrest of their leaders there was no time for further delay. On October 10, 1868, Carlos Manuel de Céspedes freed his slaves and issued a manifesto explaining the reasons for and objectives of the revolution.

García was one of the people drawn to Céspedes. Because of his background and family connections, García had joined the revolutionary army as a colonel. Operating always in his own backyard, he demonstrated his military leadership sufficiently to be promoted to major general.[6] The rebel forces he commanded, though outnumbered and outgunned, succeeded militarily using guerrilla tactics,[7] and Spain regarded him as one of the few insurgent leaders worthy of the name.[8] The war lasted ten years, but García participated only until September 1874, when he was captured in a daring raid led by a Spanish officer, Lieutenant Francisco Ariza y Gómez. Ariza had learned that important rebels were to hold a conference in a wooded encampment some twenty-five miles from the port city of Manzanillo. Taking ten of the hundred troops he'd brought with him, Ariza surprised García, his chief of staff, and his aide, while the remainder of his troops opened fire on the unprepared rebels, killing thirty-six of them. It was at first mistakenly reported that García was one of those killed.[9]

Later photos of García show a distinct scar above his nose, the result of a wound inflicted during this attack. It was not, however, the result of Spanish gunfire. García managed to get off a couple of shots attempting to defend himself, but quickly realized he was going to be captured. Preferring death to imprisonment, he held his revolver under his chin and pulled the trigger. According to one account, this was not a spur-of-the-moment decision. Earlier, in that very camp, he had been asked by his good friend Felix Figueredo what he would do if captured by the Spanish. García replied, "Nothing. I would not fall into their hands; my revolver has six bullets—five for the enemy and the last for me."[10] This is consistent with a much-repeated anecdote in which García assures his mother that he will never let the Spanish take him alive. When she hears that he has been captured, she says, "No! That is not my son." On being told that he survived a self-inflicted gunshot to the head she says, "Ah. . . . That is my son."[11]

The slug, which was fired at a forward angle into the roof of his mouth, came out between his eyes, leaving him alive and conscious but unable to speak. A short while later he wrote a note asking for soup, stating that he had eaten nothing for the past thirty hours. And then, apparently having a change of heart regarding the desirability of death to dishonor, he demanded the attention of a surgeon. A doctor saw to his wound but held little hope for his survival. Yet García managed to live long enough to be taken to Santiago, where he was treated in the Principe Alfonso hospital. From there he was transported to Havana and held in Morro Castle, and eventually he was taken by the mail steamer *Méndez Nuñez* to the Spanish port city of Santandar as a prisoner of war, arriving there on March 5, 1875.[12] So pleased was the Spanish government with his capture that the minister of war sent a telegram to the captain general calling it a "signal triumph" and confirming with approval the promotion of Ariza to captain.

After two months in Santandar, García was again moved, this time to the prison of San Francisco in Madrid. Bad as jail was, even there rank had certain privileges—including being allowed visitors. His good Hispanic mother, Lucía Íñiguez y Landín—usually referred to as Cía—abandoned several daughters and a developmentally disabled son in Cuba to be near Calixto ("son of my soul and of my heart") and was able to visit him regularly. There was also a group of Cuban students living in Madrid who saw him often. Unfortunately, their love and enthusiasm for the prisoner caused him to be sent to a much worse prison in Pamplona; the officials became aware of a plot the students had concocted to free him and, for security reasons, the government had him "confinado en oscuro y húmedo calabozo" (confined in a dark and humid dungeon). Often cold, sick, and hungry, he remained there until June 8, 1878.[13]

After being granted amnesty, García moved with his family to New York.[14] Once there he revived the Comité Revolucionario and wrote its manifesto calling for a new war to overthrow Spanish rule.[15]

He was joined in this effort by Antonio Maceo, another important figure in the independence movement and who was at that time in Jamaica. Maceo was the son of Marcos Maceo, a Venezuelan who had served in the Spanish Army, and Mariana Grajales, a woman born in Cuba of black Dominican parents. Grajales was a fierce supporter of Cuban independence and encouraged her sons to join the rebel army. Even today she is known as the Mother of Cuba, with schools, squares, and organizations named for her. Maceo enlisted as a private at the start of the Ten Years' War and rose through the ranks to become a general. Then as now, having one black parent usually determined one's racial definition. Known as the Bronze Titan, he was devoted not only to independence from Spain but also the abolition of slavery and equality for blacks and was the most prominent among mulatto and black officers who were ready once more to battle the Spaniards.[16] Many enslaved Cubans who had in the Ten Years' War remained obedient to their masters now saw a new opportunity to gain their freedom.

The proportionately high number of men of color who embraced the latest stage of the insurrection gave Spanish officials the opportunity to characterize it not as a struggle for Cuban independence but as a race war, with its goal being the creation of a black republic. The ruse worked, and nearly all the white liberals and generals disassociated themselves from this latest effort. To counteract the perception that it was a black rebellion, García ordered Maceo to remain in Jamaica rather than to lead an expedition to Cuba where he was to have taken command of the forces in Oriente Province; a white general, Gregorio Benítez, would instead take his place. But things didn't go well.[17] By the time García sailed from New Jersey on March 26, 1880, with twenty or so men, it was all but over. He traveled first to Jamaica and then to the coastal town of Aserradero in what is now the province of Santiago de Cuba, landing on May 7.[18] The Spanish authorities were aware of his arrival and, surprisingly, managed to keep this news from two of the more important black generals, José Maceo (Antonio's brother) and

Guillermo Moncada, both of whom, thinking they were part of a lost cause, surrendered on June 1. Without them, García had no hope for success, and on August 3 he too surrendered.[19] The aborted revolution became known as La Guerra Chiquita, the Little War.

This time around, the Spanish had no intention of turning García loose. He was taken once again to Spain as a prisoner and was probably lucky he wasn't shot. One can only imagine how he felt to be back aboard the mail steamer *Méndez Nuñez*.

With the Little War effectively crushed, the authorities in Spain were less interested in punishing García than in keeping him out of Cuba. Accordingly, he was released from prison on October 12, 1880, after giving his word that he wouldn't leave the country. This time his mother, Cía, stayed in Cuba, but in April 1882 his wife and children left New York to join him in Madrid. He supported them by taking a position with the Bank of Castile, a branch of the Bank of Madrid, of which an old schoolmate was a director. He also taught French and English, and for a while held a teaching post with the Association for the Education of Women. The years went by quietly enough; his family grew, his oldest daughter married an Anglo-American dentist, and his father died. Then, in December 1887, came disturbing and tragic news from Havana. His first-born son, Calixto García Veléz, had in a fit of jealous rage murdered his beautiful young wife and then committed suicide. Life somehow went on.

Calixto García Veléz was not the only son named for García. In 1873 García was told that his wife, Isabel, and other family members had been killed by the Spanish. At the time he was involved in one of what, apparently, were many affairs while in the field. Believing himself a widower, he married Leonela Enamorado Cabrera. In June the following year she bore a son whom they named Calixto García Enamorado. Three months later García was captured and discovered that Isabel hadn't been killed. After the custom of the time, the younger Calixto lost the right to his father's family name and became simply Calixto Enamorado. At age twenty-one he would join the rebel forces and participate in many significant battles. As a result of his bravery he was regularly promoted, and at the end of the war in 1898 he was made brigadier general. One of his father's sisters then legally adopted him so that he might gain the family name and become Calixto García Íñiguez Enamorado. He went on to be a government official, politician, and novelist, dying in 1951.[20]

There was one odd incident that speaks to García's character. On September 19, 1886, he and his son Carlos were on the balcony of the family's huge fourth-floor apartment, one of the many houses in which they lived during their fifteen years in Madrid, when they heard sporadic gunfire in the distance. García assumed it was a revolt instigated by General Arsenio Martínez-Campos y Antón, the republican who was later to be military commander and governor general in Cuba. Then he heard someone below calling loudly for the porter to open the front door. This person asked if this was the house in which General Calixto García lived, and if so, he had an urgent need to see him. Although fearful that the government might somehow mistakenly have assumed he would be mixed up in a purely Spanish political battle and that this might be a trap, García left the balcony and entered the house to face the intruder. He immediately recognized Francisco Ariza, the daring young lieutenant (now a captain and not so young) who had captured him in San Antonio twelve years earlier. Ariza had no intention of capturing him again. He explained that it was not Martínez-Campos who had initiated the quickly foiled insurrection but another general named Villacampa, and that he, Ariza, had thrown his lot in with him. Now he was in need of sanctuary. According to Carlos, García turned to his wife and said, "Prepare a room for Captain Ariza; we have to hide him." Ariza stayed until it was safe to leave and, through the good offices of Martínez-Campos, was insinuated back into the army.[21]

Through it all García stayed true to Cuba and the fight for independence. He continued corresponding with compatriots and invited members of the local Cuban colony to his home, which a friend described as "the headquarters of the Cuban insurrectionists in Madrid."

Cuban liberation remained a live topic among most of the veterans of the Ten Years' War and the Little War. Chief among them was the

Cuban-born poet, journalist, and orator José Martí. In 1892 he established El Partido Revolucionario Cubano (popularly referred to as the junta), whose purpose was "to obtain, with the united forces of all men of good will, the absolute independence of the island of Cuba, and to foment and aid that of Puerto Rico."[22] Over the next three years, things moved inexorably toward the call for revolution, which Martí issued in April 1895. He landed in Cuba himself on April 11, was appointed major general of the Liberation Army on April 16, and was killed in a skirmish on May 19, upon which Tomás Estrada Palma took over party leadership.[23] This time there was to be no turning back; Antonio Maceo and Máximo Gómez were in command.[24]

García's compatriots wanted him back to help lead the struggle, and they established a subscription fund to raise money to pay for his and his family's departure from Spain. On August 4, 1895, his fifty-sixth birthday, García wrote to Estrada Palma, saying that since the beginning of the new revolution it had been his most ardent desire to join the struggle "but, unfortunately, the deplorable state of my health prevents my attempting that enterprise." His condition was well known, and as a result, the authorities neglected to watch him as carefully as they might. One day in October he was asked if he would be leaving to join the revolution. "It would be impossible," he answered, "because I am very sick." The following day he left for Paris, later arriving by boat in New York City. Waiting for him were Estrada Palma and others connected with the Revolutionary Party. He was taken to the home of a Dr. Menocal where, after a short rest, he met well into the evening with virtually every important Cuban in the New York area.

García spent the next couple of months in New York being watched by men from the Pinkerton Detective Agency, hired by the Spanish government, and by U.S. officials trying to prevent him from filibustering, a serious violation of U.S. neutrality laws. At one point he evaded those watching him, but the truth came to light on January 28, 1896, when the ship on which he'd sailed, the steamer *J. W. Hawkins*, foundered at sea forty-five miles from the Barneget, New Jersey, lighthouse. The passengers and crew who hadn't drowned were rescued by various ships in the vicinity. Among the survivors were Calixto and Carlos García.

Captain Henry Denyse of the tug *Fred B. Daizell*, to which the two generals were transferred from a rescuing schooner, was asked by a reporter if the Garcías were on board.

García and his son were both on board, and 68 others besides— seventy in all. They had no baggage or dunnage of any kind; that is, none except García had any. He had two valises, and both of them were bursting full with greenbacks.

Did you see the greenbacks?

I did.

The reason Capt. Denyse was so sure of the number on board was because he was paid one dollar each to carry them into New York.[25]

According to the *Hawkins* mate, the ship was struck by a severe storm and sprang a leak. The pumps were choked with coal, so every man began bailing, but their buckets couldn't keep up with the water pouring in. Even jettisoning the bags of coal on deck didn't help. This came as no surprise to Captain Denyse. "Did you ever see the *Hawkins*? No! Well I have and I wouldn't go as far as Staten Island in her."[26] A spokesman for the junta had an equally low opinion: "She was not fit to cross the East or the North River."[27]

Up to the point when the boat began to leak, the expedition had gone quite well. Conductors on the crosstown 138th Street trolley cars who were questioned later reported an extraordinary number of "dark, black-eyed fellows" boarding their cars at every stop: "No one spoke a word. They kept looking over their shoulders out of the windows, as if they were afraid of something. Some of them were fine-looking fellows, with good clothes and silk hats. Others were rough-looking men, in slouch hats and buttoned-up overcoats. They all got out in a body at Locust Avenue, and walked north." There was a pier at the foot of Locust where the *J. W. Hawkins* was being loaded for its departure at around 1:00 A.M. The fact that García and so many others were able to reach the pier and board the boat without arousing the suspicion of anybody but trolley car conductors was something of a surprise considering that the Spanish had Pinkerton agents watching him. When the Spanish consul was asked how the filibusters left the city undetected by the agents, he replied testily, "I do not know. That is what I am trying to find out."[28] Speaking for the Pinkerton agency, a representative said, "Our rules prohibit the admission that our agents have been detailed to service in any direction. This, of course, applies to the Hawkins expedition."[29]

García's next filibustering venture occurred later that month in New York. It involved the *Bermuda*, a 223-foot steamer purchased some time earlier by John D. Hart, a Philadelphian known to have been associated with other rebel expeditions to Cuba. The ship drew attention when it was placed in dry dock and completely overhauled, including having its bottom scraped and painted, over a very busy two-day period. The captain took out clearance papers for Colombia on February 23, but by then Pinkerton agents and U.S. marshals were watching developments very carefully; they even knew which tugs had been hired to transport freight and individuals to the ship.

On the evening of February 24 a dozen Pinkerton agents and eight federal officials hid themselves aboard the revenue cutter *Hudson*, which steamed to the vicinity of the *Bermuda* and lay in wait with lights out, hidden behind a huge coaling vessel. After watching fifty or so men board the steamer from a tug, the *Hudson* closed in for the kill as the *Bermuda* was weighing anchor. With revolvers drawn, marshals climbed over the railings. As soon as the ship was under their control, marshals aboard the *Hudson* picked off the supply boats, eventually confiscating thirty to forty tons of war matériel and arresting 159 individuals, including García. García was one of five arraigned; the men were charged with violating a federal statute prohibiting any military enterprise against a state with whom the United States was at peace. Then, at the behest of the Spanish consul, further charges were brought in connection with the fiasco involving the *Hawkins*. Late in the day the men were finally released on bail, García's being $2,500. On March 11 the five were indicted by a federal grand jury. And though the arms shipment intended for transport on the *Bermuda* had been confiscated, it was believed the ship was once again loaded with arms and ready to sail. One member of the Cuban junta was very critical of the operation:

General Garcia is a very patriotic man and a good fighter, but he lacks the caution necessary to fit out such an expedition as that on the Bermuda. . . . Instead of the Bermuda lying in the upper bay, awaiting her cargo and the men who had volunteered for the expedition, she ought to have been out to sea beyond the reach of Spanish spies who are watching every movement of the patriots. It was folly to suppose that an expedition of such magnitude could be fitted out at this port and successfully evade the detectives of the Spanish Government.[30]

García apparently took this criticism to heart. Barely three weeks later, he and a few others were involved in a complicated ruse to avoid watching eyes. They left Philadelphia by tug on March 15, ostensibly heading for the Delaware Breakwater. During a fog the next afternoon they doubled back up the Delaware River to Camden, New Jersey. From there they took a special train to Tuckahoe, New Jersey, where they boarded the steamboat *Atlantic City*, a small ship normally used during the summer tourist season. The Cubans must have felt safe from surveillance on the ship, because it stayed in port until the morning of March 18, when it steamed to Ocean City, New Jersey. Its purpose in sailing, according to papers filed with the custom house, was a demonstration cruise for potential buyers. Once beyond the three-mile limit, the rebels boarded the waiting *Bermuda* and were headed for Cuba.[31]

This time the ship was under the command of "Dynamite Johnny" O'Brien, a well-known filibuster who acquired his nickname after secretly transporting sixty tons of dynamite to Colón, Cuba.[32] Having been frustrated in the past, García was very pessimistic about successfully reaching Cuba this time, but O'Brien reassured him: "Take my word for it. This time we will get you there." There were, however, complications, not the least of which were the two pilots on board. One of them, it turned out, was a traitor whose job it was to lead them into a trap. The other was merely incompetent. When the steamer reached Cuba, the pilot who had been bribed intentionally misidentified a lighthouse, saying they should continue along the coast for another thirty-five miles. Fortunately, O'Brien was correctly able to identify the light and knew exactly where they were; he physically kicked the traitor off the bridge and piloted the ship himself to the prearranged landing site, a small harbor near Baracoa on Cuba's extreme northeast coast. And so on March 25, 1896, General Calixto García, now changed into full uniform, stepped onto Cuban soil for the first time in fifteen years.[33]

To deal with the renewed conflict, the Spanish authorities appointed an infamous officer from the Ten Years' War, General Valeriano Weyler y Nicolau. Approximately 300,000 peasants—especially family members of revolutionaries—were concentrated into camps with inadequate housing, little food, and no medical attention; tens of thousands died of starvation, mistreatment, and disease. In the meantime, thousands more middle-class Cubans fled the country, while many who stayed behind were arrested and exiled to Spanish prisons and African penal colonies. Before the year was out, the insurgents' numbers had increased to 50,000—a number, however large, that merely equaled the number of fresh troops that Weyler had brought with him. The total number of Spanish troops then stood at 200,000.[34]

When García landed at Baracoa, Weyler had been in Cuba nearly two months, and his extreme measures were well under way. By common agreement, Gómez concentrated his troops in the western provinces, and Maceo in the central.[35]

The fight to free Cuba from Spain is nearly always referred to as the Spanish-American War, though the American participation in Cuba lasted only a few months and was confined to two naval battles, one land battle, and a few firefights. The real fighting had been going on for three years between the Cubans and the Spanish, and the *insurrectos* pretty much controlled the sparsely populated eastern end of the island. By the time Rowan reached the small city of Bayamo—which García's forces had just taken from the Spanish—there were in all of Cuba perhaps 40,000 poorly equipped Cubans fighting well-armed but ineffective Spanish regular soldiers and volunteers. Though they numbered nearly a quarter million, many thousands of Spaniards died of disease and many thousands more lay in hospitals. One estimate put the effective number of Spanish soldiers at 55,000.[36]

In spite of enormous amounts of money raised for their assistance and dozens of filibuster attempts, there weren't nearly enough weapons to arm the rebels.[37] The lucky ones carried captured Spanish Mausers, technically superior weapons to the Winchesters, Remingtons, and Springfields toted by their comrades. While a Spanish soldier carried 100 to 150 rounds of ammunition, a rebel usually had 4 or 5 rounds. The dearness of their weapons and the motivation of their cause made the Cubans more effective shooters than the Spaniards. The German-designed Mausers had a range four or five times that of the American-made rifles, but that advantage amounted to little when the rifles were in the hands of the barely trained Spaniards.

To make up for the difference in numbers and weapons, the Cubans developed a highly organized force of guerrillas who were able to rely on peasants not only for support but also for information regarding Spanish troop movements.[38] At the end of three years, the guerrilla tactics, the climate, and disease had caused 100,000 Spanish casualties, and the soldiers still on their feet were far from being in a proper state of readiness.[39] A British observer wrote, "It makes one sad to see the quality of the expeditions packed off in heartless shoals to Cuba, boys, to look at, at fifteen or sixteen, who have never held a rifle till this moment, and now are almost ignorant which end it fires, good lads—too good to go to such uneven butchery—with cheerful, patriotic willing faces, but the very antithesis of a soldier."[40]

Another British writer traveling in Spain interviewed a returned invalid in early May 1898 before word had reached them about the Spanish defeat in Manila Bay. The soldier damned everybody from Weyler to the Cuban volunteers fighting the rebels to the rebels themselves, but saved his special curses for the United States. In response to the question, "Does Spain wish to keep Cuba?" he answered,

> The officers and *empleados* [civil servants] do in order to fill their pockets, but Spain is sick of Cuba. There is hardly a village that has not some of its number dead in Cuba, hardly a village where someone has not come back a wreck, as I have, to tell his friends about Cuba. But we will not give up Cuba to those thieving

Yankees without a fight. Those Yankee hogs have insulted us, and we must fight them to the death. If it were only "Cuba Libre" we should not so much mind that, but we know the Yankees mean to steal the island and make much money out of it. Look you, the Yankee loves nothing so much as money; everybody knows that. He never did anything for any country unless with the hope of making money. He calls himself a Christian, but his God is "Don Dinero."[41]

When U.S. entry into the war became inevitable, it was the wish of the Cubans that such intervention be limited to blockading the ports and providing the rebels with arms and ammunition. Deprived of food, ammunition, and medical supplies, the Spanish soldiers would be at the mercy of the strengthened Cubans. Such a strategy would also mean that one foreign army (Spain's) would not be replaced by another (America's). This would leave the Cubans free to rule their own country after their victory. The American generals favored this approach because they had no wish to send large numbers of their soldiers into Cuban jungles to suffer as the Spanish had done.[42] There was no question, though, that American troops would land in Cuba and that military cooperation between the two armies was essential.

On the morning of May 1, the news quickly spread throughout Bayamo that Gervasio Savio had come from Jamaica with an envoy from the American government. Around noon they arrived at the recently established military headquarters with "the Cuban flag . . . hanging lazily over the door from an inclined staff." Leaving Rowan standing by his horse, Savio advanced to the door and was admitted. He was carrying the telegram from Estrada Palma indicating that the Cubans should have full confidence in the bearer. After a short wait, Savio was presenting Lieutenant Andrew S. Rowan to General Calixto García, whom Rowan later called "a splendid old man . . . a Chesterfield in manner."[43] Rowan was given a glass of rum and some breakfast, after which he and García got down to business. One of those present, Colonel José Portuondo y Tamayo, acted as interpreter. Rowan evidently made a good impression; as Brigadier General Enrique

Figure 3. Lieutenant Rowan, looking like a local mailman, hands an envelope to a grandfatherly General Calixto García in a 1945 advertisement for the National City Bank of New York, which at the time of publication had eight branches in Cuba. J. W. Wilkinson/Citibank.

Collazo later noted, "Rowan was of average height, well formed, broad shouldered, and good looking. His frank and candid eyes denoted intelligence and resolve, his manners were refined, and his conversation showed him to be cultured and a perfect gentleman."[44] Leaving Rowan with the general's son, García and his staff consulted in private at some length. They had no intention of allowing Rowan to reconnoiter the area and to report his observations; nor did they want him to return with a written message that could be misinterpreted. To make sure that the War Department was given the exact information—and only that information—that would serve its purposes, it was decided that three officers would accompany Rowan back to Washington, D.C. Furthermore, they would leave as quickly as possible.

It was at this point that Rowan botched his mission.[45] He should have refused the offer and insisted on staying. He hadn't been sent there as a messenger boy; he was a trained military observer dispatched to Cuba, as Major Arthur L. Wagner wrote in his memorandum of February 26, to "keep the War Department informed as to the strength, efficiency, movements and general military situation." The idea was for him to stay in Cuba, to "accompany the Insurgent Forces," and to send back dispatches.[46] One problem with the latter was that he had destroyed his line of communication to the War Department through U.S. consul Louis A. Dent when he insisted that the consul disassociate himself from the mission.

Even though Dent claimed to be acting in the best interests of the government and with no personal feelings in the matter, Rowan had definitely gotten under his skin. On the very day that Rowan left for Cuba, Dent sent a report to the secretary of state detailing his strenuous efforts to make the mission a success and pointing out Rowan's base ingratitude: "I consider that his action . . . was characterized by neither good taste, judgment nor discretion. He placed me in an embarrassing position with the Junta people; incurred for me the personal enmity of the representative of a powerful news corporation, and almost destroyed the plans of his government." His next sentence, however, made him equally complicit with Rowan in the failure of the mission: "By my withdrawal he nullified the arrangement which I had to keep open communication with him, and provide for his despatches."[47]

Rowan might have tried to negotiate his way out of this fix, but he didn't. Instead, he left Jamaica knowing he had no ready means to keep the War Department informed about the military situation. From this it can be inferred that he had no intention of staying in Cuba and sending back reports. When García was later criticized for dealing directly with Rowan and disregarding the Cuban civil government, Colonel Cosme de la Torriente y Peraza pointed out that the consul was at some distance and that Rowan was in a great hurry to return to the United States.[48]

The officers García designated to accompany Rowan were Collazo, Lieutenant Colonel Carlos Hernández, and Lieutenant Colonel Dr. Gonzalo García Vieta. The Cubans carried with them military data, maps, and other material, including a message from García written in English that read, "To the Secretary of Ward [sic] U.S.A.—Dear Sir: I confer into Gen. E. Collazo my entire confidence full powers to slate [sic] in view to you giving particulars of importance verbally, of great value for further intelligence between that Department and this Army."[49] According to Collazo, there was a note written in Spanish repeating this information that added, "Mr. A. S. Rowan has completed his mission to my complete satisfaction and I would be very pleased if you were able to place him under my command." García would never have written these words if Rowan had fully informed him of his assignment. Rowan referred to it obliquely when he later recounted his trip, pointing out that García "by his quick conception and speedy acceptance of conditions had saved me months of useless toil." He seems totally to have forgotten why he was sent. What he took back with him was a snapshot provided by the Cubans, not the continuous reporting of events and developments that Wagner had convinced Adjutant General Henry Clark Corbin would be forthcoming. Rowan did say he would like to have had a chance to "look around me in these strange surroundings" but promptly answered, "Yes, Sir!" when asked if he could proceed that day.[50] "It was evident that General García was a 'to-day' man. No '*mañana*' man was he."[51] After a 5:00 P.M. meal, Rowan was told it was time to go. He hoped that Savio would have been a part of the expedition, but García wouldn't permit it; Savio's services were needed elsewhere. There were others who could provide an escort.

And so, within hours after his arrival in Bayamo, Rowan and the three officers were on their way to Cuba's north coast. In addition to an escort, they were accompanied by two sailors familiar with the coastal waters. These men, it was thought, would be valuable should the United States send back requested supplies. They didn't stop until midnight, setting up camp near the Cauto River. On the move again at sunrise, they perceived a four- or five-hundred-man force of Cuban soldiers near the war-ruined town of Victoria de las Tunas, which, Rowan noted, was "razed to the ground." That night they camped at the foot of a hill called Damanuecos. (This may or may not have been the actual name of the hill. Rowan sometimes misunderstood Spanish names.) Somehow aware that the boat in which they would leave Cuba needed sails, they spent the day making them from their hammock canopies. They climbed the hill the next morning, and Rowan saw a huge palm forest stretching north through which they would have to pass. In addition to heavy brush that made the journey difficult, there was also *guao*, the Cuban version of poison ivy, which apparently made a painful impression on Rowan. After leaving the jungle behind, they passed by a fortress with walls of coral rock and finally arrived at the coast. Here they found saltworks (*salinas*) where seawater was boiled in huge kettles to obtain salt for the Cuban rebels, the work being a form of punishment for military malefactors.[52] It had taken five days, and Rowan, without bedding, suffered from the cold every night as he had since his arrival. He was completely deprived of sleep one night by sand fleas.

At sunset on May 5 in Manatí Bay, they "drew a little cockle-shell of a boat from under a mangrove bush." There was room for only five of the party in the fourteen-foot boat, so Vieta was sent back. This was a pity because Vieta, a relative of García's, was a medical doctor familiar with tropical diseases and might have been able to offer useful aid to the Americans.[53] With food gathered from the forest and the sails they'd patched from hammock canopies, they set out at 11:00 P.M. Even with only five on board, the boat was low in the water. "It was desperately hard rowing," Rowan later wrote, "and the big waves were continually washing over the gunwales, wetting our stores and keeping us busy bailing. All night long we worked steadily without a wink of sleep.

At dawn the next morning the man at the helm called out, 'un vapor'—a steamer. This was followed by 'dos vapores, tres vapores, caramba, doce vapores'—twelve steamers."[54]

What they were seeing was the U.S. North Atlantic Fleet commanded by acting rear admiral William Sampson. His ships, which had been blockading Havana, were steaming east in the hope of intercepting a Spanish squadron under the command of Admiral Pascual Cervera y Topete. Cervera was known to have left the Cape Verde islands on April 29, probably heading for Puerto Rico. Unfortunately for Spain, Cervera's collection of warships was in a pitiable state of readiness. His flagship, the armored cruiser *Infanta Maria Teresa*, had malfunctioning electric motors serving the turret and ammunition hoists, and the breechblocks of some guns either didn't fit or were missing. The *Vizcaya's* hull was so barnacle-ridden that its speed was cut dramatically; in addition, several of its batteries were defective. The turret of the *Almirante Oquendo* wouldn't turn and couldn't be repaired. The one ship that could have given them a fighting chance, the new cruiser *Cristóbal Colón*, was without the four guns of its main batteries, and nobody knew why they hadn't been installed or where they could be found. Of the remaining vessels, only three torpedo boats were more or less fit for service.

Reports of the fleet's departure from Spain had thrown Washington into a tizzy. Unknown to Cervera was the extraordinary fact that while he and his captains were slowly crossing the Atlantic in vessels of questionable seaworthiness and reduced firepower, they were also terrorizing the East Coast and disrupting American invasion plans. So long as their whereabouts remained uncertain, they controlled America's war strategy.[55]

Rowan and his companions in the "cockle-shell" boat continued sailing—and bailing—northward. The next morning they stopped for a brief rest on a key south of Andros Island, the largest of the Bahamas;[56] in the afternoon they met up with a small sponging steamer that carried them into Nassau. According to Rowan, they were "promptly set upon by the most rapacious quarantine highwaymen that can be found anywhere. Mr. McLane, the American consul, finally rescued us, and on the second day we were off for Key West in the schooner

'Fearless.'" Rowan's crediting the American consul makes perfect sense, but Enrique Collazo claimed a Cuban agent, Indelacio Salas, was instrumental in obtaining their release. Perhaps it was both.[57]

Incommunicado for the past few weeks, Rowan didn't learn until he arrived in Nassau that his journey had been reported in detail in the press.[58] On April 27, an Associated Press report with the dateline Kingston, Jamaica, appeared in newspapers across the United States. Reporter Elmer Roberts had at least waited until after Rowan landed in Cuba before telling all he knew, but what he knew could have come from only one source—Rowan himself. "Lieutenant Rowan is on his way to the camp of General Calixto Garcia," Roberts wrote. "He will represent the War Department in arranging for the co-operation of the insurgents in the invasion of Eastern Cuba by the forces of the United States. The time and place of invasion will be controlled by events and the character of Lieutenant Rowan's dispatches." The account continued with further details, but Roberts was not aware that Dent was no longer involved in transmitting Rowan's intelligence: "A courier with Lieutenant Rowan's dispatches to the War Department will probably leave General Garcia's camp next week."[59] Dent's April 23 cable to Assistant Secretary of State William Day, noting that Rowan's expedition was to start and that he (Dent) had withdrawn his connection with the enterprise, crossed the desk of Alvey Adee, the second assistant secretary, who saw the potential for trouble and sent it immediately by courier to the adjutant general, Henry Corbin.[60] By this time Corbin would have been aware of the controversy surrounding Roberts. This would explain the publication of an article with the dateline, Washington, April 25, that appeared in the *New York Times* two days before Roberts's article was published. In it, newspaper correspondents and publishers were warned that they shouldn't publish what they knew. A federal law enacted in 1806 had included the provision: "Whosoever shall be convicted of holding correspondence with or giving intelligence to the enemy either directly or indirectly, shall suffer death, or such other punishment as shall be ordered by the General or a court-martial." The *New York Times* article went on to note that "General Corbin has not yet found occasion to renew this order," but the threat that he would do so if necessary was apparent. The article did note that there was no record of a correspondent's ever having been shot for violating the order.[61]

On April 28, the day after the articles about Rowan appeared, Dent sent a coded telegram to the State Department: "Am informed that Roberts associated press correspondent given out here full particulars Rowan's mission and sent story home also if story told to me is true Rowan gave him full confession deceiving me as to the object his mission."[62] Adee immediately sent Corbin a copy.

The next day, a new warning was published pointing out that if correspondents continued to be indiscreet when it came to publishing war news, the whole lot of them could be banned from the theater of operations, a fate almost worse than being shot.[63] But this was an empty threat; the War Department had not hesitated to use newspaper reporters as information gatherers and, when it suited its purposes, as information disseminators. What it didn't want was for them to act independently, but there was probably never a time in history before or since when war correspondents had such freedom of movement. As the war progressed, it was sometimes difficult to distinguish between correspondents and combatants.[64]

None of this was what Wagner had foreseen when he proposed sending his good friend Rowan to Cuba, and it must have distressed him greatly; however, when Dent's message was passed on to him by Corbin, he loyally defended his friend and colleague, stating, "I do not believe Mr. Dent's statement. I know Lieut Rowan to be a discreet officer. I believe him to be a victim of malice or ignorance on the part of other people." Notably, he added the words "or ignorance" in pen to the typed note, perhaps realizing that to describe the career diplomat's motive simply as "malice" would undercut his defense of Rowan.[65]

Roberts continued to give Dent fits, finally causing him to send a coded cablegram to Day on May 4 asking that the correspondent somehow be recalled immediately: "Owing to his publication here Spanish Consul has requested the Government to investigate and to prosecute all parties connected with the Rowan expedition. The government has complied." It had to. Jamaica was a neutral country, and those assisting Rowan could be regarded as engaging in an act of war. Dent, who probably saw himself spending time behind bars, was showing signs

of paranoia. In the cablegram he wrote, "Roberts will make a dangerous witness, and being inspired by most bitter animosity against me,
he would undoubtedly expose my connection with the affair. Please act
immediately. The steamer for New York leaves tomorrow morning." He
wanted Roberts on it. John Moore, as assistant secretary, responded the
next day to say that he had communicated with the Associated Press,
but he indicated no sign that Dent's wishes would be carried out. This
lack of news disturbed Dent to the point that he considered allowing the junta people to take Roberts to Cuba in order to get him off
the island. Then he backed down and pleaded once again for the State
Department to get Roberts recalled "and thus end a most disagreeable
incident, and eliminate a disturbing element."[66]

The newspaper coverage of Rowan's mission had been read with
some anxiety by his family. On May 6, his father wrote Wagner asking
if the reports were true and promising to keep any information Wagner
might impart strictly confidential. Wagner replied with assurances
that he was "confident [Rowan] would reach his destination in safety,
and that he will emerge from the war with an enviable reputation. I do
not expect to hear from him in some weeks." Imagine, then, his surprise three days later when he received the following coded message
sent from Nassau: "Am safely with García's representatives and please
telegraph wife."[67] Keeping a promise he'd made to Rowan's father,
Wagner immediately notified him of this development;[68] someone else
in the office sent a similar telegram to Rowan's wife in Atchison,
Kansas. Wagner, no doubt dumbfounded by the telegram from Nassau,
must have been equally surprised the following day by newspaper
reports stating that Rowan had accomplished his mission—which he
most definitely had not.[69] Yet six days later Wagner, now assistant adjutant general, was in Tampa himself and sent a note to Rowan lauding
him for completing his journey and noting that the "dangerous mission has been executed by you to my complete satisfaction," almost the
exact words written by General García.[70]

How can we account for Wagner's unabashed embrace of Rowan's
actions? To begin with, he appears to have genuinely liked the junior
officer; perhaps he saw something of himself in Rowan. Their per-
sonalities in some respects were not dissimilar—particularly their

disputative natures and superior attitudes regarding other officers. One can imagine their privately sharing disdainful chuckles. Both men were inclined to send formal, if rancorous, complaints up the line on those occasions when they sensed they'd been disrespected.[71] As the officer who argued to send an agent to Cuba and who personally selected Rowan for the job, Wagner was responsible for any missteps in the operation. The only way to avoid criticism was to act as if Rowan had done exactly as he'd been instructed.

The news of Rowan's arrival in Nassau did not reach Kingston until late in the day on May 10, by which time Roberts had successfully negotiated with the junta people for his transportation to Cuba. The previous evening Dent made one last desperate attempt to have him recalled, and finally learned from a late-night cablegram that Rowan was to return to the United States. The Roberts affair degenerated into exchanges of charges and countercharges; some of these involved Dent's deputy consul, L. B. Mosher, who resigned on May 12 to become a correspondent for William Randolph Hearst's *New York Evening Journal*. At times the exasperated Dent appeared to be close to a mental breakdown.[72]

On May 13, a month after he had landed in Jamaica, and still unaware of the controversy surrounding his return, Rowan reached Key West. From there he sailed to Tampa and a waiting press corps eager for details. Port Tampa, on Florida's western coast, had been chosen as the point of embarkation for the assault on Cuba. The invading forces were designated as the Fifth Corps.[73] Thousands of troops had been pouring in, and the area was ill suited to receive them. Even less ready for the gathering of thousands of troops and mountains of matériel was the War Department itself. As Secretary of War Russell Alger later wrote, "The Army, or any great part of it, had not been mobilized since the Civil War. The problem was in all respects a new one, and it was presented in a form that aggravated its inherent obstacles."[74] The supply officers simply didn't know their jobs. According to Wagner, who reported on the situation later, "though all worked energetically, there was all the friction attendant upon the hurried solution of an important practical problem by untried men."[75] A typical example of the confusion caused by inexperience was the handling of bills of lading for the thousands of freight cars carrying supplies. The bills of lading identified the contents of the 13,239 freight cars providing supplies for the eventual 28,195 men slated to be transported to Cuba and 17,460 to Puerto Rico, or one freight car for every 3.45 men.[76] Instead of being posted on the outside of the cars, the bills of lading were mailed separately, as was the practice at the time. But the tiny post office was overwhelmed by the crush of mail for the troops. (By the middle of May, three to five regiments were arriving daily, and every soldier among them was receiving letters from family and friends.) Without breaking the railroad cars' seals, there was no way of knowing whether a car carried clothing, horse equipment, ammunition, siege guns, or commissary stores. And because of inadequate sidings at Tampa, many cars were sidetracked miles from the city, their whereabouts unknown for weeks. In time, trains were backed up as far as Columbia, South Carolina. When describing the snafu months later, Commissary General of Subsistence Charles P. Eagen put a positive spin on it by writing that it was caused by "the celerity with which the troops and their supplies were concentrated at that place."[77] As Wagner pointed out, the troops and their supplies should have come together long before arriving in Tampa. That port was chosen for the "*embarkation of completely mobilized troops*, not as [a point] of organization and supply" (Wagner's emphasis).[78]

As it developed, they had more time in Tampa to sort things out than had been anticipated. As long as Cervera's ships remained a "fleet in being" as opposed to a fleet in fact, U.S. warships couldn't be spared to protect the convoy that would carry the troops.[79] This meant that the invading force had to stay put, and staying put meant living in absolutely miserable conditions. Poultney Bigelow, writing for *Harper's Weekly*, described the scene:

> The poor men have to sleep on the ground in the heavy, dirty sand. Their sweaty clothing picks it up, and their food is full of it. Every whiff of hot air blows fine dust about, and every horse, cart, or even passing person adds discomfort to men already miserable. How little it would cost to have the camp sprinkled

once or twice a day! Or at least the government might have provided rough boards from which the men could have sawed themselves a few feet of flooring.

We are in the habit of pitying the soldier of Europe as hardly treated. For downright neglect, I have seen nothing to beat the way the American is treated by Uncle Sam.

Who is responsible for this meanness which is seriously affecting the health of our men?

In this hot climate we yearn for fresh fruit and vegetables, for anything that will quench thirst and at the same time cool the blood. Meat and all heating things we try to avoid by a wise instinct. The troops, however, are supplied with only that which is most unseasonable—greasy pork, and beans of that brown quality that makes one ready to spend the rest of the day in a watermelon-patch. I found officers with nothing but these rations, because the commissary had nothing else, and they could not afford to send for other things from the town. Is it a wonder that the men develop abnormal thirst, and rush off to satisfy this craving as best they can—some with plain water, some with milk-shakes, some with beer, some with other compounds? The result is that already the camp doctors are busy every morning with men and officers suffering from varying degrees of dysentery. We hush this up as well as we can, but to do so altogether is impossible.[80]

For diversion, the men spent considerable time drinking, gambling, fighting, and whoring.

The senior officers, on the other hand, spent their days trading old war stories among the ornamental brick and silver-tipped minarets of the Tampa Bay Hotel, a sprawling five-story complex that covered six acres with a casino, a ballroom, a peacock park, wide verandahs, and 511 guest rooms; Richard Harding Davis, one of the more celebrated war correspondents of the day, wrote that it was "larger than the palaces which Ismail Pasha built overnight in Cairo, and outwardly not unlike them in appearance."[81] This unlikely complex existed because it was the terminal point and home port for Henry B. Plant's

railroad lines and steamships. A self-made millionaire, Plant had purchased bankrupt Southern railroads after the Civil War and consoli-
dated them into a single system. The hotel was built as a destination
in itself to lure Northern passengers aboard the trains. According to
some accounts, Plant managed to convince Secretary of War Alger
that Port Tampa, some nine miles from the city of Tampa, was the
appropriate embarkation point for troops being sent to Cuba, thus
guaranteeing considerable traffic for his rail lines. To sweeten the deal,
two floors of the hotel were reserved for officers and their wives.[82]
While later accepting no personal responsibility for choosing Tampa,
Alger pointed out that the location was suitable for a small force, but
"it would hardly have been selected for the purposes of the Santiago
expedition had so large a force been under consideration at the time."[83]

Theodore Roosevelt later mentioned being shocked that businessmen might try to arrange war preparations to increase the profits of
their corporations, noting that "one morning a very wealthy and influential man, a respectable and upright man according to his own lights,
called on me to protest against our choice of Tampa, and to put in a
plea for a certain other port, *on the ground that his railroad was entitled to its share of the profit for hauling the army and equipment!*"
(Roosevelt's emphasis).[84]

It was to the Tampa Bay Hotel that Rowan was taken—"bronzed
and hidden in an old Panama hat," according to Davis—to regale the
hundred or so reporters with details of his adventure.[85] "One Cuban
in the bush," he told them, "is equal to two Spaniards. They will fight
hard, and they are absolutely essential to our army, of which they
would be the eyes and ears."[86]

Perhaps it was the unaccustomed experience of seeing a hundred
pencils busily scribbling down his every word that made Rowan think
he could jump the chain of command. Whatever the reason, he put
himself in an untenable position vis-à-vis General Corbin by tele-
graphing directly to Secretary of War Alger, informing him of his
arrival in Tampa with García's dispatches and representatives. The telegram ended up on Corbin's desk, who wrote back to Rowan, "Your
telegram, addressed to Secretary of War, has been received. You are

directed to proceed to this city and report to the Adjutant General of the Army to whom you should have addressed your telegraphic communication. On completion of this duty, you will be relieved from all further duty in this office and proceed to join your regiment."[87] As a result, Rowan's reception in Washington was not as welcoming as the one he'd received in Tampa, though he was permitted to meet with the cabinet and to receive congratulations from President William McKinley for his efforts.[88]

Washington was a smallish city in 1898,[89] and in all likelihood Rowan had already set eyes on the president at some government ceremony or other, but there's a strong possibility he may have unwittingly seen McKinley twice before. In June 1864, when McKinley passed through Gap Mills as a young lieutenant with General David Hunter's retreating Union troops, it's not hard to imagine a seven-year-old boy drawn irresistibly to the awesome sight of the marching troops.[90] The second sighting is a near certainty. In 1880, during Rowan's third year at West Point, McKinley was one of twelve members of the Board of Visitors appointed to evaluate conditions at the academy. He was on the Education and Library Committee—which was highly critical of the low admissions standards—and there's little doubt that during his ten-day visit McKinley and Rowan would have crossed paths. Rowan would have had no reason to remember a black-frock-coated, obscure congressman from Ohio, nor would McKinley have remembered one of many young uniformed cadets.[91]

Their 1898 meeting was quite cordial but, unknown to the president, Corbin was ready to court-martial Rowan for blabbing to reporters—specifically to Roberts. If Rowan hadn't realized this possibility when he landed in Tampa, the curt telegram from the adjutant general would have alerted him. He might also have been warned by someone—Wagner, perhaps. In any event, the day after receiving the telegram Rowan hied himself to a justice of the peace and swore in a deposition that he was "in no way responsible . . . for any notices that appeared in the American and English press" between April 23 and May 9 concerning his mission to Cuba. He acknowledged that he had discussed his mission with Elmer Roberts, but had done so at the urging of "the Consul" (never once referring to Louis Dent by name), and that Roberts had agreed "to say nothing of the journey." He admitted to going along with Roberts's request to accompany him to Cuba, but when he learned it was not to be permitted, he so informed Roberts, and the joint venture was canceled. In the last paragraph of the deposition, Rowan preemptively swore that "any statement, official or otherwise, made by the U.S. Consul, Kingston, Jamaica, that is at variance with the above statement or statements is not in accordance with the truth."[92] He didn't explain the reasoning behind his assumption that Dent might have a different, and therefore untruthful, version of what happened in Jamaica. The statement was read by Corbin and passed on to the Department of State, where it was determined on May 28 that Rowan's and Dent's statements "in regard to the refusal to allow Mr. Roberts . . . to accompany the expedition, do not substantially differ."[93] Wording it in that way and narrowing the focus to that single topic would seem to have gotten Rowan off the hook. Had the State Department based its determination on what he may or may not have told Roberts, he would have been in deep trouble: on that count there were very substantial differences between what he claimed and what Dent charged.[94]

By the end of May, Rowan was an internationally famous war hero. While staying in the Washington area, he was able to visit with his mother-in-law, who happened to be in Baltimore. According to one newspaper account of his presence in that city, he "attracted more attention than Buffalo Bill."[95] This was no small compliment in 1898. What especially endeared Rowan to the public was his unassuming demeanor. The public would not have understood nor would it have taken kindly to his being court-martialed merely for talking to the press. Didn't this "brave soldier" and "daring officer" undertake a "perilous journey" in which he "freely dared every risk to which a soldier may be subjected" in order to complete "one of the most gallant and brilliant exploits in our military history"? And when asked about his mission, hadn't this paragon of duty and loyalty stated simply, "I was ordered to go, and I went"?[96] The United States was at the beginning of a great patriotic war, and to court-martial this modest war hero would have been a serious blunder.

It would also have made Major General Nelson A. Miles look ridiculous. He had personally interviewed Rowan[97] and was impressed to the degree that he decided Rowan would be a worthy addition to his staff, to which he was assigned on May 20.[98] On May 23, in a letter that was released to the press, Miles recommended to Alger that Rowan be promoted to lieutenant colonel and assigned to one of the regiments of "immunes."[99] These were men—mostly African Americans—believed to be immune to diseases and infirmities peculiar to the tropics.

The notion of "immune" troops was based on flawed intuition, and an examination of Civil War records would have demonstrated this. Of the 125,239 cases of typhoid fever among whites, 31,115 (24.8 percent) died. Among the 11,623 cases among African Americans, 3,581 (30.8 percent) died. During the Spanish-American War, the mortality rate for typhoid among whites was 10.3 percent; among African Americans it was 24.2 percent. The morbidity rate among whites was considerably higher, but this can be accounted for by noting that the majority of white soldiers were volunteers new to the hygienic practices of soldiering; the majority of African Americans were experienced members of the regular army who knew how to set up a camp and take care of themselves.[100]

In his letter Miles pointed out that Rowan had journeyed across Cuba, met with García, and brought back critical information. "This was a most perilous undertaking," he wrote, "and, in my judgment, Lieut. Rowan performed an act of heroism and cool daring that has rarely been excelled in the annals of warfare."[101] On that same day Rowan received a letter previously sent to him in Kingston and finally forwarded to him in Washington. Written by his seven-year-old daughter, it read:

Dear Papa:
    I am wearing my hair braided. Look out that the Spaniards don't catch you.
    Hurry and come home the cherries will be ripe by the time you get here.

With love and kisses
Elizabeth Rowan[102]

Instead of going home, Rowan was ordered on May 31 to report to an examining board in Tampa to evaluate his fitness to be promoted to lieutenant colonel. Following this examination, he did a bit more traveling before returning to Washington, where he was commissioned on June 20 and assigned to the Sixth Regiment Volunteer Infantry. He acknowledged his assignment, but instead of reporting for duty, remained with General Miles. Miles was apparently taken with Rowan and could see no reason for wasting his time and talents commanding troops that Miles was sure would never be deployed.

CHAPTER 4

America Takes a Step toward Empire

Even though war with Spain had not been declared, it was deemed inevitable, and orders were issued on April 15, 1898 to send specific battle-ready regular army units to Chickamauga Park, Georgia; Mobile, Alabama; New Orleans, Louisiana; and Tampa, Florida. In most cases the regulars would leave before the arrival of masses of volunteers. These Southern locations, it was reasoned, would lessen travel time to Cuba and better acclimatize the men for duty in a tropical country. In order to institute important reforms, the bill introduced in early March 1898 by John A. T. Hull, the chairman of the House Committee on Military Affairs, was rewritten to satisfy the U.S. National Guard. The new version authorized an expansion of the regular army to approximately 61,000 and provided that half the expeditionary force be composed of volunteer regiments and guardsmen. The army immediately began signing up new recruits, but not indiscriminately. Out of 127,798 applicants, 77 percent were rejected.[1]

One provision of the bill authorized the creation of three volunteer cavalry regiments. Secretary of War Russell Alger, aware of Theodore Roosevelt's eagerness to participate in the conflict, and perhaps to get him out of Washington, D.C., offered Roosevelt the command of one of the regiments. Tempering humility with egotism, Roosevelt acknowledged his lack of command experience but credited himself with the wisdom to recognize this temporary shortcoming, noting that it would take him an entire month to acquire the skills to be a colonel in the cavalry. This delay would slow down the regiment's organization and, as a result, he might miss the war altogether. He therefore declined the commission but did agree to accept appointment as a lieutenant colonel if command of the regiment was given to his friend Colonel Leonard Wood. Thus was born the Rough Riders, officially called the First United States Volunteer Cavalry—an unlikely collection of cowboys, frontiersmen, Native Americans, and Ivy League collegians.[2] Roosevelt ordered a tailored uniform from Brooks Brothers,[3] settled his affairs as assistant secretary of the navy, and on May 15 joined the regiment, already well organized, at Camp Wood outside San Antonio, Texas.[4]

It was to the Rough Riders' great advantage that they were isolated from other volunteer troops and under the command of a line officer who recognized the necessity of a sanitary camp. "Hygienic conditions," Roosevelt later boasted, "were as good as any regular regiment."[5] Their fellow volunteers were quartered in appallingly unhygienic conditions and suffered from many illnesses. The generic cause, as Alger put it, "was Camp Pollution; specifically, the cause was due to ignorance or neglect on the part of officers, coupled with the inexperience of the newly enlisted soldiers. It is an axiom of military life, that there is nothing of which the recruit is so prodigal as his health."[6] Soldiers were allowed to pitch their tents too close together, too near latrines, and in poorly drained sites. Furthermore, no serious efforts were made to prevent men from defecating wherever they found it most convenient. This was an epidemic awaiting only the introduction of disease.[7]

Brigadier General Collazo and Lieutenant Colonel Hernández, the two officers assigned by General Calixto García to accompany Andrew Rowan back to the United States, met with Secretary Alger and General Nelson A. Miles to discuss the military situation in eastern Cuba. Eventually they accompanied Miles back to Tampa. On June 2, Hernández was transported back to Cuba to deliver a message from Miles to García, requesting a number of actions to be taken to support a landing by U.S. troops.

This was the first definite news that García had of the impending invasion, and he quickly composed a response agreeing to take measures at once to carry out the recommendations. He also passed along data regarding Spanish forces.

In the meantime, Admiral Cervera's fleet had finally been located at the French island of Martinique in the Caribbean, and intelligence indicated that it would be heading for Havana with much-needed supplies. Instead, Cervera departed for Curaçao to rendezvous with a collier carrying five thousand tons of coal, but the collier wasn't there. Having to go somewhere, and with barely enough coal to make the trip, the squadron left Curaçao on June 15 for Santiago Harbor in southeastern Cuba.

The Flying Squadron under Commodore Winfield S. Schley had been assigned the task of protecting America's east coast. When the general whereabouts of the phantom Spanish fleet that had been haunting that vicinity were finally known, Schley (pronounced *Sly*) was free to sail south. But to where? Not guessing that Cervera would head for Santiago de Cuba, a city unconnected by rail or even decent roads to the rest of the island, Admiral William Sampson dispatched Schley, with four warships and a number of smaller boats, to Cienfuegos on Cuba's southern coast—three hundred miles from Santiago. On May 19, reports of Cervera's actual location began coming in, but Schley refused to believe them and, unknown to Sampson who had ordered him to Santiago, stayed put.

After a series of misunderstandings, blunders, and delays, Schley's squadron finally arrived at Santiago de Cuba early in the evening on May 27, still not knowing that Cervera's fleet was moored there. It wasn't until two days later that the Americans knew for certain.[8] Their task then became obvious—to blockade Cervera in the port.

The entrance to the harbor was quite narrow, and Schley had been ordered by Sampson to sink the coal transport *Merrimac* in the channel. This would effectively eliminate Cervera's ships from further participation in the war. There were problems with such a maneuver. First, the harbor entrance was mined; and second, a number of batteries on shore could easily sink the collier before it reached its objective. A young naval constructor, Richmond Pearson Hobson, was entrusted with the mission, the details of which he designed. The plan failed—the ship being sunk where it would cause no problems to the Spanish—and the few men on board were presumed dead.[9] The following morning Hobson, clinging to the sunken ship's lifeboat and accompanied by all seven of his men, hailed a Spanish launch. Admiral Cervera himself helped Hobson board and acknowledged his bravery by exclaiming, "Valiente!"[10] Hobson joined Rowan as one of the few popular heroes of the war.

Back in Tampa, Major General William R. Shafter, whose job it was to assemble troops for the attack on Cuba, was struggling against all odds to sort out men and supplies and to load them on transport ships. His specific orders from Miles were to land his troops near Santiago de Cuba and assist in capturing the harbor and the Spanish squadron. Shafter was sixty-three years old when selected for this difficult task; he had been a soldier for thirty-seven years and had risen to the rank of brigadier general the previous year, having come to the attention of high-ranking officers in Washington upon being awarded the Medal of Honor in 1895 for distinguished gallantry in battle during the Civil War.

Shafter was a tough old bird and, in spite of his lack of experience commanding large numbers of troops, was considered a sensible choice to head up the invading force.[11] There were some who considered his appointment politically motivated. Unlike the dashing Miles, a potential Democratic contender for the presidency, Shafter had no political aspirations.[12] He also had no talent for bringing order out of chaos. If it weren't for his staff of regular officers, things would have been even worse.[13] Colonel Wood, the nominal commander of what were in fact Teddy Roosevelt's Rough Riders, wrote of Tampa, "Confusion, confusion, confusion."[14]

When orders were finally given to board the ships at Tampa Bay on June 6, some units, fearful of being left behind, commandeered trains to make the nine-mile journey from Tampa.[15] Because of a shortage of space on the ships—the invading force had grown from 6,000 to 25,000—the cavalry horses were left behind along with some 8,000 soldiers. For the next week, the units that had managed to get on the ships suffered in the Florida sunshine, not moving out of Tampa Bay, while the navy investigated a report that Cervera's fleet had somehow escaped from Santiago de Cuba. The accommodations on the ships were so bad that Teresa Dean, a correspondent for *Leslie's Weekly*, wrote, "With horrible stench in my nostrils, with my head dizzy, my eyes blinded, and my senses sickened with the close, hot, thick atmosphere of one transport, I staggered to [one officer] and said: 'Can those boys, our boys, live even to *get* to Cuba?' "[16] The men weren't permitted off the ships, but the officers' horses were disembarked "for the simple reason that they began to die," as Roosevelt wrote to his friend Henry Cabot Lodge.[17] The convoy finally started its thousand-mile journey on June 14, eventually reaching its destination June 20.[18] At that point in history it was, as Richard Harding Davis wrote,

> the largest number of United States troops that ever went down to the sea in ships to invade a foreign country. . . . The thought of twelve thousand men on thirty-two troop ships and their escort of fourteen war-ships . . . brings up a picture of a great flotilla, grim, sinister, and menacing, fighting its way through the waves on its errand of vengeance and conquest. But as a matter of fact the expedition bore a most distinct air of the commonplace. It moved through the succession of sparkling, sunlit days, over a sea as smooth as a lake.[19]

In the meantime, Sampson learned that General García would be arriving at Aserradero, eighteen miles west of Santiago de Cuba. It would make sense to arrange a meeting between García and the American commanders before the soon-to-arrive troops disembarked. Accordingly, on June 18 Sampson sent his chief of staff, Captain French Ensor Chadwick, to Aserradero aboard the *Vixen*.

García and some of his staff members went on board the *Vixen* to be transported to Sampson's flagship, the *New York*. The *Vixen* was tossed about by the swelling sea, and once aboard the *New York* they held a meeting of sorts, about which Sampson later wrote, "My impressions of General Garcia were of the most pleasant character. He was a large, handsome man, of most frank and engaging manners, and of most soldierly appearance. He remained some time on board, though, unfortunately, so sea-sick that he was obliged to lie down during the whole of his visit."[20] García asked if, when General Shafter arrived, they might confer on land, and this was agreed to. The next afternoon the major conferees sat on boxes under a palm-leaf roof in an open hut examining a blueprint map. Shafter wore his loose-fitting blue jacket with its double row of brass buttons, Sampson was in fresh white duck, and García wore a slouch hat, linen uniform, and high leather boots. The meeting lasted an hour or so, and it was decided that the troops would be disembarked at Daiquiri,[21] seventeen miles east of Santiago, with the ultimate goal of marching on that city. García pointed out that contingents of Spanish soldiers, numbering in the hundreds, were stationed at various key points along the coast. The plan called for the warships to shell these installations to clear them out while Cuban forces created a diversion to occupy Spanish troops to the west. The plan worked, and the Americans faced no serious Spanish opposition at any point during the landing.

The only proper harbor available along Cuba's southeast coast was Guantánamo, a prohibitive fifty-five miles from Santiago, which was why Daiquiri had been chosen. Daiquiri, being an open roadstead, offered no protection from the trade winds that at this time of year produced a heavy surf on the coral reefs. The single facility for unloading ships was a small wharf, and there was no time under these conditions to build a proper one.[22] Early in the morning of June 22, war ships shelled the area sufficiently, as one captain put it, "to drive out the whole Spanish army in Cuba, had it been there."[23] Disembarkation was complicated by huge swells. The transports stood many hundreds of yards offshore, their captains fearful of the dangers posed by the heavy seas. "The army," as Henry Cabot Lodge noted, "had neither lighters nor launches. They had been omitted, forgotten, or lost, like an umbrella, no one knew exactly where; so the work of disembarking the troops fell upon the navy."[24] Men and matériel were carried in fifty or more longboats and launches loaned by the nearby navy ships and manned by bluejackets. The soldiers, heavily laden as they were with rifles, ammunition, haversacks, and other gear, found it extremely difficult to climb from the ships into the boats, but eventually all made it. Packhorses and mules were simply forced overboard. In their confusion, some of the animals swam out to sea and drowned; others, exhausted by the mile-and-a-half swim to shore, were dashed on the rocks by the heavy surf. In all, including those that died en route from Tampa, at least fifty animals were lost. One of Roosevelt's two horses was among the victims, an event that caused Roosevelt, after "snorting like a bull, [to] split the air with one profanity after another."[25] Two soldiers also drowned when one of the boats overturned; Roosevelt's reaction to their loss has not been recorded.

The one highlight of the first day occurred when an American flag was unfurled above a Spanish blockhouse on a nearby peak. Stephen Crane, who was present, wrote that "all burst into a great cheer that swelled and rolled against the green hills until your heart beat loudly with the thrill of it. The sea, thronged with transports and cruisers, was suddenly ringing with the noise of steam whistles from the deep sea-lion roar of the great steamers to the wild screams of the launches." The last of the troops and artillery made it ashore on June 26, but it wasn't until the next day that they were provided with sufficient ammunition. Once it was ashore, an efficient method of distributing the ammunition to the front was established.[26]

Regular army troops were issued Norwegian-made Krag-Jorgensen rifles, which used smokeless powder for ammunition, while volunteers carried Springfields, which required black powder. The Krag was a superior weapon to the Springfield, and the smokeless powder didn't reveal the position of the person firing it; this advantage was so obvious that volunteers, whenever they were able, appropriated any Krags left unprotected. Only one volunteer unit was issued the Krag-Jorgensen, and it should come as no surprise that it was Roosevelt's Rough Riders.[27]

Rowan's trek through Cuba occurred too late for the intelligence he gathered to have done much good for the invading army. Too many decisions had already been made. Had he gone a year earlier, when Major Arthur L. Wagner first wanted to send someone, things would certainly have progressed more smoothly and at less expense. On the other hand, what useful information he provided regarding the terrain seems to have gone unheeded. For example, Quartermaster General Marshall Ludington had gone to extreme lengths to obtain sufficient mule-drawn wagons, both to use in camps in the United States and to carry supplies in the field. These would have worked fine around Havana, but there was no point in taking them to southeastern Cuba, where there were few roads. The few roads that existed were usually impassable, even though Shafter had a thousand men continuously working on them. Most of the two hundred wagons transported there remained in the ships' holds; of course, this is exactly where they would have remained, even if there had been a use for them, since there were insufficient lighters to carry them to shore.[28]

On June 24, the Rough Riders and two other units were ordered to advance on Santiago; they were told by Cuban general Demetri Castillo Guany that Spanish troops were temporarily dug in near a fork in the road called Las Guasimas. Nevertheless, they walked into an apparent ambush, and when it was over, eight Rough Riders were dead and thirty-four were wounded. Another eight from the First and Tenth Regulars were also dead. The Rough Riders had wanted first blood, and they got it. In spite of having superior numbers, the Spanish were driven off, and the Americans continued their march.[29]

There were two more military objectives before the assault on Santiago could begin. The first was the village of El Caney, some six miles northwest of the city. According to Alger, Generals Henry W. Lawton and Adna Chaffee considered the taking of El Caney "a mere incident" in the Santiago campaign—something that would occupy only a couple of hours.[30] The next assault would take place on San Juan Hill, barely a mile and a half east of downtown Santiago. As July 1 dawned, 5,400 American soldiers stood ready to attack the 520 Spanish soldiers at El Caney; another 10,000 Americans were ready to advance on the 521 Spaniards occupying San Juan and Kettle Hills. Following Shafter's orders, García and his insurgents were heading northwest of Santiago to cover the right flank of Lawton's infantry division. In spite of their bedraggled appearance, they moved quickly, arriving at their position by 6:45 A.M.[31] Their purpose was to prevent an approaching Spanish force under the command of Colonel Frederico Escario from entering the city and joining the existing troops.[32]

The battle at El Caney began with artillery fire at 6:30 that morning. This was the battle that was supposed to last two or three hours, but it lasted ten hours and cost the Americans 438 casualties, including eighty-one deaths.[33] A few miles to the south, the artillery assault on San Juan Heights began at 8:00 A.M. and was silenced shortly thereafter by more accurately placed return fire from the Spaniards. This left the advancing troops without that support. As they marched, Private Charles Post, a former newspaper artist, saw a surreal figure on a horse: "The horse was not big but the man was, and tall: his legs and white socks hung well below the horse's belly. Dressed in black civilian clothes as if he had just stepped over from New York, he wore a jaunty flat-brimmed straw hat with a scarlet hatband and a scarlet tie to match." It was William Randolph Hearst.[34] Hearst had earlier visited García's headquarters, where the general presented him with a bullet-torn Cuban flag.[35]

The steep Kettle Hill stood between the Americans and their objective; it was up Kettle Hill—not San Juan Hill—that Teddy Roosevelt gallantly, if foolishly, led his dismounted Rough Riders and two dismounted black cavalry regiments. Only afterward did they join the assault on San Juan Hill. It was in this later action that two Spanish soldiers jumped up and fired at Roosevelt. "As they turned to run I closed in and fired twice, missing the first and killing the second," he would write later. He was using a pistol reclaimed from the battleship *Maine*,[36] and later he told reporters, "I made a vow to kill at least one Spaniard with it."[37] And in a letter to his friend Henry Cabot Lodge he boasted like a schoolboy, "Did I tell you that I killed a Spaniard with my own hand when I led the storm of the first redoubt?"[38] At times, when reading histories of the war and Roosevelt's part in it, it's possible to believe the Spanish-American War occurred so that Roosevelt might have the opportunity to kill a man legally, even if it meant shooting him in the back. Other people were firing nearby, and he may not have shot anyone at all, though he surely believed he did.[39] For his display of heroism in leading the charge, Roosevelt later lobbied for a Medal of Honor, an activity perceived by some as unseemly. The medal was not awarded, and his wife later said that not receiving it was one of the greatest disappointments of Roosevelt's life. President Bill Clinton, in one of the final acts of his presidency, eventually granted the posthumous award on January 16, 2001.[40]

At the end of the day, the Americans were entrenched on the San Juan Heights at a cost of 1,385 casualties, more than double those of the Spanish. Of the American casualties, 205, or 15 percent, were killed. Although the Americans had every military advantage at this point, the fight was gone out of them.[41] Even the officers felt their position was untenable and discussed retreating. They didn't consider the desperate situation of the Spanish, who had almost no food, little ammunition, and no way to escape. As early as June 10 there were reports of death from starvation among civilians. The Spanish, when fleeing the village of Siboney, left a flag flying over a blockhouse. It was spotted by Wagner, who had been temporarily placed in command of an advance guard, and he ordered it taken down. "As I was in command," he later wrote, "and as the flag was pulled down by my order and duly turned over to me, I claim the honor of having captured the first Spanish flag that was taken in Cuba."[42] It might have been a children's game.

At 8:30 A.M. on July 3, Admiral Cervera, sailing aboard the *Infanta Maria Teresa*, bravely led his fleet out of Santiago Harbor. He hadn't wanted to go, preferring to use his guns to protect the city rather than to lead his ships to certain destruction outside the harbor. In Havana, Governor General Ramón Blanco y Erenes, Cervera's immediate military superior, saw it differently. Not capable of understanding the situation, or perhaps not willing to understand it, he ordered Cervera by cable to make an attempt at escaping in order to avoid a moral defeat by remaining in the harbor. The six ships moving at six hundred yards apart flew huge silken battle flags above their swabbed decks and polished brass work.

At a later time in history, this lineup would be considered similar to a row of targets in a rifle gallery, but in 1898 naval gunnery hadn't progressed to the degree one might imagine. Of the 5,752 shells fired by the *Brooklyn*, the *Oregon*, and the *Indiana*, only a very small number struck their mark. The percentage of hits for the variously sized guns was in the 1.1 to 3.1 range.[43] Fortunately, the ships had great stores of ammunition and were able to accomplish their task by hurtling massive numbers of shells. Less than five hours after Cervera's flagship steamed out of the narrow entrance of the harbor, the squadron was destroyed; 323 Spaniards were dead, with 151 wounded. The Americans suffered three casualties: one killed and two wounded. In the midst of battle, the sailors on board the *Texas* cheered as the *Vizcaya*, the second ship, burned and exploded. From the bridge of the *Texas*, Captain John W. Philip "dropped his glass, held his hand out with a quieting gesture," and admonished them: "Don't cheer, boys! Those poor fellows are dying." This was typical of the developing attitude toward the once-hated Spanish. Cervera, who had to swim to shore, was rescued by U.S. sailors and spent the duration of the war in Annapolis. He was considered a hero throughout the United States.[44]

The Americans made strenuous efforts to rescue Spanish sailors and to give first aid to those in need. Captain Robley Evans of the *Iowa* described his feelings regarding the rescue work of those under his command: "So long as the enemy showed his flag they fought like American seamen, but when the flag came down they were as gentle and tender as American women."[45] There was at least one report of Cubans taking potshots at sailors stranded on a sunken sandbar after swimming from their sunken ship.[46] Yet Lieutenant Charles W. Hazeltine, who commanded the armed yacht *Hist*, noted that several of the Spanish sailors his ship rescued "had been given first aid by Cubans on shore." He also reported that the Cubans "did not fire on the Spaniards. In fact, when our boats were taking the Spaniards from the beach, the Cubans rendered valuable assistance."[47]

By pure coincidence, Shafter sent the following note on July 3 to General José Toral, the current commander of the Spanish troops as Cervera was leaving the harbor.

> Sir: I shall be obliged, unless you surrender, to shell Santiago de Cuba. Please inform the citizens of foreign countries and all women and children that they should leave the city before 10 o'clock to-morrow morning.[48]

Toral didn't receive the note until 4:00 that afternoon. In his reply he stated there would be no surrender, but he would advise the foreign consuls and citizens of Shafter's message. This left insufficient time for an evacuation by 10:00 the following morning, and the foreign consuls asked that the bombardment be delayed twenty-four hours. Shafter readily acceded, and some 22,000 people left the city.[49] As the standoff continued and the refugees starved, the American soldiers fared little better. They were plagued by torrential rains and steaming afternoons, disgustingly rotten food, voracious body lice, and tropical fevers. Land crabs and vultures feasted on their dead bodies—even those buried weeks earlier, because the rains had washed them from their shallow graves.[50] Still, they had apparently won the battle and were on the verge of winning the war.

At this point Rowan had still not reported for duty with the Sixth Volunteer Infantry, which was in the process of mustering in 904 enlisted men in three different cities in Tennessee.[51] The army wasn't in the habit of assigning surplus officers to a unit, and there was no question his presence was missed. His commanding officer, Colonel L. D. Tyson, had written to Adjutant General Corbin on July 2 asking that the new lieutenant colonel be ordered to report "at the earliest practicable moment as his services are urgently needed to assist me in the organization of my regiment." All he got in answer was a one-sentence telegram informing him that Rowan was on duty with Miles, "who states that his services cannot be spared at this time."[52] Yet Rowan's assignment didn't seem that critical; by July 11 he had been put in charge of a transport ship carrying troops off Santiago.[53]

In spite of a long string of mistakes stretching beyond the assembly of the troops in Tampa, by early July the Battle of Santiago was essentially won; all that was left to do was to get the Spanish to surrender. Instead of acting from a position of power and laying down conditions of surrender, Shafter, perhaps weary of the whole business and certainly not feeling well, seemed willing to give away the store. After a few days' exchange of overly respectful letters between the commanding officers, he sent a following telegram to Alger, noting, "I am in receipt of a letter from the Commandant of Santiago de Cuba, who proposes to march out of the city with arms and baggage and not to be molested until he reaches Holguin, surrendering to the American forces the territory now occupied by him."

The reply from the president through the adjutant general was curt. It instructed him to "accept nothing but an unconditional surrender."[54] And when Shafter didn't reply quickly enough, Alger shot off another telegram asking if the surrender was complete, adding, "We are await-ing the conditions with impatience."[55] It was to be exactly what the administration wanted, but the Spanish requested that the word "capit-ulation" be used in place of "surrender" in all documents. Like good winners, the Americans immediately agreed to this change.

Like a beautifully dressed toreador moving in for the kill after the picadors had done their work, Major General Miles arrived from Washington to metaphorically slip his sword between Toral's shoulder blades. Accompanied by Major-General Joseph Wheeler and Shafter, he had face-to-face meetings with Toral on July 13 and 14, during which the terms of capitulation were established.[56] García was not invited to participate in the meetings with Toral, and in fact was not even made aware that they were taking place.[57] Leaving Shafter to clean things up, Miles set off, with Lt. Colonel Andrew Rowan in tow, for what was assumed to be an easy campaign in Puerto Rico.

After a certain amount of haggling, the surrender of Santiago took place at 9:30 on the morning of July 17 beneath a huge ceiba tree east of the city. It was a day filled with a great deal of pomp and circum-stance, with mounted American soldiers, smartly dressed Spanish troops, formal salutes, grave courtesies, and the playing of national anthems. From the point of view of the *insurrectos*, these final days were seriously flawed.[58] No Cuban officers were involved in the nego-tiations, the signing of the surrender, the formal turnover of the city, or the grand ceremony in the plaza. It was there that the "United States flag was hauled to the masthead [atop the palace and at] the same moment twenty-one guns were fired and the band of the Sixth Cavalry struck up 'Hail Columbia!'" One wonders if the choice of songs was intentional. One of America's de facto national anthems until "The Star-Spangled Banner" was officially designated in 1931, "Hail, Colum-bia!" derives its name, of course, from Christopher Columbus, whose arrival in Cuba four hundred years earlier had established Spain's dominance over the island.[59]

Santiago was not surrendered to the combined Cuban and Ameri-can forces, but "to the prowess of American arms."[60] Furthermore, the Spanish were to continue running the city. There were a number of rea-sons for all of this, not the least being that Shafter had no intention of sharing the victory with García's ragtag, mostly black *insurrectos*. In addition, the Americans had come to identify with and respect the Spanish more than the Cubans they came to liberate. From their arrival, the Americans disdained their Cuban allies. The soldiers felt the Cubans could not be trusted and would steal anything they could get their hands on. And, of course, there was out-and-out racism at work. One officer wrote that a Cuban is "a treacherous, lying, cowardly, thieving, worthless, half-breed mongrel; born of a mongrel spawn of Europe, crossed upon the fetiches of darkest Africa and aboriginal America. He is no more capable of self-government than the Hottentots that roam the wilds of Africa or the Bushman of Australia."[61] In spite of such widespread feelings, there were many in the military who took an opposing view. During an address given at the Army and Navy Club some years later, Brigadier General Edward J. McClernand said, "The work of García and his men in the campaign . . . was harshly judged by many. When we consider their poor arms and equipment, the wonder is not that they accomplished so little, but that they did so much."[62]

Another serious concern was that the Cuban soldiers would exact revenge against the Spanish. The *New York Journal* reported that fifty Spanish prisoners turned over to the Cubans were killed. Alger wrote Shafter asking if this were true and, either to his credit or to his lack of faith in the accuracy of the *Journal*, he noted that he and other members of the administration did not believe it.[63]

The Americans, for the most part, came to view the campaign against Spain as a sporting contest between worthy opponents—akin to a Yale versus Harvard football match. Yes, people were suffering, starving, and dying, but that was the nature of the game and had nothing to do with personal animus. The symbol of the Spanish presence in Cuba, the "evil butcher," General Valeriano Weyler, was replaced in American minds by Admiral Cervera, who had personally rescued the heroic Hobson from Santiago Harbor much as the captain of an opposing team might lend a hand to help a dazed quarterback to his feet. This was not how the Cubans saw it; they had suffered too hard and too long, and the fear among some Americans was that the Cubans would use the occasion for plundering the city. When it became known that the Cuban soldiers would not be allowed into Santiago, an Associated Press reporter noted that "deep mutterings were heard among General Garcia's men. It was evident the Cubans were greatly disappointed at the step taken by the American commander, for they had confidently counted upon having Santiago turned over to loot and plunder as they had sacked [D]aiquiri, Siboney and El Caney."[64] There had been no plundering in those locations, but such was the Americans' low opinion of the Cubans that this accusation was easily believed. When asked by a Cuban officer why the city was to remain in the control of the Spaniards, Shafter replied, "The Spaniards are not our enemies. We are fighting the soldiers of Spain, but we have no desire to despoil her citizens."[65]

General García was quite naturally angry and insulted, both personally and as a son of Cuba, by his exclusion. He withdrew his troops from the vicinity, taking the road to Jiguaní, some fifty miles northwest of Santiago. After consulting with his officers, he sent by special courier to General Máximo Gómez Baez, the Cuban commander in chief, his resignation as commander of the Cuban Army for the east,[66] and on July 19 he sent an emotional letter to Shafter expressing his displeasure.[67]

Shafter replied the next day, noting his surprise and regret that García should regard himself "in any way slighted or aggrieved," and went on to explain why things had gone the way they did,[68] but it is doubtful that this letter had any ameliorative effect. As military historian David Trask pointed out, "Had Shafter extended to García a modicum of the courtesy he lavished upon General Toral, he might have minimized the tensions that built up between the Americans and the Cubans."[69] Copies of García's letter were quickly circulated and appeared in the U.S. press on July 22. American officials were taken by surprise—especially because Shafter had given them no word of the letter's existence.

As far as the Americans were concerned, they had not intervened in an insurrection but had defended themselves from attacks by a country that had declared war against them; Cuba was not the issue, but merely one theater in a much wider conflict. The battle cry for the Americans was "Remember the *Maine!*" and not "Cuba libre!" The realities of a declared war seemed to trump the stipulations of the Teller Amendment, particularly the fourth resolve, which stated unambiguously that "the United States hereby disclaims any disposition or intention to exercise sovereignty, jurisdiction, or control over said Island except for the pacification thereof, and asserts its determination, when that is accomplished, to leave the government and control of the Island to its people."[70] The detail deviling the process would be in determining precisely when the pacification was accomplished. And it should be remembered that what Congress creates it can also repeal. Even before the troops landed in Cuba there was a movement afoot for annexation.[71] As Henry Huntington Powers, professor of economics at Stanford University, pointed out in the fall of 1898, the Washington Doctrine—national isolation—quickly faded away under the present circumstances:

> Most striking of all, perhaps, is the way in which we have forgotten what we set out to accomplish and have become engrossed in new interests. Starving *reconcentrados* and struggling Cubans are crowded quite into the background of our imagination to make room for our own larger prospects and new ambitions. . . . We started to free a weak and oppressed people whose sufferings near our borders attracted our attention and appealed to our sympathies. We expected when this was done to go about our business as though nothing had happened. . . . With the prospect of invasion by American capital and American population [Cuba's] acquisition is as good as assured. We seem likely within a twelvemonth to have changed our ideal of isolation for that of empire and to have gone a long way toward its realization.[72]

CHAPTER 5

The Creation of an American Myth

With Havana and the rest of the island cut off from Spain by the blockade, the war in Cuba was effectively over. Next to be subdued was Puerto Rico, and this brings us back to Andrew Rowan, who had accompanied General Miles there.

Rowan, in charge of the troop ship *The City of Macon*, sailed to Guantánamo and from there, as a part of Miles's invasion force, to Guánica on Puerto Rico's southwestern coast, arriving there on July 25, 1898.[1]

Miles's choice of a landing site was influenced by information provided by one of Rowan's fellow members of the Military Information Division, Lieutenant Henry H. Whitney, a thirty-one-year-old West Point graduate. He, too, was sent on a secret mission: as Rowan sailed out of Manatí Bay, Whitney left Key West aboard the battleship *Indiana* and was transferred to one of publisher William Randolph Hearst's correspondent ships, the *Anita*. After the *Anita* docked at Charlotte Amalie on the island of St. Thomas, Whitney disembarked and stayed behind. Like Rowan, he sought help from an American consul—in this case, Philip C. Hanna, the consul from San Juan who had left Puerto Rico when the situation with Spain became serious. Hanna assisted Whitney in obtaining passage for Puerto Rico on the British merchant ship *Andarose*, during which time Whitney posed as an ordinary seaman. The ship made unscheduled stops along the Puerto Rican coast—paid for by Whitney at sixty dollars each—so that he could go ashore and make observations. At one point the *Andarose* was boarded and searched by Spanish soldiers alerted by news stories to the possibility of his being aboard. Fortunately, they took no notice of H. W. Elias, the sweaty, coal-dusted stoker hard at work in the boiler room. Had he been identified, Whitney would have been shot as a spy.

As Whitney worked his way along the coast, sometimes traveling inland and presenting himself as a British seaman, traveling sales-man, or sports fisherman, he collected vast amounts of information regarding topography, defenses, weaponry, lighthouses, roads, and other strategically important data. His fluency in Spanish (he was in the top quarter of his class in Spanish at West Point) allowed him to travel easily through the country, gaining useful insights into the sentiments of the locals.[2]

When the *Andarose* eventually sailed for New York on June 1, Whitney traveled with it, arriving there on June 8. He left immediately for Washington, D.C., and the next day accompanied Secretary of War Russell Alger to an interview with President William McKinley. As a reward for completing his daring mission, he was promoted to the rank of captain and, along with Rowan, was assigned to Miles's staff. Miles later wrote, "The information he gained concerning the position of the Spanish troops, the topography of the country, the character of the inhabitants, the resources and amount of supplies available, and especially his reports of the conditions of the harbors, I afterward found to be most important."[3] The day after Miles and his troops landed in Puerto Rico, the French ambassador in Washington, acting for Spain, delivered a note from Madrid to the White House admitting defeat and asking for an end to the war. Secret negotiations began, while hostilities in Puerto Rico and the Philippines continued.[4]

The campaign in Puerto Rico wasn't quite the "gran' picnic an' moonlight excursion" that Finley Peter Dunne's fictional character Mr. Dooley called it,[5] but it was nothing compared with the difficulties that had been encountered in Cuba. On separate occasions, both Richard Harding Davis and Stephen Crane, while moving ahead of advancing troops in Puerto Rico, had villages turned over to them as if they were conquering generals rather than newspaper correspondents.[6]

Many Puerto Ricans seemed pleased to find themselves in the hands of the Americans. Francisco Magia, the *alcalde* (mayor) of Juaco, wrote,

"Today the citizens of Puerto Rico assist in one of her most beautiful feasts. The sun of America shines upon our mountains and valleys this day of July, 1898. It is a day of glorious remembrance for each son of this beloved isle, because for the first time there waves over it the flag of the stars planted in the name of the Government of the United States by the Major General of the American Army, Señor Miles."[7]

While he was in Puerto Rico, Rowan met Crane, who took an immediate dislike to him. He later wrote that Rowan was "personally a chump and in Porto Rico where I met him he wore a yachting cap as part of his uniform which was damnable." There was no doubt some jealousy at work because of Rowan's lionization in the press after his journey to Cuba. "He received the praise of the general of the army," Crane wrote, "and got to be made a lieutenant col. for a feat which about forty newspaper correspondents had already performed at the usual price of fifty dollars a week and expenses."[8] Recalling the willingness of Elmer Roberts to accompany Rowan on his mission from Jamaica to Cuba, there was some truth to this assertion.

Shortly thereafter, Rowan himself became something of a correspondent: *McClure's* magazine wasted no time soliciting an article from him recounting his journey.[9] Rowan's article, "My Ride across Cuba," was described by an editor's note as "the simple, straightforward [tale] of a man who is unconscious that he has done anything remarkable." Rowan tended to overwrite, and one has to suspect the piece received considerable editing—particularly the terse first paragraph.[10]

Miles's troops were progressing nicely in Puerto Rico when on August 13 the United States and Spain signed a protocol ending the hostilities. As Davis put it, "The campaign was nipped by peace."[11] In three weeks in Puerto Rico, three Americans had been killed and forty wounded. During the entire course of the war, 1,577 American servicemen were wounded, another 280 died of battle injuries, and 2,565 died of disease and other ailments. The vast majority of those deaths occurred among volunteer troops who had never left the United States; these were the victims of the army's lax attitude regarding established sanitation practices in encampments.[12]

With the fighting at an end, Miles decided that Rowan would be the perfect man to travel through Cuba evaluating conditions there. On August 22 Rowan was given his formal orders to "ascertain the condition and disposition of the inhabitants of the island, the status of any civil or military government, the condition of the lines of communication by road, telegraph or railway, the topography of the country, the character of the streams, the various industries, and other information of importance and interest."[13] He was to be accompanied by Lieutenant Charles F. Parker of the Second Artillery. They departed Ponce on August 31 on the brightly painted side-wheeler *Gussie*, traveling first to Gibara on Cuba's northern shore, not far from Manatí Bay, the place from which Rowan had departed Cuba a few months earlier. When they headed south from Gibara on September 4, Cuban general Luís de Feria Garayalde provided them with horses and an escort. During his second trip through this countryside, Rowan looked about him through different eyes, noting, "The blight of war fell heavily on those eastern provinces. The country is a desert—void of life beyond any district we saw. The roads are mere trails, losing themselves in seas of grass and underbrush, needing a native guide to find them at all times.... There were men in the woods, but it took long search to find their wretched huts of palm bark." This time there was no fear of being shot as a spy. In fact, he had no fears at all. "The striking thing is the perfect order enforced by the insurgents," he wrote. "Traveling is safe as in any state in the Union. Indeed, I am not sure that I would not take more precautions on a horseback journey there than here. Half the time we traveled without escort, only a guide accompanying us, and we slept in hammocks in the open, picketing our horses, but taking no other measures to insure their safety or our own."[14] After two days in Santiago they headed west toward Manzanillo on the Gulf of Guacanayaba, about fifty miles northeast of Belic, where Fidel Castro would land the *Granma* fifty-eight years later.[15] From here they sailed across the gulf to Santa Cruz, where they paid a visit to the administrative headquarters, obtained fresh horses, and headed inland to Puerto Principe, today called Camagüey. Rowan wrote, "After Puerto Principe, our route was a catalogue of hunger-ridden cities with deserts between them . . . until we reached Havana and plunged west into Pinar del

Rio. At Placetas we struck the sugar country. What cane fields the insurgents had spared promised an abundant yield, enough perhaps to foot up a third of a full crop before the insurrection began. Down in the Pinar del Rio the same thing is true of the tobacco crop—good, what there is of it, and one pound where there were three before." He believed there was insufficient food on the island, even if, that is, "the poor had money to purchase it." One plan under consideration that he thought might be the "simplest and in the end the only practical way" of solving the poverty problem was "to pay the Cuban army and send the soldiers back to their farms and plantations . . . for it is the mothers and fathers, the wives and children of the insurgents who are in the direst need." And unlike many of his fellow soldiers, Rowan had nothing but praise for the Cuban fighters: "The insurgents deserve some consideration. They made tremendous sacrifices when they went into the woods. They have endured privations without end. Their officers are superior to Spanish officers of the same grade in intelligence and bravery. If the bottom had not dropped out of the Spanish war after the battle of Santiago the American army would have found them invaluable allies in their advance upon Havana."[16]

One can only speculate on what the final outcome of the Cuban insurrection would have been had the United States not intervened. There is no doubt that many thousands more Spaniards and Cubans would have died of wounds, disease, and starvation. Spain would probably have increased its naval presence around the island, greatly reducing the military supplies reaching the *insurrectos* and, perhaps, in the end slaughtered enough Cubans to quell the rebellion. On the other hand, the Spanish people were losing any enthusiasm they might have had for retaining Cuba; no one can know for sure, but perhaps the rebels would have eventually worn them down. We can, however, be certain that when the fighting was over, neither side—Spanish nor Cuban—would have put Santiago to rights in any way approaching the level achieved by recently promoted brigadier general Leonard Wood.

Wood, who served with distinction in the West, had been a highly regarded army surgeon in Washington before the war. It was there that he became friends with Theodore Roosevelt, and the two of them were given permission to raise the regiment that would become known as the Rough Riders—Wood as colonel, Roosevelt as lieutenant colonel.[17] At the end of June, Wood was given a battlefield promotion to brigadier general and after the capitulation was ordered to take charge of Santiago. Even in the best of times, Santiago was no model of hygiene; sea captains claimed they could smell it ten miles out at sea. After the siege, it held 100,000 residents—double its usual number—and many of them were dying, if not already dead, of various diseases. A thousand buzzards circled overhead, and millions of flies buzzed below. "Men could not bury the dead fast enough," Wood wrote, "and they were burned in great heaps of eighty or ninety piled high on gratings of railroad iron mixed with grass and sticks." Wood burned the dead and fed the living, issuing 20,000 and more rations a day. He created a police force, established a yellow fever hospital, put down looters, cleared the jails of all but murderers, forced food vendors to lower their prices, cleaned the streets, had the scavenger dogs killed and burned, bought medicines and food for the sick Spanish soldiers, improved the sewage system, and listened to a thousand tales of woe from ordinary citizens. The death rate eventually went down from two hundred per day to twenty.[18] It is difficult to imagine any Cuban being in a position to have accomplished what this thirty-nine-year-old American was able to do.

As a sign of their newly established friendship, Major General Lawton, who was appointed military governor of the province, invited General Calixto García Íñiguez to visit the city of Santiago, and García chose to go. His entry was triumphant, complete with a marching band and an escort of mounted cavalrymen. As many as 10,000 people crowded the central plaza. That night there was a gala reception at the San Carlos Club, and American army officers in dress uniforms mingled with their Cuban counterparts and prominent civilians. García gave a laudatory speech in which he noted what a great country it was that would send the sons of millionaires, who had nothing to gain, to die by the side of Cubans. "Our gratitude to the United States of America will be eternal."[19]

It will be remembered that when García successfully left the United States for Cuba in February 1896, he was under indictment and had skipped out on $2,500 bail. In March he had written an open letter to the people of the United States, stating,

> I am fully aware of the obligation which I have contracted to stand trial for my alleged violations of the laws of your country. I have not remained to face the consequences of my acts, simply because I feel that I have a higher duty to perform as a soldier and a Cuban. . . . Should I fail, my death will expiate, I hope, in your eyes, any possible offense for which I might have to stand trial there; should I survive, I give you my word as a man and a soldier, to return to your country and cheerfully abide by the consequences which the laws of the country may visit upon me.[20]

An editorial in the *New York Times* the following day noted,

> There is a delightfully solemn kind of humor in the promise of Gen. Garcia to come back and stand trial on the charge of violating our neutrality laws just as soon as the task of freeing Cuba, on which he is now engaged, has been accomplished. . . . And if he comes back, representing a new nation instead of an enslaved province, his re-arrest and trial are not likely to end in anything very severe. Perhaps the offended dignity of our courts might necessitate a sentence of imprisonment in a banquet hall for three or four hours, with hard work at speechmaking, but for one trained in guerrilla warfare that prospect need not shadow life with horrid apprehension.[21]

This is close to what happened when he returned to New York as president of the Cuban Commission to confer with McKinley regarding the future of the island.

Six weeks after they began their journey, Rowan and Parker had traveled over two thousand miles on horseback through difficult country.

On September 29, while they were still meandering through Cuba, Colonel L. D. Tyson, the officer to whom Rowan was officially assigned, heard through the grapevine that his regiment, now at

Chickamauga Park, Georgia, would soon be going to Cuba; and here he was, still without a second in command—and still in the dark as to Rowan's whereabouts. Once again he wired Adjutant General Corbin asking that Rowan be ordered to join him. And once again he was told that Rowan was on special duty, but that upon its completion he would be directed to join the regiment.[22]

Rowan and Parker left Havana on Saturday, October 15, on board the Ward Line SS *Orizaba*, arriving in New York the following Wednesday afternoon after having sailed through a ferocious storm along the East Coast.[23] Parker was suffering from a fever, but a reporter found Rowan at the Windsor Hotel appearing "as hale and hearty as if he were returning from his Summer's vacation. . . . He is a wiry, compactly built little man, with mobile countenance, swarthy skin and a stubby, black military moustache."[24]

Rowan left New York for Washington on October 20 to prepare and present his final report to the War Department. That same day a lengthy interview with Rowan appeared in the *New York Times*, and an editor at *McClure's* immediately dispatched a letter to Rowan in Washington asking for the opportunity to publish an account of his latest travels.[25] For whatever reason—perhaps time constraints—he wrote only his official account, and it was fairly dry, concerned chiefly with roads, streams, topography, and other topics that would be of interest only to an occupying army.[26]

Miles was pleased with the quality of the data Rowan and Parker brought back and later wrote that they "obtained most valuable information concerning that country and the present condition of its inhabitants, which is both of political and military interest."[27] Many of Rowan's personal observations printed in the *Times* interview involved the deleterious effects the war had had on the country and the people, but the trip left Rowan convinced there would never be a serious disagreement between Cuba and the United States: "Throughout the interior of the island I heard nothing but gratitude expressed by the people for the part we played in gaining their freedom. All seem to realize that sooner or later their country will become a part of the United States, and have no idea that they can maintain an independent government for long, but they want to be free and try their hand at self-government for a limited period from a mere sentimental standpoint." Near the start of their journey, Rowan and Parker visited General García's camp at Jiguaní. Of the general he said, "He is one of nature's nobleman. He is intellectually a great man, and I don't think that any other nation under the circumstances can turn out a better soldier."[28]

On November 17 García sailed for New York aboard the *Segurança*, the ship that had served as Major General Shafter's seagoing headquarters off southeastern Cuba the previous June. To avoid any demonstrations in Havana harbor, García boarded the liner after first departing by tug from nearby Playa de Marianao.[29] A delegation of Cubans and their sympathizers, including "Dynamite Johnny" O'Brien, rode out by tug to greet the *Segurança* when it arrived in New York harbor on November 21. When they boarded the liner, it was a "scene of animated greetings, the conspicuous feature being the Spanish embraces. Gen. Garcia towered above all the others, broad, heavy-chested, and bronzed." After passing through customs, García held a news conference at which he said that after a few days' rest the commission would travel to Washington. Once there, they would meet with President McKinley. In answer to a reporter's question regarding annexation, he quickly responded, "No annexation. The people of Cuba rely on the good faith of the United States. It is necessary for the American troops to occupy the island until order is established, but not forever." It was dark when the general made his way to the pier to meet what appeared to be most of New York's Cuban colony, including two of his sons. He was forced to shake hand after hand before eventually reaching his home on Lenox Avenue in Harlem,[30] and it may very well have been this wholesale handshaking that introduced the slight cold he developed within the next few days.

García left for Washington on November 30, having stayed in New York a little longer than planned. He and other commission members made their first call at the White House on December 2, meeting with the president in the Cabinet Room for an hour and a half. No one present would later discuss the meeting, saying only that it was of an agreeable nature. The next night, in spite of his cold's having gotten worse, García attended the annual dinner of the Gridiron Club, along with 160 other guests, including the president, Admiral William Sampson, Shafter, and a number of foreign dignitaries.[31] Within days the cold had developed into pneumonia, and by December 9 García's condition was a cause for alarm. He died on Sunday, December 11, the day after the signing of the Treaty of Paris that officially ended the war between Spain and the United States.[32] Until the very end, García's thoughts were with the rebellion. In a delirium as he lay dying, he gave orders to his son for a battle he believed would take place the following day with four hundred Spaniards. Immediately after he died, his body was prepared for burial and placed on a bier. As the *New York Times* described it at the time, "A large Cuban flag served as a covering, and the head was placed on one of smaller dimensions. The face and bust were left exposed to public view. The features had a lifelike appearance and gave no indication of the sufferings which the General had borne. Just above the head rested a magnificent floral piece of red and white roses and a cross of palms tied with a white ribbon. By direction of Gen. Miles a detachment of soldiers from Battery E, Sixth Artillery . . . was detailed as a body guard."[33] García's body lay in state in the Raleigh Hotel the following day as hundreds of visitors paid their respects. Floral tributes crowded the room. That night his remains were placed in a black, cloth-covered casket for temporary interment in a vault the following day at Arlington National Cemetery, eventually to be moved to Havana for final burial. The funeral, at St. Patrick's Catholic Church, was filled with all the stately pomp and circumstance one would expect in Washington. Not present among the crowd of military officers, American and Cuban politicians, and religious leaders from around the country was his widow, who was tending their seriously ill daughter, Mercedes, in Thomasville, Georgia. To add to Señora García's sadness, Mercedes died on December 27, unaware that her father had preceded her in death; her body, like that of her father, would be returned to Cuba.[34]

The news of García's death left a feeling of gloom among Cubans everywhere. Yet there was also the expressed declaration among the various factions that his death may have removed one more complication in the resolution of Cuba's future. In Havana, Cubans took offense at continued public entertainment during the period of mourning and forced theaters to close. The management of the Gran Teatro de Tacon, which was filled with Spanish officers, refused to close it; the result was a small riot in which three Cubans were killed and one Spanish officer and one Cuban were wounded. The melee continued inside the Hotel Inglaterra, where a French citizen was wounded while sitting at a table. Even though the Spaniards were now officially vanquished, they were to remain, under the command of General Adolfo Jimenez Castellanos, the established force for law and order in Havana until January 1, 1899. To prevent further altercations Castellanos issued an order closing coffee shops in the central city at 6:00 P.M., preventing the passage of private carriages through that area in the evening, and forbidding the gathering of groups near the hotel. In addition, all theatrical entertainment and public balls were temporarily prohibited.[35]

It wasn't until February 4, 1899, that García's body was transferred to the U.S. gunboat *Nashville* for passage to Havana, and the Cubans made plans for an impressive ceremony. The body arrived in Havana Harbor on February 9; somber booming from the guns at Morro Castle and American ships in the harbor announced its arrival. Flags everywhere were lowered to half-mast, their poles topped with black streamers. Once offloaded, the casket, followed by bareheaded Cubans and accompanied by a funeral dirge, was taken by hearse to the municipal council chamber, where it would lie in state until the public funeral two days later.

On Saturday, February 11, six black horses pulled a black-draped artillery caisson bearing García's casket. The caisson slowly made its way through the thronged but quiet streets of Havana, preceded and followed by the most elaborate funeral cortege ever seen in the city. It traveled the four miles to the Colón Cemetery, where the bodies of American sailors who had died aboard the *Maine* had been buried a year earlier.[36]

Even in his final moments above ground, García was a source of controversy. As the procession moved through the streets, it became apparent to some that among the bands, the American soldiers, the many hearses filled with flowers, and the dozens of societies, there were no Cuban soldiers. At the cemetery, the person designated to give an oration was not there. A final salute was fired by an American squad, and taps was played by an American bugler. The problem, as ever, had to do with hurt feelings. In recognition of his senior rank on the island, Major General John R. Brooke, the military governor, was to ride in a carriage directly behind García's casket. Forty or so members of the Cuban Assembly thought they were to march immediately behind Brooke, but were outraged to discover they had been pushed even farther back in the procession, behind the carriages for the general's staff and an American cavalry troop. This distance from García's body would, they felt, dilute their importance in the eyes of Cuban citizens along the route; they therefore withdrew and ordered every Cuban soldier out of the procession. Somewhat to their surprise and satisfaction, the soldiers obeyed. That afternoon and evening, the cafés were filled with Cuban officers denouncing Brooke and declaring that McKinley should call him home. The brouhaha ended quickly enough, and the next day the city erupted with abandonment and gaiety as the Cubans celebrated Carnaval.

Had it not been for a few months of headline popularity, García would have occupied as little space in the American mind as his compatriots Máximo Gómez and Antonio Maceo. For his part, Andrew Rowan would eventually have joined his friend Richard Pearson Hobson in the small pantheon of forgotten Spanish-American War heroes.[37] Yet because of some late-night scribbling by a long-haired megalomaniac named Elbert Hubbard, García's name lived on as metaphor, and Rowan became a celebrity.

Hubbard was the proprietor of the Roycrofters handicrafts company in the village of East Aurora, New York, not far from Buffalo. Where the name Roycrofters came from depended on when you asked him; at one time he said it was from the respected English printers Thomas and Samuel Roycroft, and at other times he claimed to have chosen the name because it translated into king's craft, or work fit for a king.[38] In fact, Hubbard acquired the name from Harry P. Taber, a business associate who established the Roycroft Press (named for the English printers) to publish a magazine, *The Philistine: A Periodical of Protest*, which he founded with Hubbard and another partner. It was also Taber who

Figure 4. Elbert Hubbard wearing his trademark Stetson, long hair, and flamboyant soft bow tie. Library of Congress.

designed the Roycroft orb-and-cross trademark. Being involved with the press fit in perfectly with Hubbard's desire to be a published author, and at the start he was a contributor to the *Philistine* under Taber's editorship. The periodical didn't quite catch on, and Taber couldn't afford to continue subsidizing it. Hubbard, who had money to invest, bought him out and became the sole owner in November 1895.[39] His decision to own a publishing company had been influenced by a visit the previous year to William Morris's famous Kelmscott Press in the London suburb of Hammersmith.[40]

Under Hubbard's management the *Philistine*'s circulation grew and, inspired by Morris, he expanded the publishing business to include artsy limited editions of books. In spite of Hubbard's motto, "Not how cheap, but how good," Roycrofter products never reached the quality of Morris's. George Bernard Shaw, whose essay "On Going to Church" Hubbard reprinted in 1896,[41] at one point referred to Hubbard as a "pseudo-Morrisian."

In time Hubbard further emulated Morris by manufacturing craft items, eventually producing hundreds of objects, from hammered-copper bookends to large pieces of furniture; it was, however, the publishing end of the business that most appealed to him, particularly the *Philistine*, and it was this that resulted in his fateful connection with García and Rowan. It started during a dinnertime debate that occurred on George Washington's birthday in 1899,[42] a couple of months after the war had ended. Hubbard's son Bert was insisting that Andrew Rowan was the true hero of the war because of the manner in which he had carried the message to García. At first his father was having none of it, but then suddenly he gave in. As Hubbard remembered the incident some three years later, "It came to me with a flash! yes, the boy is right, the hero is the man who does his thing—does his work—carries the message. I got up from the table, left the rest of the family there, went into the next room, and wrote 'The Message to Garcia.'"[43] Hubbard's essay begins,

In all this Cuban business there is one man [who] stands out on the horizon of my memory like Mars at perihelion. When the war broke out between Spain and the United States, it was very necessary to communicate quickly with the leader of the Insurgents. Garcia was somewhere in the mountain fastness of Cuba—no one knew where. No mail nor telegraph message could reach him. The President must secure his co-operation, and quickly.

What to do!

Some one said to the President, "There is a fellow by the name of Rowan will find Garcia for you, if anybody can."

Rowan was sent for and given a letter to be delivered to Garcia. How the "fellow by the name of Rowan" took the letter, sealed it up in an oil-skin pouch, strapped it over his heart, in four days landed by night off the coast of Cuba from an open boat, disappeared into the jungle, and in three weeks came out on the other side of the Island, having traversed a hostile country on foot, and delivered his letter to Garcia—are things I have no special desire now to tell in detail.[44]

One can understand Hubbard's unwillingness to go into any detail. In the first few paragraphs he fabricated nearly all the facts. Furthermore, the details of Rowan's journey, fictional or otherwise, had little to do with the purpose of the essay. Hubbard continues,

> The point that I wish to make is this: McKinley gave Rowan a letter to be delivered to Garcia; Rowan took the letter and did not ask, "Where is he at?"
>
> By the Eternal! There is a man whose form should be cast in deathless bronze and the statue placed in every college of the land. It is not book-learning young men need, nor instruction about this and that, but a stiffening of the vertebræ which will cause them to be loyal to a trust, to act promptly, concentrate their energies: do the thing—"Carry a message to Garcia."[45]

The "fellow by the name of Rowan" is never mentioned by name again. The remaining twelve hundred or so words are devoted to a few hyperbolic examples demonstrating the utter worthlessness of 90 percent of America's workers. Those today who complain that people don't work as hard as they did in the old days might find it instructive to read Hubbard's raillery of the old days:

> We have recently been hearing much maudlin sympathy expressed for the "down-trodden denizen of the sweat shop" and the "homeless wanderer searching for honest employment," and with it all often go many hard words for the men in power.
>
> Nothing is said about the employer who grows old before his time in a vain attempt to get frowsy ne'er-do-wells to do intelligent work; and his long patient striving with "help" that does nothing but loaf when his back is turned. In every store and factory there is a constant weeding-out process going on. The employer is constantly sending away "help" that have shown their incapacity to further the interests of the business, and others are being taken on. No matter how good times are, this sorting continues, only if times are hard and work is scarce, this sorting is done finer—but out and forever out, the incompetent and

unworthy go. It is the survival of the fittest. Self-interest prompts every employer to keep the best—those who can carry a message to Garcia.[46]

There's much more of the same as Hubbard fudges his way to a desired number of column inches. During the course of his complaining, allusions to a "first mate with knotted club" and "the toe of a thick-soled No. 9 boot" suggest there may even be instances when physical violence on the part of an employer is a justifiable last resort. But he ends on a positive note, sighing as he dreams of the perfect worker:

My heart goes out to the man who does his work when the "boss" is away, as well as when he is at home. And the man, who, when given a letter for Garcia, quietly takes the missive, without asking any idiotic questions, and with no lurking intention of chucking it into the nearest sewer, or of doing aught else but deliver it, never gets "laid off," nor has to go on strike for higher wages. Civilization is one long anxious search for just such individuals. Anything such a man asks shall be granted. He is wanted in every city, town and village—in every office, shop, store and factory. The world cries out for such: he is needed, and needed badly—the man who can CARRY A MESSAGE TO GARCIA.[47]

Hubbard later claimed that the essay "leaped hot from my heart, written after a rather trying day, when I had been endeavoring to train some rather delinquent helpers in the way they should go." His son Bert, who was sixteen at the time, later remembered it somewhat differently: in a reminiscence published after his father's death, he stated quite plainly that the essay was directed solely at him for having committed some boyish deviltry, the nature of which he chose not to disclose. He also intimated that the argument about Rowan's heroism might never have occurred.[48] Of the father and son, young Bert is the more believable if only because there's considerable evidence that his father didn't feel obliged to spoil a good story by sticking to the facts.[49] What motivated Elbert Hubbard doesn't matter; what matters is what happened afterward.

The fifteen-hundred-word piece was written in order to fill what were some still empty pages of the March 1899 edition of the *Philistine*. "I thought so little about it," Hubbard wrote, "that we ran it in without a heading." And it might have ended there, passing into journalistic oblivion, as have all his other *Philistine* essays. But as Hubbard himself acknowledged, "the combination of theme, conditions of the country, and method of circulation were so favorable that their conjunction will probably never occur again." There were requests for additional copies—a dozen here, fifty there, and finally an order from the American News Company for a thousand copies. "I asked one of my helpers which article it was that had stirred things up. 'It's that thing about Garcia,' she said."[50]

After completing his tour of Cuba, Rowan was shuttled here and there. In November 1898 he was in New York, where he was joined by his wife, Ida. From there they made the long train ride back to Atchison, Kansas, for a short visit. He was finally ordered to join the Sixth Volunteer Infantry Regiment, but he never made it. Instead he was told to accompany Redfield Proctor, who wanted to make a postwar tour of Cuba. Ida accompanied him on the three-week trip, during which they visited Cienfuegos, Havana, Matanzas, and Pinar del Rio.[51] Back in the States, Ida returned to Atchison, and Rowan went to New York City.[52]

Ida Rowan's Kansan sensibilities were shaken by nearly everything she saw in Cuba. There was nothing she cared for, from the weather to the women. Everything was dirty, including the people, the houses, and Morro Castle. The food was tasteless, the hotels crowded, and the shopkeepers dishonest. Surprisingly, the only thing she found palatable in Havana was the water.[53]

Again Rowan was ordered to join the Sixth, now in Savannah, and this time he reported for duty. Ironically enough, his job was to muster out the troops he'd failed to muster in. During its brief existence the regiment had lost thirteen men to disease (in spite of their being "immunes"), and another forty-eight had deserted.[54] After a few more weeks on special duty assisting with the mustering out of other units, Rowan himself was mustered out, costing him his lieutenant-colonelcy. This was customary with officers specifically promoted to such positions in volunteer units, which, it was assumed, were temporary assignments. Anticipating being reassigned to the Nineteenth Infantry Regiment, which had been in Puerto Rico and was returning to the States,[55] Rowan requested a month's leave of absence and was granted twenty days with the proviso that it "not extend beyond the date fixed for the departure of the Nineteenth Infantry from Camp Meade, Pennsylvania for the Philippine Islands." He spent part of the time visiting relatives back in West Virginia, where, according to the Charleston *Daily Gazette*, he "expressed his happiness at being once more able to breathe in the pure air of his Monroe home."[56]

One of the readers of Hubbard's essay in the *Philistine* was George H. Daniels, an executive with Cornelius Vanderbilt's New York Central Railroad, who commented,

> When I opened *The Philistine* for March, and glanced through its interesting pages, the title, "A Message to Garcia," struck me as peculiar, and I felt confident that underneath it would be found something of unusual interest. I . . . read the article aloud to my Secretary, and as I finished it I remarked, "This is the finest thing of its kind I have ever read."
>
> Immediately there passed through my mind the names of a thousand men and women I wanted to have read the message and appreciate it as I did, and I at once wired this to Mr. Hubbard: "'A Message to Garcia' is superb; please print us 1,000 copies. This article should be read by every citizen of our great Republic."[57]

Daniels was engaging in a bit of dissemblance here. To begin with, the piece in the magazine had no title, and the other details are a little shaky; however, he did order a thousand copies of the essay printed as a pamphlet on handmade paper,[58] and Hubbard quickly provided them. The copyright date was April 17, 1899.

George Daniels was something of a character himself. As a young man he had quit school to fight with the Union army during the Civil War, eventually becoming a steamboat pilot. After being discharged, he traveled to the West and began his career as a railroad man. In time he became the head cheerleader for rail travel in the United States and was described by a contemporary as "*the* man to address railroad assemblies on all sorts of occasions [and] the most brilliant of speakers."[59] Another writer described him as "a rosy, good natured man who looks like a Methodist bishop."[60] One of his duties for the New York Central was overseeing the production and distribution of pamphlets titled the Four Track Series. Titles ranged from *Block Signals on the New York Central* (number 17), to *Health and Pleasure on America's Greatest Railroad* (number 5), to *Two Days at Niagara Falls* (number 9). All carried house ads and paid advertisements. "A Message to Garcia" was pamphlet number 25, and an explanatory statement in the first edition read, "This homily, first printed in The Philistine Magazine for March 1899, caused the edition to be exhausted within three days after its publication. The matter is now re-printed in this form by request of Mr. George H. Daniels, General Passenger Agent of the New York Central, for distribution among those discerning ones who appreciate a good thing." No sooner had Daniels mailed copies to his thousand closest friends than he ordered a second edition of a thousand, and then a third.[61] Realizing he had a moneymaker on his hands, Hubbard printed up an additional thousand copies for sale in his own shop. He changed the design somewhat, and chose the word "preachment" rather than "homily" to describe the nature of the essay, and that is what it was called thereafter. At some point Daniels ordered 100,000 copies. This was in the days of the so-called jobbing platen presses from which a deft lad might, for a short while, get a thousand sheets an hour printed on one side.[62] Hubbard had three of these foot-operated presses and, taking his other printing obligations into consideration, calculated it would take him up to two years to fill the order. That didn't suit Daniels, who asked for permission to have them printed elsewhere, agreeing to pay Hubbard a royalty.

After five editions of 100,000 each, the railroad revised the design,[63] and for its "second half-million edition" produced a slick, four-by-eight-inch, thirty-page booklet printed and engraved by Rand McNally with a full-color cover illustration of, presumably, Rowan staring at García's mountain fastness in the distance. Inside were original drawings illustrating various passages in the essay; photos of Rowan, García, and Hubbard; scenes along the railway line; a short bio of Hubbard; and a few pages of advertising. The back cover contained a map showing the New York Central's routes from New York north to Montreal and west to St. Louis. Also added were dozens of encomia written by newspaper and magazine editors, clergymen, railway executives, educators, and the like, each seemingly trying to outdo the other in lavish praise: "Every word in it has the ring of Gospel truth" (the rector of one of the most prominent churches in New York); "It contains more sound horse sense to the square inch than anything I have read in a long time" (a manufacturer in Central New York); "one of the most useful little books to young men that has ever been written" (the secretary of the Prison Association of New York); "It is an epic. It ought to be pasted with the Golden Rule in the hat of every boy in the land" (a prominent lawyer of Troy). And Mr. Albert Leonard, dean of the College of Liberal Arts at Syracuse University, wrote in the *Journal of Pedagogy*, to later be quoted in the New York Central tract, "We do not recall anything in the whole range of English literature that is more likely to incite the young to energetic and high endeavor than this preachment of Mr. Hubbard's. The less than dozen pages in this pamphlet contain the complete philosophy of success in any undertaking in life. Many a youth who would otherwise do life's work in a half-hearted and careless way will be led to make the most of himself through the reading of 'A Message to Garcia.'"[64] Well, perhaps. But there were some who saw it differently. As a letter writer to the *New York Times* pointed out, "Our supremacy in commercial and industrial affairs disproves assertions that when asked to deliver "a message to Garcia," the average man will merely "look at you out of a fishy eye" and ask foolish questions. On the contrary, the great majority of young men attend to their tasks faithfully and with a desire to please their employers, anxious to have their services appreciated and suitably rewarded."[65] And this was among the milder criticisms. George H. Heafford, Daniels's counterpart at the Chicago, Milwaukee, and St. Paul Railroad, dismissed it as "a gratuitous insult even to the lowest average of intelligence and ability." In a letter to Daniels he referred to the essay as "an outrage upon civilized humanity which should be resented by everyone."[66]

None of this kept the presses from their relentless task of printing ever more copies. Jules Zanger, who has written extensively about American literature, explains this phenomenon by suggesting that Hubbard managed to "catch, perhaps inadvertently, the precise tone—threatened, angry, irritated—and the value structure of the American business community at the turn of the century, and to articulate them in terms with which that community could immediately identify."[67] The immediate effect on Hubbard was to make him considerably more famous—and wealthy—than the bric-a-brac he and his Roycrofters were cranking out could ever have done. On May 22, three months after writing "A Message to Garcia," he and George Daniels spoke by invitation at the 115th meeting of the New York Universalist Club at the St. Denis Hotel in New York City. There were 122 members and guests present, the largest turnout ever. Daniels spoke briefly about the phenomenal success of "A Message to Garcia"; Hubbard spoke at length about himself. Rowan had also been invited to attend, but was on leave in faraway Kansas at the time of the meeting. He did send a letter to Hubbard stating, "Give my regards to Daniels [and] tell him he is a good fellow, but that he's kicked up a great deal of dust about a small matter."[68]

Daniels had sent a copy of the "Message" to Rowan, who wrote to Hubbard on May 1, while he was still in Savannah, "You have done me entirely too proud in that beautifully written essay but to show you that I am not mad I take the liberty of enclosing ten dollars with the request that you enter my name among the subscribers to the *Philistine*, also six copies of *A Message to Garcia*." Hubbard replied, thanking him for the ten dollars and noting that "you certainly did your work and did it well and my heart goes out to all such." There's a joke somewhere in his next sentence, which reads, "Then, after you did your work you did not let all the girls in the land play tiddledywinks with you in an osculatory way raising interesting questions for the bacteriologist."[69]

By the time Rowan began his leave of absence, he had achieved the status of a major war hero. On June 1 he was honored in Atchison with a huge reception at the Byram Hotel sponsored by the city and the First

Presbyterian Church. According to the *Atchison Daily Globe*, it "broke the record in Atchison, both in attendance, and in the magnificence of the decorations." The article continued,

> The parlors of The Byram were very handsomely decorated for which credit is largely due J. Wallenstein, of the Boston Store, and his window trimmer, Max Dannebaum. The name "Rowan" appeared in electric lights above the receiving party, and on either side were enormous American flags made of bunting. At the top of a pedestal stood an American eagle, and on the mantels were banks of natural flowers. Both of the greenhouses contributed great quantities of palms. American flags and bunting were displayed everywhere, and it is generally agreed that the decorations were much the handsomest ever seen in the city. . . . Thirty gallons of ices were ordered for the reception, and it was served at three tables by six young ladies, assisted by a corps of colored waiters.[70]

To entertain the crowd, estimated at between fifteen hundred and two thousand, there was a twenty-two-man orchestra, fifteen of whom were "crack musicians from St. Joe and Kansas city, imported for the occasion." Their first number was a march written for the reception by "Professor" J. H. Davies of Atchison titled "A Message to Garcia."[71] William Allen White, who was present, lauded the orchestra for "a particularly good concert" and called the reception "one of the best ever given in Kansas," crediting its success to the "high standard in intelligence" to be found in Atchison. And, he added, "best of all, no one was allowed to make a speech or sing a song. In any other Kansas town, some fool would have broken in with a speech, or some woman would have sung a song, or at least some elocutionist would have sneaked into the service, and made people tired."[72] A writer in the *St. Joseph Herald* praised the excellence of the affair, pointing out that the people of Atchison were famous for the quality of their public celebrations. "Other towns have attempted to imitate," he wrote, "but there is only one Atchison 'Corn Carnival.'"[73] Celebrities from around the state attended, including Governor W. E. Stanley and his wife. A rumor later circulated that the governor, a Methodist, danced at the reception, but this was repudiated in the columns of the *Atchison Daily Globe*. Little Elizabeth was there in the company of her grandfather, A. B. Symns, but she didn't join her parents in the reception line. Rowan was wearing a new pair of white kid gloves, and by the end of the evening they were stained nearly black from the shaking of so many hands. Ida laid them away as a souvenir of the occasion, saying she wouldn't "clean them for the world."[74] The one sad aspect of the affair was the absence of Ida's mother; she had been suffering for the past year from a malignant abdominal tumor and was unable to attend.[75]

Otherwise, this was about as good as it could get for an infantry captain from Union, West Virginia. Rowan was the kind of man every mother wished her son would grow up to be. It is apparently true that Rowan enjoyed all the attention; on June 29 he wrote to Hubbard from Fort Meade, "Thank you for boosting me so far along on the road to fame."[76]

The war with Spain officially ended with the signing of the Treaty of Paris on December 10, 1898. Cuba was to be occupied by the United States until pacification was complete; then it was to become a sovereign nation. Puerto Rico and other Spanish-ruled islands in the West Indies, and the island of Guam in the Ladrones, were ceded to the United States outright; the Philippine archipelago was also ceded—sold, in fact, to the United States for $20 million.[77]

But there was one problem with Spain's selling the Philippines to the United States: the Filipinos themselves wanted independence. On June 12, 1898, Emilio Aguinaldo y Famy, the leader of the Filipino insurgents and nearly always referred to as charismatic, had already declared their independence "under the protection of the mighty and humane" United States.[78] He should have gotten better assurances from American officials first.

Rudyard Kipling's notorious poem "The White Man's Burden" appeared in the February 1899 *McClure's* magazine; it reads in part,

Take up the White Man's Burden—
Send forth the best ye breed—

Go bind your sons to exile
To serve your captives' need;
To wait in heavy harness,
On fluttered folk and wild—
Your new-caught, sullen peoples,
Half-devil and half-child.[79]

If taking up the burden meant fighting the Filipinos for their own land, so be it. Captain Andrew Summers Rowan of Company I of the Nineteenth Infantry Regiment boarded the transport *Tartar* in San Francisco on July 24, 1899, to do his share.[80]

CHAPTER 6

Exactly Where Are the Philippines?

The events that led to Andrew Summers Rowan's departure for the Philippines occurred 378 years earlier, when Ferdinand Magellan landed in the archipelago while on his famous voyage; Magellan is given credit for being the leader of the first expedition to circumnavigate the globe even though he was murdered in what came to be known as the Philippines before accomplishing his goal. Only one of his five ships, the *Victoria*, completed the westward circumnavigation, returning to Spain after an incredibly difficult voyage of nearly three years. Before he was killed by inhabitants of the small island of Mactan off Cebu in the Philippines, Magellan, a native of Portugal, claimed the archipelago for Spain on Easter Sunday 1521. On the basis of that claim Spain assumed possession of the islands.

The essentially Spanish Christian culture imposed on them left the poorly educated natives unable to compete with the Spanish, who continued to treat them as a conquered people. There were uprisings now and then, but they were doomed from the start. The fragmented tribal nature and relative backwardness of native societies prevented their being able to compete politically or militarily with the Spanish.[1]

Things began to change in 1869 with the opening of the Suez Canal. Passage time to Spain was cut from two or three months to just one, and goods and people began to flow in both directions. From 1867 to 1894, trade increased by more than 300 percent. This created business opportunities not only for the colonizers but also the colonized. A new upper middle class arose among the Filipinos, who saw themselves as equals to the Spanish in every way. As such, they agitated for social change.

It wasn't independence from Spain that concerned the *ilustrados* as much as having the same rights and privileges as Spanish citizens.[2] They wanted not revolution but reform: they wanted the Philippines to become a Spanish province represented in the *cortes* (parliament)—a change that would mean converting from military to civil rule. As citizens they would have the rights guaranteed in the Spanish constitution.[3] Much of the work for reform was carried out in Madrid and Barcelona by Filipino students with the assistance and encouragement of Spanish liberals.[4] It was only after they realized the reforms would never be made that they spread their propaganda among the masses. Filipinos were ready for it, and they wanted more than mere reforms.[5]

A grassroots organization, the Katipunan, was formed with the ultimate goal of overthrowing the Spanish through armed revolt. Membership grew slowly, exploding in 1896 to 30,000. One recruit was twenty-six-year-old Emilio Aguinaldo y Famy, son of a landowning family in Cavite.

On August 31, 1895, Aguinaldo had taken control of his own town and called a public meeting during which he announced his resignation as municipal captain and appointed himself the local military commander. The next day he issued a manifesto to his counterparts in nearby towns, and the rebels quickly controlled all of Cavite Province but the peninsula jutting into Manila Bay.[6]

General Ramón Blanco y Erenes, governor general of the Philippines who would later succeed Valeriano Weyler in that same capacity in Cuba, had under his command four thousand troops, but two thousand of these were Filipinos, and the remaining Spanish troops were widely dispersed.[7] When Blanco cabled Madrid reporting recent developments, members of the government were outraged to learn that the lowly *indios* dared to confront their imperial rule. Troops were dispatched at once and, in Manila, Spanish residents called for the slaughter of the wretched Filipinos. Thousands of civilians were arrested and imprisoned. Some were executed. The Spanish attacked the town of Nasugbu, killing over a hundred rebels and an untold number of women and children who had taken refuge in a church. (They retained some of the women to satisfy the sexual needs of the soldiers.) In the town of Lemery they did the same. Shortly thereafter Aguinaldo issued a manifesto calling for the creation of a revolutionary government patterned somewhat after that of the United States (with a nod to the French Revolution): "People of the Philippines, the hour has come to shed our blood to achieve our right to liberty. Let us band ourselves about the flag of the revolution, whose motto is Liberty, Equality, and Fraternity!!!" The manifesto spelled out in detail how the people should organize themselves along republican lines, and it designated the titles of those who would lead this new government.[8]

Aguinaldo's forces in Cavite Province, anticipating a counterattack from the Spanish, did what they could to acquire arms and ammunition and to build defenses. In spite of primitive communications and a poorly trained army—some people were armed with only bows and arrows—they managed to hold off the Spanish for more than six months.[9]

At a stormy meeting of the Katipunan, Aguinaldo, who wasn't able to attend the meeting, was elected president. Filipinos continued to be recruited into the Katipunan, and the fighting continued with no lessening of intensity. A new governor general, Fernando Primo de Rivera, thought it was obvious that the revolutionaries were not going to be defeated by brute force. He was also quite aware of the great cost in pesetas and lives the two revolutions—in Cuba and the Philippines— were imposing on Spain. When he was approached by Dr. Pedro A. Paterno, a well-known Filipino lawyer in Manila, to propose a truce with the revolutionaries, Rivera took him up on it.

Negotiations dragged on for months while the fighting continued. Finally, on December 20, 1897, the rebels ratified a pact that provided for the departure of Aguinaldo and his chief aides for Hong Kong and for the surrender of all arms to the Spanish. In exchange the Spanish promised to make three payments totaling 800,000 Mexican dollars to the revolutionary government,[10] also agreeing to many concessions. Aguinaldo later wrote that he "entered into a secret pact" with Rivera for further provisions including that the Philippines be granted two representatives in the Spanish *cortes* and that equal opportunity be given to Filipinos for government posts.[11] In a proclamation declaring the end of the revolution, dated Christmas Day 1897, Aguinaldo wrote, "I lay down my arms because continuing the war will produce turmoil and evil in place of happiness. This is not the end sought by the insurrection."[12] On December 27 Aguinaldo and thirty-six fellow insurgents boarded the steamship *Uranus* and sailed for Hong Kong. Four days later Rivera cabled the news to Spain, noting, "Today is the day I can effusively cheer: *Viva España!*" It would seem that all had gotten what they wanted.[13]

In fact, the Spanish may never have intended to carry out the reforms, and Aguinaldo readily admitted that he and the other leaders had agreed even before they'd gotten the first dollar that the money was to be used to buy arms should the Spanish not fulfill their end of the deal. As it turned out, Aguinaldo was paid 400,000 Mexican dollars, only half of what had been agreed upon, and none of the reforms were made. The pact did not bring peace, but barely a short truce. The revolution resumed.

It was at this point that Americans began to pay attention to what was going on. An insurrection halfway around the world held little interest for a populace saturated with news about an insurrection on its front doorstep, but this began to look like news.

The Military Information Division (MID) was at this time concentrating all its resources on Cuba; reports and evaluations of the situation in the Philippines were not being collected and analyzed in the same fashion as those from the Caribbean island. There was no Philippines desk at the State Department, nor was a specific individual in the MID accumulating information about the struggle in that country and who the key figures might be. Until his departure for Hong Kong, Aguinaldo was barely mentioned in the U.S. press. But the Filipinos were quite aware that the possibility of war existed between Spain and the United States.

Commodore George Dewey's presence in Asian waters and his readiness to do battle with the Spanish, it will be remembered, was due largely to Theodore Roosevelt. Like all senior naval officers in 1898, Dewey had seen no action since the Civil War, and then only as a young lieutenant serving under his hero, Admiral David Farragut. In his autobiography Dewey wrote, "Valuable as the training of Annapolis was, it was poor schooling beside that of serving under Farragut in time of war."[14] If he were to follow in Farragut's footsteps it would have to be now.

There was a command vacancy in the Asiatic Squadron, but another officer, John A. Howell, was similarly keen on that appointment. Roosevelt favored Dewey for the job because he admired his expansionist sympathies and his willingness to act independently. When Roosevelt learned Howell was being recommended for the job by a powerful Republican senator, he urged Dewey to approach his fellow Vermonter, Senator Redfield Proctor, and ask for his help. That very day Proctor called on William McKinley and got the president's promise that Dewey would be commander of the squadron.[15] Roosevelt later wrote, "I would have preferred to see Dewey get the appointment without appealing to any politician at all. But while this was my preference, the essential thing was to get him the appointment. For a naval officer to bring pressure to get himself a soft and easy place is unpardonable; but a large leniency should be observed toward the man who uses influence only to get himself a place in the picture near the flashing of the guns."[16] Once he had Dewey in place, Roosevelt took steps to make sure the commodore would be ready for war when it came. This was no spur-of-the-moment activity, but the result of a well-thought-out plan, the result of long discussions between Roosevelt and other navy personnel. His chance came on February 25, 1898, when John Davis Long, secretary of the navy, left him in charge for the day. Among the many orders Roosevelt sent out—some of which were later canceled by Long—was a message to Dewey aboard his flagship *Olympia*: "Secret and confidential. Order the squadron, except Monocacy to Hongkong. Keep full of coal. In the event of declaration of war Spain, your duty will be to see that the Spanish squadron does not leave the Asiatic coast, and then offensive operations in Philippine Islands. Keep Olympia until further orders."[17] Long let this order stand, and following its dictates, which Roosevelt had anticipated, Dewey prepared the ships for battle by removing personal belongings, wooden appointments to reduce the danger of fire and flying splinters, and other flammable objects. In addition, he had the *Baltimore's* hull scraped and all the ships repainted from white and buff to wartime gray.[18]

The Spanish fleet commander, Admiral Patricio Montojo y Pasarón, was fully aware of Dewey's preparations and of the probability of a naval battle in Manila Bay. At the behest of merchants who were concerned for their waterfront property,[19] Montojo took his decrepit squadron eight miles southwest of the city and anchored in a slightly curved line from the eastern tip of the presque isle on which Cavite is located. Dewey arrived as anticipated. Following his famous order to Captain Charles Gridley at 5:40 A.M., the guns aboard the American ships blasted away rapidly and methodically as they sailed around a five-mile-long racetrack-shaped course at a moderate six miles an hour. At this speed the ships should have been nearly as vulnerable to enemy fire as the stationary Spanish flotilla was to them.[20] And, in fact, there were a number of hits on American ships; some of them were close to being disastrous but, as it turned out, caused no great damage.

After two hours the Americans withdrew because Dewey had been misinformed about a possible shortage of ammunition. While it turned out that there was no shortage, Dewey took advantage of the moment to rest and feed his troops. Taking a break in the middle of a battle to eat breakfast furthered his reputation as a daring and nonchalant warrior. Having eaten, the sailors returned to their task of bombarding the Spanish. At 12:30 P.M. Montojo surrendered, with only one of his ships still afloat.[21] Some the Americans had sunk; others had been scuttled by the Spaniards to avoid turning over possibly useful ships. As far as maneuverability and firepower were concerned, Dewey was able to report that the American squadron "was in as good condition after as before the battle."[22] In all, Dewey's ships fired 5,859 shells and managed to hit their targets only 142 times—a success rate of less than 2.5 percent.[23] The Spanish ended up with 371 dead and wounded; the Americans had only nine slightly wounded and one sailor dead of heat prostration.[24]

At one point Dewey suggested to the Spanish captain general of Manila that they share use of the telegraph cable to Hong Kong. When the captain refused, Dewey ordered the cable to be dredged from the bottom of the bay and cut. As a result, no immediate word of the battle's outcome traveled much farther than the environs of Manila. It was known in Washington, D.C., via a message sent before the cable was cut that a battle had occurred and that there was considerable destruction and loss of life, but that was all. In the meantime Dewey carefully prepared his blockade of Manila. This prevented the three newspaper correspondents who had accompanied the squadron from making the 650-mile trip back to Hong Kong so they might cable their stories. They finally departed along with Dewey's official dispatches aboard the cutter *McCulloch* on May 5 at noon and arrived in Hong Kong forty-eight hours later. It wasn't until then that Aguinaldo, along with everyone else, learned the outcome of the battle. He had expected to be taken back to Manila when the ship departed, but the captain had no orders to do so and returned without him.[25]

The reporters aboard the *McCulloch* had an agreement with Dewey specifying that the navy's reports were to be sent first. The correspondents' detailed stories would follow at the news rate of sixty cents per word. One of the reporters, Edwin Harden, had the bright idea of sending a shorter message at the urgent rate of $9.90 per word to his newspaper, the *New York World*; this would guarantee its arrival five hours before any of the other accounts, including the official naval reports. As it turned out, the *Chicago Tribune* scooped even the *World*; when the urgent cable was called in to the *World* by the telegraph office at 4:30 in the morning, a *Tribune* reporter who happened to have been participating in a poker game took the call. Because the *Tribune* had a contractual right to the *World*'s wire service, he immediately called the Chicago paper, repeated Harden's story word for word, and thereby scooped every other newspaper.[26]

The nation was ecstatic and piled on Dewey every honor possible, appending his face and name to everything from a self-playing music box, to a laxative, to a public square in Boston,[27] and he was celebrated in poetry, prose, and song.[28] The newly promoted rear admiral took the adulation in stride and, far from being the "modest, unassuming man" as he was described at the time in an article in *Munsey's*, accepted it as his due.[29]

Aguinaldo, who had made his way back from Hong Kong two weeks after the battle, installed himself, with Dewey's concurrence, at the Cavite arsenal in the former home of the Spanish naval commandant. On May 24 he issued the following proclamation:

Filipinos:

The great North American nation, the cradle of genuine liberty, and therefore the friend of our people, oppressed and enslaved by the tyranny and despotism of its rulers, has come to us manifesting a protection as decisive as it is undoubtedly disinterested toward our inhabitants, considering us as sufficiently civilized and capable of governing for ourselves our unfortunate country.

Did he really believe his words? Or was he hoping to paint the United States into a corner? He added, "In order to maintain this high estimate granted us by the generous North American nation we should abominate all those deeds which tend to lower this opinion, which are pillage, theft, and all sorts of crimes relating to persons or property with the purpose of avoiding international conflicts during the period of our campaign." Aguinaldo then enumerated the respectful behavior toward lives and property that would be expected of Filipinos, and he promised summary executions for murder, robbery, and rape.[30]

Aguinaldo's return was the sign Filipinos had been waiting for. They not only volunteered in droves, but nearly every one of the 12,000 Filipino soldiers attached to the Spanish army went over to the insurrectionists. Hardly believing their eyes, the Americans saw a Filipino revolutionary force come into being overnight, and where they once doubted the possibility of an assault on Manila they now began to wonder if the Filipinos might defeat the Spanish. It appeared that the Spanish-American War and the Filipino insurrection had become intertwined, if not entangled. Dewey admitted in a letter to Washington that "these people are superior in intelligence and more capable of self-government than the natives of Cuba, and I am familiar with both races."[31] Aguinaldo proclaimed that at noon on May 31 all Filipinos should arise for an armed defeat of the Spanish. The new insurrection was triggered three days earlier than planned when a Spanish force attacked the small barrio of Alapang, where arms were being distributed to the Filipinos. By midafternoon the insurrectionists were victorious, and Aguinaldo, who had been in command, raised the new Filipino flag for the first time. During the month of June the insurrection spread through the islands; by the end of the month Manila was besieged, and Aguinaldo was in a position to present terms of surrender to the governor general, Don Basilio Augustín.[32]

Augustín was in a tight spot, and he knew it. His only real hope lay in the arrival of a second Spanish fleet, one that was powerful enough to blast the Americans out of the water and carried sufficient additional troops to defeat the insurrectionists. As it turned out, he was saved the ignominy of surrendering to the uncivilized *indios* by the arrival of American troops.

On the surface, the Santiago and Manila campaigns share many similarities. Before American intervention, both of the tropical island countries were Spanish colonies converted, in large part, to Catholicism. In Cuba and in the Philippines, long before the war with the United States, the Spanish faced widespread insurgencies among native populations. After the war began, Spanish fleets in the two countries were completely destroyed by American ships, which themselves suffered little damage. And once the Spanish were expelled, American armed forces took control of the administration of the countries.

There were important differences between the two campaigns, one of the more obvious being the manner in which they were organized. Where Major General William R. Shafter was over his head in Tampa, Florida, Major General Wesley Merritt had things pretty much in hand in San Francisco, the embarkation point for the Philippines. The stories diverge completely following the Spanish surrender.

The Cuban insurgents were more or less convinced that within a reasonable amount of time they would control their own country; they were therefore willing to cooperate with the Americans.[33] This wasn't the case with the Filipino insurgents. Many were encouraged by Aguinaldo to believe that once the Spanish were defeated, they would become a free and independent republic.

What Aguinaldo didn't comprehend was that the "mighty and humane" United States wouldn't take on the expensive task of protecting the Philippines from the predations of others just to guarantee the existence of a new independent nation. Talk of annexation began immediately after Dewey's victory. Many Americans would have been satisfied with just the Port of Manila to serve as a coaling station and a military base from which the United States might support American trade in Asia. But the nature of the archipelago was such that it couldn't be tasted in small bites. It was a matter of either gobbling up all seven thousand islands or going hungry. One essential problem was that almost nobody but the Filipinos themselves believed they were capable of self-government. Some other country, it was assumed, would have to rule them. Germany and Japan were two prime candidates, but neither of these was acceptable to most of the rest of the world. There were, as far as McKinley was concerned, only two possibilities: Spain or the United States, and it certainly wasn't going to be Spain.[34]

Dewey's major problem was what to do with Manila Bay now that he had it. He had done precisely as he'd been ordered, and as Roosevelt had confidently foreseen. Now what? Dewey believed his guns could bombard Manila and force the Spanish to surrender the city, but he didn't have enough personnel to occupy it afterward. Clever as Roosevelt had been, neither he nor anyone else in the administration had considered the possibility of having simultaneously to occupy Cuba, Puerto Rico, and a third island nation halfway around the world.

Privately comparing himself to Farragut at New Orleans during the Civil War, Dewey notified the administration that he could take Manila at any time, and he estimated that 5,000 troops would be necessary to occupy the city.[35] This was a totally unrealistic assessment, yet it happened to be the exact number that General Nelson A. Miles had earlier recommended, and he later quoted Dewey to justify his own assessment.[36] Dewey's estimate of 10,000 Spanish troops in the Manila area was very close to being accurate, but beyond that he didn't know much more about what was going on in the Philippines than did Miles.[37] Merritt, who was put in charge of the expedition, managed to convince the War Department to increase the number of troops to 12,000.[38] Eventually, and over Miles's objections, the force was further increased to 20,000.[39] But what they were to do when they got there wasn't precisely established; McKinley, even after spending considerable time praying,[40] was unable to come up with definitive orders for the disposition of the Philippines.

There was considerable pressure for annexation, both within the government and without. Business interests saw it as an opportunity to expand their markets in Asia, but they may have had an inflated view of the Philippines as a potential buyer of American goods. According to a British Foreign Office report, the total value of Philippine imports in 1896 was $10.6 million ($304.4 million in 2015 dollars); exports approached nearly twice that amount: $20.2 million ($580.1 million). The United States accounted for slightly over 1.5 percent of imports and nearly 25 percent of exports, much of that for hemp and sugar.[41] Even if the Philippine trade was limited in the past, things would change once the Spanish were gone.

Furthermore, Manila would provide an Asian military outpost and home away from home for business enterprises. Churchmen, too, saw opportunities for expansion. As the Presbyterian periodical *The Evangelist* put it, "Where war has opened the door the church may enter."[42] Many of those who opposed annexation did so because they sincerely believed in the highest of American ideals. On the other hand, there were anti-annexationists who were aghast at the possibility of Filipino "mongrels" becoming American citizens.[43]

In September 1898 the *Literary Digest* published the results of a poll of approximately three hundred major daily newspapers regarding the disposition of the Philippines. Of the 192 that responded, 44 percent favored assuming ownership of the Philippines, 33 percent approved only of establishing a naval base there, and barely 3 percent wanted the United States to pull out entirely. Two-thirds of the newspapers that identified themselves as Republican favored American possession of the entire archipelago, compared with only one-third of the Democratic newspapers. Regionally, the number of newspapers favoring total ownership was 42 percent in New England; in the rest of the Northeast 59 percent; 29 percent in the South; and 57 percent in the West.[44]

Little by little, average Americans, though not particularly familiar with details concerning the Philippines and basing their opinions on second- and thirdhand reports, favored expanding America's influence overseas.[45] As Mr. Dooley said to his friend Mr. Hennessey in Finley Peter Dunne's *Mr. Dooley in Peace and in War,*

> "Suppose ye was standin' at th' corner iv State Sthreet an' Archy R-road, wud ye know what car to take to get to th' Ph'lippeens? If yer son Packy was to ask ye where th' Ph'lippeens is, cud ye give him any good idea whether they was in Rooshia or jus' west iv the' thracks?"
>
> "Mebbe I couldn't," said Mr. Hennessy, haughtily, "but I'm f'r takin' thim in, annyhow."[46]

President McKinley, typically keeping his thoughts to himself, may very well have seen the opportunity for expansion right from the start. Then again, he may have been gradually turned in that direction by growing public opinion and the views of his advisers. It's possible— even likely—that there was no plan at all. This will never be known.[47]

General Merritt, a West Point graduate, has been described as "representative of the best of the United States Army of his day. A fine looking man of strong will and wide experience . . . highly competent, and at the same time modest and agreeable." He fought in the Civil War, was present at the Battle of Appomattox, and in the 1880s was superintendent of the West Point academy.[48] He was also a military theorist and had pieces published in professional journals.[49] On May 12, 1898, Merritt was officially notified by Adjutant General Henry Clark Corbin that he was to "repair to San Francisco, Cal., and assume command of and organize troops assembled there" for the purpose of sailing to Manila. But exactly what would those troops do when they arrived in Manila? If Major Arthur L. Wagner's MID hadn't a great deal of information about Cuba, it had even less about the Philippines, and because an invasion of the Philippines had not been anticipated, there was no time to have someone "carry a message" to Aguinaldo. The MID was in the process of compiling a comprehensive report that would have considerable information regarding climate, geography, political divisions, religion, and education—and even a few maps—but nothing regarding Spanish troop placements.[50] In any event, it wouldn't be available for months. Fortunately, by May 1 the MID had completed maps of Luzon and Cavite Province.[51] Notably, it was learned in 1899 that the director of the Jesuit Observatory, the Reverend José Algue, was supervising the production of a series of thirty highly detailed maps of the more important islands in the archipelago; all the technical work had been executed by native Filipino draftsmen. Wagner, in the meantime, had been reassigned to Miles's staff to engage in secret intelligence work involving Cuba.[52]

In a letter to McKinley on May 16, Merritt asked eight pertinent questions that showed how little information the army had.

First, What is the total strength of the Spanish forces in the island?

Second, How much of this force is in or about Manila?

Third, What proportion of the troops is Spanish and what native?

Fourth, What amount and caliber of field artillery have they?

Fifth, Can we operate field artillery, or will mountain artillery alone be practicable?

Sixth, What number of horses can be had in or near Manila? What work are they equal to?

Seventh, What food supplies is it imperative to bring?

Eighth, Will bridge trains be needed, and how much?

In this same letter Merritt goes on to admit that he does "not yet know whether it is your desire to subdue and hold all of the Spanish territory in the islands, or merely to seize and hold the capital." Without knowing the answers to any of these questions, Merritt, Miles, and others in the War Department were making very specific recommendations regarding the makeup of the expeditionary force. On May 19 McKinley issued a statement to Russell Alger, the secretary of war, regarding the goals of the expeditionary force, and Alger later forwarded the statement to Merritt. The army of occupation was to have "the twofold purpose of completing the reduction of the Spanish power in that quarter and of giving order and security to the islands while in the possession of the United States."[53] This could be construed to imply that Merritt was to subdue and then occupy the entire archipelago, but it doesn't quite say so. McKinley was still keeping his long-range intentions to himself—or waiting to see what course future developments might indicate.

By the end of the month, Merritt still didn't have the answers to his eight questions for the simple reason that no one knew the answers. Like everyone else, he'd read the newspaper stories about Rowan's adventure in Cuba and was impressed. Because he was in San Francisco he would have heard none of the Washington scuttlebutt about Rowan's involvement with Elmer Roberts or the fact that Rowan had ended his mission early. Accordingly, Merritt telegraphed Corbin on May 29 requesting Rowan's service as an intelligence officer. "The paucity of information in regard to the islands is so great that the services of this officer would be of inestimable advantage to the success of the expedition." Keeping his opinions to himself regarding Rowan's value as an intelligence officer, Corbin replied the next day, saying that by order of Secretary of State Alger, Rowan was engaged in the organization of a volunteer regiment, adding, "It is suggested that you name some other officer." Desperate as he was for intelligence, Merritt was unwilling to give up. He wired Corbin back, offering Rowan the job of chief of the MID's Philippine Expedition and the rank of lieutenant colonel: "I respectfully request his detail and assignment here. His services are much desired by me." To refuse such a request from a major general in charge of a large expedition would not have been likely under ordinary circumstances, but again Corbin turned him down, saying that Rowan's current assignment was "of first importance." Rowan had little command experience, and there had to be many officers more capable than he of organizing a regiment. On the other hand, he was one of a handful of officers with experience in gathering intelligence. When Corbin insisted that Merritt "think of the name of some other officer in connection with duties you desire to assign to Colonel Rowan," Merritt seems to have read between the lines and knew enough to drop the subject.[54]

CHAPTER 7

A Glorious Undertaking

Much has been made of the sometimes comic-opera bungling by the military during preparations for the Santiago, Cuba, campaign. There was considerably less evidence of this in the site chosen for assembly and embarkation for Manila. San Francisco, a lively city of 330,000, was a much better choice than Tampa, Florida; it had excellent rail connections, port facilities, telegraph and telephone service, and an army general depot. Moreover, the California First Infantry Regiment and the Third U.S. Artillery were already in place.[1] Best of all, it was under the command of Major General Wesley Merritt.

Feeling secure in its immensely moated castle, the United States had no compelling need to plan for large troop movements across the continent. In the West, the rail lines were somewhat sparse compared with those in the East, and rolling stock couldn't be manufactured overnight. Sleeping cars, in particular, were in short supply, so many soldiers rode in day cars. This was an improvement over Civil War rail transport thirty-some years earlier when soldiers were shipped like freight in boxcars and cattle cars, or even on flatcars. Under the circumstances, the railroads did an excellent job; unlike the army, they were in the business of moving large quantities of people and goods. And although it was "taxed to the utmost," the only real breakdown reported in the San Francisco area was a derailment, and this might have occurred in any event.[2]

The first members of the Eighth Army Corps, as the expeditionary force was designated,[3] arrived on May 7, 1898. Trains carried the troops into Oakland, and from there the men were ferried across the bay to San Francisco where they marched to the Presidio, a U.S. military reservation since 1848. Weary from their journey, many of them away from home for the first time, and hungry as bears, the volunteers found themselves sadly unappreciated and totally disregarded by the locals. Even the weather gave them the cold shoulder; as a reporter for the *New York Times* noted,

> All night long the rain which commenced falling yesterday noon continued to drench the 3,000 men camped at the Presidio awaiting orders to proceed to Manila to relieve Admiral Dewey. The Presidio is a sea of mud, and the troops, most of whom are lacking proper clothing to withstand the cold and damp, are suffering greatly, but the men do not complain. Although their tents are surrounded by miniature lakes, and small rivulets course through the camps underneath cots and shakedown beds, not a whimper is heard. Last night was the most disagreeable yet experienced by the men; fires would not burn, and the troops had to content themselves with cold lunches and an occasional cup of hot coffee.[4]

The lack of any kind of welcome went on for the first six days, until the city's newspapers shamed the citizenry into action. As soon as civic organizations such as the Red Cross and Salvation Army took up the responsibility of greeting the new arrivals, everything changed.[5]

Until Commodore Dewey's victory in Manila Bay, all the news about the probable war with Spain concerned activities in the East. When San Franciscans finally realized their city had become part of the glorious undertaking to defeat the ignoble Spaniards, they enthusiastically joined in the fun, delivering pies and cakes to the camp. As always, there can be too much of a good thing; at one point the officers had to ask them not to bring the volunteers any more goodies: "Many of them are gluttons and as a consequence are troubled with indigestion."[6] With or without the treats, people flocked to the barriers surrounding each regiment's lot to talk to the soldiers.

Additional accommodations were going to be needed to encamp the growing number of troops, and a new site was chosen.[7] Camp Merritt, as it came to be called, was an abandoned racetrack covered with six inches of sand and subject to frequent visits from cold winds, rain, and fog. The damp, salty air was new to the Plains States boys who first arrived here, and they didn't care for it at all.[8] According to the adjutant general of Nebraska, it took little time before "the camp was complete, and, with its regular, well-ordered streets and tents, presented a neat and military appearance."[9] He painted a pretty picture, but as army medical department historian Mary C. Gillett has noted, "sanitation presented problems as it had at every other camp where eager neophyte soldiers and their inexperienced officers gathered. Typhoid as well as the inevitable measles soon appeared."[10]

When the call went out on April 25 for 125,000 volunteers, Secretary of War Alger notified the state governors of the number and composition of volunteer troops they were to provide and urged them to use National Guard units for this purpose. A great number of units, in order to meet their quota, signed up eager young men on the spot—men with no experience or training.[11] Many volunteers were lacking weapons, uniforms, and all other manner of equipment. Some of the young men arrived in San Francisco in virtual rags and depended on the Red Cross to provide them with clothing and shoes.[12] William Allen White, writing from his perch in Emporia, Kansas, noted that up to that point, the "principle martial duty the national guards had to perform before they were mustered out was to precede the fire company and follow the Grand Army squad in the processions on Memorial Day and the Fourth of July."[13]

Before any plans were known regarding an expeditionary force, the navy had contracted with the Pacific Mail Steamship Company to have the *City of Pekin*, a 428-foot steamer, carry ammunition and supplies to Dewey. Any extra space was to be used for the transport of troops and their supplies. Two other Pacific Mail ships contracted for by the army, the *City of Sydney* and the *Australia*, were also being refitted to carry troops. This was no simple matter. Among the modifications they needed bunks and galleys, and it had to be determined that they were seaworthy before entrusting them with thousands of American soldiers' lives.

Merritt was busy on the East Coast, and it would be some days before he would arrive in San Francisco, so Major General Ewell S. Otis was offered the post of second in command. He was ordered to assist in the troops' organization, which he did to great effect. Merritt arrived in San Francisco May 26 and stayed at the elegant Palace Hotel, performing his executive duties in the nearby Phelan Building. He sent and received frequent wires to and from Washington, D.C., met with reporters, dictated letters, and attended social functions. Only once was he observed formally inspecting the facilities at Camp Merritt, where Otis and his staff worked and lived in tents. The drilling and training went on relentlessly.[14]

The day finally came when the first troops, under the command of Brigadier General Thomas M. Anderson, were ordered aboard the three transports that were to carry them to Manila: the *City of Pekin*, the *City of Sydney*, and the *Australia*. At 7:00 a.m. on May 23 a bugle sounded, and hundreds of tents were collapsed and prepared for shipment. At 8:00, under a clear blue sky, the soldiers of California's First Regiment, each encumbered with forty pounds or more of blanket roll and heavy knapsack, marched to the waiting ships. This was the hometown unit, and San Franciscans gathered en masse to see them off. It must be remembered that the Cuban convoy didn't leave Tampa until June 14, so the men in San Francisco were the first soldiers ever to leave the North American continent to engage in battle with a foreign enemy. What started as a proper march in formation was transformed into an unorganized attempt by single individuals to fight their way through a mob armed with fistfuls of flowers.[15] A reporter for the *New York Times* described the scene:

> There was one continuous roar of cheers, flags were waved frantically, and people along the line, as they recognized some friend among the soldiers, rushed out and grabbed him by the hand to say good-bye. When Market Street, the main business thoroughfare, was reached the crowd was enormous. People on their way to work lingered to see the soldiers pass. The cheering of the crowd grew in volume, and nothing like the sight on Market Street was ever seen here before. Many weeping women followed along after the soldiers, as though loath to let them out

of their sight, and even men were not ashamed to show their emotion.

It wasn't only the civilians who were emotional; as one officer commented, "If we had let go of ourselves for an instant we should have cried our way to the ship."[16] The *New York Times* reported,

As the marching men neared the water front bombs were fired, steam whistles blown, and every device imaginable for making noise was put into full operation. The jam at the dock was something terrific. In vain the police and the mounted signal corps attempted to keep the crowd back. The people rushed on the dock in the wake of the soldiers. Arrived at the dock, the volunteers were marched on board the transport without delay. It took considerable time for each man to be assigned to his quarters, but this task was accomplished with but very little confusion. After the soldiers were once on board the ship, the police with difficulty cleared the dock and the gates were shut.[17]

The scene remained as frenzied on the water as on land:

[The soldiers] climbed to the rigging and swarmed all over the big ships, shouting and cheering like mad. The bay was alive with small craft of every description, and huge ferryboats were pressed into service to accommodate the eager crowds and carry them to the head of the Golden Gate, that a last farewell might be said.

The big transports steamed slowly along the water front, and the crowd on shore raced along to keep them in sight. The noise made by patriotic citizens on sea and shore was something terrific. Every steam whistle in the city appeared to be blowing, cannon were fired, and the din lasted for fully an hour.[18]

Then they were at sea. The frenetic activity in which the soldiers had been engaged for the past few weeks suddenly stopped, and now they spent a little over an hour a day in calisthenics and drill, and not even that on Saturdays and Sundays. On Sundays their only organized activity was a church service. Weather permitting, they showered with seawater, and on specified days they tended to their laundry. Otherwise, according to Oscar Davis, their days were spent "loafing on the hurricane deck, watching the flying fish, and speculating on the end of man, in particular the man who went to the Philippines as a private." This was, however, no pleasant ocean cruise. The galleys were totally inadequate, and only by operating around the clock were they able to prepare two meals a day. The bunks in some cases were built in long rows, four high and seven deep, with no intervening aisles, meaning that men had to crawl over one another to get to their bunks. This created hellish ventilation problems. And as one officer delicately put it, passageways between the tiers of bunks would have prevented "some of the inconveniences resulting from seasickness." Not only were living conditions inadequate; so were clothing and supplies. Brigadier General Anderson, the commanding officer for the journey, had been assured there was a six-month supply of stores. He was appalled to discover that some men had only one set of underwear, and many of these were destroyed by the equipment used to fumigate them.[19]

The first port of call for the troop ships was Honolulu, where they joined the cruiser *Charleston*, which was carrying ammunition for Dewey.[20] Cheering crowds met them at the wharves, and the following day a gigantic feast was laid out for the soldiers.[21] This wasn't mere island hospitality; the point was to impress upon the visiting soldiers what a wonderful place Hawaii was and what a wonderful addition it would make to the United States, if only it were annexed. The soldiers, it was hoped, would convey the benefits of annexation to their elected representatives in Congress.[22] Annexation had been the goal of the American businessmen who had engineered a revolt in Hawaii some five years earlier, though it was far from the desire of the native Hawaiians and Asian immigrants who had been lured there to work as laborers.[23] After a pleasant two days in Hawaii, the three troop ships, accompanied by the *Charleston*, continued their journey west.

When the flotilla arrived in Manila Harbor at 5:00 P.M. on June 30 it had traveled 7,246 miles in thirty-six days—too long a period,

Anderson felt, for a tropical cruise. The temperature, which might have suited a passenger cruise ship, was far from ideal. With the ships settled into eighty-two-degree water, a considerable amount of meat was spoiled in what should have been cold storage areas below deck; it had to be thrown overboard. Fortunately, no soldiers experienced the same fate. In spite of having so many men packed into uncomfortable quarters, the medical staff on the *City of Pekin* was faced with only influenza, minor surgery, one case of "acute mania," and a serious spinal injury caused by an accidental fall through an improperly guarded bunker hatch. Two more convoys followed, with improvements having been made in the way of bunks, galleys, and other arrangements for the troops.

The day following Anderson's arrival in Manila, he and Dewey called on Emilio Aguinaldo at Cavite. In spite of his very positive-sounding language regarding the "great North American nation," Aguinaldo must have had his doubts. During the initial meeting with Anderson, he asked outright if the United States intended to recognize his government. Anderson told him that he was "acting only in a military capacity . . . and had no authority to recognize his government." Aguinaldo returned the visit a few days later and rephrased the question. He wanted to know if the United States intended to "hold the Philippines as dependencies." Again, Anderson admitted quite honestly, he couldn't say. He did point out that in 120 years as an established country, the United States had acquired no colonies. Aguinaldo responded by noting, "I have studied attentively the Constitution of the United States, and I find in it no authority for colonies and I have no fear."[24]

There were around nine thousand Spanish and four thousand Filipino troops in Manila,[25] and few of them, no matter what their ethnicity, were going to give the Americans much trouble. Secret negotiations had been going on for some time to surrender the city under terms that would cost few lives but save the honor of the Spanish officers.[26] The gist of the agreement was that if the ships did not fire on Spanish-occupied areas of the city, the Spanish artillery would not fire on the U.S. fleet; there was, however, no agreement on limiting the use of deadly force among foot soldiers. There had to be an appearance of resistance, and any casualties that might occur would be the price of saving the Spanish officers from the threat of trial by court-martial.[27]

The Battle of Manila began at exactly 9:35 A.M. on August 13, 1898, when the *Olympia* fired on Fort San Antonio Abad located a mile and a quarter south of the city center. The guns aboard other ships joined in, as did an army battery on land. This went on for nearly an hour, inflicting only a moderate amount of damage and no casualties. There were no casualties because, by prearrangement, the fort was unoccupied. When the shelling stopped, American troops quickly moved in, and the American flag was raised above the parapet. Elsewhere, Filipino and American troops engaged the Spanish in earnest. As agreed upon, a white flag was hoisted over the city, but because of weather conditions and battle smoke, it wasn't seen by the ground forces until 1:00 P.M., at least an hour and forty minutes after it had been raised. When the Spanish flag came down and the Stars and Stripes went up in its place at 5:43 P.M., scores of combatants were dead or wounded.[28]

The shame is that there would have been no battle had Dewey and the governor general arrived at an agreement regarding use of the cable back in May. With the cable uncut, both sides would have been aware in a timely manner of what was going on in the rest of the world; they would have known that the war between Spain and the United States had effectively ended with the signing of the armistice in Washington at 4:30 P.M., August 12, just a few hours before the shelling had begun.[29]

At 9:00 the evening before the assault, Anderson received orders from Merritt to notify Aguinaldo that he must forbid his insurgents, who were fully prepared to take part in the battle, from entering Manila. Anderson later wrote that the Filipinos "received Merritt's interdict with anger and indignation. They considered the war as their war, and Manila as their capital, and Luzon as their country." Nevertheless, orders were orders, and Anderson placed a battalion of North Dakota volunteers at a bridge the insurgents would have to cross to get into the city.

Anticipating problems with the insurgents, Merritt sent orders via the repaired cable to the adjutant general the day after the battle, reading, "Since the occupation of this town and suburbs the insurgents on outside are pressing demand for joint occupation of the city. Situation difficult. Inform me at once how far I shall proceed in forcing obedience in this matter and others that may arise. Is Government willing to use all means to make the natives submit to the authority of the United States?" The answer was, in a word, yes; the response from Adjutant General Corbin couldn't be clearer: "The President directs that there must be no joint occupation with the insurgents. The United States in the possession of Manila City, Manila Bay, and harbor must preserve the peace and protect persons and property within the territory occupied by their military and naval forces. The insurgents and all others must recognize the military occupation and authority of the United States. . . . Use whatever means in your judgment are necessary to this end."[30] The future was set.

As in Cuba, it was assumed that the chief preoccupations of the native population were rape and pillage. Merritt made this clear in a later report when he praised his troops, "a large proportion of whom were newly organized and hastily equipped and very few of whom had ever participated in an engagement," for preventing "rapine, pillage and disorder. . . . [This] was an accomplishment of which only the law-abiding, temperate, resolute American soldier, ably and skillfully handled by his regimental and brigade commanders, was capable."[31] Yet, according to Anderson, the American soldiers weren't nearly as law-abiding as Merritt portrayed them. "Our soldiers," he wrote, "to get what they considered trophies, did a good deal of what the Filipinos considered looting. A number made debts which they did not find it convenient to pay."[32]

Winning a sham battle with an armed fleet at your back was one thing; dealing with the mind-boggling complications of reconstructing a government, mollifying an armed insurgency, and coping with the exigencies of a large force of volunteer soldiers thousands of miles from home was something else. Once the Battle of Manila was over, Merritt wasted little time asking to be relieved of his command; on August 26 he was ordered to "proceed without delay to the city of Paris, France," to confer with the peace commission.[33] He might have preferred reassignment to the States, but who could turn down an all-expenses-paid vacation in the City of Light at the height of *la belle époque*? It appears to have been a great social event. The commission members were accompanied by their wives, "who could not resist the lure of the Paris shops."[34] Merritt's replacement was Elwell S. Otis, his workaholic alter ego in San Francisco.

At the time of his appointment as military governor of the Philippines, Otis was sixty years old and a veteran of both the Civil War and several Indian campaigns. A bullet wound to the head during the Civil War troubled him for the rest of his life,[35] and perhaps this accounted for his nearly total lack of a sense of humor. Frederick Funston wrote that one "would about as soon think of cracking a joke in his presence as of trying to pull his beard."[36] Surprisingly, for a man of his generally dour personality, Otis cultivated extravagant sideburns that caused him to resemble a family dog. In spite of his friendly appearance he was not well liked, and contemporaries as well as modern historians vied to create insulting remarks about the man.[37] As in San Francisco, he circulated little, remaining closeted with paperwork; no doubt this suited his personality better than did dealing with people. He was no diplomat; on September 8 he sent Aguinaldo a long letter, part of which read:

> It only remains for me to respectfully notify you that I am compelled by my instructions to demand that your armed forces evacuate the entire city of Manila, including its suburbs and defenses, and that I shall be obliged to take action with that end in view within a very short period should you decline to comply with my Government's demands, and I hereby serve notice upon you that unless your troops are withdrawn beyond the line's of the city's defenses before Thursday the 15th instant, I shall be obliged to resort to forcible action and that my Government will hold you responsible for any unfortunate consequences that might ensue.

One historian has called this "one of the most arrogantly worded ultimatums in the annals of American diplomatic history."[38]

During the month of September, the Military Information Division published a compilation entitled *Military Notes of the Philippines*. The material was gathered from sources as varied as *National Geographic*, *Encyclopedia Britannica*, *British Admiralty Reports*, and *Revue des Deux Mondes*. Following eighty-one pages of categorized data (on harbors, minerals, trade, etc.) were another two hundred pages of detailed descriptions of provinces, districts, and important islands, along with a number of maps. An introductory note acknowledged the inclusion of "inaccuracies [but] it is believed that they can be readily amended as American reports are received."[39] Flawed and incomplete as it might be, it was better than the scattered bits of information it replaced.

Back at the White House, President McKinley's prayers finally paid off. On October 26, in response to a request for explicit instructions, McKinley had Secretary of State John Hay cable the peace commission that annexing just Luzon wouldn't work. "Leaving the rest of the islands subject to Spanish rule, or to be the subject of future contention, cannot be justified on political, commercial or humanitarian grounds," the cable read. "The cession must be of the whole archipelago or none. The latter is wholly inadmissible, and the former must therefore be required."[40] It was done. Nearly a month later, during a visit in his office by a delegation of Methodist Episcopal dignitaries, McKinley took the opportunity to explain to them why he had concluded to annex all of the Philippine islands:

> When . . . I realized that the Philippines had dropped into our laps I confess I did not know what to do with them. I sought counsel from all sides—Democrats as well as Republicans—but, got little help. I thought first we would take only Manila; then Luzon, then other islands perhaps also. I walked the floor of the White House night after night until midnight; and I am not ashamed to tell you, gentlemen, that I went down on my knees and prayed to Almighty God for light and guidance more than one night. And one night late it came to me this way—I don't know how it was, but it came: (1) That we could not give them back to Spain— that would be cowardly and dishonorable; (2) that we could not turn them over to France or Germany—our commercial rivals in the Orient—that would be bad business and discreditable; (3) that we could not leave them to themselves—they were unfit for

self-government—and they would soon have anarchy and mis-rule over there worse than Spain's was; and (4) that there was nothing left for us to do but to take them all, and to educate the Filipinos, and uplift and civilize and Christianize them, and by God's grace do the very best we could by them, as our fellow-men for whom Christ also died.[41]

In addition to his prayers, McKinley was also influenced by public enthusiasm for annexation he encountered during an eleven-day speaking tour of six Midwestern states in support of Republican candidates for Congress. During his fifty-seven stops, he repeatedly heard cheers whenever he intimated that the United States should retain the Philippines. He never came out and said it, but his supporters knew exactly what he was talking about. When, ten days after the trip ended, voters rewarded him by returning a Republican majority in both houses, McKinley knew he could proceed with the only course that seemed to him to be tenable.[42]

In the treaty of peace that was finally concluded in Paris on December 10, Spain "relinquished all claim of sovereignty over and title to Cuba," ceded to the United States "the island of Porto Rico and other islands . . . in the West Indies," along with the island of Guam, and ceded the Philippines in exchange for $20 million.[43] In reference to this last article, Speaker of the House Thomas Brackett Reed remarked, "We have about 10,000,000 Malays at $2.00 a head, and nobody knows what it will cost to pick them."[44]

On December 27 the text of McKinley's famous "benevolent assimilation" proclamation was cabled to Otis. In it McKinley declared the United States had acquired sovereignty over the entire archipelago and that a military government would, therefore, occupy and administer "the whole of the ceded country." "However," he pointed out, "we come, not as invaders or conquerors, but as friends, to protect the natives in their homes, in their employments, and in their personal and religious rights."[45]

The day after its publication Aguinaldo issued a response that was reprinted in *La Independencia*, an insurgent newspaper, in which he protested "most solemnly against this intrusion of the United States government on the sovereignty of these islands."

The American-Philippine War was a can of worms; to this day even the official name is uncertain and the date of its actual ending is in dispute. The one thing usually considered beyond doubt is its beginning. Unlike most wars, the start of this one can be narrowed down not only to a precise time but to a single shot. As the story goes, on the night of February 4, 1899, Private William "Willie" Grayson of Company D, First Nebraska Volunteer Infantry Regiment, shot and killed a Filipino soldier.[46] This was not the first time that such a thing had occurred, but this particular incident didn't stop at a protest or an investigation; it immediately triggered a firefight that was to last for years.

At the moment Grayson fired his shot there were some 19,000 American troops in and around Manila.[47] Outside their defensive positions were an estimated 20,000 Filipinos, some of them in a series of blockhouses built a kilometer apart by the Spaniards to protect the city during the revolution. Others occupied various newly built earthen fortifications.[48] Tension between the two armies, already high, grew more so as the Filipinos continually made attempts to control unoccupied intervals between American commands. Nervous sentries were quick to fire at enemy soldiers who may or may not have been there.[49] Taunts were exchanged. At about 8:45 P.M., Grayson and another soldier, Orville Miller, were on outpost duty when they encountered three Filipinos in an area where, Grayson claimed, no armed Filipinos should be. After an exchange of one-word challenges ("Halt" and "Alto") Grayson fired his rifle. "There was no time to lose," he later said, "and so I brought my first Filipino down; and I tell you, there was a little feeling of safety and satisfaction when I heard him groan." He and Miller raced back toward their camp; "I shall never forget that little trip that night."[50] Grayson evidently had forgotten one small detail: in another version he claimed that he and Miller, while on the run, killed two more Filipinos who were blocking their way.[51] A Filipino inquiry into the start of hostilities a month later has American soldiers firing on Filipinos engaged in a legitimate patrol between blockhouses. No one disputed the fact that the Americans fired first, and no one challenged Grayson's claim that he was the person who did the firing. There is, however, no report by either side of anyone's having been shot, let alone killed, during the initial firing. We have only Grayson's personal testimony.[52] In a statement for the U.S. Senate, he testified that after the shooting he said to fellow soldiers on patrol, "Line up, fellows; the niggers are in here all through these yards."[53] Thus began the second Battle of Manila, and this one was no sham.

CHAPTER 8

Captain Rowan in Command

The *Tartar*, with Captain Andrew Rowan aboard, left San Francisco at midnight on July 24, 1899, and at that hour there was, presumably, no jolly flotilla to accompany it out to sea. On board were eight companies of the Nineteenth Infantry Regiment—twenty-eight officers and 948 noncommissioned soldiers—under the command of Colonel Simon Snyder. Rowan was commander of Company I. Among other matériel, they carried two hundred rounds of .30-caliber ammunition per man.[1] Also on board, if George Daniels's intentions were successful, were three hundred copies of "A Message to Garcia" and a hundred copies of "How It Came to Be Written," which he shipped to New York Central Railroad's agent for the West Coast with instructions to get them into Rowan's stateroom before he embarked.[2] There is no record of Rowan's having received the pamphlets or, if he did, how he disposed of them. The *Tartar* arrived in Manila on August 21. A message to Attorney General Corbin from Major General Otis informing him of the transport's arrival noted "all well; no deaths."[3]

The Nineteenth was one of the units sent to replace the state volunteers whose original mission, so they thought, was to whip the Spaniards. The volunteers hadn't counted on being bogged down on miserably hot, rainy, tropical islands battling disease and the never-before-heard-of Tagalog. Furthermore, in spite of their bravery and willingness to fight, there was a streak of antimilitarism—stemming, no doubt, from their populist roots—that prevented them from becoming the sort of obedient soldiers that officers desire. The men were, in many respects, the "frowsy ne'er-do-wells" decried by Elbert Hubbard. They were not only unwilling to carry the message to García but were also writing to their families and hometown newspapers complaining about being asked to do so. It wasn't long before their elected officials were hearing the complaints as well. The administration of President William McKinley had no choice but to respond;[4] on March 3 Otis received a cable from Secretary of War Russell Alger instructing him to send back the volunteers as "rapidly as possible."[5]

By the time Rowan went ashore on August 22, the war had spread throughout Luzon, the island on which Manila is located, and into the Visayan Islands. The principal Visayas—Bohol, Cebu, Leyte, Masbate, Negros, Panay, and Samar—lie in a cycladean belt near the center of the archipelago.

It was to the Visayas that parts of the Nineteenth Infantry were sent to replace the First Tennessee Volunteers. Company I, under Captain Rowan, sailed aboard the transport *Indiana* on September 13. They arrived off Cebu City on September 18 and landed the following day.[6]

Cebu is a long narrow island of 1,707 square miles and situated more or less in the center of the Visayas; it stretches 139 miles north and south and is never more than twenty miles wide. A mountain range with heights reaching over three thousand feet extends the entire length, with only six passes from east to west.[7] The population at the time was a little over half a million.[8] Cebu City is located on the island's east coast, halfway between the northern and southern tips. With a metropolitan area population of over 35,000, it was the Philippines' second city and the commercial center of the Visayas.[9] The Cebuanos hadn't participated in the insurrection of 1896, but in the two years that followed, agents of the Katipunan successfully organized underground cells. On April 3, 1898, five days before Rowan set out on his mission for Cuba, the new revolt against Spanish rule began. They were unaware, of course, that Commodore George Dewey's Asiatic Squadron was in Mirs Bay and would, in just three weeks, be steaming toward Manila. As they skirmished with the Spaniards they couldn't have begun to guess their unlikely future. There was regular communication by boat with Manila, so they learned fairly quickly the result of the Battle of Manila Bay, but not what that result would mean. Rumors of every sort spread through the island, creating total confusion. The only thing certain was that

Spain's colonial rule was coming to an end. And, indeed, it did on December 24, 1898, when the Spanish flag came down forever. Control of a sort was transferred to a caretaker government.

By the time Private Willie Grayson fired his fateful shot on February 4, 1899, relations between the Americans and Filipinos had already deteriorated to the point that both sides were preparing to do battle with each other. On February 5 Emilio Aguinaldo issued orders to the Cebuanos to prepare for war; a few days later, Juan Climaco, the well-connected son of a Chinese mestizo family, was selected as chief of staff for war preparations. For weapons, the army would have to rely on spears and bolos, there being barely two hundred firearms—some of them ancient— and eight thousand rounds of ammunition on the island.

The old boxing axiom "a good big man will beat a good little man" is equally true in the deadly sport of war. At the time of the Philippine-American War the average Filipino male was slightly under five foot three and weighed not quite 116 pounds. The average American recruit accepted into the army in 1897 was slightly over five foot seven and weighed just over 147 pounds. In close combat a Filipino with a bolo— the Filipino version of the machete—would be no match for a trained American soldier wielding a nine-pound Krag-Jorgensen rifle topped with an eleven-inch bayonet. At a distance the Americans had an even greater advantage; those who weren't already experienced riflemen when they joined the army received excellent training in weapons handling and marksmanship as new recruits. John Bass, writing in *Harper's Weekly*, repeated a "yarn" that may or may not have had any basis in fact, but did illustrate an attitude toward Filipinos among American soldiers:

A Filipino convict had climbed the prison wall and was running for dear life through the open. Two long-legged Tennesseans were on guard duty. They kneeled to fire.

"I don't guess it's more than three hundred yards," said one, quietly. "I reckon it's most five hundred," said the other, as if he were discussing the weather. The prisoner was running like a deer, and rapidly approaching the undergrowth around innumerable little huts, where he would be safe.

"Call it four hundred," suggested the first Tennessean, in a conciliatory tone. They adjusted their sights, aimed, and fired. The escaping convict fell, and the two Tennesseans went out to bring in what was left of him. "If he's hit in the head, it's my shot," said one. "I aimed low, acco'din' to a'my regulations," drawled the other. The convict was found with one bullet through the back of his head and another through the lower end of his spine. They know how to shoot in the mountains of Tennessee.[10]

If this casual approach to killing seems not quite believable, it's worth noting a report issued little more than a month earlier that stated, "In the path of the Washington regiment and Battery D of the Sixth Artillery there were 1,008 dead niggers and a great many wounded. We burned all their houses. I don't know how many men, women and children the Tennessee boys did kill. They would not take any prisoners."[11] Although the Filipino soldiers outnumbered the Americans, barely half of them had rifles, and those who did were notoriously bad shots. This was caused in part because the rear sights had been removed from their rifles by Spanish officers, leaving the native soldiers useful as cannon fodder but ineffective in case of a revolt. And due to a critical shortage of ammunition, there was little target practice, leaving them with little experience in aiming a weapon. In many cases they didn't aim at all, but simply held their rifles over a parapet and fired in the general direction of the Americans. This was not a display of cowardice but a rational decision made after having seen too many of their compatriots' heads blown away by American riflemen.[12] When it came to large-bore weapons, there was no contest at all. Between the army's West Point–trained artillery officers and their cannon and the navy's shipboard cannon, the Filipinos were hopelessly outgunned.[13]

In September the USS *Indiana* arrived with two battalions of Tennessee Volunteers and units of the Nineteenth Infantry. Also on board was Colonel Simon Snyder, who was the newly appointed military commander of Cebu. Considering the number of troops on hand, Snyder and his fellow officers decided the time had come to confront the

Filipino guerrillas in battle. On the morning of September 21, four columns of soldiers, comprising eight hundred officers and enlisted men, advanced on the Filipinos' positions five miles west of Cebu at a place called Bocaue. In little over forty-eight hours the Americans had succeeded in driving out the guerrillas, capturing seven forts, including their smoothbore cannon, and fourteen other entrenched and fortified positions. A private with the Sixth Infantry was killed, and four other Americans were wounded. Enemy losses were estimated at forty. Among the captured Filipino arms were three small seventeenth-century brass cannons.[14]

Companies I and K of the Nineteenth Infantry under Rowan's command were left behind to secure the site. Following orders from Snyder, Rowan and seventy-five of his soldiers set out on October 1 to reconnoiter the country west of their position and to "develop or occupy the works of the enemy beyond the Bocaue range." They happened on two previously unknown and well-concealed forts, both deserted. Their objective, Rowan wrote, was "a formidable looking work near Mount Compensa, high above us, but showing no signs of being occupied." He chose a route that seemed to be the easiest to ascend and directed an advance guard under Second Lieutenant J. L. Bond to precede the main body. After a short while, Bond reported that it was impossible to proceed. Rowan thought differently:

> This did not agree with my own impressions. I went forward and took command of the advance guard and continued the advance. A little over halfway up the slope several Filipinos were seen looking down from the crest above us on the right and left flanks. A few volleys were promptly fired at them and we saw them no more. After attaining the hogback we continued the ascent in the direction of the fort in a heavy rainstorm, followed by a dense fog. When the mist lifted, the advance guard found itself on a small knoll about 100 yards from the fort. I ordered two volleys fired into the work. There was no return fire and no sign of life. Under these circumstances I considered it safe to advance with the few men composing the advance guard. The fort was found deserted.[15]

The entire detachment camped nearby for the night, the next morning ascending the mountain, the highest point in the area. To the west they could see the mountains on the nearby island of Negros and the strait that separated it from Cebu. The country was, understandably, sparsely inhabited, and what few natives there were fled from their advance. On the way back the soldiers captured one Filipino who "could give no satisfactory account of himself." He was eventually sent to Snyder's headquarters.

Rowan suggested that a detachment of only twenty-five or so men would suffice to hold the present camp. This would free the men of Company K for other duty. He wanted to take the remainder of his men to an advanced position in the Jacupan Valley, from where they might guard the forts and be more easily supplied. He requested "about twenty coolies" to help with the move. Others of his company under Lieutenant James Little were busy destroying the Filipino forts. During the operation only one man was adversely affected by the mission; suffering from exhaustion, he was under the care of the medical officer, Captain Bratton. Rowan made one request of Snyder on behalf of his soldiers: "This rough country and hard campaigning done by Company I and K have worn out the shoes of the men, and permission is requested for a new issue as soon as possible." This probably says as much about the quality of the shoes as it does about the hardness of the campaigning; whatever the case, Snyder agreed with all of Rowan's requests and recommendations.[16]

In spite of the American presence in the Jacupan Valley, Filipino guerrillas moved back into the area. At one point they engaged in a heavy firefight with the soldiers of Company I, but the Americans suffered no casualties, nor did they come into physical contact with the Filipino guerrillas.[17]

Rowan's fame hadn't faded away with his departure from the United States. The state of West Virginia, only thirty-seven years old at the turn of the century, had few nationally known native sons. Andrew Summers Rowan was easily the most famous of these, and state officials hoped to capitalize on his name. On January 4, 1900, the entire delegation of West Virginia's congressional representatives—which is to say, four in number—called on President McKinley to lobby for Rowan's being awarded the Medal of Honor. McKinley, of course, agreed that Rowan deserved a medal and left the representatives believing that he would do all in his power to make sure Rowan was justly recognized.

Encouraged, Representative David E. Johnston, representing the Third District, which included Monroe County, wrote to Brigadier General Corbin, the adjutant general, urging him to recommend Rowan for the Medal of Honor; Johnston's three colleagues added their signatures to the letter. In his recapitulation of Rowan's mission, Johnston perpetuated Hubbard's fantasy, having Rowan crossing "from the Florida coast in an open boat to Cuba" to deliver his message. Corbin, it will be remembered, had been on the verge of bringing Rowan up before a court-martial; he certainly wasn't going to recommend him for the nation's highest military honor. While he did acknowledge the "gallant and meritorious service performed" by Rowan, he also quoted the specific language describing the conditions for awarding the Medal of Honor: "Distinguished bravery or conspicuous gallantry which shall have been manifested in action by conduct that distinguishes a soldier above his comrades and that involves the risk of life or the performance of more than ordinarily hazardous duty." Without going into any details of Rowan's mission, Corbin added, "Applying the rule to the case under consideration the Secretary of War desires me to say that while he is satisfied that the meritorious services of Captain Rowan on the occasion in question were highly creditable to himself and to the service, he does not feel that he would be justified in regarding it as meeting the conditions laid down in the rules in question." And that was that.

During the second week in January, and unknown to the folks in Washington, D.C., Rowan was distinguishing himself in battle in the Sudlon Mountains. The Filipino guerrillas should have learned the lesson during the Battle of Bocaue that with their small numbers, odd assortment of weapons, and limited experience and training they were no match for a professional army during an out-and-out battle. Nevertheless, they were unwilling to give control of the central region of

Cebu to the Americans. And the Americans, having chased the Filipino guerrillas off Bocaue, certainly weren't going to let the Filipino soldiers stay in the Sudlon Mountains. Snyder ordered Colonel Edward J. McClernand, commander of the Forty-Fourth U.S. Volunteer Infantry, to clear them out. McClernand was an excellent choice; he had held a number of important posts during the war with Spain, and though he had seen no action in that war, he was an experienced Indian fighter. He had been engaged in a number of campaigns, including being part of the expedition that rescued the remnants of General George Armstrong Custer's command at Little Bighorn, and he was eventually awarded the Medal of Honor for distinguished gallantry against the Nez Percé in 1877.[18]

McClernand was to accomplish his task in the Sudlon Mountains with three companies of his own regiment, the Forty-Fourth; three of the Nineteenth; and one of the Twenty-Third. No one thought it would be easy. The Filipinos had between six hundred and a thousand men positioned in twenty-five forts along a four-mile front high on a precipitous mountain. McClernand was to make a frontal assault at any point of his choosing, while three additional companies of the Nineteenth under Major John G. Leefe attacked the left and rear. Rowan had placed a field gun high on a mountain that gave a full view of the Filipino earthworks. McClernand was impressed, and ordered a second gun positioned nearby. It was only with strenuous effort and the use of block and tackle that the guns were placed. There being no artillery officer in his command, McClernand requested that Captain William P. Evans, who was stationed in Cebu, be permitted to examine the site. Using an "excellent" map prepared by Rowan, the range for each fort was determined by a plane-table survey. Evans proved their accuracy by firing a few test shells into a number of forts—causing, it was hoped, a demoralizing effect on the Filipino soldiers. Copies of the map were given to each battalion and company commander.

On January 5 McClernand met with Snyder and Leefe in Cebu City to go over the final details. The men were to be in position at a preselected site for an early morning assault on Sunday, January 8. Inclement weather Saturday night thwarted the plan somewhat, but they came reasonably close. The rain-soaked soldiers got what rest they could lying down among the boulders along the river bank. At 4:30 A.M. they were quietly awakened for breakfast and an hour later were in position at the foot of the mountain where a field hospital was established. Shortly after 6:00 the troops started their two-mile ascent up the slope. Three hours and ten minutes later, having experienced considerable heat, rough terrain, and rifle fire, the first troops planted their colors on the summit. As more soldiers followed, they drove the Filipinos from one fort to the next. At one point the Filipinos made the decision to stand and fight. As McClernand later reported, "This fort, built on a high knoll, was of earth, and forty feet square; the embankment on three sides at the top was about five feet thick, and on the fourth not less than ten feet; the earth was held in place by well-laid sod, and had the enemy held on resolutely, we must have met with great loss. Some of them fought bravely. They would stand up, exposing a good part of their bodies above the parapet, fire and then drop down. Fortunately for us they were poor marksmen."[19] It took but a half hour to drive them out. When it was over, the Americans suffered only two men wounded; this small number was due in large part to the Filipino guerrillas' inability to fire their rifles accurately, but it had also been a well-executed assault. As Marrion Wilcox later noted, "Much credit is due to the battalion and company commanders for the skillful manner in which they advanced their commands by echelon up the mountain, and for the well-directed volleys which kept down the fire of or so demoralized the enemy as to render his fire wild and ineffective." McClernand also credited Evans's "ability with which he performed the [artillery] duty assigned him."[20]

Rowan, if something of a prig who enjoyed the perks of office, was a good company commander, never hesitating to experience the same uncomfortable and dangerous conditions he ordered his soldiers to endure; yet one has the impression this was more through a sense of noblesse oblige rather than being one of the boys. He was the leader; they were the led. As a West Point graduate, he had more in common with those above him in the chain of command than with those below. Over time Rowan developed the unlikable characteristic of ingratiating himself with superiors while demeaning and even bullying those he considered his inferiors. He seems particularly to have targeted junior commissioned officers as the recipients of verbal attacks. In the presence of other officers on board the *Tartar*, for example, he referred to Second Lieutenant Arthur F. Cassels of the Seventh Artillery as a "son-of-a-bitch," and in December 1899 he asserted that Bond was "a scoundrel, a liar, and a thief." Bond was the officer whom he had pointedly indicated in an official report was lacking in tactical judgment during the October 1 assault of Mount Compensa.

Rowan's unfortunate habit of badmouthing junior officers became very public in January 1900, a couple of weeks after the Battle of Sudlon. It seems that First Sergeant Samuel Hollaway, apparently under orders from Rowan, was riding in Cebu City on a horse that had been assigned to acting assistant surgeon Harold L. Coffin. When confronted, Hollaway refused to surrender the horse to Coffin, even after being ordered to do so by Second Lieutenant Leon L. Roach. He would surrender the horse only under orders from Rowan. Flummoxed, Roach wrote a note to Rowan, put it into a sealed envelope, and handed it to Hollaway with orders to deliver it. When Rowan read the note standing outside his tent, he said in a voice loud enough to be heard in nearby tents that Roach and Coffin were "sons of bitches and liars." Not satisfied with saying it once, he repeated the remark twice more. At least two other officers—Lieutenants Cromwell Stacey and James H. Bradford—clearly overheard him. Bradford repeated the story to his friend Roach, who, greatly incensed, preferred charges against Rowan:

> Charge I.—Conduct unbecoming an officer and gentleman, in violation of the 81st Article of War . . .
> Charge II.—Conduct to the prejudice of good order and military discipline, in violation of the 62nd Article of War.

In the specifications beneath each charge he detailed the circumstances.[21]

The charges were filed with the regimental adjutant, Captain Frank McIntyre, who referred them to Major Thomas C. Woodbury, Rowan's battalion commander. After reading the charges, Woodbury offered Rowan the opportunity to submit a written statement in his defense.

Instead Rowan handed Woodbury identical countercharges that he was preferring against Roach. Furthermore, he charged Bradford with conduct unbecoming an officer and a gentleman for having talked to Roach. In his charge, Rowan claimed that Roach's specifications were "absolute and baseless lies." Incredibly, in the attempt to portray himself as the victim of "false, slanderous and defamatory statements," he resorted to some highly charged language himself. Bradford—who incidentally was the only West Point graduate among the junior officers involved—came in for some particularly sharp barbs, being referred to parenthetically as "a meddling and malicious liar." According to Rowan, Bradford overheard "fragments of a conversation [by eavesdropping] which he reported in a cowardly and contemptible manner [and which in turn caused] Roach to write out a series of false charges and specifications." Woodbury ordered the three men known to be present, Bradford, Stacey, and Hollaway, to submit written statements describing what they had heard. Bradford and Stacey stated quite unambiguously that they heard Rowan call Roach and Coffin "liars and sons of bitches." Sergeant Hollaway, on the other hand, stated just the opposite—that he had not heard any such statements. He claimed that Rowan had told him only that he had done the right thing in not giving up the horse. Woodbury questioned Rowan, who eventually admitted, in a hedging fashion, that he did make the statement attributed to him, but meant the words only "conditionally." Though he declared that the language Rowan used should "under no circumstances" be applied to another officer, Woodbury came to the unlikely conclusion that the charges against Rowan could not be substantiated.

The regimental commander, Colonel Snyder, was not buying it. To him it was "plain that Rowan did use highly improper language in speaking of the [two] officers." He was also of the opinion that Rowan's charges against Roach and Bradford could not be maintained. Nonetheless, he decided that in the "interest of harmony and to avoid the scandal that would arise from the trial of four officers of the regiment [I am] desirous that the matter be dropped."

When Roach learned of this, he was furious—so furious, in fact, that he submitted the matter to Adjutant General Corbin, in Washington.

In his letter he said he had been informed that Woodbury had recommended there be no trial in order to prevent a scandal. The letter fairly boiled with anger: "I then asked what redress I was to have for being called such a vile name and referred to in such a manner that it is now a matter of common talk both among officers and enlisted men. . . . As the matter now stands, I can not expect to command the respect of a single enlisted man in the regiment and my status as an officer in this Regiment is practically *nil.*" Writing to Corbin was one thing. Seeing any action taken was another. To begin with, it took over a month for the letter to reach Washington. Corbin was no fan of Andrew Rowan's, but he did have a war to run, and he passed Roach's letter on, without comment, to Major General Miles, the commanding officer of the army. Miles's office sent the letter back to the Philippines, where it would arrive six weeks later on the desk of Major General Arthur MacArthur, then the commanding general of the Division of the Philippines. The next step down the chain was Brigadier General Robert P. Hughes, who commanded the Department of the Visayas in Iloilo; he referred it to his inspector general. Its being a matter of honor and not of criminality, the investigation had to wait until an officer was visiting Cebu City on other business. That finally occurred in September, and by then, of all the principals involved, only Bradford remained in the vicinity. The investigating officer could do nothing more than read through the original documents, which were still on file in the regimental adjutant's office. On November 15, ten months after the event, the office of the judge advocate of the headquarters division of the Philippines submitted a memorandum succinctly summarizing the events of the previous January and severely criticizing Rowan. He then wrote:

> That Captain Rowan used the language reputed to him is strongly borne out by his evident ready use of intemperate and unjustifiable language as shown in the specifications to the counter charge he brings against Lieut. Bradford and wherein he appears to feel privileged to denounce him. . . . As unfortunately there appears to be no disposition on the part of Capt. Rowan to apologize for the stinging imputations he has cast upon his juniors,

no other recourse save trial by General Court Martial appears to be open by which to quicken his recognition of the wrong he has done to himself and them.

It looked like Roach was to get his day in court. But as things turned out, it was precisely because he so badly wanted his day in court that there would be no trial. In his letter to Corbin he devoted too much space to himself; it was clear that his chief object was the desire for revenge. In handing down a resolution, a writer in the judge advocate's office pointed out that "preferring charges against an officer of the army [is] a duty calling for the exercise of the most conscientious discretion, [and] should not be made a vehicle for venting personal spleen." But he wasn't letting Rowan off the hook, adding "before resort is had to a trial, it is thought that a direct appeal should be made to Capt. Rowan, that in view of his own good reputation and of his services in which the Army has a common interest and pride, he ought to recognize the wrong he has done and publicly apologize to each of the officers whose reputations he has with such trivial provocation assailed." Rowan took a why-didn't-you-say-this-in-the-first-place approach to this last paragraph, claiming this was the first time he was aware that an apology "would be a satisfactory adjustment of the case." And so, little more than a year after the offending statement was made, a written apology was sent to Lieutenant Roach—one that was really no apology at all. "I am in receipt of a communication from the Headquarters of the Division of the Philippines directing that I make an apology to you for the use of 'unseemly language.' I hereby do so without reserve and you are at liberty to consider this written statement to cover such language as you believe to have been used by me in reference to yourself on any occasion, although I am convinced that you have never been correctly informed in this matter." One can almost hear the gnashing of Roach's teeth.

After receiving his telegraphed assignment as commander of the First Battalion of the Nineteenth Infantry Regiment, Rowan immediately set about surveying his subdistrict with an eye for the suitability of the various locations where units of soldiers were stationed. In Cebu City he arranged for transportation north and was furnished with the gun-boat *Panay* under the command of Lieutenant J. M. Luby. On February 9, 1900, the boat steamed slowly up the east coast, not reaching Danao, barely twenty miles away, until night. It was here that Rowan became aware of a serious shortcoming. When the *Panay* signaled the shore, there was no answering signal. He later suggested to the adjutant general that isolated posts be provided with signaling devices and be required to communicate with vessels at night. Early the next morning the *Panay* arrived at Sogod, yet another twenty miles up the coast. After inspecting conditions there, Rowan issued a number of orders that were to take effect immediately. First he had some "shacks" destroyed that he felt might furnish hiding places for enemy combatants who could creep up on the troops, fire a volley, and immediately disappear into the bush. Some of these shacks were in fact the homes of local residents. All the more reason they should be destroyed, he felt, because "innocent inhabitants" could also provide protection for *insurrectos*. He ordered outposts to be established on the foothills and day patrols in the vicinity of the village.

Back on board the *Panay*, Rowan proceeded another six or seven miles up the coast to Borbon, which he felt was equally deficient as Sogod as a location for the troops stationed there. It did have the advantage of being only a day's march from Bogo, which was located near the Canal de Dayagon that separates the island of Cebu from its northernmost portion, but the road was in poor condition. He returned to Sogod and sailed again on February 12, landing with thirty men for Point Nailon, just a few miles from Bogo. After capturing some of the locals who were pressed into service as guides, the soldiers marched overland to Bogo, surprising the citizens. In the meantime the *Panay* carefully threaded its way through the reefs in the narrow channel and anchored near the town. As military commander, Rowan ordered the local *presidente*, Pedro Rodriguez, to report to him.

Rodriguez, as Rowan noted, was an intelligent man who saw no advantage in lying when questioned about aid and comfort given locally to the *insurrectos*. He readily admitted that supplies had been, were, and would be furnished to the *insurrectos* stationed in the nearby hills, but he claimed that after the Battle of Sudlon, the Cebuano leaders were inclined to wait and see what decisions were to be made by the U.S. Congress regarding the ultimate disposition of the island. That was all well and good, but Rowan warned him that a state of war would exist against the entire population as long as they were perceived to be aiding the enemy.

Again on board the *Panay*, Rowan and his soldiers passed through the canal and continued their survey down the west coast, stopping in Balamban. Here he called on Colonel McClernand, his commanding officer during the Battle of Sudlon, who advised him on the state of affairs in his section. Rowan and his men continued their investigation of the northern part of the island, stopping here and there to question the locals, none of whom was as forthcoming as Rodriguez. He also ordered other officers, including company commanders, to pursue investigations within their bailiwicks. Because of his length of time in the army—now going on twenty years—Rowan was senior to most other captains who crossed his path.

There is little doubt that Rowan was aware of General Leonard Wood's success in cleaning up Santiago de Cuba. He may or may not have been influenced by Wood, but when he was made commander for the first time of a defined military district, Rowan acted in a similarly decisive and dictatorial fashion, if not achieving the same ends. He was particularly put off by the Filipinos' lackadaisical approach to civic hygiene, and ordered the natives of Sogod ("a filthy place") to clean up their village. He was so gratified by the results that he determined to issue the same order for all the coastal towns in the district. As soon as that was completed, he would press natives into work details to repair the road from Danao to Bogo.[22] In Bogo he ordered the streets and plaza cleaned and the drains opened, and insisted that the locals remove debris from under their houses and stop throwing garbage there. In fact, they were to obtain portable garbage cans for this purpose. At one point Rowan complained that he wasn't "obtaining as much assistance from the people of the city" as he would have liked, but insisted this wouldn't deter him from cleaning the place up, including satisfying all the sanitary recommendations made by the military doctors. Each building, public or private, was to have its own outhouse "provided with a non-leakable wooden latrine of sufficient capacity for two day deposits." No detail was too small to escape Rowan's attention, including the disposition of privy contents. Captain Bratton pointed out that "it has been found that the dangers of infection from this source is almost nil" and suggested it would be put to better use as fertilizer rather than dumped in the bay, where "some of it would undoubtedly be washed back on the shore." Furthermore, the natives were to use the latrines.[23]

To prepare the Port of Bogo militarily Rowan had the channel marked in the bay by a series of bamboo buoys with white flags so that steamers might approach the wharf more closely than ever before. In spite of Rowan's attention to detail, not all preparations went smoothly. Even as late as the middle of April, property belonging to Company I had not yet arrived. As a result, the men were unable to be fully ensconced in their new quarters.[24] To protect his command, Rowan used the natives as a barrier. "If I am attacked," he pointed out, "the suffering will necessarily fall upon the town which is between my position and the foothills." Within his area was the home of Pedro Rodriguez, the only building suitable for a hospital. Rodriguez agreed to rent the house to the army for forty Mexican dollars a month, an amount Rowan considered fair, though he still had to plead his case to higher-ups.[25]

Whenever he ventured forth, Rowan habitually made careful notes of the local terrain, road conditions, arable land, and other features of military interest. His previous experience along the Canadian border, in Guatemala, and in Cuba left him particularly prepared for this activity. There existed a map of Cebu prepared by the Spanish, but it was only the roughest of guides—little more than a suggestion—of the geographical and civil features of the island. Rowan let it be known to the chief engineer officer of the Eighth Army Corps that he was eager to make a transit and plane table map of Cebu. Somehow or other, Brigadier General Robert P. Hughes learned of this and had an underling write Colonel Snyder, commanding officer on Cebu, offering the suggestion that he appoint Rowan to the task: "While not wishing to dictate in any way in the matter he believes it would be to the best interests of the service if Captain Rowan could be so detailed. . . . The [Spanish] map of Cebu is very faulty and we absolutely need just such a map as

Captain Rowan proposes to make. . . . The District Commander asks that you will consider this matter and act as promptly as possible if you deem it practicable or desirable to make the detail."[26] It was an offer Snyder could not refuse. On May 17, Rowan was assigned to be engineer officer. Busy as he was commanding the subdistrict of Bogo, he was unable to apply himself to the degree he would have preferred and by the middle of June had completed only a preliminary outline for the triangulation of the area. It wasn't military action that occupied him as much as creating a pleasant and sanitary environment for natives and soldiers alike. On June 30 he reported to Snyder that he had had the houses whitewashed. Furthermore, "I have issued orders that occupants of houses be held responsible for the cleanliness of the premises and for the streets fronting on their property. The Presidente has provided carts which will pass through the streets daily and pick up all the refuse & cart it to the outskirts where it will be burned."[27] He didn't say what the punishment would be if people disobeyed. Maybe they'd heard enough fearful stories about American soldiers that threats were unnecessary. At one point Rowan reported having five natives in custody who had been observed "acting in a suspicious manner." Even though no one believed they were guilty of any crime, they were to be released, he wrote, only when "their innocence can be established." This was a typical example of the sort of arbitrary and absolute power American soldiers had over the native population for whom they had little respect. The feeling was mutual.

If things weren't bad enough, word reached Rowan that plague had broken out in the city of Cebu, and he was forced to quarantine the Port of Bogo against vessels from the city. This lack of communication by water with Cebu made life miserable for everyone—shippers, soldiers, and civilians.

Among the Filipino leaders there were the inevitable disagreements over who would be running the show. Faced with a militarily threatening situation, and in accordance with the Decree of June 18, 1898, the civil government was dissolved, and the military chief of the highest rank—at this time, Arcadio Maxilom—assumed control. During the course of the war, Maxilom usually had approximately two hundred armed soldiers under his command—fewer than could be found in two U.S. companies. Until the middle of January 1900 he organized them following standard military practice and had them stationed in fixed positions. When it became clear they couldn't match American firepower he concluded that it was "necessary for us to adopt guerrilla tactics" and reorganized his troops accordingly. Confrontations between the Americans and the Filipino guerrillas became a series of ambushes and surprise attacks.[28]

It was about this time that Rowan received a chatty letter from Daniels telling him what a great reception *A Message to Garcia* was receiving in Washington and that he'd been told President McKinley himself said it "was one of the most remarkable things he had ever read." He also told Rowan that copy number 500,000 of the essay had been mailed to A. B. Symns in Atchison, Kansas—Rowan's father-in-law.[29]

After receiving information that Filipino soldiers were gathering in the hills west of Borbon, Rowan ordered Lieutenant Little, with fifty men, to capture or engage them. The soldiers were to travel down the spine of the central range so they might look for evidence of Filipino military activity along either coast, eventually returning to Bogo. It was a miserable trip, much of it spent in the rain while trudging along muddy paths. A number of the men became ill. During the return trip Little observed a "sullen disposition" among the residents of Tabogan; this was exactly how Maxilom had ordered them to behave.[30] The tired, footsore soldiers were not in their best ambassadorial mood, and apparently entered and searched houses at will, finding evidence of a Filipino military presence. Most of the male residents had flown the coop, no doubt realizing they might be arrested for any or no reason. The women left behind were not gracious hostesses when it came to providing drinking water to the troops. And when Little tried to borrow a *banca*—a native boat—to carry some of the sickest men back to Bogo, he was refused. That being the case, he simply took one.

In July 1900, Rowan sent a report to McClernand, who now commanded the Second District, Department of the Visayas, which included Rowan's subdistrict.[31] In it he told of a conversation with the *presidente* of Medellin and confirmed his opinion that the leading people in his subdistrict had a great antipathy to the word "provisional" preferring much to be assured that whatever form of government they adopt will be a fixed (fijo) form not subject to change. Why they have adopted this view is unknown to me. Some think that the present arrangement is better than the proposed arrangement (Order No. 40). . . . They cannot understand the decentralizing feature of the order and seem to be unable to distinguish between municipal government and provisional government. No amount of explanation seems to be sufficient to teach them that the purpose of the orders is to place local affairs entirely in the hands of the people of the district.[32]

Nevertheless, Rowan believed that everything was in readiness for an election later in the month and that rival candidates were in the process of positioning themselves for various offices. All that was needed was for him to impart explanations and instructions. In time elections were held, with Rowan supervising the swearing in of officials. Thwarting his best efforts at organizing the natives, whom he thought were "very much like children [and] easily terrorized," were four individuals he identified by name. First on his list was Pedro Rodriguez, "a thorough poltroon," who would limit American influence in the area. The second was Rodriguez's cousin, Leoncio Mansueto, who was elected *teniente alcalde* (deputy mayor) of Bogo. Rowan was under the impression that Mansueto had come to Cebu as Aguinaldo's representative; and though he hadn't sufficient evidence to convict him of any crimes, he wanted McClernand to void his election and instruct the citizens to elect someone more suitable. So much for placing "local affairs entirely in the hands of the people." Then there was the pastor of the Bogo and Tabogan districts, Padre Inocente, "a very wily man." According to Rowan he used his "sacred office" not as a "means of improving the morals and spiritual welfare of the people" but to secretly influence them to oppose the United States. "He did the same thing against the Spaniards and altogether he is a very undesirable person in the district." Last he named Padre Angel of San Remigio, "a kind of spy [who] has spread a species of dumb terror throughout San Remigio District." He told McClernand that he was prepared to take "the most serious action against these four enemies of our country."[33]

On September 12 Rowan sent Lieutenant Stacey with a detachment of soldiers to Sogod. He had heard that a group of Filipino guerrillas was occupying the convent and had captured one of his native runners. The soldiers' first act on entering the town at 8:00 the next morning was to shoot a Cebuano for no other reason than that he was carrying a bolo. It was his misfortune not to have left town with everybody else. The only other individuals remaining were malefactors locked up in the police station. They claimed Maxilom had come and gone. With no Filipinos in the convent, the Americans decided to bivouac there themselves. Fearful that nearby houses might be set afire by rebels during the night, thereby putting his soldiers in danger, Stacey took the preemptive step of ordering the houses burned early that afternoon. The American soldiers had little experience with this sort of thing, and when the fire finally burned itself out, the entire town was gone, including the convent. With no place to sleep, Stacey marched his men to Borbon, arriving there near midnight.[34]

Still trying in late September to apply General Order No. 40 to the communities in his district, Rowan sent Stacey and twenty-five men south to Tabogan, a municipality yet unorganized. As Rowan noted, the area produced the best tobacco on the island and was, therefore, a rich source of contributions to the Filipino cause. Stacey's orders were to hold an election, tolerating "no excuses" from the villagers for there not being one; but if it proved impossible, he was to gather the names of trusted individuals who would then be appointed under Article 56 of the General Orders. Rowan was well aware that the town was "poorly situated for defense," and he ordered Stacey to put a squad of men into trenches in the nearby hills and to let the people know they would be shot if they approached within rifle range of the outpost. Stacey was also to assume ownership of as many boats in the area as he deemed necessary for a quick escape by water should the need develop. In the end, there were no elections held in Tabogan. In spite of Rowan's expectations of having a "solid block of American districts," as far south as Bolon he and his lieutenants managed to organize only three: Bogo (the first municipality on Cebu to be organized),[35] Medellin, and San

Remigio. This was not bad considering that in the remaining 80 percent of the island a total of only six more towns were organized.[36] The election in San Remigio was not without its problems. Irregularities were noted at Second District headquarters and duly pointed out to Rowan. Not denying there were "some serious errors," Rowan responded, as he often did to criticism, with a numbered list of items intended to justify any actions he may or may not have taken. McClernand, to whom Rowan sometimes addressed his letters as "My Dear Colonel," let the matter rest.

In between skirmishes and organizing activities, Rowan's efforts at creating a sustainable infrastructure in the district were paying off. He built roads, installed telegraph lines, made plans for improvements to the canal on which Bogo is situated, and contemplated the construction of bridges over all streams south of Maravilla. He also managed to acquire thirty horses (but unfortunately no blacksmith) for the creation of a mounted detachment to be divided among the troops occupying the towns of Bogo, Malagasi, and Maravilla.[37] At one point he wrote home asking to be sent lettuce, radish, and onion seeds. The Filipino diet consisted for the most part of rice and fish,[38] and the only fresh vegetables available to the soldiers were onions and potatoes shipped from the States—and those only after a lengthy journey.[39]

Earlier in the year Rowan had become embroiled in a controversy with the medical staff.[40] He had accused a hospital steward of allowing a small amount of rations to disappear without a proper accounting, writing on July 1, "In my opinion these rations were never received here, or if they were, they were improperly used and Pvt. (now Act. Hospital Steward) Gregg should be made to pay for them and perhaps tried as well." The matter soon involved the chief surgeon in Cebu, Major W. F. Lippitt, who didn't try to hide his irritation: "If [Rowan] can prove his assertions of dishonesty, I would request that he be instructed to prefer charges against Steward Gregg, that the facts be brought out by a Court. If not able to substantiate them, Capt. Rowan should be instructed that such charges not lightly be made against a Non-Commissioned officer." He then added, "It can be proved that the articles mentioned herein were received at Bogo, properly used and properly accounted for." Lippitt's irritation was understandable. There was a serious shortage in the Philippines of surgeons and qualified hospital workers, and many of the physicians were civilian doctors under contract; just as they were getting the hang of things, they returned to the States.

Slightly more than 10 percent of soldiers became casualties as the result of combat injuries. These and the illnesses expected of any population—hernias, appendicitis, and so on—kept the medical staff busy, but they were not overwhelming. The difficulties were compounded by poor diets, exhaustion, rain, heat, and endemic diseases such as malaria and typhoid—to say nothing of gonorrhea, syphilis, dysentery, and diarrhea.[41] And here was Rowan complicating Lippitt's life because of an apparent clerical error regarding a few dollars' worth of hospital rations. This was not the last time that Rowan would irritate the major; in October he wrote to McClernand complaining about Lippitt's medical department, noting that "this station is inadequately equipped with Medical Supplies and Appliances. This thing has gone on so long that I do not feel like entrusting the matter to the Medical Department any longer. This station has been in existence for six months and has never been provided with scales. The consequence is that when we happen to have medicines on hand, they can only be administered by guess work." Following up on the implied criticism in "when we happen to have medicines on hand," he complained that his medical officers had only enough quinine for two or three days: "A great many men are suffering with malarial fevers which easily yield to quinine, but quinine is not now to be had. Requisitions have been made, apparently only to be dishonored." The only two items he specifically referred to were scales and quinine, but he suggested a lack of smallpox vaccine when writing, "My outlying detachments are stationed in infected districts; both Tabogo and Lambusan having cases of smallpox. I have recently occupied Malagasi, some distance away, but I intend to station the Surgeon there. He can be of little use, however, unless he is properly provided with medical supplies." Smallpox was indeed a problem throughout the Philippines, and all American troops were to be immunized. In spite of this, there were some who contracted the disease from infected Filipinos. To prevent this, a massive attempt was made to eradicate the disease among the native population by "forcible vaccination and revaccination," if necessary; it wasn't until February 1900 that the program was extended beyond Luzon, however, and Rowan was justified in being fearful that his troops could become infected.[42] It was the tone of his letter and his going over Lippitt's head to make his case that caused trouble. He compounded the problem when he wrote, "The fact that the Medical Department, as far as this sub-district is concerned, is a failure, may require me to withdraw my outlying detachments and throw the districts, which now believe they will be protected by American troops, without adequate protection."

Who knows where it all might end?

McClernand, whom Rowan expected to "correct" the situation, could do little more than pass the letter on to Lippitt. The chief surgeon was beside himself and suggested the letter "was evidently written in haste, and without knowledge of the facts." He pointed out that, since the middle of June, only four requisitions had been received from Bogo and only the last—which was received six days after Rowan's letter was written—requested quinine. He acknowledged that Bogo had no scales, but pointed out that since nearly all medicines were provided in tablet form, rather than powders, scales were unnecessary. Liquids, obviously, were measured by volume. But if Rowan wanted scales, he should have them; and as soon as newly requisitioned scales arrived from the supply depot in Manila, they would be shipped to Bogo. Lippitt was at a loss to name any other medical appliances that the Port of Bogo lacked, nor could any be named by three medical officers who had been stationed there. Furthermore, no one had ever requested any appliances other than a fountain syringe, which had been sent. Regarding smallpox, Lippitt stated that five thousand units of vaccine had been sent to Bogo since June, adding, "Particular directions were given to act. asst. Surgeon Christensen now on duty at Bogo to see that the men of the Command, and the natives of Bogo and Medellin were vaccinated thoroughly . . . and if the Commanding Officer, Bogo, desires that the people of any particular point in his Sub-Dist. be vaccinated he can have it done as he sees fit." But it wasn't quite that simple. The soldiers could easily be vaccinated, but there were far too many natives, and they were much too spread out for army personnel to effect the vaccinations. It might have been possible to hire Filipinos to do the work, but they sometimes faced the possibility of being kidnapped by guerrillas.[43] None of this was the result of a lack of vaccinations on hand, and Rowan was wrong to imply otherwise.

Lippitt didn't think it was a good idea, in any event, to send a surgeon to the small detachment at Malagasi: "The larger part of the command will be in Bogo, the Hospital will be in Bogo, all seriously sick should be sent to that point where they can be properly cared for, and that is the point where the surgeon should be on duty. I would therefore recommend that instructions to that effect be issued to the Commanding Officer, Bogo." He concluded by saying that all requisitions had to be approved by the authorities in Iloilo, but the situation being an emergency, he would have the quinine shipped at once.

McClernand was not pleased with Rowan's letter, and immediately returned it to Rowan with Lippitt's response: "It is desired officers refrain from unnecessary criticism of others, uselessly exciting animosity and frequently interfering with cordial cooperation in the transaction of public business. Most officers are doing their best and doing well. The surgeon at Bogo can be sent to Malagasi occasionally, as circumstances require. Generally, the Commanding Officer will require him to be in Bogo to attend the sick in hospital there." Rowan couldn't leave it at that, however. Both Lippitt and McClernand had used the third person when referring to Rowan, and he now did the same: "The Commanding Officer at Bogo writes few letters hastily and none without sufficient knowledge of the facts, to warrant all the statements he makes." He labored on to make his case, but it was weak. Though he claimed he could refute "nearly every statement" Lippitt made, he chose not to: "I do not feel it proper to say more than to disclaim any intention of 'exciting animosity' or 'interfering with cordial co-operation in the transaction of public business.'" His original letter, he wrote, "was intended to be a statement of a condition which I felt sure the District Commander would remedy at once and was in no sense a criticism upon anybody."

McClernand had had enough and passed the correspondence to Lippitt with instructions not to respond. The incident was an example of Rowan's increasing irascibility, no doubt brought on by the continuing stresses of being a commander in a war zone.

In early December another incident occurred revealing Rowan's intemperate behavior involving a junior officer, Lieutenant Little, whom he had previously praised in dispatches to McClernand.[44] It seems there was a balance due from the authorities at San Remigio on an assessment levied by the United States. The acting *alcalde* managed to get the money together and sent it to Rowan in Bogo, who duly signed a receipt for it. The money was to be sent on to McClernand's office in Cebu, and since Little was to leave for that city, Rowan had the money taken to Little's quarters along with a receipt for him to sign. In a similar situation in the past, on delivery of other funds, Little had been unable to get a signed receipt in turn, and he didn't want to chance a repeat of that experience. Accordingly, he carried the money back to Rowan's office, informing him he could not sign the receipt. Instead of allowing him to explain, Rowan said, "You must sign it. It is your duty to sign it and if you do not I will place you under arrest." When Little steadfastly refused, that's exactly what happened, and Rowan ordered him to his quarters. On his way out of Rowan's building, Little happened to see the Spaniard with whom he ate his meals and asked this person to deliver his dinner to his quarters. Rowan saw this encounter and angrily demanded to know why Little stopped to talk to someone. Little tried to respond, but Rowan kept yelling, "Go to your quarters." In response, Little yelled back that he would do so at his leisure.

Rowan then proceeded to prepare formal charges and specifications against Little. The next day he mailed them to McClernand with a cover letter in which he gave a brief account of the matter and explained that he had signed a receipt "in order to expedite public business. In return I believe that I am entitled to at least some little protection— such at least as is granted in the ordinary business affairs of life." He signed the letter, "Your friend." Specifically, he charged Little with "Disobedience of Orders, in violation of the 21st Article of War," "Breaking arrest, in violation of the 65th Article of War," and "Disrespect to his Commanding Officer, in violation of the 20th Article of War."

As in the Roach case, it was Major Woodbury who tried—successfully, this time—to defuse the matter. He pointed out that no officer is bound to sign a paper, even under orders, if he has sufficient reason for not doing so. He also didn't think Little had broken arrest by speaking to the person who provided his meals. As far as the third charge—showing disrespect—yes, he was guilty of that, but "he has been sufficiently admonished. . . . I recommend that the matter be dropped."

Back in the States, someone finally got around to publishing a pamphlet rebutting Hubbard's assessment of American workers.[45] The writer, a board game designer named C. G. Harger Jr., had no concern with Rowan's carrying a message to García, but only with Hubbard's exploitation of that mission to rail against employees. Unfortunately, Harger wasn't much of a writer. A reviewer for the *Washington Post* offered this critique of the pamphlet:

> Compared with what might reasonably and truthfully be said on the subject, his arguments are lame and incomplete [and he fails] to emphasize with sufficient force the fact that the picture drawn by Mr. Hubbard is grossly exaggerated and in many respects utterly absurd. . . . Mr. Harger might justly have pointed out the unreasonableness of expecting the employee to cheerfully and industriously drudge year after year, with little if any improvement in his own financial stature in order that someone else will reap the entire benefit. . . . An insignificant advance in salary, grudgingly bestowed and thinly spread over long years of faithful work, is poor encouragement to unceasing effort and sustained endeavor. Why should a man be expected to maintain a cheerful alacrity and unfaltering devotion to his employer's interests under such adverse conditions?[46]

The reviewer continued for a couple more paragraphs. It's a pity he hadn't written the pamphlet instead of Harger; it might have achieved a respectable circulation instead of disappearing with barely a trace.

Hubbard and the *Philistine* were, by this time, so well known that Bert Leston Taylor, a humor writer for the *Chicago Daily Tribune*, was able to parody him in his newspaper column without having to identify his target. Instead of Fra Elbertus (Hubbard liked to style himself as if he were a monk toiling at his labors), Taylor's character was Fra McGinnis. The writing style was dead-on Hubbard. Fra McGinnis was a dully platitudinous, somewhat lascivious poseur with grand notions of his own worth; he presided over the Boy Grafters (Roycrofters), selling locks of his abundant hair—even pillows filled with it—and wrote enthusiastically about work, though he preferred to sit around thinking grand thoughts.

Excerpts from *The Bilioustine*, as Taylor named his travesty, appeared with some regularity in the *Tribune* and were collected into two actual bound editions closely resembling Hubbard's periodical. The humor was heavy-handed and appealed to reviewers perhaps more for the person being satirized than for the quality of the writing. The *Denver Republican* noted, "As a well-aimed shaft of ridicule there is nothing to equal it. As a piece of humor it is a gem." A reviewer in the *Chicago Journal* commented, "The Fra Maginnis [*sic*] of 'The Bilioustine' proves to be a more entertaining character than the original Fra, while his writings are much cleverer and contain a great deal more common-sense than those of his model."[47]

CHAPTER 9

An Idyllic Spot to Spend the War

In late December 1900, Andrew Rowan and a detachment of twenty-one men were sent to the Philippine island of Bohol to assist in the repair of telephone lines along the island's southeast coast. When the Spanish left Bohol in December 1898, the island became, in effect, a tiny independent nation with its own federal government under the leadership of Don Bernabe Reyes; yet it swore allegiance to Emilio Aguinaldo. In spite of this it wasn't considered important enough to warrant the deployment of American troops and was barely mentioned in official dispatches to Washington, D.C. On July 4, 1899, General Otis had informed Adjutant General Corbin that he was "about" to extend control to Bohol,[1] but it wasn't until March 17, 1900, that troops landed—Companies G and C of the Forty-Fourth Infantry Regiment under the command of Major Harry C. Hale.[2] Accompanying them was Major George P. Scriven with the Signal Corps, who described what they found, noting that "the houses are often of wood and of a very good class; the people show every evidence of comfort, and well being; the expression of their faces is open and kindly and for the most part they seem well fed. The women are very modest and wear more and better clothing than the bean poles of Panay, and the men though wearing often a mere [idea?], still manage to appear modest. The better class of men wear coat and trousers like other civilized people." Scriven was quite taken with the Boholanos, especially the women: "The women are modest in appearance and prettier than others, they have finer complexions and their mouths and teeth do not seem as fouled by the use of beetle-nut; they are larger, too, with more curves to their figures and flesh on their bones than have the willowy, bamboo shaped houris of Panay. They seem very modest and unsophisticated too and [according to military surgeon] Dr. Furbush, there is no venereal disease on the island."[3] It seemed like an idyllic spot to spend the war. Another soldier, First Sergeant E. W. Cissell, also appreciated the Boholan culture, going so far as to compare the "weird and peculiar" singing of the natives to a scene from Gounod's *Faust*. Yet he saw past the smiling faces and noticed that the "natives were scared to death when the United States soldiers came." After all, they had to wonder if they'd traded in one set of tyrants for another. "But in less than a month," Cissell continued, "they were thoroughly reassured."[4]

After the Spanish left the island in 1899, it was ruled by the Junta Provincial of Bohol, which, after coping with Cebuano bandits in the north, created a peaceful, relatively prosperous society. Instead of leaving things as they were, Hale ordered the junta to be disbanded. Even though they vastly outnumbered Hale's forces, the Boholanos, armed with little more than bolos and spears—and aware there were thousands more American soldiers in the Philippines—had no choice but to accede while secretly planning otherwise.[5] Then, on August 31, a detachment of U.S. soldiers was attacked near the town of Carmen. War had come to Bohol.[6]

This was the situation when Rowan and his detachment of twenty-one men arrived to assist in the repair of telephone lines between Jagna, on the southeast coast, and Ubay, on the northeast. On December 15 they left Jagna at 7:00 A.M., replacing poles as needed. As they continued up the coast toward the town of Guindulman they noticed there were no natives working in the fields, nor were they in evidence along the road. Looking back, they could see people coming out to the road to watch them from a distance. When they reached the halfway point to Guindulman, they became aware that the houses were deserted. Rowan kept the men as closely grouped as possible, but their line was (by necessity) thin as they passed through a rock cut known locally as Kabantian Pass. The cut was about twenty-five yards long and, at the center, about twelve feet deep. The road itself was some eighteen feet wide, with ditches on both sides. Rowan later wrote this report:

> When the detachment entered this cut they were attacked, without warning, from all sides at once by bolomen who cut, stabbed,

and slashed at them front and rear. The attack was so sudden and overwhelming that all we could do was stand still and fight and that is just what we did. It was a hand to hand fight and every man done his duty. It did not last over a minute and a half but by that time we had killed nineteen of them and wounded probably fifty, who ran, or crawled, away as soon as shot. When the fight was over I found that I had three men killed and five wounded, so that it was impossible to follow them with the remnant of my force as there would be none to take care of the wounded. A. A. Surgeon E. P. Rockhill, U.S.A., took charge of the wounded at once and though severely cut himself paid no attention to himself until everyone else was attended to. The condition of the wounded made it imperatively necessary that I return to Jagna which I did, bringing the wounded men in a cart and the dead across our horses to Duero, and on a boat from Duero to Jagna where we arrived about 11 P.M. that night. The wounded were at once redressed and made as comfortable as possible and the dead were prepared for burial.[7]

After returning to his subdistrict on Cebu, Rowan started up where he'd left off, overseeing the election of new government officials and making sure they acted in accordance with his dictates. There was little that missed his attention, even going so far as to change the name of the municipality of Cauit to McClernand. He did so, he said, because there were "so many *Cauits* already in the island of Cebu, the word, (in Vasayan), simply meaning *the point*."[8] It also offered an easy opportunity to honor his "dear" colonel, Edward J. McClernand.

In addition to such mundane chores as swearing in village officials and planting telephone poles, Rowan and his soldiers were kept busy arresting suspicious Cebuanos and chasing down rumors of guerrilla incursions throughout the district. Spies seemed to be everywhere. Rowan locked up one woman he had "important information against" and whom he was expecting would confess as soon as she tired of prison life.[9] Had she been a man, she could have expected harsher methods to extract intelligence; torturing suspects to obtain information was a common practice in the archipelago. A favorite method was called "the water cure," and as Brigadier General Frederick Funston, who claimed he'd never seen it applied, described the process, "The victim is bound and a canteen [of water] forced into his mouth. . . . His head is thrown upward and back, and his nose grasped by the fingers of the torturer. Strangulation follows as a matter of course. When the victim is about suffocated the application is released, and he is given a chance to talk on recovery or take another dose of it. The operation is brutal beyond a doubt, but hardly fatal."[10]

It's probably true that Funston never saw the torture applied; generals rarely participated in such events, and in many units there were low-ranking soldiers specifically assigned to this duty. Another method of applying the water, which was often dirty, salty, and gritty, involved a five-gallon can with a hose that was shoved in the prisoner's mouth, forced open by a club or cartridge case. Sometimes there was a second hose shoved in the man's nose. He might also be held, with his mouth forced, open under a running faucet. What Funston didn't mention was that the water had to be expelled from the victim in order for more to be introduced a second and third time. This was done by pressing on the man's stomach and sometimes by laying him on the ground and jumping on his stomach. Not surprisingly, the victim would soon confess to whatever charge was made against him—if he survived. Funston's claim that the water cure wasn't fatal wasn't true, and surely he knew it. One notorious case involved a Catholic priest who denied knowing the location of buried guerrilla gold. The site was never discovered—if, in fact, there was any such site—because the "water cure squad" managed to kill the priest. The soldiers were sworn to secrecy, and the body was buried beneath an army baseball field. Funston was certainly right when he described the procedure as "brutal." In some cases blood would come out of the victims' eyes, ears, and mouth. One American soldier, Charles E. James, a first lieutenant with the Thirty-Sixth Volunteer Regiment, reported he had the water cure administered to him while a prisoner of the guerrillas following a three-day forced march without food. He claimed not to have divulged any information nor to have suffered any ill aftereffects: "I strangled once, but

one quick cough ended it." One is left to conclude that either the Filipinos were not as adept at applying the water cure as their American
counterparts or that the man was lying.[11]

In the meantime Rowan had not been forgotten at home. On January 22, 1901, the West Virginia legislature passed a joint resolution
honoring him for having "volunteered his services to the President
[and then entering] upon his important mission." Other details were
incorrect, such as having him walk "one hundred and fifty miles into
the interior" to find García, a distance that would have taken him
through Bayamo to the northern shore of Cuba. Nor did he, on his
return, wire "the President the information he desired." Nevertheless,
it was so resolved: "That the thanks of the people of his native State of
West Virginia be and are hereby returned to Captain Rowan for the
distinguished services rendered to his country in a period of great
emergency, and that the successful manner in which he filled his trust
marks him as a man of bravery and patriotism, scarcely paralleled in
history." It was further resolved that a copy of the resolution be
engrossed and sent to him,[12] but there is no record of Rowan's having
received or acknowledged the resolution.

On November 1, 1899, President McKinley's life had become a bit more
difficult when his vice president, Garrett A. Hobart, died. Hobart was
a genial man with an excellent mind who ably presided over the Senate.
Furthermore, he was a personal friend and confidential adviser to the
president.[13] His wife, Jennie, helped Ida McKinley get through her
troubled days and acted in her stead when the first lady was out of
sorts.[14] Their disappearance from Washington was a serious loss.
Hobart's death also posed a new problem for the Republicans: who
would replace him on the ticket for the upcoming presidential election? A possible choice was Theodore Roosevelt. The problem was
that Roosevelt was anathema to the Ohio political boss, Mark Hanna,
who considered him a madman. On the other hand, New York's political boss, Thomas Platt, thought it was the perfect job for Roosevelt.
After the war in Cuba, Roosevelt had won election as New York's
governor, and Platt wanted him out of there because he was not

cooperating with the cozy few who ran the statehouse. Roosevelt readily admitted all this.[15] For his part, he preferred being a state chief executive than a national second banana, and on February 12, 1900, he issued a statement: "In view of the continued statements in the press that I may be urged as a candidate for Vice President, and in view of the many letters that reach me advising for and against such a course, it is proper for me to state definitely that under no circumstances could I, or would I, accept the nomination for the Vice Presidency." He slyly added, "And I am happy to state that Senator Platt cordially acquiesces in my view in the matter."[16] At first Roosevelt truly did not want the job, but he was convinced to change his mind. He indicated his new intentions when he showed up at the convention in Philadelphia wearing a slouch hat that evoked the one from his Rough Rider campaign and, by this simple act, stampeded the delegates into choosing him.[17]

A mostly happy population isn't likely to throw out a president who had recently won a war—especially when his running mate is a hero of that war. Issues such as imperialism and the insurrection in the Philippines were important only to the Democrats. The Republicans concentrated on—and accepted credit for—the booming economy. In the end McKinley won with 65 percent of the electoral votes.[18] And so, on March 4, 1901, William McKinley, with Roosevelt as his vice president, was sworn in for a second term.[19]

The Americans on Bohol had not forgotten the ambush of Rowan and his soldiers at Kabantian Pass. In addition to conducting a general campaign against insurgents on the island, they were motivated in their efforts by a desire for revenge. Having intelligence regarding encampments in the vicinity of Lonoy, one of Jagna's satellite barrios, the Americans planned a hike to rout them. The Boholanos learned of the proposed attack and prepared a surprise attack of their own by digging trenches alongside a path they were certain the Americans would take. Unfortunately for them, the Americans had spies of their own and were tipped off to the proposed ambush. On March 8, instead of following the expected path, four platoons of soldiers surprised the Boholanos, who were unable to clamber from their trenches. In the bloodbath that followed, over 406 guerrillas were killed; only seven got away. The Americans suffered three dead and ten wounded.

On April 18, 1901, Rowan returned to Bohol, this time accompanied by his entire company. They arrived by boat in the horseshoe-shaped harbor of the village of Jagna on the island's southeastern coast. At the time of Rowan's landing, Bohol had a population of 248,000 scattered among a hundred or so municipalities and countless rural settlements. The 1,429-square-mile island is fairly hilly, with peaks reaching as high as 2,600 feet. Bohol constituted a Philippine province, the capital being Tagbilaran in the extreme southwest corner of the somewhat oval-shaped island. Jagna, with a population of 13,491,[20] was considered a pueblo, or small city. Smaller villages were designated as barrios.[21]

Company I was there to replace Company C, Forty-Fourth Infantry, which was to leave the island the following day. Captain James L. Anderson, commander of Company C, took Rowan on a tour of the quarters currently occupied by the men of the Forty-Fourth—and into which Rowan and his men would soon move. As was the custom in the Vasayas, the enlisted men occupied the local convent, the only building capable of accommodating up to fifty men. The whereabouts of the building's former occupants was never mentioned. Anderson also filled in Rowan and his junior officers on the current military situation in the vicinity; as they were already aware, it was not good.[22]

To begin with, most of the men of Jagna were presumed to be among the *insurrectos* in the hills surrounding the pueblo. Rowan reported Anderson's telling them that the *insurrectos* "were in the habit of coming into the town at night and remaining until the early morning hours sometimes dressed as women." There had been attempts by bolomen to kill or injure American soldiers, and the assumption was that it was not safe for soldiers to walk about unarmed. Anderson also reported that *insurrectos*, not satisfied with killing Americans, "had committed atrocities by digging up the dead American soldiers and cutting off their heads and otherwise mutilating their bodies." He felt that only a very few citizens of Jagna could be trusted.[23]

Considering developments in the recent past—the ambush that Rowan and his men had experienced at Kabantian Pass, and the Lonoy Massacre—it would be surprising if they trusted any of the locals. One previously friendly resident—the *alcalde*, Francisco Acala—had been kidnapped the previous month and was never seen again. When Anderson's troops pursued the kidnappers, they came across a small group of Boholanos that they claimed were Filipino guerrillas; they killed nine of them and wounded five. One of the dead was a woman, as was one of the wounded. There were no casualties among the Americans.[24] It is little wonder that Rowan reported the "sullen demeanor of the people naturally inclined me to the belief that the presence of Americans was not desired there." Lieutenant Cromwell Stacey and the company doctor, Lieutenant J. K. Ashburn, both expressed their definite impression of unfriendliness among the natives. This would have been equally obvious to the rest of the company; Rowan claimed that in spite of the locals' demeanor "the men and the officers treated the people with the greatest consideration. . . . There was no reasonable request made by anybody that was not granted." It requires a stretch of credulity to imagine Rowan and the men in his command, all of them aware of the ambush just four months earlier, treating the locals with "the greatest of respect." They had just spent a year and a half shooting and being shot at by Filipinos, a people they routinely referred to as "niggers."

It wasn't merely the attitude of the natives that concerned them but also their strategic position. Rowan was well qualified to judge the topographical situation, and he didn't like it. The pueblo was situated on the beach and surrounded by nearby hills. To the east stood a hill with a 250-foot crest barely four hundred yards away from the convent and hospital. Another hill with similar specifications stood to the west, and there was also high ground to the north that commanded the pueblo. As another officer who surveyed the town put it, "the troops were practically in a trap."[25] It will be remembered there were nearly a quarter million Boholanos; and here was Company I, composed of only 175 men, virtually isolated from the other commands on the island but for an easily cut telegraph wire. Typhoid fever lurked in the vicinity, and two members of the Forty-Fourth were on sick call when they arrived. Everyone in the company was well aware of the dangerous situation in which they found themselves, and they wouldn't have been in a frame of mind to treat the "sullen" Boholanos in a friendly manner.

After taking command on April 19, Rowan set about familiarizing himself with the physical nature of the countryside. This required going out daily with a small detachment, and even such a simple routine as this had its dangers. Anderson had warned Rowan that concealed bolomen would attack both flanks of a column and inflict serious wounds with their bolos before the soldiers could effectively use their rifles. Assuming that the *insurrectos* had rifles and cannons, he determined that it would be necessary to place outposts on at least two of the surrounding hills to prevent their being used as assault positions. The hospital, with its flammable straw roof, was of special concern.

Finding himself in this untenable situation, Rowan hoped to pacify the area by convincing the *insurrectos* to abandon their mountain retreats for life back in the pueblos. On different occasions he talked to the local leaders, explaining his desire for peace and promising that returning bolomen would be "treated properly." On April 28 he asked the Jagna authorities to bring in their counterparts from nearby pueblos so that he might discuss the issue with them. He apparently did not understand that the presence of Company I in their midst was not merely nettlesome to the natives but was considered to be an occupation by a belligerent force preventing their independence as a people. This soon after the Lonoy Massacre, the *insurrectos* had no reason to believe or trust an American army officer. Nor did they want to. Simply giving up and settling for life under American rule was not a choice.

The following morning at about 6:30, four men were seen entering the town from the east. Two wore ordinary native garb, one was wearing a uniform of sorts, and the fourth wore blue trousers and a shirt. They passed in front of the convent in which Rowan was already at work in the orderly room. After attending to a few duties, he put his uniform in proper order and left the building to perform his role at muster, which was scheduled to occur at 7:00. Following muster he inspected the barracks and hospital and then resumed his office work.

One of the routine chores for the soldiers was dumping their trash in the bay. The company's first sergeant, William McCreight, detailed Corporal Charles Daly to oversee the loading of a small boat and the eventual dumping. The boat was situated on the beach, with six unarmed soldiers nearby, and ready to push off. They were not far from Rowan's personal tent.

The four Filipinos, whose whereabouts had been unknown for the past two and a half hours, were seen leaving the police station shortly before 9:00. One of the two men in native dress left the other three and walked the short distance to Rowan's tent. Not finding the captain there, he left with a paper in his hand and walked directly toward Corporal Daly, who was standing barefoot in the water. Private S. A. McMahan, who was nearby, said to Daly, "There is a nigger looking for you. He wants to speak to you."[26] Daly turned, took a few steps toward the native, and accepted the paper that was handed him. As he looked it over, the native drew a concealed bolo from his shirt and stabbed him under the breastbone. He then went after McMahan, who tried to get away, and stabbed him in the back. As McMahan fell forward on his hands and knees, the native quickly walked away.

The soldiers with the boat happened to be turned away at that moment. It all happened so quickly and quietly that none of them was aware that anything was amiss until Daly, after being stabbed, yelled, "Look out, men." The soldiers took this as a warning regarding the presence of a snake. A fifth soldier, who was carrying Daly's shoes and leggings to the barracks, turned in time to see the native withdraw his bolo from Daly's stomach. Daly rushed toward the barracks to warn the other soldiers, crying, "Get your guns!" As he neared the convent, he fell. The soldiers inside, thinking they were under attack, grabbed their rifles and ran to the beach. Someone yelled, "Shoot that man." Another said, "He killed Daly."[27]

Rowan, in the meantime, had returned to his tent only moments after the native's entrance and exit, and was just about to unbuckle his pistol belt when he heard the commotion. He quickly left his tent and saw the native walking down the beach. The man was looking at the soldiers who were running toward him. A couple of men raised their rifles, as if to fire. Rowan called out, "Don't shoot that man, he seems to be a simple native. Don't kill him simply because he has a bolo in his hand."[28] No one fired, and Carl F. Peters, who was corporal of the guard that morning, walked up to the native and put his right hand on the man's shoulder. He ordered Private W. Bodkins to take the bloody bolo and then he pushed the native toward the guardhouse.

Rowan, who had heard the remark about Daly's being killed, saw a man being carried to the hospital. He rushed over, expecting to find Daly, but instead saw McMahan. He asked about Daly's whereabouts and was told that he was lying near the convent. He ran over to him. Dr. Ashburn, who was in the hospital, had seen McMahan being carried his way and gave orders to make preparations to receive him. As Peters and the arrested native neared the street, a number of soldiers, perhaps as many as thirty, surrounded them. While the corporal still had his hand on the man's shoulder, two or three shots rang out, and the native fell dead. Rowan heard the shots, and a soldier reported to him that the native had been killed while trying to escape.[29] He sent a soldier to fetch the doctor, who arrived immediately. Within moments, Daly was dead, just fifteen minutes after he had been stabbed.

Rowan had the company formed and told the men that Daly was dead—assassinated—and warned them not to allow any natives to approach near enough to cause injury without first making them expose enough of themselves to demonstrate they carried no concealed weapons; he suggested twenty feet as the nearest they should be allowed to stand. By this time Rowan realized that it was he who was the original target of the native, and he noted that he was going to post a guard at his tent. And by now thoroughly irate, he told the company he had no doubt they would have the opportunity to kill at least a hundred of the enemy in retaliation.

After the men were dismissed, a burial detail was assigned. Their own digging tools having been misplaced, they visited the home of Padre Filomeno Orbeta, the Jagna parish priest whom someone remembered using such tools in his garden. According to Corporal Charles L. Hamilton, who was in charge of the detail, the priest asked him why he wanted the tools. When told they were needed to dig a grave, the priest said, "Cosa, Capitan patay?"[30] *Patay* is the Visayan word for *dead*, and it's likely that a soldier in the middle of a war in the Visayas would be acquainted with it. On the other hand, why would a Spanish priest use a Visayan word when speaking to an American soldier? What he meant by using the Spanish word *cosa* (thing) in that context is uncertain. Hamilton told him, no, it wasn't the captain, it was Corporal Daly who had been killed. Following this exchange, the priest let the men have the tools. Another soldier, Corporal Thomas Stalcup, was quartermaster that day, and it was he who had to admit earlier that the company's digging tools were lost. He, too, remembered that the priest had a pick and shovel, so he went to the priest's house. The priest told him only that he did not have the tools, not bothering to mention that he had already lent them to Hamilton. Then, according to Stalcup, the priest said, "El Capitan patay." Stalcup also told him that it was not the captain, but Corporal Daly, and made it a point to make sure he understood. Stalcup was followed in turn by Private John E. Watson, who was with the Hospital Corps. He was slightly acquainted with the priest and decided to visit him. According to Watson the first thing the priest said was, "Cosa, esta hombre patay Capitan?" *Patay* could also mean "to kill."[31]

Private Robert P. Taylor, who had previously seen the group of men that included the murderer, was on guard duty when he noticed four men coming down the street. Taking Privates H. C. Jones and C. V. Davies with him, he arrested the men and turned them over to William Frye, the corporal of the guard. When Frye reported their arrest to Rowan, Rowan ordered him to keep them outside doing prisoner work, such as toting water and cutting weeds. Frye sent two of them under the care of Jones to the rear of the convent, an area surrounded by a four-foot-high stone wall. According to Jones, after reaching the area the two men began to run. He told them to halt three times. When they didn't stop, he fired, hitting one in the head and the other in the back, killing each of them with just one bullet apiece. Jones then called for Frye, who was apparently nearby. Frye sent Jones to the guardhouse and reported the shootings to Rowan. When told the prisoners were killed while trying to escape, Rowan asked no further questions but ordered Frye to have the bodies carried out to the road where they were to be left with the body of the native killed earlier.

Shortly thereafter Sergeant Hansjosten, who was provost sergeant at the time, ordered Davies to take the other two men to the same walled area. Just as before, the two men started to run. "I suppose they were scared at what happened to the other two," Davies later allowed. He said he warned them twice to halt, and when they didn't, he loaded his gun and shot one in the back, killing him instantly; the other required four bullets. They were laid in the road with the others.

Rowan ordered the *principales* of the town to be rounded up and asked to identify the men. None could, or they were reluctant to admit they could, even though it was believed by some of the soldiers that the man in uniform was a policeman from Jagna. The reluctance of the Boholanos to identify the men is understandable, considering that they appeared to have been killed for no other reason than that they were thought to have known Daly's murderer. Rowan later noted that "they left very quickly and had very little to say on the subject." He telegraphed Major Woodbury, now military governor of the island and commanding officer of the troops, informing him of Daly's assassination at 8:55 A.M., including the fact that the murderer had first gone to his tent. In his reply Woodbury acknowledged that Rowan had a narrow escape, adding, "Being on the ground, you can judge best what steps to take." Shortly afterward he sent another message ordering Rowan to join him late in the day, May 3, at Dimiao (another coastal town some fifteen miles west of Jagna) with fifty armed men equipped and provided with rations for four days. Noting the difficulty in finding bearers to carry supplies, he suggested hiring carabaos. He told Rowan to let him know when he would be leaving Jagna.[32]

Rowan had other plans. Believing that the assassination attempt seemed "to have been the reply of the people to my effort to terminate the revolution by peaceful means," he had already decided to take military action in the Jagna area. Accordingly, he ordered a roundup of male Boholanos—*hombres*—to act as carriers. One detail was led by Corporal F. L. Lightcap and another by Sergeant Peter Scanlon. Rowan made it a point to order the noncommissioned officers not to shoot any of the natives. Lightcap's group went north, and Scanlon's west. Before the afternoon was over, soldiers had captured a few dozen natives and incarcerated them in the guardhouse. During the roundup, they forced their way into homes, searching for both *hombres* and war contraband. The latter was defined as anything of a military nature, including the new Filipino flag. These flags were common on Bohol after the Spanish left, and it would have been natural to display this symbol of newly acquired independence—unaware, as the Boholanos would have been in 1899, of any future plans the United States might make regarding the status of the Philippines. Unfortunately for them, it was the standard practice of the soldiers in Company I, with Rowan's approval, to burn "abandoned" buildings in which war contraband was found; many houses in Jagna contained flags, and many were set afire that afternoon.

Without mentioning that he was collecting bearers for his own expedition, Rowan replied to Woodbury, "Carabaos impossible. Suggest that I go North and clear out my district. Can you not use 'K & M' Companies on your proposed expedition? My men will be worn out carrying extra supplies to Dimiao. Wish to speak to you personally and confidentially at 4:00 P.M. today, if convenient."[33] Woodbury called him at 4:00, and Rowan detailed his plan to lead an expedition north in a circuitous four-day route that would bring him back to Jagna. Woodbury sanctioned the expedition and asked when he would start. Rowan told him they would leave at 4:00 the next morning. The two men left the phone with two different interpretations of what had been agreed on: Woodbury thought Rowan would be leaving the next morning on the four-day expedition, while Rowan thought Woodbury understood he would be leaving the following morning to make investigations in the immediate vicinity of Jagna, not on the four-day trip. Things were further complicated by Woodbury's suggesting that Rowan might connect with Captain F. G. Lawton, who would also be leading an expedition north of Valencia, another nearby coastal town; but Woodbury admitted that due to unknown conditions, it was uncertain they would meet up and cooperate on a joint mission.

Included among the *hombres* rounded up were the *principales*, a Chinese merchant, and three Spaniards, two of whom were employed by the Tabacalera Company. Pedro Avalle, the agent of the company, was told to gather up all his books and money, which he turned over to the first sergeant after being taken to the convent. Though he spoke little if any English, he understood that all the buildings belonging to the company were to be burned. When he asked if he could pay his compliments to the captain, he and the other two Spaniards were taken to Rowan's tent, where they were told to stay until after Daly's funeral, which was to be held at sunset.

Rowan read a standard burial service, said a few words about Daly, and reminded the men once again that they must be wary. He told them that the town seemed to be infested with assassins and they must go armed at all times with bayonets affixed—even to the water closet. In all, he spoke about fifteen minutes. Instead of the usual small detail firing three shots over the grave, Rowan had the entire company fire as a "special mark of esteem" for Daly who, after all, had died in Rowan's stead. At some point in the ceremony Lieutenant Ashburn noted smoke perhaps a half mile to the west and brought it to Rowan's attention. When asked later if the fire was started by members of Company I, all those interrogated asserted it would have been impossible since every soldier was present or accounted for at the assembly; yet the only proof of attendance was a verbal response to a roll call—something easily faked, particularly if the noncommissioned officers were complicit. Rowan claimed it would have been a "physical impossibility for any enlisted man to have fired the town."[34]

As soon as the funeral was over, Rowan sent Lightcap with two or three men of his squad to investigate the fire, warning them that it might be a trap and to make sure that it didn't spread anywhere near the hospital. He then rejoined the Spaniards in his tent and invited them to dinner. Rowan ordered two bottles of California wine to be served with the food. While they were eating and chatting, Avalle noticed through the flap opening that a fire was burning in the direction of the company buildings. He asked if he could go see. Rowan gave his permission, but said he would not be responsible for his life if he chose to go. At that point Scanlon entered the tent and showed Rowan war contraband that had been found in a company building. Avalle, who didn't understand what was being said, found his neck suddenly in Scanlon's grip. He was taken to the guardhouse and searched, and soldiers found his documents and a considerable amount of money that he hadn't turned over earlier—some of which belonged to him, some to the company. Prisoners confined in the guardhouse were normally not allowed to retain valuables, and the money was confiscated along with a silver watch and gold ring. He was never to see any of it again.

There had been a number of reports concerning *insurrectos* entering the pueblo at night and sneaking out at dawn. Rowan decided to assemble detachments at 3:00 in the morning to travel surreptitiously to Jagna's exit points so they would be in position to apprehend any early morning departures. Five squads were assembled, two led by McCreight, and the other three led by Hansjosten. Instead of staying near the edge of Jagna, McCreight marched his men five or six miles east to the pueblo of Duero, where they waited on the outskirts until it was light enough to see. Finding "all the houses tenantless," the soldiers searched them for contraband. They burned at least a dozen houses and perhaps the entire village—or that may have occurred as a result of the fire's spreading. Hansjosten took his twenty-four men to the west, claiming they traveled no farther than a mile and a half, burning every house along one particular stretch of road and firing at some supposed Filipino guerrillas; they returned to town four or five hours later. Residents of García Hernandez, six miles away, claimed that twenty-five American soldiers entered their town and set fire to it. No one disputes the fact that García Hernandez was destroyed by fire that day, but no soldier in Rowan's command would admit to having been there. No other attachment of American soldiers was in the area.

That day more houses burned in Jagna. Rowan claimed this was due to heavy winds that blew embers from one rooftop to another. That afternoon, according to his account, "the fire crossed the plaza and burned the houses around it notwithstanding my earnest effort to avert such a catastrophe." Even his tent and kitchen were burned in places.

The following morning, May 2, he set out with a detachment to investigate the extent of the damage to the telephone line, which was obviously not working. He didn't get very far before hearing the whistle of a steamer entering the bay and, knowing it would be carrying important correspondence, turned back. There were two sacks of mail, much of which required his attention for the rest of the day. The following morning he again left the pueblo, this time going a mile before having to turn back in response to another steamer whistle. This time it was the *Troy*, an official steamer whose arrival might require his presence. The next day, May 4, was the day he had planned to travel north on the expedition he had described to Woodbury, but he was occupied during the afternoon making preparations. Still believing that an armed insurrection was imminent, Rowan and a detachment of mounted soldiers set out early the next morning.

That afternoon, Woodbury arrived in Jagna and was surprised to learn that Rowan had set out on his mission earlier that day—the mission that he, Woodbury, had ordered him to begin on May 1. Furthermore, he was told that Rowan had a good many bearers, bearers Rowan had left him believing were unobtainable. Woodbury's visit to Jagna had been prompted by a series of reports. It began with a notice he'd received saying that García Hernandez had been burned by American soldiers. This news left him flabbergasted. He could assume only that Rowan had disobeyed his orders and embarked on a different expedition than the one they had discussed. Then he was told that Jagna was also burned and that natives were shot in the streets. With the telephone lines cut, Woodbury could not immediately determine the truth of the stories. After reporting the details to district headquarters, he was ordered to go to Jagna to investigate for himself.

At Jagna he questioned soldiers concerning the death of Daly and reconstructed the sequence of events up through the shooting of the natives attempting to escape. He also learned of a sixth native shot in the back while under guard, another case of a prisoner supposedly trying to escape, though no one saw him running. In the guardhouse, Woodbury discovered the many prisoners being held there. Unable to question Rowan, who wasn't expected back for a few days, Woodbury left things as they were and went to Cebu, though he did leave a letter behind.

While this was going on in Jagna, Rowan and his soldiers were continuing on their expedition. In spite of their guide's incompetence—or, perhaps, intentional delaying tactics—at midmorning they discovered a small guerrilla outpost and then a larger encampment that had been a Filipino officer's headquarters. Letters found among the abandoned materials led Rowan to believe it had been the camp of

General Pedro Samson. They pressed on and around 2:00 P.M. were assaulted by large rocks tumbling down on them from a previously prepared fall. As the soldiers dashed aside to escape the stones, some of them were wounded by bamboo spikes placed there for that purpose. Rowan's horse jumped into the spikes and was wounded seriously enough to cause its death. When Rowan clambered off, he received a painful bamboo stab in his lower left leg near the knee that penetrated to the bone. Notwithstanding the tumbling rocks, the soldiers charged an occupied line of trenches and breastworks some hundred yards ahead. A small force of guerrillas vanished down previously cut exit paths.

The soldiers went on, eventually reaching Mayana, one of the barrios associated with Jagna. It had been a difficult march, and things got worse during the night. It rained from 10:00 to 3:00, leaving the men thoroughly soaked in the morning and surrounded by a thick fog. Ashburn determined that two men who had been wounded the previous day could not continue and would have to be carried on litters. Rowan was forced to conclude that they must return to Jagna by the most direct route possible. This meant traveling through the same defile in which they'd been bombarded by rocks the day before. Aware of the danger in advance, soldiers fired a number of rounds to chase off any guerrillas who might be positioned to push off stones. Farther along the trail they came under rifle fire on two occasions but managed to get through unharmed, eventually arriving in Jagna around 5:00 A.M. Other than having possibly disaccommodated Samson, the expedition was a failure. Two men were in the hospital, Rowan's horse was dead, and Rowan's leg wound had worsened, leaving him unable to walk unaided.

Things weren't improved when he read the letter left behind by Woodbury, which contained no cordiality, only the tone of a superior addressing a junior officer: "I must impress upon you the fact that the Philippine Commission has now this island under its protection, and all of the officials of the town are responsible to that body, through the Civil Government." He was telling Rowan, in other words, that it was not he who ran Jagna, but the city officials. Furthermore, the burning of the pueblo, if done by soldiers, "is not in accordance with General

MacArthur's orders." He also ordered Rowan to repair the telephone line, noting that he, Woodbury, was responsible for making sure that "the troops on this island conduct themselves in accordance with existing orders. Therefore I must be informed by telephone when and where you wish to send an expedition. . . . Under the orders that I have, you will see that no officer or soldier burns any house in any town or anywhere else, unless it is used by the *insurrectos* for defensive or offensive purposes, that is, armed *insurrectos*." He pointed out that he had not interfered with the prisoners, not knowing why they were confined, but unless Rowan had serious charges against them, they were to be released. He informed Rowan that he would be back in a few days and that Rowan was to be there to meet him. He ended with, "You will not order any more expeditions until after my visit."[35]

Two days later Woodbury arrived in Jagna carrying orders temporarily relieving Rowan of his command and directing him to accompany Woodbury back to Tagbilaran. Ashburn insisted that Rowan would be in no condition to travel for a few days. Having no choice but to accept the doctor's medical opinion, Woodbury agreed to Rowan's staying behind, but proceeded to look further into the circumstances surrounding recent occurrences in Jagna.

In his report to the adjutant general's office for the Second District, which included Bohol, Woodbury noted that he "proceeded to investigate the origin of the fire and other incidents connected with the affair." He was told about the many rifle cartridges and Filipino flags that had been discovered in the houses, but he could not find out "who or by what authority men had gone to Garcia Hernandez." It soon became evident to him that "all the company had made up their minds to know nothing about it. They said that the fire at Jagna must have been started by natives."[36]

The seventy prisoners, including the employees of the Tabacalera Company and Jagna city officials, one of whom had been forced to act as a bearer, were still incarcerated. "I asked why the officials of the town had been confined," Woodbury wrote, "and was told for supposed complicity in the killing of Corporal Daly." After learning from Rowan that there were no serious charges against any of the Boholanos, Woodbury ordered them released. The stories of the two Spaniards and the

Chinese merchant differed greatly from those of Rowan and his soldiers. They denied having any contraband and told of their buildings being looted before being burned. Manuel Gonzales, the second Spaniard who dined with Rowan, said that Rowan had told him he was going to burn all the houses that were found to contain contraband. Woodbury also learned that the priest's sister reported being robbed of money, jewelry, and other items. At one point he asked Ashburn if Rowan had been drinking on the night of April 30. Ashburn acknowledged he had, but "not enough to impair his faculties." After officially relieving Rowan of duty, Woodbury appointed Lieutenant Stacey company commander. Woodbury left, taking the Spaniards and the Chinese merchant with him.

As temporary company commander, pending Rowan's reinstatement, Stacey took a detachment of men on May 8 to García Hernandez to investigate conditions there and to look into the matter of the missing telephone line. He found the road completely desolate, with every house having been burned. The pueblo itself was completely burned but for the church, and dead carabao, horses, and pigs lay in the streets. Some seven miles of line had been cut and carried off. On May 10 Stacey established an outpost on a hill just outside of town. Two days later, at 3:00 A.M., a Filipino force of three cannons and as many as fifteen rifles began firing on the company area. The outpost was able to hold the Filipinos in check until the company had formed into land squads placed at strategic points. The exchange of gunfire lasted about a half hour. The next morning the bodies of three dead guerrillas were seen, but there were no casualties among the soldiers. The hospital building was the camp's most vulnerable point, and Stacey decided to move all hospital facilities into the church. The next night, from 8:30 to 2:30, firing continued intermittently with no casualties reported on either side.

Later that day Woodbury returned by launch to Jagna. It was then that he learned the details of the destruction of García Hernandez and all the houses along the road from Jagna. Stacey also told Woodbury about a box containing 120 pounds of church silver that Watson, the hospital corpsman, had discovered in a small boat. It was at first suspected of having come from García Hernandez but was subsequently identified as belonging to the Jagna church. There was no doubt in anybody's mind that it had been stolen from the church and placed where it was found by personnel from Company I.

Woodbury questioned Rowan again, asking if there were any soldiers whose testimony he should hear. Rowan said he could think of none. Woodbury had also asked Rowan for a "full report on the transactions at Jagna and of any expeditions"; what he got was a one-page statement regarding the fires and Rowan's lack of knowledge about them. In the last sentence Rowan declared that he did not believe Duero had been burned at all. When Woodbury asked him if this was all he wanted to submit, Rowan curtly replied, according to Woodbury, "something to the effect that he thought it would suffice."[37]

The following morning Woodbury returned to Tagbilaran, taking Rowan with him. That afternoon he questioned officials that he'd ordered summoned. They told him that on the morning of May 1, about twenty-five American soldiers entered the town from the direction of Jagna. After shooting the place up, killing four men, wounding one woman, and looting the municipal building, they set fire to the town. Two women were burned to death. The soldiers left in the direction of Jagna.

Rowan had not made it clear to him that the aborted hikes he began on May 1 and 2 were what he later claimed—investigatory hikes of the immediate area.[38] Nor had he made it clear that when he left on the May 4 expedition, he thought he was following a plan that Woodbury had approved. This, combined with stonewalling and denials, left Woodbury believing that Rowan and the men of Company I were guilty of gross misconduct and were lying about it. In a report on May 15 to the adjutant general, Woodbury stated,

> This burning has been a very disastrous event for this Island, and has seriously embarrassed the Provincial Government and has created a feeling of unrest among those peacefully inclined. I believe that nearly all the towns on the Island desire peace and that most of the Presidentes have joined the Federal Party.
>
> It is scarcely creditable that on May 1st, the day that I directed a military movement and on which Captain Rowan said he

started, that twenty-five men could leave their station and burn and kill in a town five or six miles away, at about 6:30 in the morning; and no one knew they had gone. . . .

I can make allowances for the feelings of the men when a comrade is assassinated but I cannot understand such a lack of restraint and discipline as is manifested here.

There cannot be two ways of managing affairs and two commanding officers on the Island.[39]

The guerrillas continued their night attacks on the camp through the month of May. With nearly 30 percent of his troops on sick report, Stacey was prevented from counterattacking. Forty soldiers against an estimated eight hundred Filipinos in the surrounding forest were hardly enough. Stacey thought their position was impregnable, but eventually Woodbury ordered Company I to be withdrawn from Jagna and reassigned to Tagbilaran. Still feeling strongly that the incidents surrounding the company's short stay in Jagna did considerable harm to relations with the Boholans, he issued General Order No. 20 on June 1: "No house in this Sub-District will be burned, unless the same is used by the insurrectos as a place from which to fire on troops, and even then an investigation will be made to ascertain whether the insurrectos have taken possession against the wishes of those living there. There will be no killing of unarmed natives nor any unjustifiable shooting of others." Woodbury was no doubt correct in his assessment of American-Boholano relations. It was reliably reported that the flag of the *insurrectos*—the cause of so much of the burning—now flew openly over Jagna.

A few days later Captain Edwin T. Glenn with the Office of the Judge Advocate in the Vasayas was ordered to investigate the Jagna affair. He arrived in Tagbilaran on June 8 and the next day began questioning, under oath, all the officers and men of Company I that he felt could contribute any useful information. Later in the month he questioned others who were stationed at Loon, a pueblo twenty or so miles north of Tagbilaran. Eventually this amounted to some one hundred individuals. The questions and answers were taken down in shorthand and later typed. Because the typed transcripts were not available for reference, Glenn had to rely on his memory and on handwritten notes to keep dozens of details straight; as a result, he did a poor job of following up on discrepancies, of which there were many. Men reported seeing Daly's murderer standing still when he was shot, alternately walking slowly, walking briskly, or running. They reported hearing one shot, two shots, or three or more shots, yet not one member of Company I saw anyone fire a rifle. It is next to impossible not to turn one's head in the direction of nearby rifle fire, but apparently no one did. Nor did anyone happen to be standing next to or behind the shooter or shooters. There was one man who did see something. Private Joseph Linsey, a member of the Signal Corps and not of Company I, claimed that as he was looking out a window he saw the man shot not by one of those guarding him but by a man in a white shirt. Glenn didn't follow up on this at all, and the impression is that, under the circumstances, it didn't matter who shot the prisoner; it was a just execution for an obviously guilty murderer.[40] The same was true for the other five unarmed Boholanos killed that day who, it was assumed, were part of an assassination plot. The fact that they lingered in the vicinity might have suggested they had no reason to run. Glenn asked no questions indicating he had any doubts about the circumstances surrounding their probable guilt or their deaths. He showed no curiosity about their identification or the disposition of their bodies, and readily accepted any statements about them made by the soldiers.

He interrogated the men closely about the burning of García Hernandez. There was only one group of soldiers anywhere near the town on the day it was burned—three squads led by Sergeant Hansjosten who, under questioning by Glenn, indicated on a map that he and his men had traveled about a mile and a half west of Jagna, but no farther. He admitted his soldiers burned most if not all of the native houses just west of Jagna after they were found to contain contraband. They were gone four and one half hours, sufficient time to walk to García Hernandez, burn it, and return, but he insisted they had not done so. Many of the men in that detachment were questioned, and each of them remembered they had traveled "about a mile and a half" west of Jagna. It is the only consistent bit of data in all their testimony, which raises the suspicion of their having been coached to say it. During questioning, Glenn often reminded the men that they were under oath, but this never caused a single soldier to retract a statement.

Glenn was given the names of certain Boholanos who it was thought might contribute materially to his inquiry, and he submitted their names to the governor of the island, Aniceto Clarin. Had Glenn been able to question them he might have considered things differently, but in spite of repeated tries, none of the people would come forward. In the company of Clarin, Captain Lawton, and a dozen or so soldiers, Glenn traveled aboard the SS *Troy* to Jagna and García Hernandez. Although he didn't go ashore in either town—at Clarin's insistence—he was able to discern the damage done by fire. Using the governor as intermediary, he learned that no one would talk to him. From what he was told and from what he observed himself, Glenn was certain that Clarin was merely a figurehead and had no authority on the island.

He traveled to Loon to question the remainder of the soldiers, and then to Cebu to take statements from Pedro Avalle, the Tabacalera agent, and two Filipinos, Catalina Casabas and Manuel Ababa. Avalle told him what had occurred to him the afternoon of the day Daly was murdered—that he was told to gather up all his record books and money, which he then turned over to a first sergeant, and how Rowan invited him and the other two Spaniards to dinner. He had been arrested again in Rowan's tent, after which additional company money, his personal money, a silver watch, and a wedding ring were taken from him and never returned. The soldiers who took these items kept him facing one direction while they searched him from behind; he never saw who they were. Glenn pointed out that he should have turned the money over to the first sergeant along with the other money and books and that he was to blame for its being stolen.

Casabas asserted that the four men described as companions of Daly's murderer were local policemen and that it was rumored that the murderer was a crazy person from Duero.[41] Glenn made no serious attempt to follow up on Avalle's or Casabas's stories.

Glenn was told by three different soldiers that after Daly's death Padre Orbeta asked, on three different occasions, if it were Rowan who was killed even though he always got the same answer. Instead of finding this unlikely, Glenn used the priest's supposed words to lead the soldiers into suggesting that the padre had anticipated and was somehow involved in Daly's murder and that Rowan was the intended victim. Furthermore, on that very morning a hospital corpsman out buying eggs for breakfast had difficulty obtaining them and found the natives unfriendly. In addition, Lieutenant Stacey, who was not in Jagna at the time of Daly's murder, said that Captain Anderson of the Forty-Fourth had told him the guerrillas boasted that sooner or later they would kill the commanding officer in Jagna. Another officer in Cebu reported to Glenn that officers of the Forty-Fourth had told him the same thing. Was this a mere coincidence? In his final report Glenn transmuted this froth into solid gold evidence and concluded that "all this would seem to indicate beyond a reasonable doubt that the intention of the assassin and his associates was to kill or assassinate Captain Rowan, but also that the people of Jagna, as represented by the officials, particularly by the padre, who, by the way, was especially selected by the former district commander for that pueblo, possessed *absolute knowledge* that the assassination of Captain Rowan was to take place that morning" (emphasis added).[42] The point wasn't to find the people of Jagna—by way of the padre and *principales*—guilty, but to demonstrate that the men and officers of Company I were innocent. Glenn continued,

> In view of the foregoing, it is not recommended that any further action be taken in regard to the killing of the assassin or of his associates, not only because of the inability to prove who killed the assassin, but also because it would be impossible, even if deemed expedient, to prove that his associates were not killed in attempting to escape, and for the further reason that in my judgment the laws of war not only condemn in the strongest terms assassinations committed in this way as being contrary to the usages of modern warfare, but declare that they are abhorred as outrageous, and the strongest retaliation should follow such murders.[43]

As far as the burning of the towns is concerned and Rowan's culpability, Glenn noted that "the evidence fully justifies this burning as an act of war. In fact if the conclusions reached from the evidence are correct this town should have been burned, and such being the case the Commanding Officer there at the time should have given the necessary orders, and in his failure to do so he erred. This action would have given this burning more of an official air and have eliminated some of the features that are now subject to criticism."[44] Rowan's sin, if any, was that he *didn't* order the burning of Jagna.

There was no denying the discovery of the box of silver taken from the church. Glenn condemned the looting and recommended that Rowan be directed to investigate the matter. As far as Avalle's money, watch, and ring were concerned, his failure to turn these items over to the proper authority as he was directed made him responsible for the theft. On the other hand, "as it is a matter affecting company discipline"—and apparently having nothing to do with justice or honor—Rowan was to be directed to "investigate the subject, and if it is possible to locate the party taking this money, that he be brought to trial."[45]

Then there was the matter of Rowan's disobeying Woodbury's orders. Under Glenn's questioning, neither man would cede the other was correct, but Glenn chose to side with Rowan. "I am forced to conclude," he wrote, "that Captain Rowan did not in word, act or intent, disobey the instructions or orders which he received." He didn't note whether or not he was influenced by Rowan's ad hominem defense that "a conversation at close hand with Major Woodbury is very difficult for me to understand under ordinary circumstances, and still more difficult, and almost impossible to understand him when he is talking over the telephone or when he has been drinking." As a result of his investigation, Glenn recommended that Rowan be reinstated as commander of Company I.[46] Had it helped that Glenn's and Rowan's paths had crossed at West Point in 1877? It probably hadn't hurt.

Up to this point in his report, Glenn was doing fine as far as the army brass was concerned. A week after the report was completed, Brigadier General Robert P. Hughes, district commander of the Visayan group,[47] followed Glenn's recommendations that Rowan be restored to duty and that the investigation into the burning of García Hernandez and the theft of the church silver be pursued. Glenn went beyond what he was instructed to do when he offered his military analysis of the situation at Jagna, however. It made sense to include a few paragraphs regarding the conditions in the town prior to Daly's murder, but he overstepped when he wrote, "From a military standpoint, in my judgment, Jagna was unwisely selected as a station for troops in the first instance." He went on to describe the vulnerability of the post due to its being located directly on the beach and situated between two hills, noting that, "in short, the troops were practically in a trap." Perhaps he wanted to further vindicate Rowan, or he may have honestly believed his military opinion was of value, but Hughes, a highly respected officer who had risen from private to lieutenant colonel in the Civil War, didn't appreciate this gratuitous advice from an underling. At the end of Glenn's report Hughes wrote, "It is believed that after a little further consideration [Glenn] will not adhere to his remarks on the advisability of occupying Jagna. The purpose was to get the troops into the worst nests of our new subjects. He has shown Jagna was of that character and had I known it was to be abandoned I do not think it would have been done. If dominated by two hills, they should have been occupied by out-posts." What Glenn hadn't stopped to consider was that Hughes might have been the very person who ordered the troops sent to Jagna.

News of the incidents in Jagna and the subsequent investigation was slow to reach the newspapers. The first mention of any aspect of the story appeared in the *Manila Times* on June 2: under the headline, "Capt. Rowan Wounded," there were a few sentences describing—incorrectly in almost every detail—the bamboo stab in Rowan's leg. It wasn't until June 18 that any mention of the larger incident appeared in the States, and only as a single paragraph in the *Oakland Tribune*, datelined Manila. It mentioned that Rowan was under investigation for the burning of a town in retaliation for the assassination of a corporal. As a result of the burning, it noted, "the people, inflamed with rage, rejoined the guerrilla general, Samson."[48] The same story, reprinted the following day in the *Washington Post*, carried the subhead, "Act of Weylerism Drives Pacified Natives Back into the Field."[49] To ascribe the tactics of General Valeriano "The Butcher" Weyler to an American army officer was a serious insinuation. Other newspapers picked up the story and in their headlines emphasized the Filipino reaction to the burning: "Captain Rowan's Act Caused Insurrection to Be Renewed" and "Renew Hostilities in Bohol Because Capt. Rowan Burned a Town." An article in the *Atlanta Constitution* even omitted the reference to Daly's murder.[50]

On June 27, the *Manila Times* published a fuller but garbled account that was apparently based on Glenn's investigation but before he concluded that Rowan was innocent of any wrongdoing.[51] That news finally reached the American public on July 18 in an abbreviated form,[52] but by then it was old news, and not even Rowan's name could keep it alive—except, of course, in localities with which he was associated. In an editorial in the July 25 *Monroe Watchman* it was pointed out that his acquittal was "entirely in harmony with the expectations of his friends," and that Rowan "is not only a trained and intrepid soldier but one thoroughly imbued with the virtue of dutifulness. Those who know him best could not conceive it to be true that he transgressed the laws of civilized warfare."

The writer went on to point out that Rowan had never been fully rewarded for putting his life in peril when he "penetrated the Cuban jungles and 'carried the message to Garcia,'" and suggested the oversight was intentional due to the discovery by the Republican administration that Rowan was a Democrat. He may have braved "tribulation, or distress, or famine, or peril, or sword" (a paraphrasing of Romans 8:35) in the service of his country, "but if a Democrat naught but obscurity must be his portion."[53]

Before the incident faded away completely, the *United States Army and Navy Journal and Gazette of the Regular and Volunteer Forces*, a weekly tabloid of military news and information, published an editorial on July 27 titled "Burning Filipino Towns." Although the writer notes that Rowan was exonerated, he takes it for granted that Rowan did, in fact, order the burning:

> The noise that has been made over the alleged burning of a native town in the Philippines by Capt. A. S. Rowan, Nineteenth Inf., must puzzle those acquainted with the methods common in the fighting in the Archipelago. One would imagine Captain Rowan to be the only officer who ever ordered that sort of thing.

If those who are making the clamor would read the official reports on the various expeditions, scouts and "hikes," they would often see this ending to reports: "Stores and barrio (village) burned." In this particular case by Captain Rowan, it is stated by Captain Ralph Ingalls, who has just come from the Philippines, that the place burned, raised by the sensationalists to the dignity of a "town," was a collection of huts that could be rebuilt in almost a day, the whole damage to no more than $150.

The burning of barrios has proved one of the most effective ways to keep the natives in order and to prevent outbreaks of assassinative malignity.... Now, the fact is nobody is shot . . . at these burnings, which are matters of such form that the natives are out of the huts long before they are set afire. Little of value is destroyed in these fires. More than one American officer has been disgusted at the sight of Filipinos letting useful articles being consumed in the houses while saving, often at great risks to their own lives, their game cocks with which they could continue their gambling.[54]

The *Journal* took a hard line on the insurrection, as did the *Manila Times*, which reprinted the piece in September.[55] Rowan expressed his indignation at the turn of events in a fifteen-page typewritten memorandum, at the end of which he concluded:

I believe . . . [t]hat suspending me from duty while my command was present was illegal and not contemplated by the articles of war, and that its effect was bad, and that it tended to weaken discipline and deprived the Government of the services of an officer against whom no charges could be brought within the prescribed limit, and that it deprived the Government of his services when sorely needed, and that the chief result of this suspension prevented the proper inquiry into the conditions, which resulted from the assassination of Corporal Daly, by the only officer who was present on the ground and who was more familiar with the conditions than any other officer.[56]

On September 7, 1901, there was room for only one story on the front pages of America's newspapers. The day before, at the Pan-American Exposition in Buffalo, a troubled young man named Leon Czolgosz put two bullets into President William F. McKinley. It was 4:00 P.M. when Czolgosz, with a newly purchased .32-caliber Iver-Johnson revolver hidden by a white handkerchief, approached the president at a public reception in the Temple of Music and fired the two shots. Czolgosz was immediately attacked by men in the crowd, and McKinley, who was helped into a chair, said, "Don't let them hurt him." The McKinleys had been staying at the mansion owned by John G. Milburn, president of the exposition, and it was there he was taken after first being examined at the exposition's emergency hospital.[57]

Czolgosz confessed to a personal bitterness that intensified after listening to a speech by the notorious anarchist Emma Goldman. "Her doctrine that all rulers should be exterminated was what set me to thinking so that my head nearly split with the pain. Miss Goldman's words went right through me and when I left the lecture [in Cleveland] I had made up my mind that I would have to do something heroic for the cause I loved." He denied having any accomplices, which apparently was true.[58] This, however, did not stop a spate of arrests of anarchists around the country.[59]

At the time McKinley was shot, Vice President Roosevelt was with Senator Redfield Proctor on Isle de Motte, Lake Champlain, Vermont, where a thousand people had gathered for the annual outing of the Vermont Fish and Game League.[60] The vice president received the news by telephone at 5:30, leaving him stunned. "As soon as he realized the meaning of the terrible news," a member of his party reported, "a dazed look of unmistakable anguish came to his face, and tears immediately filled his eyes." A second communication suggested that the president's wounds were not necessarily fatal. "That's good," he was reported as saying, "it is good. May it be every bit true." Somewhat relieved, Roosevelt traveled by yacht to Burlington, where at 8:15 he boarded a special Rutland Railroad train that would take him directly to Buffalo,[61] arriving there at 1:00 in the morning. After conferring with the doctors at Milburn House, he issued a statement. "When I came here this morning I felt a hundred years old," Roosevelt said. "I did not think there was any hope. The situation is still very grave, and we may lose our President within a few hours, but the best surgeons and physicians to be secured are at his bedside and they say he will get well. We must be prepared for the worst, but we have got the best of reasons for hoping for the best."[62] Two days later, confident that McKinley would recover—and typically having no fears for his own safety—Roosevelt left Buffalo for his home at Oyster Bay, New York.[63]

The nation was at war, and the president was barely surviving an attempted assassination. Under such circumstances at almost any other time in history, the vice president would have been expected to be in the nation's capital, protected by armed guards and ready to assume, if necessary, the duties of president of the United States. Roosevelt chose this moment to leave Oyster Bay and join his family, on vacation at the Tahawus Club, a private fishing and hunting lodge in the Adirondacks, nine miles from the nearest telephone. Furthermore, he left the club with guides for an extended hike deep into the forest. Earlier that morning, September 13, his secretary, William Loeb, telephoned the Tahawus post office to forward a message he'd received from Elihu Root: "The President appears to be dying and members of the cabinet in Buffalo think you should lose no time in coming." The message had to be carried by wagon to the lodge and then by a guide who managed to locate Roosevelt while he was having a late lunch along the trail on Mt. Marcy. He finished his lunch, then seems to have deliberately dawdled, not leaving until a second telegram arrived. He then took a waiting wagon at 10:30 P.M. Loeb had arranged for a special train to carry him to Buffalo,[64] and it wasn't until he boarded the train—around 5:00 A.M. the next morning—that Roosevelt learned McKinley had died nearly three hours earlier. After his arrival in Buffalo he delayed the taking of the oath of office until midafternoon. (Whether this was to maintain decorum, to avoid any appearance of eagerness, or for some other reason will never be known. In his autobiography, Roosevelt glosses over the assassination, his vacationing in the Adirondacks, and his assumption of power in a single paragraph.[65]) When he was sworn in by Judge John Raymond Hazel of the federal court at Buffalo at precisely 3:30 P.M.,[66] the country had been without a president for thirteen hours and fifteen minutes. Before taking the oath he made a declaration: "I wish to say that it shall be my aim to continue, absolutely unbroken, the policy of President McKinley for the peace, the prosperity, and the honor of our beloved country."[67] As he explained later to his friend Henry Cabot Lodge, "It is a dreadful thing to come into the Presidency this way; but it would be a far worse thing to be morbid about it. Here is the task, and I have got to do it to the best of my ability; and that is all there is about it."[68]

Thus, at least for the time being, the situation in the Philippines was to remain exactly as it had been.

Rowan's part in the Jagna affair had no effect on his reputation among enlisted men or fellow officers. Soldiers serving under Hughes were notorious for the severe measures they took against Visayans whom they regarded as uncivilized "indios."[69] Hughes may have bridled at reading unsolicited criticism from Captain Glenn, but he was not above seeking advice from underlings, particularly those whom he considered experts in their field. On July 23 he cabled Rowan in Tagbilaran, acknowledging that Rowan was "more familiar with the interior of Cebu than any officer over there" and asking for his tactical suggestions for taking possession of a fifty-mile-wide strip across the island from the city of Cebu to the west coast. Rowan, who had in the meantime resumed his command of Company I, was leading his soldiers from Tagbilaran to Tubigon, a small city on the northwest coast. He responded to Hughes as soon as he received the forwarded message, and his ability to envision terrain from a military point of view allowed him to reply in detail, noting the relative density of forest lands, the availability of trails, the possibility of obtaining water-borne supplies, and the like.

Secure in his exoneration and with the apparent approval of the senior commander in the Visayas, Rowan continued his heavy-handed tactics against the Boholanos, driving them out of their forts and capturing many arms. After one rout they found a list of officers for the entire island, showing names, titles, and assignments. At the top of the list was General de Brigada Pedro Samson, *jefe superior.*[70]

Near the end of October, the *insurrectos* back on Cebu had had enough. What few of them were left—sixty officers and 470 men—surrendered, giving up 150 rifles and six brass cannons. Hughes notified the current military governor and commander of U.S. forces in the Philippines, Major General Adna R. Chaffee, who advised him to waste no time moving on to Bohol.[71] Accordingly, on November 4, Hughes landed another four hundred troops on the west coast of the island, not far from Tubigon. As the burning and torture increased so did their wearying effects on the soldiers; in October Rowan described the situation in a letter to his wife Ida as "discouraging." It had been more than two years since they had seen one another. Officers' wives could, if they were able, travel to the Philippines, but Rowan told her it would be inadvisable.[72] One of his soldiers, Corporal Henry K. Dulabahu, didn't seem quite so depressed when he wrote to his parents in Massillon, Ohio, to say, "We expect the niggers on Bohol to surrender any day now, and I hope they do, as I am getting tired hiking after them. . . . We have a base ball club. We went over to Cebu, and we didn't lose a game. The captain is proud of us. He paid $104 for an outfit for us. We had one game at Cebu on Christmas."[73] The assault was successful, and 365 Boholano guerrillas surrendered on January 14, 1902.[74] By February 1, William H. Taft, the civil governor of the Philippines, predicted a bright future for the islands, noting, "The Filipino is attached first to his town and, second, to his province, and he is, I think, now forming an attachment for the name of Filipino. On that pride of country and on the Filipinos' desire for education, I base my hope on the success of what we are doing in the islands." Taft's rosy view was a few months premature, but there remained only two serious holdouts: the easternmost Visayan island of Samar and the province of Laguna, on the island of Luzon.[75]

Brigadier General Funston, a wiry, fearless man only five feet, five inches tall, had first seen combat as a volunteer artillery officer in Cuba with Máximo Gómez in 1895, his previous occupation being a botanist with the U.S. Department of Agriculture. After Funston's return from Cuba just prior to the war with Spain, the governor of his home state of Kansas, John W. Leedy, appointed him commander of the Twentieth Kansas Regiment. Funston arrived in the Philippines after the Spanish surrender but distinguished himself in battle against the insurrectionists and was awarded the Medal of Honor and promoted to brigadier general of volunteers. He was due to be mustered out in early 1901 when he devised a plan for the capture of Emilio Aguinaldo.[76]

Documents turned over by a defector named Cecilio Segismundo revealed that Aguinaldo was asking for four hundred volunteers to join him at Palanan, a small municipality on Luzon's east coast. Funston received permission for himself and three other officers to pose as prisoners captured by a sham force of guerrillas led by Segismundo. The plan was quite complicated and involved faked documents, a nighttime landing, and a march of over one hundred miles, during which they came close to starving. The plan worked, but not without great endurance and considerable luck. Aguinaldo was captured, and Funston returned triumphantly to Manila.[77] MacArthur called the operation "brilliant in conception and faultless in execution"; he hoped it would result in a "speedy cessation of hostilities throughout the archipelago."[78] It may have done so, but the war was nearing an end. As a reward, Funston was soon transferred from the volunteers to the regulars with his brigadier-generalship intact, a fact resented by West Pointers among his fellow officers.[79]

By May 4 the outcome of the war was so certain that President Roosevelt cabled a victory message to Chaffee: "Accept for the army under your command, and express to General Davis and Colonel Baldwin especially, my congratulations and thanks for the splendid courage and fidelity which have again carried our flag to victory. Your fellow-countrymen at home will ever honor the memory of the fallen, and be faithful to the brave survivors who have themselves been faithful unto death for their country's sake."[80] On May 28 Rowan boarded the transport *Sherman* for his return trip to the United States.[81]

CHAPTER 10

Major Rowan in Love and War

Angel Island in San Francisco Bay is about one square mile in area and was occupied by Native Americans for centuries before the Spanish arrived. When Andrew Rowan landed there on June 21, 1902, it was the site of Fort McDowell, which served primarily as a discharge camp to process soldiers returning from the Philippines.[1] Rowan was there on July 4 when Theodore Roosevelt issued his proclamation declaring that "the insurrection against the authority and sovereignty of the United States is now at an end." The president went on to grant "a full and complete pardon and amnesty to all persons in the Philippine Archipelago who have participated" in the so-called insurrection.[2] In terms of casualties, this war had been more expensive than the War of 1898—4,000 Americans, 20,000 Filipino soldiers, and probably a quarter of a million Filipino civilians were dead or not to be found.[3]

Rowan stayed in command of his company until July 22, after which he spent nearly two weeks on sick leave in the general hospital. Following his discharge from the hospital on August 4, he began what was to have been a four-month leave of absence. This was cut short by his appointment to a cushy job in Kansas, not far from Atchison, where his family lived. It would be his responsibility to teach military tactics to students at the Kansas State Agriculture College and Applied Science in Manhattan (now Kansas State University). Manhattan, settled in 1855, was a quiet little town with a population in 1902 of about 3,500; the enrollment at the college was 1,574. It would be a good place for Rowan to rusticate after his difficult two years in the Philippines, and it was only about eighty miles from Atchison.

He reported for duty on September 12. KSAC president Ernest R. Nichols, who would have been aware of Rowan's fame as the carrier of the message to Calixto Garcia Íñiguez, informed the inspecting officer, Major Daniel H. Brush, that Rowan was "all that could be expected." Brush, who inspected the cadets on June 11, 1903, added in his official report that Rowan was "very efficient and qualified for the duty."[4] One can picture Rowan, with his bristly mustache, lecturing the young men on lines and bases of operation, advance and rear guards, and the attack and defense of an outpost, illustrating the textbook cases with actual examples from his experiences in Bohol and Cebu; he knew too well that one day their lives might depend on lessons learned in his classroom. Military discipline and form were no less important, and in the spring of 1903 his students participated in twenty-seven company drills, twenty-four battalion drills, eight dress parades, and two reviews and inspections. At one point Rowan's enthusiasm caused him to receive a rebuff from the War Department. In a quarterly report he suggested changing the General Order that established the rules for student cadet programs; he wanted to substitute "a minimum per cent (say 80) instead of a fixed numerical (100) enrollment in [a college's] military department," thus increasing student participation in his program from 250 to 800.[5] This would give him a command approaching the size of a regiment. In offering this suggestion he made two mistakes. First, he hadn't discussed the matter with KSAC's administration, and, even worse, it appeared as if he were trying to tell the members of the War College Board how to run their affairs. He received a curt reply from the adjutant general's office that ended with a snide comment regarding Rowan's assessment of the number of students that could be made to participate in his program; as a further reminder to keep his nose where it belonged, the letter was directed to the college president, to be passed on to Rowan.[6] But this was just army politics. There was worse to come.

The first public hint that Rowan might be in some kind of trouble at KSAC was a cryptic squib in the *Students' Herald* of April 9, 1903: "[W]hat is the matter with a College detail for an army officer? At least in some cases it seems about as easy for them to sit still and draw pay as it does for a stone to lie still and gather moss. A big name abroad doesn't always come home with a soldier. A prince in a foreign land may be a pauper at home. Of course we have no specific case in mind, but we have no doubt that some of our cadets at least can call up instances where the remarks apply." It's impossible to know whether Rowan read this; surely no one would have pointed it out to him. He would definitely not have been aware of a letter mailed on July 25 to "His Excellency, Theodore Roosevelt, President, U.S.A." by Mrs. Mary A. Browne, corresponding secretary of the Manhattan Women's Christian Temperance Union, requesting that he give his personal attention to a matter of grave interest to the ladies of its membership:

> Current opinion as freely expressed in this vicinity is to the effect that the military instructor in the Kansas State Agricultural College, Captain Rowan, somewhat famous for "carrying the message to Garcia" is in his personal habits most unfit to be of service in the training of our boys. Charges of drunkenness are often made against him. . . . The great interest you have manifested in the need of good character for American citizens assures us that you know that our young men should have only good teachers, and we hope for an immediate investigation, that if you learn that charges are true you will bring about a change before the college opens this fall.[7]

In those days a letter to the president could get action.[8] In this case Roosevelt passed it on to Elihu Root, the secretary of war; from Root's desk it went to the acting adjutant general, Lieutenant General W. P. Hall, and then on to Lieutenant General Samuel Baldwin Marks Young, president of the War College. On August 24, not quite three weeks after the letter was written, Young urged the immediate removal of Rowan. He also recommended that "the officer who succeeds him be selected with special reference to the statement contained in [the] last paragraph of President Nichols's letter," referring to the killer letter sent by the KSAC president verifying everything Mrs. Browne had written and then some. According to Nichols, Rowan was so drunk on the previous commencement night that he was "unable to appear in company." In the last paragraph referred to by Young, Nichols wrote, "We have a large number of young men here and I wish we might have a detailed officer who was entirely free from vices to take charge of the drills.

Kansas being a prohibition state, drunkenness is, of course, especially noticeable." Nichols never explained why he overlooked the drinking problem when he told Brush that Rowan was "all that could be expected." On August 26 Rowan was officially relieved from duty and ordered to rejoin his regiment at Vancouver Barracks in Washington. Nichols suggested three possible replacements, but added that if none of these were available, "any good clean man would be acceptable." Within a month a presumably abstemious first lieutenant, Pearl M. Shaffer, was assigned to the post.[9]

Rowan accepted being relieved from duty at KSAC with military grace—at least in writing. There were no excuses offered, no huffing or puffing, and for good reason: his behavior was inexcusable, and he knew it. Furthermore, on September 10, the same day he acknowledged his dismissal, he also submitted a request to the adjutant general for a three-week leave of absence due to a serious illness in the family.[10] And he had yet one more reason to behave quietly: just two days earlier he had been saved from total ignominy by being ordered to report for duty as an umpire during army maneuvers—essentially, war games—at West Point, Kentucky, and at nearby Fort Riley, Kansas. Only the most competent officers were chosen as war game umpires because it was they who controlled the flow of information between the two opposing "armies" as each side carried out its maneuvers.[11]

The maneuvers were being held because, in spite of having won the war with Spain, the land forces hadn't performed spectacularly well. One has to wonder what the outcome would have been against a highly functioning European army instead of Spain's pathetic force. Congress had begun looking into matters since shortly after the war ended, and then president William McKinley's new secretary of war, Elihu Root, had dedicated himself to reforming the creaky military machine.[12] One thing was beyond dispute: the national guardsmen, for all their patriotic enthusiasm for war, were unfit to fight in one. Simply put, the majority of guard units were poorly financed, organized, trained, and supplied. Their yearly encampments often more closely resembled social events than military exercises, complete with dances and family participation.[13]

Gossip about Rowan's sad fate would have traveled quickly through army circles in Washington, and he was no doubt indebted to his old friend and senior officer at the Military Information Division, Colonel Arthur L. Wagner, for these assignments. Wagner was chief umpire for the maneuvers,[14] and Rowan's selection at this precise moment was surely no coincidence. This is not to suggest that Rowan wasn't qualified; indeed, his battlefield experience and topographical expertise made him an excellent choice. The maneuvers were not to start until the end of September 1903, and Rowan was granted leave with the understanding that there be no delay in his arriving in Kentucky at the designated time.

He left Manhattan after the college shut down for the summer and went on vacation with Ida and Elizabeth, and possibly other members of the Symns family, in Ishpeming, Michigan. (Ida's mother would not have been among the vacationers, having died on September 14, 1900.[15]) The Symnses had a connection in Ishpeming—their good friends Dr. and Mrs. Theodore A. Felch were former residents of Atchison, where Dr. Felch had practiced medicine for many years and may have been the Symns family doctor.[16] Whether Ida traveled there to consult with Felch or became sick later is unclear, but on September 10 she was seriously ill—so ill, Rowan asserted, that it would not be possible for her to join him in Vancouver, Washington, where he was to reunite with his regiment after completing his duties as umpire.[17]

Keeping to his word, Rowan reported for duty in West Point; this would have been his first meeting with Wagner in nearly five years. Two weeks later he was again acting as umpire at Fort Riley. Because of Fort Riley's proximity to Atchison, Rowan was able to see Ida before leaving for Vancouver. He departed in time to arrive on November 21 in order to resume his duties as company commander.

Ida died on New Year's Eve 1903, though how she died is something of a mystery. Under normal circumstances, the *Atchison Daily Globe* printed every bit of news that floated through the transom, but the newspaper gave only the basic facts concerning Ida's death. Because of her marriage to Andrew Rowan, the news of her death was picked up by the Associated Press and widely reported around the country—but without any details other than that she'd died at home. When Ida's mother died, the *Globe* devoted many column inches describing her illness, but for Ida there was virtually nothing.[18] One can assume only that the editor of the *Globe*, perhaps at the behest of the family, chose to protect the Symnses' and the Rowans' privacy.

Being sent to the Vancouver Barracks, just a few miles north of Portland, Oregon, and across the Columbia River, was considered a plum assignment. The climate, the scenery, the location, the parklike facilities, and the fairly easy duty made it seem more like a pleasant suburb of Portland than a military base. It was a great place to be a soldier—that is, unless you had a drinking problem and your wife had recently died.

Rowan didn't do well in Vancouver. One of the few good things to happen was an operation in February to relieve the discomfort of internal hemorrhoids. In his first efficiency report, his commanding officer, Colonel Joseph H. Huston, wrote that Rowan "takes but little interest in his company duties and performs them in a very perfunctory manner." On a number of occasions Huston reproved him in writing, calling attention to derelictions of duty. "Many of these," he wrote, "were the result of intemperance." Worst of all, he charged that Rowan's "habit of criticism of his superiors is such as to be a menace to discipline."[19] This was serious. Yet Rowan's soldierly qualities pulled him through. His ability to judge topography from a military point of view, for example, put him in good stead with certain superiors—Brigadier General Funston, for one.

It just so happened that the Vancouver area had been selected as the site for further joint maneuvers. Funston, who was in command of the Department of the Columbia, realized that Vancouver Barracks, however pleasantly situated, hadn't the space for expansion or for engaging in large-scale military maneuvers. When he did some reconnaissance in the American Lake area south of Tacoma, Funston took two principal advisers with him—Major R. G. Ebert of the medical department and Captain Andrew S. Rowan. After a careful two-day examination, the site was chosen for maneuvers in which members of the Washington and Oregon National Guard would join regular army units for ten days of war games. More than 270 officers and 3,739 soldiers were involved. The maneuvers were a huge success, and Major General Arthur MacArthur was on hand for a grand review on the final day. In addition to directing the survey on which the official map was created, Rowan was chief assistant umpire.[20]

With his value in this capacity now established, Rowan was sent off in August to officiate at maneuvers at Camp Atascadero, situated on the 25,000-acre Henry Ranch in San Luis Obispo County, California. It was a massive effort involving five thousand soldiers and one thousand horses commanded by MacArthur,[21] who, out of necessity, would have conferred with the umpires from time to time, further establishing Rowan's favorable connections in high places. MacArthur was reported as being "delighted" with the exercises,[22] and later wrote that the experience was "of incalculable benefit to all."[23] Many of the enlisted men among the National Guard weren't quite so happy. They particularly objected to having been marched at double time without food or water through scratchy underbrush. Some asserted they would stay in the guard only "long enough to get out of it."[24] This sort of griping wouldn't have found a sympathetic ear with Rowan, who had been through much worse himself when it wasn't a game and the bullets were real.

As soon as the maneuvers were over, Rowan left on a month's leave of absence. The camp was located north of Los Angeles, about a third of the way to San Francisco, and Rowan spent at least part of his leave in that city. He had, in fact, stopped off in San Francisco on his way to the maneuvers. On August 8 an engagement announcement appeared in the *Oakland Tribune* noting that Captain Rowan was to marry the well-known clubwoman and divorcée Josephine Morris de Greayer. Rumors of a possible marriage had circulated the previous month but seemed so unlikely to the Symns family back in Atchison that they were inclined not to believe them.[25] In San Francisco, however, the details of the pair's becoming acquainted were apparently so well known through society gossip that it wasn't necessary to relate them, only to hint that the affair could have come right out of a romance novel. The reporter called the union "singularly appropriate," going on to write,

There is a touch of the autumnal about it for both of the parties
are more than forty and both have been married before. Mrs. De
Greayer's first marriage was not a happy one and Captain Rowan
is a widower with a growing daughter. Mrs. de Greayer has seen
a great deal of sadness for she was for many years sadly over-
borne by a blind brother who needed much care. In spite of this
she was always cheerful, often gay and merry, and she is one
of the most refined women in San Francisco. Literature and
clubs are her fads, and she is fond of theatrical folk—Miss Ida
Conquest is an old and dear friend.[26]

The marriage, according to this writer, was to take place at the home
of Mrs. de Greayer's intimate friend, Mrs. J. O'B. Gunn, at a date and
time to be determined by the needs of her fiancé. The happy couple
would then spend part of their honeymoon at El Paso de Robles, a
small town near Camp Atascadero, while Rowan attended to his duties
as umpire.[27]

The situation would require all of Rowan's military logistical skills.
The maneuvers were to begin on August 13, and everyone involved was
expected to be there by August 10.[28] Under normal bivouacking conditions, even high-ranking officers are expected to stay in the encampment. How was Rowan, merely a captain, to spend his nights with
Josephine? There was a health spa and resort hotel in El Paso, but it
would have been packed with wealthy summer visitors.[29] Had Rowan
or Josephine the foresight to wire ahead in time to reserve a room? And
what was he to use for daily transportation between the war games and
the bridal chamber? It would appear to have been an impetuously
conceived plan. Rowan did marry Mrs. de Greayer, though not as the
Tribune writer reported; they instead were married in the late afternoon on August 7 in the Swedenborgian church on Lyon Street in San
Francisco.[30] A reporter for the *San Francisco Call*, which regularly
mentioned Mrs. de Greayer's activities on its society page, scooped
his—or probably her—colleagues to write:

The words that joined the soldier and the lady were spoken by
the Rev. Mr. Worcester, while the birds in the trees without

warbled the wedding march. There was no retinue, no gaping crowd—not even a chattering friend—to break in upon their happiness. The service over, the happy pair withdrew from the little gray church and disappeared in the shadows. Only the "cabby" knows where they went and he has the dark secret hidden within his breast.

But one thing the friends of the pair are sure—they must soon come out into the open, for the gallant captain is due at Camp Atascadero for maneuvers. And then may the sweet stupidities of congratulations be said.[31]

Undoubtedly there was no end to the "sweet stupidities" when the pair finally did return to San Francisco and the new Mrs. Rowan was feted by her friends at a luncheon on September 26. Each of the ladies present was given a signed copy of "A Message to Garcia."[32] The luncheon was but one of a series of events including a theater party, an informal musicale, and a tea.[33] Josephine was quite popular among society women, and her name and face were familiar to readers of San Francisco area newspapers. In a feature article, the *San Francisco Call* once noted that she was one of the "few society women who find time for constant active philanthropic work."[34] Josephine participated in charity sales, the opening of a maternity home for the poor, and various other good works. Her most notable achievement was the establishment of a public library for the blind in August 1902, a cause to which she devoted herself after the death of her brother.[35]

At the time of their marriage, Josephine was living in the St. Dunstan, a fashionable hotel and apartment house at the corner of Sutter and Van Ness.[36] It can be seen that Rowan, who lived on no more than his captain's pay, had greatly improved his financial situation by marrying a woman who, according to one report, had "a fortune in her own right" and who had been pursued unsuccessfully by other men.[37] It was, commented a reporter in the *Call*, "the climax of his achievements—but what might not have been expected of the 'man who bore the message to Garcia'?"

The question of how they met remains only partially answered. According to one newspaper account they were introduced by none other than Elbert Hubbard, but no details were given.[38] In any event, they met and married, and Josephine, eager to partake of her new life as an army officer's wife, accompanied Rowan to Vancouver where her gregarious nature quickly made her an active participant in the social life of the camp. They lived on Officers' Row, a pleasant group of buildings where children frolicked in the gardens—officers' children, that is; the children of enlisted men were forbidden by regulations to play there.[39] And when Rowan—his reputation and qualifications as a military officer having been reestablished—was sent back to the Philippines, Josephine went with him. She returned to San Francisco before their departure in April 1905 to visit with friends and to take part in the Mardi Gras festivities, where she was a "center of interest."[40]

When Roosevelt issued his peace proclamation declaring amnesty for Filipinos who participated in the insurrection, he pointedly exempted "the country inhabited by the Moro tribes."[41] After the United States government acquired the Philippines from Spain it assumed greater ownership than the Spanish could honestly claim. Although the Spaniards insisted otherwise, there were two chiefly Islamic areas outside their control—the Sulu Archipelago and the island of Mindanao.[42]

Thanks to the many years of Spanish rule over the central and northern islands, the Americans' self-appointed task to Christianize and civilize the Filipinos was made simpler because 80 percent of the population was already Christian—Catholic, to be specific. The real challenge was to be found among the Moros.

In August 1901, Brigadier General George W. Davis became the first military governor of what was called Moroland, the Muslim areas of Mindanao and Sulu. He instituted policies that reflected the new thinking in the American military—that it was time to begin exercising control in the south. Davis took a stand against practices Americans found particularly offensive—polygamy, slavery, and piracy—and had patrols sent out to survey the territory and gather information. Inevitably this led to conflict, and as the fighting increased, so did Moro casualties. The Americans had all the military advantages they held in the northern islands and they used them. And almost worse for the Moros than the military defeats were the cultural changes that were taking place: schools, hospitals, roads, health regulations, taxes, and land surveys. Society was being transmogrified before the Moros' eyes, and they didn't care for it.[43] For their part, the Americans found a land and people straight out of history books and boys' adventure tales. As one officer put it, "Over here we are living in the midst of feudalism and slavery, with pirates and bloody murder."[44]

Unlike the islands in the north, which had civilian governments, the Moro Province, as it was then called, continued to be ruled by the American military. Major General Leonard Wood, Roosevelt's commanding officer in the Rough Riders and the postwar military organizer of Santiago de Cuba, took over as military governor of the province on August 6, 1903. This would never have happened had he not been transferred from the volunteers to the regulars with his rank of brigadier general intact, then enjoying a further promotion. As in the case of Frederick Funston, most regular officers were incensed, and it may even have been worse in the case of Wood. With no military training and only eight weeks in command of a volunteer unit, he was catapulted over the heads of 509 existing senior officers. This was due in large part to his personal ambition, strong political connections, and reformist frame of mind.[45] As president, Roosevelt was now Wood's commander, and a few days before assuming his new job, Wood wrote to his friend Roosevelt, "I shall make a sincere effort to have peace, but with the distinct understanding that the territory belongs to the United States and that its troops and officers, while engaged in the performance of official duty, military exercises, etc., must not be molested, and that they in turn will respect the property and rights of the inhabitants. If they still insist, as they may, upon a row, it won't amount to much. I think one clean-cut lesson will be quite sufficient for them, but it should be of such character as not to need a dozen frittering repetitions."[46] The tone of this letter indicates that Wood was prepared to do whatever was necessary to exercise control over the Moros. There was little he observed about them that he liked. On December 16, 1903, he wrote to William Howard Taft, the first civil governor of the Philippines, "The people of these islands are Mohammedans. Their faith teaches them that it is no sin to kill Christians, and it is taught by the priests to believe it is commendable. They are nothing more nor less than an unimportant collection of pirates and highwaymen, living under laws which are intolerable."[47] Wood's experience in Cuba taught him something that would affect his strategy for career advancement: he learned that zealous attendance to administrative duties necessitated stepping on a lot of toes and angering many people. Yes, one's superiors would be impressed, but that was not the sort of approval that led to higher commands. What were needed were combat successes, and that's what he went looking for in Moroland.[48] In April 1904, Wood reported to the adjutant general of the Philippines Division how he intended to establish his orderly government. "Our conciliatory and good natured policy with them resulted," he noted, "in the establishment among them of the firm conviction that we were both cowardly and weak and out of this conviction grew an absolute contempt for our authority. Firmness and the prompt application of disciplinary measures will maintain order, prevent loss of life and property and permit good government and prosperity among these people. Dilatory tactics, indecision and lack of firmness will result in a carnival of crime and an absolute contempt for our authority in this region."[49] Wood's notion of orderly government had almost nothing in common with that of the Moros, and he was to use these differences to goad them into fighting him. A fearless campaigner himself, Wood finally succeeded in finding an important Moro leader on the island of Jolo, Panglima Hassan, who was prepared to take him on. When this particular bout ended, fifteen hundred Muslims were dead, many of them noncombatants, including women and children; only fifteen Americans died. The campaign could accurately be described as an exercise in wanton murder and destruction.[50] Wood persevered in his campaign to destroy anything and anybody that appeared to him to threaten American domination of Moroland. "While these measures may appear harsh," he explained, "it is the kindest thing to do."[51]

On May 12, 1905, Captain and Mrs. Andrew S. Rowan arrived at Malabang, a small port town on Illana Bay on the southern coast of Mindanao. There was a slight hitch getting off the army transport, USAT *Buford*, which had run aground,[52] but they eventually were taken to Camp Vicars, some twenty-five miles inland on a high plain overlooking Lake Lanao. The lake—created centuries earlier when a lava flow blocked a deep mountain canyon—covers 145 square miles in northwestern Mindanao.[53]

Barely a month after his arrival, Rowan was ordered to report back to Malabang at 10:00 P.M. on June 21 to meet with a board of officers to determine his fitness for promotion to major. One of the six board members was his and Josephine's friend, Captain Arthur B. Foster. Among the various matters upon which Rowan was examined was his tactical ability, as measured by a written response to a preset problem involving two evenly matched but differently composed military forces. With his understanding of terrain, his personal wartime field experience, and his latterly acquired knowledge as a maneuvers umpire, he was able to write a succinct two-page answer that was found to be perfectly acceptable by the board. On the same day he received a physical examination, which he readily passed. None of his previous black marks was deemed serious enough to disqualify him, and before the day ended the board declared him to have the "physical, moral, general efficiency and professional qualifications" to perform the duties of an infantry major in the U.S. Army. His commission was sent from Washington, D.C., on October 13, and he took his oath of office on November 28.

The plan all along was for Rowan to command the Third Battalion of his old unit, the Fifteenth Infantry Regiment, which had been stationed in the Presidio in Monterey since 1902. The Fifteenth was scheduled to leave the United States on November 7, meaning it wouldn't arrive at Mindanao until December.[54] In the meantime, Rowan continued serving with the Nineteenth. The Fifteenth Regiment eventually marched into Camp Keithley, located to the west of Lake Lanao, at 10:30 A.M. on December 11. A later writer described what they would have seen: "As one climbs the last ridge and enters Camp Keithley he is impressed by the wide open spaces and the unobstructed view across the lake and beyond. Villages on the eastern and southern shores, ten to twenty miles away, are plainly visible. Then leaping over a few miles of intervening low land, one's eyes rest upon the lofty volcanic peaks of the Butig range, which rise to an elevation of over 9,000 feet and are clothed to their unexplored summits by the densest sort of primitive dipterocarp rain forest."[55] For security reasons, vegetation had been cleared inside the camp, and barbed wire protected the perimeter,[56] but it remained a pleasant location. Josephine occupied herself with describing it poetically while Rowan attended to his duties.

Pleasant as the camp may have been, there was a war on; and on February 14 Rowan was ordered by Colonel Walter S. Scott to command Companies L, D, and H on a ten-day mission "for the purpose of arresting certain assassins said to be hiding near Orin Pass of the Butig Mountains. The assassins are protected by a band of disorderly characters and every effort will be made to capture the arms of the party and destroy it if resistance is offered."

On the morning of February 15, the men, supplied with ten days' rations (bacon, hard bread, coffee, and sugar) plus 250 rounds of ammunition per man, assembled at Marahui Wharf, where they would board two steamers to take them across the lake. Rowan, unfortunately, was drunk—not stumbling drunk, but sufficiently under the influence of alcohol that his condition was obvious to Scott when he inspected the troops. It was too late to assign another officer, so Scott permitted the mission to continue with Rowan in command. He also knew that Rowan had given explicit orders that no "intoxicating liquors," including medical restoratives, were to be carried by anyone and that when the present effects wore off, Rowan would remain sober for the remainder of the expedition. The steamers left the wharf at 2:20 P.M.

Rowan used the passage time to issue detailed orders to the commanding officers of the three companies, each of which was to act as an individual column when they marched across country to their objective. The plan worked perfectly, except their prey were long gone. The soldiers continued their march and in a few days were joined by two companies from the Nineteenth. For the remainder of their field service, which as it turned out amounted to fifteen days, they "covered a large amount of new territory hitherto unvisited by civilized man and mapped the same as well as the limited time and the single instrument, a prismatic compass, would permit." They accomplished little in the way of successful combat against the Moros, but did capture a few weapons and determined the locations of thirty-two modern rifles and pistols in the hands of hostile Moros.

The expedition, Rowan felt, could be counted a success, being as it was the initial venture into the territory by most of the officers and enlisted men. His junior officers, he thought, were too sympathetic toward the "weaklings" during the first few days out, leaving it up to him to exercise necessary discipline: "But with the hardening of the men's feet and the strengthening of their hitherto for some time unused muscles these minor difficulties disappeared and by the end of the fifteen days constant marching under difficult circumstances the command was in fine physical shape and in splendid *morale*. But as usual the wear and tear on the clothing and equipment and the absence of such commissary's luxuries, as tobacco, brought about discomfort that it should be the effort on all concerned to overcome."[57] He generally praised all the men and officers, calling special attention to a few by name. None of this prevented his catching hell from Scott, on his return, for having shown up under the influence of liquor on February 15. He was warned that a repetition of such behavior would not be tolerated. Resorting to his typical defensive sarcasm, Rowan pointed out in a response to a notation regarding the incident in his efficiency report that Scott "directed me to embark my command and proceed on my way. Evidently, he did not consider the 'influence' mentioned within, serious or he would have taken a different action."[58]

Even though rebellious activity had moderated considerably, the attractiveness of owning modern weaponry continued to tempt the Moros. On June 27 at 2:45 A.M., a sentry was seriously wounded and his Krag rifle stolen by two Moros who had easily entered the camp in the darkness.[59] This raised concern for the safety of the inhabitants of Camp Keithley, but Josephine Rowan was committed to staying with her husband until the end of his assignment. In spite of the danger of aggressive incursions into the camp, Rowan was specifically told that any troops under his command should engage in "friendly relations with the Moros living about the lake." Contact with the natives was inevitable as he led his troops on reconnaissance and mapping expeditions, as ordered by the department commander.[60] He was also appointed chief officer of a three-man board for the purpose of considering and reporting on a considerable enlargement of the camp.

Unfortunately Rowan repeated what seems to have been a congenital problem—that of publicly criticizing his fellow officers. In this case he was confined to quarters for "remarks reflecting upon the Commanding officers and officers of the garrison." A court of inquiry required him to apologize to a Captain W. A. Cavanaugh, and this, judging from previous behavior, would have irked Rowan no end.

Anticipating his departure in 1907, Rowan applied for duty in recruiting detail and somehow managed to have Senator Proctor write a favorable recommendation to fellow Vermonter Major General Frederic C. Ainsworth, who had recently taken over the office of adjutant general.[61] It did the trick: when the Rowans left Mindanao in March 1907, they knew the next assignment would take them to New York City.

Josephine was sport enough to pass a two-year tour of duty with Rowan under the comparatively primitive conditions at Camp Keithley, but she saw no reason to spend their journey back to the States in anything but first-class accommodations. They stayed for two nights at the Delmonico Hotel in Manila, one of only two hotels in that city favored by military officers—if they could afford it, and Josephine could—before sailing to Hong Kong.[62] Josephine had bought few personal items on Mindanao, where there was little to buy, but she made up for it in Hong Kong, for the most part buying clothes from such establishments as the City of Paris ("The only place in town employing Parisian dressmakers exclusively"). She bought porcelain, buttons, a silver purse, a clock, and more, eventually filling six large pieces of luggage. Over the next few weeks they traveled to Yokohama, Hakome, Tokyo, Kobe, Miyahima, and Nagasaki, where they stayed in the better hotels, such as the Imperial in Tokyo. From Nagasaki they sailed to San Francisco aboard the Japanese-owned steamer *Hong Kong Maru*, which three years previously, during the Russo-Japanese War, had been temporarily refitted as an armed cruiser. Josephine's circle back in San Francisco had been apprised of the couple's travel plans and were looking forward to her return in May.

After their arrival, Josephine remained in San Francisco renewing her society friendships while Rowan left almost immediately for Atchison to assist in the settling of his deceased first wife's estate. From

Atchison he traveled to New York to take up his post with the Coney Island recruiting office. Josephine left San Francisco on June 28 to join him, but their anticipated new life lasted only a few months. As a major with considerable experience, Rowan was too valuable an asset to leave outside the active military system. In October he learned that he was to be ordered to rejoin the Fifteenth Regiment, which, on its return from the Philippines, was sent to Fort Douglas, Utah, outside Salt Lake City. Rowan would once again take command of the Third Battalion. He reported for duty on December 19.

When Rowan arrived, the duty was fairly routine with considerable emphasis on training. The hitches of five hundred members of the Fifteenth expired in 1908, and they were replaced by new recruits. Rowan, his fellow officers, and an experienced cadre of noncommissioned officers succeeded in training them to the degree that they excelled in army rifle competitions.[63] In spite of a continuing drinking problem, Rowan managed to receive "good" to "excellent" ratings in various categories on his yearly efficiency reports.[64]

Josephine, never one to sit on her hands, busied herself in Salt Lake City with organizing a reading room for the blind, which opened on September 14, 1908.[65] Not having as wide a circle of friends as in San Francisco left Josephine free to edit and retype the scores of poems she had written over the years; while in Mindanao she had been enchanted with the exotic scenery and cranked out poem after poem describing the country and its inhabitants. Among the twenty-five or so American periodicals received in the camp was *Harper's New Monthly*,[66] edited by Henry Mills Alden, whom Rowan had met in Cuba. Presuming on that acquaintanceship, he submitted one of Josephine's poems along with a cover letter reminding Alden of their meeting. Alden remembered him well ("What days they were—those of 98!") but declined Josephine's lines on Lake Lanao, explaining, "Descriptive verse is never in our line."[67] There were, however, other periodicals that favored her sort of poetry, and while in Salt Lake City Josephine managed to place a few pieces in such magazines as *Outdoor Life* and *Lippincott's*.[68]

The population of Salt Lake City at the time was less than half that of San Francisco's. Compared culturally, the fraction would be considerably less. It certainly wasn't the stimulating environment Josephine had known all her life, and if the Rowans were to stay put, they could expect only more of the same. There were other possibilities. Growing tensions in the Far East would probably result in the Fifteenth's being sent back to Asia.[69] At age fifty-seven, Rowan was not inclined for camp life, and Josephine, three years his senior, had even less such inclination. More than likely, his health would have precluded his being sent anyway. In 1908 he was present sick or reported sick eighty-one days, suffering from chronic laryngitis and acute adenitis (swollen lymph glands).

Another possible future was indicated on his June 30, 1908, efficiency report. In response to question 18, "In the event of the outbreak of war, for what class of duty is he best suited?" Rowan's commanding officer, Colonel Walter S. Scott, wrote, "General Staff."[70]

Spending the war behind a desk, perhaps in Washington, would have delighted many older officers, but it was anathema to Rowan. Over the years he had often shown disrespect for many of his superiors, but he absolutely disdained those whom he referred to as "swivel-chair" officers.[71] He finally chose the one course over which he had the most control—retirement. On October 11, 1909, with more than thirty-two years of service behind him, Rowan submitted a request for retirement to take effect December 1. It was speedily granted.

CHAPTER 11

The Complexities of Retirement

It didn't take Andrew Rowan and his wife Josephine long to get back in the swing of things after their return to San Francisco. Best of all, Elizabeth was able to join them. It was the first time since her father left for Cuba in 1898 that she was able to live with him in an established residence. Fresh out of a finishing school on the Hudson River, she joined her father and stepmother at their new home at 1036 Vallejo Street on the summit of Russian Hill.[1]

From the time of her mother's death in 1903 and going off to school in New York, Elizabeth had been raised by her grandfather and an aunt, her grandmother having died in 1900. "Billie," as she was known to her friends, quickly took her place among the city's young socialites, even though she nearly missed that year's social season. The next summer it was announced that she was to be one of 1910's debutantes. But, alas, it was never to happen. While visiting Yosemite Park that July, she met one Thurman Alden DeBolt of Los Angeles, a former yell leader at Stanford University, and the couple became secretly engaged. DeBolt, who had graduated the previous year and was at the time working toward a law degree, was exactly the sort of young man Rowan had no stomach for. On a Monday night in August, after Billie and DeBolt informed him of their intentions, Rowan—perhaps in his cups, perhaps not—threw one of his classic tantrums and ordered DeBolt out of the house. Billie, who was no wimp herself, stood up for her young lover and was also ordered to leave. First thing next morning, after apparently spending the night together, Billie and Thurman obtained a wedding license. Billie then returned to the house for her clothes, and before the day was over the couple was married. After spending a couple of nights at the St. Francis Hotel, they left for Los

Angeles, where DeBolt had a job waiting for him. The story went around that they had eloped, but this was not the case. Josephine, who had come to regard Billie as a daughter—and perhaps recalling her own impetuous, yet successful, marriage to Andrew—accompanied the two young lovers to the church. Later she denied any rift between Rowan and his daughter, pointing out that Rowan had seen the couple off.[2]

It's a sign of the Rowans' status in San Francisco—and Billie's quick acceptance by her social circle—that area newspapers reported on the event the day after the wedding, including a front-page story in the *San Francisco Call*.

Exactly nine months later, another life-changing event occurred in the lives of the DeBolts, and it wasn't the birth of a child. It was the inheritance by Elizabeth of a $100,000 legacy from her grand-father, A. B. Symns, who had died six years earlier in a carriage-train accident in Hot Springs, Arkansas. This was one-fourth of his estate and the amount her mother would have inherited had she been alive, the rest of the fortune having been divided evenly among Symns's three other offspring.[3] One hundred thousand dollars was a huge amount of money in 1911, the equivalent of more than $2 million a hundred years later.

During the years following the first publication of "A Message to Garcia," Elbert Hubbard spoke at gatherings all over the country. What he talked about, of course, was himself and his organization.[4] Not everyone appreciated the subject matter. "The only man we know," went a review in the *Syracuse Standard*, "who has the supreme crust to charge a dollar for hearing him advertise his own goods." Characteris-tically, Hubbard quoted this and other barbs in the *Philistine*. "Every knock is a boost,"[5] he was fond of writing. In 1909–10 he entered the world of vaudeville with ten weeks on the Orpheum Circuit, for which he was paid $10,000.[6] A fellow vaudevillian, Sir Harry Lauder, referring to Hubbard's affected appearance, quipped, "Fra Elbertus is the only man in the profession who wears his makeup on the street."[7]

The resulting publicity from the tour—good and bad—certainly didn't hurt. Circulation of the *Philistine* jumped to 110,000,[8] the Roy-crofter shops eventually employed around five hundred people,[9] and

Hubbard estimated that he made $250,000 from sales and royalties of the "Message" alone.[10]

Hubbard had traveled far from his days growing up in Bloomington, Illinois, the son of a country doctor who, according to Hubbard, never made more than five hundred dollars a year.[11] Elbert left school at age fifteen, "with a fair hold on the three R's." That's probably true. For the rest of what he claimed regarding his youthful education we'll have to take his word.

I knew all the forest trees, all wild animals thereabout, every kind of fish, frog, fowl or bird that swam, ran or flew. I knew every kind of grain or vegetable, and its comparative value. I knew the different breeds of cattle, horses, sheep and swine.

I could teach wild cows to stand while being milked, break horses to saddle or harness; could sow, plow and reap; knew the mysteries of apple-butter, pumpkin pie, pickled beef, smoked side-meat, and could make lye at a leach and formulate soft soap.

That is to say, I was a bright, strong, active country boy who had been brought up to help his father and mother get a living for a large family.[12]

One thing never in doubt was Hubbard's skill as a salesman. At sixteen he was hired by a cousin as a door-to-door soap peddler, a profession at which he excelled. Three years later he joined his brother-in-law, John Larkin, in a breakaway soap company in Buffalo, where he perfected successful mail-order strategies involving premiums and a club plan in which the customers became the company's sales staff. As a direct result of his efforts, the company prospered; but in early 1893, eager to experience new adventures, Hubbard sold his share to Larkin for $75,000. One of his aspirations was to obtain a degree from Harvard University, but to his chagrin he found himself not qualified to be a full-time student—an experience that soured him on higher education forever. It was after this that he visited William Morris's community in England.[13]

Along the way he married Bertha Crawford, a small-town Illinoisan like himself. And he also became acquainted with Alice Moore, a woman more to his taste than Bertha and with whom he maintained a long-standing affair. His double life resulted in two daughters being born within a short time of one another, one to Bertha and the other to Alice.[14] By spring of 1894 rumors had gotten back to Bertha, and it took but little searching for her to find evidence in the form of letters from Alice.[15] Much to the delight of all those who enjoy the spectacle of a fallen moralizer, Alice sued Hubbard for child support, and soon thereafter Bertha filed for divorce. In January 1904 Elbert and Alice were married in Bridgeport, Connecticut.[16]

The growing circulation of Hubbard's essay continued to introduce its gallant hero to a new crop of readers, and even though Rowan hadn't lived in West Virginia since the time of his West Point days, many folks in that state continued to think of him as one of their own. In March 1911 a coal baron named Clarence W. Watson was appointed to the U.S. Senate from West Virginia to replace his predecessor, who died in office. One of the earliest bills—if not the first—he introduced, S. 2854, called for the "erection of a statue to commemorate the bravery of Major Andrew Summers Rowan, at the War College, Washington, District of Columbia."[17] His inspiration for this project was, of course, Hubbard's suggestion that Rowan's "form should be cast in deathless bronze." The body of the bill went on to briefly describe the carrying of President McKinley's message to Calixto García Íñiguez. As a matter of course it was referred to committee, and Watson tried to provide corroborating material by writing to Adjutant General Fred C. Ainsworth asking for details of Rowan's exploit, but Ainsworth wrote back noting that an exhaustive search failed to find anything; the best he could do was refer Watson to Rowan's article in *McClure's*. The chairman of the committee, George P. Wetmore, wrote to Secretary of War W. L. Stimson, who was able to give a more detailed account, but he was inclined to discourage the idea of a statue. There were, he pointed out, five vacant pedestals available for the placement of statues, and a sixth that was already occupied by Frederick the Great. It had also been proposed that statues of Ulysses S. Grant, William Tecumseh Sherman, and George Washington be placed on the college grounds.[18] "It is not," he wrote, "undervaluing the distinguished services of Lt. Rowan to say that they were not such as to entitle him to be classed with the soldiers mentioned." Furthermore, he reminded Wetmore that there was a "sort of unwritten law in this country against erecting memorials to living persons" (a policy that, it should be noted, is today sometimes overlooked).[19]

Rowan had been occupying himself during this period by writing a history of Mexico; he devoted two years to the project. And in February 1913, while staying at the Army and Navy Club during a visit to Washington, D.C., he sent a query letter to Henry Holt and Company, addressing it to Holt's son Roland, offering him the opportunity to publish his soon-to-be-completed manuscript. Holt had published Rowan and M. M. Morrison's book on Cuba, and Rowan justifiably felt he had a fair shot. Two years earlier when he began writing the book, his instinct had been good; but with the Mexican Revolution now in full swing, his timing was late.

Rather than going into details of the book's contents, Rowan's plan was to type a copy of the preface and send only that, reassuring Holt in his cover letter that there was "no better history of Mexico than mine"; his working title was *A Pragmatic History of Mexico*. He wouldn't have intended the modern popular definition of *pragmatic*—"practical in the sense of getting things done"—but a meaning current at the time: "relating or pertaining to the affairs of a community."[20] The situation in Mexico was changing more rapidly than he had anticipated. President William Howard Taft had just ordered three more battleships sent there, to be followed by two troop transports filled with soldiers to protect U.S. citizens should that become necessary. The revolution and the U.S. response were probably the only topics of conversation among the military men in the club's dining room, and Rowan decided to save time by sending the original of the preface, adding a handwritten postscript to his letter pointing out the "necessity of prompt publication." After his first publishing experience, he should have been aware of the ponderously slow procedure for transforming a manuscript into a printed book. He remembered only the cordial treatment he'd received fifteen years earlier and somehow got it in his mind that Roland Holt would reply by return mail. When he'd heard nothing after a week, he assumed that Holt must be out of town and wrote a second letter, this time asking that his preface—the only existing copy—be returned immediately. He was to be on the East Coast only a short while longer and wanted to find a publisher before returning to California.

Roland Holt was not out of town. He simply hadn't gotten around to reading the material, but he did so the day Rowan's frantic second letter arrived. Sad to say, he found it "uninteresting" and thought Rowan was planning to devote a "disproportionate amount of space to Cortez." Rowan received a polite rejection, and he returned to California.[21]

This wasn't his only disappointment while in Washington. He learned, in between his two letters to Holt, that an appointment for which he'd been lobbying—to be an active colonel in the infantry—had been turned down.[22] In a routine two-page report prepared by the office of the chief of staff for the War Department, all the positive episodes in Rowan's military record were described—but so were details of the many negatives, among them drunkenness, insubordination, and insulting behavior toward fellow officers. Had Rowan not retired, he would have been thirty-first in line for promotion to colonel. The officer writing the report found "nothing so exceptional" in his record to warrant even his reappointment to active duty in his previous rank, let alone promoting him over the heads of thirty others: "There are in the papers in his case indications of an unfortunate temperament which unfits him to command a regiment."[23]

It is the custom for retired military officers to retain, at least as a title, their highest rank achieved. It could be argued that because Rowan was a lieutenant colonel with the U.S. volunteers from May 31, 1898 to March 15, 1899, he was entitled during retirement to be referred to by that rank. His written name, then, would be Lt. Col. (Ret.) Andrew S. Rowan. Also following custom, he could be addressed simply as "colonel"—as in, "Good morning, colonel." This distinction was lost on the general public, and in the popular press he was increasingly referred to as "Col. Rowan." Thus, though turned down by the army, he managed to obtain a "folk promotion."

Word of the unfavorable report would have circulated quickly through the small military enclave in Washington, and this probably accounts for Rowan's eagerness to return to California; having meals in the Army and Navy Club dining room would not have been a pleasant experience. Yet he was not prepared to give up. Through the years he had made many friends and acquaintances, some of whom were proud to be on speaking terms with the man who carried the message to García.

Someone put a bug in the collective ear of the Richmond County (Staten Island) chapter of the Daughters of the American Revolution, and in December 1913 the corresponding secretary wrote to Secretary of War Lindley M. Garrison, expressing the chapter's amazement upon learning that Rowan had never been advanced in rank beyond major. The women asked to be informed of the "reason for this apparent neglect to reward a very brave deed," and were shortly thereafter notified of Rowan's retirement. While the members of the chapter appreciated the secretary's prompt and courteous reply, they remained unsatisfied. Writing back on January 14, they wanted to know "whether Major Rowan received *any reward whatsoever* from the U.S. Government for his services in carrying a message to Garcia. . . . If he did, what was the nature of that reward? Were his services acknowledged in *any* way. An early answer will greatly oblige." Presumably they were eventually mollified, and in a timely manner, because there is no record of their having made any further demands on the secretary of war.[24]

In April a new campaign began. On April 23 Senator John Sharp Williams of Mississippi received a telegram from an acquaintance and constituent, F. G. Jones of Jackson, who happened to be in San Francisco at the time. According to Jones, Rowan had been recommended—he didn't say by whom—to be brigadier general in command of a West Virginia brigade. "I have known Rowan personally for many years past and feel that he is an efficient and capable officer and will give extreme efficiency to the position offered." He asked Williams to promote Rowan's appointment by speaking to his senate colleague, William Chilton. Williams had no idea what Jones was talking about, but dutifully passed the telegram on to Chilton, noting that he was acquainted with Jones, whom he considered "all right."

Why the need of a West Virginia brigade? The revolution in Mexico was still going strong, and the likelihood of American intervention was increasing. As in the Spanish-American War, there were certain to be thousands of volunteers who would want to participate. Theodore Roosevelt, who was in South America, was already planning a new cavalry brigade that he would lead into Mexico. He told an American official that he had only one proviso: that there should be "a real war and not a mere exchange of bloodless talk between President Wilson and Gen. Huerta."[25]

With each incremental incident, the possibility of war increased, and Rowan wanted to be a part of it and to be bumped up a few notches. He, too, had written to Chilton, perhaps hoping that two years after the fact Chilton might have forgotten the negative report that resulted from his previous attempt. Whether Chilton had forgotten or not, he wrote again to the secretary of war: "He is now in fine health, has a splendid knowledge of Mexico and the Spanish language, and wants to serve his country." And there were others who wrote to their influential friends in government, but all to no avail. Rowan was not called to duty.

In January 1915 Billie DeBolt was back in the news, this time because she was filing for divorce. At first she claimed that her only difference with her husband Thurmond was her love for Paris and his for the United States. Her husband was, she said, a "charming and interesting man for whom I have the highest regard"; the divorce was only a matter of "convenience." Rumors of a divorce had been circulating since February of the previous year when the couple had ceased living together. Some months later Billie traveled to Europe without Thurmond. The start of World War I interrupted her stay in Paris, and it was shortly after her return that she began divorce proceedings, much to the titillation of San Francisco's society page readers. The story even made the *Washington Post*.

It seems that Thurmond DeBolt regarded her inheritance as lottery winnings and saw no sense spending his relative youth earning a living. It's also quite probable that he had learned of Billie's prospective inheritance before marrying her, and this is what had prompted him to propose. "Time and again," Billie testified, "I urged him to go to work and do something, but he didn't seem to pay any attention to me." When the judge asked if she wanted alimony, she replied, "I couldn't collect any." The judge warned her that she would never be able to collect a dime, even if DeBolt inherited a fortune, and she said, "I will take my chances." She didn't add that as a wealthy young woman she didn't need it.

When the divorce was granted in May, the *Oakland Tribune* ran a front-page story with the headline, "'Rah! Rah!' Boy Loses Bride" with the subhead, "'Message to Garcia' Maid Repenting Elopement, Is Divorced." One can imagine Rowan's reaction to all the publicity. He did sit in the courtroom during the proceedings, no doubt feeling vindicated for his behavior five years earlier when he'd thrown Thurmond out of the house.[26]

Rowan did have at least one pleasant distraction during the foofaraw surrounding the divorce. Along with everybody else in San Francisco, he visited the Panama-Pacific International Exposition, which opened in March. He had the added pleasure of being invited to, and participating in, the dedication of the Cuban Pavilion on April 10. Some months previous he'd been part of the ceremony during which the site was turned over to the special commissioner from Cuba, José Portuondo y Tamayo, one of General García's staff members, whom Rowan had last met in Bayamo.[27]

During the last quarter of the nineteenth century, many European nations followed the Prussian lead in creating huge standing armies supplemented with vast numbers of well-trained reservists. Britain, though not having well-equipped land forces, raced with Germany in building a large navy. Such preparations could lead in only one direction, and it took but one incident for the inevitable to occur. That happened on June 28, 1914, with the assassination of Archduke Ferdinand in Sarajevo. By late summer the promise of an ever more glorious age of enlightenment and progress was canceled as the biggest war the world had, until that time, ever known spread across the continent. Americans, though strongly sympathetic with the cause of the Allies— chiefly France, Great Britain, and Russia—remained neutral, in theory at least.[28] A great deal of the activity at sea involved the prevention of war materials being shipped to either one side or the other. The British relied on strong blockades to stop the ships; the Germans used submarines to sink them.[29]

On May 2, 1915, the Cunard luxury liner RMS *Lusitania* left New York bound for London. Two of the passengers aboard were Elbert and Alice Hubbard.[30] They might not have gone but for the help of President Woodrow Wilson. Incredibly enough, in November 1912 Hubbard had been indicted by a federal grand jury on six counts under the so-called Comstock Act, a law passed in 1873 to suppress *"the Trade In, and Circulation of, Obscene Literature and Articles of Immoral Use."* The last phrase referred to objects and information relating to birth control and abortion. Hubbard's crime, in the eyes of the government, was to include in various issues of the *Philistine* "certain matters . . . of an obscene, lewd, lascivious, filthy and indecent character."[31] Hubbard loved word play and couldn't resist the temptations of the double entendre.

There were those for whom the incident provided a moment of schadenfreude, such as with a writer in the *Oakland Tribune*, who wrote, "The other day the most popular idealist in all the country was indicted for sending obscene matter through the mails. . . . Hubbard writes like a man in whom double entendre has become an irremedial infirmity. Coprolitic witticisms drop from his lips as easily as slime from the man who has just emerged from a cesspool. He bemerds his readers and himself with a gusto that betrays a proneness to rank and unsavory thought. It is no wonder that he was indicted; but what a shock to his worshipers!"[32] One of the specifics in this case involved a short piece he'd written about a stenographer named Miss Mary Merryseat. Another item—a silly joke—had a direct reference to a birth control method and a cuckolded husband. Hubbard's flouting of the law was considered so serious, according to one report, that the federal authorities fully intended to give him "a hair cut"—which is to say, send him to prison. If he were to be found guilty on all six counts, he could serve a minimum of three years.[33] Fortunately, his lawyer had been alerted by a colleague of a plan to arrest Hubbard in Erie, Pennsylvania, and he helped Hubbard evade the federal officers sent there to apprehend him. Habbard took it on the lam to Buffalo, where he was allowed to plead guilty before a federal judge who was inclined to be lenient. He fined Hubbard one hundred dollars for one offense and gave him suspended sentences on the other five in exchange for a guarantee that there would be no further violations.

This was fine until Hubbard applied for a passport. He learned that as long as he had the suspended sentences hanging over him, he had lost many of his rights as a citizen and was forbidden to leave the country. Who knew what he might do next? Once free of the restrictions of the Comstock Act, he might choose the life of a fugitive pornographer and publish obscenities around the world. This is where Woodrow Wilson came in. As a hard-nosed Presbyterian,[34] Wilson may have thought the outlandish Hubbard deserved being punished for his outré behavior. In any event, he turned down the request for a pardon on the grounds that not enough time had passed since the trial. Hubbard tried again, and the second time was successful in being granted a full pardon.[35]

At this stage in his career, Hubbard was his own best product, selling his name to whoever would pay the price. When he created advertisements for large corporations, he signed them as if they were works of art. It was a short step to writing paid advertising disguised as essays. He had become, as one writer put it, the "Voice of American Business."[36] According to Upton Sinclair, Hubbard was paid five hundred dollars by Chicago meat packers for a widely disseminated negative review of Sinclair's *The Jungle*.[37] In 1914 he solicited money from John D. Rockefeller Jr. in exchange for an article in *The Fra* presenting the Rockefellers' side in a miners' strike at the Colorado Fuel and Iron Company. In this case it didn't work; the Rockefellers declined the offer.[38]

Like the rest of the passengers aboard the HRMS *Lusitania*, the Hubbards had blithely disregarded a recent ad placed in the *New York Times* by the German embassy. It warned travelers planning an Atlantic voyage that "vessels flying the flag of Great Britain, or any of her allies, are liable to destruction."[39] Hubbard told reporters before sailing that the Kaiser would probably like to make him "look like a piece of Swiss cheese" because of some insulting remarks he had written about the German leader—as if the Kaiser were one of the *Philistine*'s faithful readers.[40]

The *Lusitania* left the dock at 12:30 P.M. on May 1, 1915, and the German submarine *U-20*, with Kapitänleutnant Rudolf Schneider in command, torpedoed the ship at 4:10 p.m. on May 7. Among the 1,198 passengers and crewmen who perished were 139 Americans, including Mr. and Mrs. Elbert Hubbard. More individuals could have been saved if the ship had not sunk in just eighteen minutes. The *Lusitania* was a large ship, 785 feet long and weighing 30,395 tons; a single torpedo shouldn't have had that effect. A second explosion was heard, and some assumed it was a second torpedo; others thought it was a boiler bursting. According to Schneider's log, which there is no reason not to believe, he fired only one torpedo. In spite of British denials, the explosion heard was probably the ten tons of explosive powder contained in the 4.2 million cartridges that had been secretly stowed aboard the ship before leaving New York.[41]

After the explosion, Ernest C. Cowper, a Canadian reporter who had become friendly with the Hubbards, passed by them on the boat deck as they stood with arms linked together. Hubbard, who had been certain the Germans would not sink a ship filled with women, children, and noncombatants, said to him, "They have got us. They are a damn sight worse than I ever thought they were." The last that Cowper saw of the couple was as they entered a room on the top deck and closed the door behind them. For all his bombast, Hubbard and his worshipful wife spent their last minutes in as dignified a manner as possible.[42]

Early rumors of the sinking were discounted, but by afternoon, with definite confirmation, the dreadful fact took its toll. There was room for little else in the newspapers as every fact and supposition remotely related to the disaster was reported from various angles. Wall Street "shook from center to circumference," and stocks dropped sharply. Politicians, editorial writers, and average citizens wanted something done. Roosevelt called the sinking "an act of simple piracy . . . accompanied by murder on a vaster scale than any oldtime pirate had ever practiced before being hung for his misdeeds" and insisted that action should be taken "without an hour's unnecessary delay."[43]

Between arguments and counterarguments as the nation gradually prepared for a war it didn't want, there was still room for America's 100 million souls to tend to their personal lives. On October 22 Elizabeth DeBolt set about normalizing her life by joining with a new husband in the office of a justice of the peace in Greenwich, Connecticut. To avoid publicity she claimed to be the daughter of a certain Andrew Rowan who lived in Brooklyn. Rowan had lived in Brooklyn while stationed at the Coney Island recruiting office, and that is perhaps why she chose that particular locale. The ruse worked for a couple of weeks; it wasn't until November 5 that the story appeared in the *Oakland Tribune* and, being stale news by then, it warranted only four short paragraphs on an inside page.

Lieutenant Joseph Mason Deem was the sort of son-in-law Rowan could approve of. A graduate of the U.S. Naval Academy at Annapolis, class of 1909, he had been appointed commander of the 161-foot G-class submarine SS *Seal* the previous February and was stationed in New London, Connecticut. It is uncertain how and when Mrs. DeBolt and Lieutenant Deem met. The submarine with Deem in command left New York the previous March for a cruise on Chesapeake Bay, followed by stays in Charleston, South Carolina, and Newport, Rhode Island, before returning to New London on October 18, just four days before the wedding. After her return to Paris, according to one news report, Billie had made the decision to remain temporarily in New York and to conduct her affairs by telegraph. Once matters were concluded, she planned to return to Paris, war or no war. Of course, this was all pre-*Lusitania* thinking. It was also before meeting Lieutenant Deem, who, by coincidence, happened to be stationed in New York at the same time as she was conducting her affairs by telegraph.[44]

The following March, when General John J. Pershing entered Mexico with 6,600 men in pursuit of Pancho Villa,[45] Rowan was still sitting atop Russian Hill twiddling his thumbs, his familiarity with Mexico, his knowledge of Spanish, and his combat command experience all going to waste. He had heard that in the event of war with Mexico he might be given a desk job. Still not wanting that fate, he pitched himself again on April 18, this time to a new secretary of war, Newton D. Baker, writing, "To place, as is proposed, a man of my physique, health, experience and service on a swivel chair, as a watchman at an abandoned post in the middle of the continent, and, at the same time, to send to the front inexperienced officers, however capable, in high command seems to me taking an unnecessary risk at the country's expense." On the same day he also wrote to the adjutant general, tendering his service with the troops "in case they are needed." He mentioned his overland travel through Mexico after leaving Guatemala and said he was working on a history of Mexico for which he was creating his own maps and "otherwise, keeping in touch with the topography of that country." No longer was he shooting for brigadier general, but he did ask that he be given the rank he would have held had he remained on the active list—namely, that of colonel of infantry. A reply from the adjutant general's office informed him that his letter had been received and would be filed for reference "in event that the services of retired officers shall be needed."[46] An optimist could make something of that.

Among Thomas A. Edison's many ventures was his production of short nonfiction films of both everyday occurrences and important events, such as McKinley's inauguration in 1897 and the preparations for war in 1898. As the public lost interest in "actualities," as such films are referred to by historians, he turned to drama and adventure films. One of these was the five-reel *A Message to Garcia* directed by Richard Ridgely and released in 1916. Elbert Hubbard is given credit as the writer, but the film bears as little resemblance to his essay as the essay did to Rowan's adventure. Shot for the most part in Cuba, it covers considerably more ground than the essay, including the sinking of the *Maine* (photographed in miniature) and footage of General Valeriano "The Butcher" Weyler y Nicolau, played by Ray Fairchild. A treacherous Spanish spy, Rosa Gonzales (Helen Strickland) attempts to subvert Rowan (Robert Conness), but he is aided by a young Cuban woman named Dolores (Mabel Trunnelle), and it is she who helps him complete his mission. According to a review in the *Reno Evening Gazette*, "[the movie] shows shootings and fighting and escapes and all that sort of thing, but the heroine shines through it all. Miss Trunnelle is a mighty pretty girl on or off the screen."[47] Dolores eventually gives her life so that Rowan might deliver his message to García. One can only imagine Rowan's reaction. Perhaps this is one of the reasons he was so eager over the next twenty years to retell the story himself.

The year 1916 brought an election, and Woodrow Wilson managed to hold onto his job as president due in part to the slogan, "He kept us out of war," even though he personally felt it misrepresented his position. And as peace advocates and war proponents battled it out in Congress and in the press, Wilson took measures to improve the country's military might.[48] Finally, after one German transgression after another, the Congress assembled on the night of April 2, 1917, in a capitol building guarded outside by the Second Cavalry and inside by swarms of Secret Service agents and police, to listen to President Wilson deliver his war message. Among his recommendations was to create an army of 100,000 men in addition to the already existing regular army and national guard units.[49] Major Rowan, just about to turn sixty, desperately wanted to be among them.

A week earlier when it was all but certain the United States would join the war, Senator William E. Chilton, still willing to champion Rowan's cause, wrote to Secretary of War Newton Baker to remind him of the many endorsements on file recommending Rowan as a brigadier general and even major general of volunteer forces in case of war: "His message to Garcia, if no other services, deserves recognition, and I shall be most sincerely pleased if this son of West Virginia can be recognized and given active service. I wished to take up this matter with you personally, but at these times you are so overworked that I hesitate to encroach on your time." Even in such hectic times, letters from senators were answered, and Chilton was duly informed by someone in the adjutant general's office that his letter was "placed on file for consideration in the event that a volunteer army shall be called into service." William M. Ingraham, the assistant secretary of war, also wrote to Chilton, saying the recommendation had been passed along to the president. When Rowan learned of this, he wrote Ingraham, "I am as ready now to go forward at the President's command in any capacity desired as I was when called upon by Mr. McKinley to go to Cuba."[50]

He never heard back.

Roosevelt experienced the same fate. He was still fondling his plan to organize a new cavalry unit, now stepped up to a division or more, though he wanted to lead only one of its brigades. For months he pictured in his mind the exact configuration it would take, including the particular individuals he would recruit. Every time he brought the subject up to Baker, he heard pretty much the same as Rowan: "Thanks. Don't call us, we'll call you." And, as with Rowan, he never got the call. When he finally appealed directly to Wilson, whom he'd vilified over and over in recent years, he was rebuffed.[51]

In the meantime Rowan had been approached by a publisher in Boston— Small, Maynard and Company—to write his personal account of his journey to Cuba. This, then, was to be his contribution to the war effort and he gave it a ponderously long title, more typical of the nineteenth century than of the twentieth:

How I Carried President Mckinley's Message to García

The Military Results and the Civil Consequences
A Twice Told Tale
Addressed
To American Soldiers and Sailors of Two Wars
and
To All Americans
Who Wish God-Speed to Their Brothers
In Jungle or Trench
On Land and Sea

After some historical background, Rowan launched into a self-serving, sometimes florid account, complete with classical allusions and reflective digressions. For the most part he expanded on the *McClure's* article of eighteen years earlier, though he was not above borrowing from Hubbard's fantasy version: "Wagner is said to have replied to the President, 'There's a fellow by the name of Rowan, will find García for you if anybody can.' "[52] There is one passing reference to Louis A.

Dent, the American consul, and not a word of Associated Press reporter Elmer Roberts.

Rowan had never forgiven General Henry Corbin for the sharply worded telegram Corbin had sent him in Tampa, Florida. It had been an embarrassing moment and had taken the glow off his triumphant return. He'd kept the original copy and at some later date penciled a note across the bottom: "Corbin denied to me that he'd ever authorized any such telegram. It was probably dished up by the contemptible Major Wm. H. Carter his underling and who became a major genl— God save the [undecipherable]."[53] Rowan's referring to Carter as "contemptible" may have had more to do with the man's achievements than with any specific wrongs he'd committed. Carter, who had graduated from West Point eight years before Rowan, had been awarded a Medal of Honor for "distinguished bravery in action against hostile Apache Indians" after rescuing wounded soldiers while under heavy fire. He was a respected military reformer, a well-known contributor to periodicals and encyclopedias, and, for a while, Rowan's commanding officer in the Visayas. But perhaps his most egregious sin was having been called back to active service in 1916 at age sixty-five to serve as a "swivel-chair officer" during the Great War. Worse yet, he was awarded a Distinguished Service Medal for his efforts.[54]

Corbin died in 1909, leaving Rowan free to attack him viciously. Not mentioning him by name, but assuming anyone who mattered would know who he meant, Rowan accused Corbin of everything from cowardice in battle to cheating at cards. Furthermore, according to Rowan, Corbin, who had been a personal friend of Rutherford B. Hayes, usurped presidential powers, forged another general's name on official documents, and was overwhelmingly blackballed from an exclusive club in Washington in spite of being endorsed by the president and secretary of state. The club's members "evidently did not cherish the idea of having their pockets picked by an established jackleg even at the behest of high government officials. . . . However, this swivel-chair general was not through with me." It will be remembered that it was Corbin, while still adjutant general, who put the kibosh on Rowan's receiving the Medal of Honor; this was another nettle. Rowan admitted he was never under fire in Cuba, but "evidently, the swivel-chair expected me to attack the 216,000 Spaniards with my little Smith and Wesson." He was mentioning these incidents, he wrote (perhaps disingenuously), "in the interest of the faithful verity of history"; it was nothing personal. The manuscript, which would have amounted to little more than a hundred pages in book form, was never published.[55]

During this same period, he wrote a 4,500-word essay titled "Pacifism and Its Cure—Universal Training." Part jeremiad, part appeal to patriotism, and part strategic policy analysis, the piece was written in reaction to an article in the May 1918 *Atlantic Monthly* titled "The Pacifist at War" by the psychologist Henry Rutgers Marshall. Never mentioning the author, Rowan responded to the title, commenting, "Of course, there is no such thing, for as soon as a pacifist goes to war he becomes a patriot. A patriot is one who obeys without question the call of his country in peace and in war; a pacifist is one who would unsex his country in time of peace so as to deprive it of virility in time of war thus inviting war." He went on to dissect various of Marshall's assertions.[56] There's no record of the article's being published, though it most certainly would have been submitted somewhere.

He had previously spoken out on the matter of the peace movement and disarmament. In 1914, while addressing a manufacturers' luncheon in Oakland, he charged that Andrew Carnegie and David Starr Jordan "have started and fostered a fad that is stripping this country of its defenses and is spreading the seeds of helplessness. These are popgun policies. . . . This nation may soon be in a strange position: robbed of its soldiers and its fighting spirit, a situation that we will regret only too late when grave peril threatens us."

By 1922 the Rowans were spending their summer months in a second home they'd built in Mill Valley, a small town across the Golden Gate from San Francisco. The quiet isolation of the rustic summer home at One Rowan Way, a short street in the Blithedale Canyon high above the village, contrasted sharply with their crowded Russian Hill neighborhood.[57] Rowan was even able to enjoy relaxing in a prototype of a modern hot tub—an earthen mound behind the house lined with concrete—in which he soaked in water heated by the sun.[58] Much as he liked the tranquility of the place—and for all his celebrated modesty—he seems never to have turned down an invitation to speak to any group that would have him. The Golden Gate Bridge was yet to be built, but ferry service was frequent, and Rowan often made the trip back to San Francisco and points beyond to retell the details of his adventure. Nor did he overlook the locals, and according to an article in the *Mill Valley Record*, he was applauded "with all the lust and zeal that enthusiastic youth can give" after speaking to the students at an Old Mill School assembly.[59]

That same year there was a strong movement to have Rowan officially, if belatedly, acknowledged with a suitable award for embarking on his famous mission. Eighty-three-year-old Lieutenant General Nelson A. Miles made three trips to the War Department on Rowan's behalf, speaking personally with Secretary of War John W. Weeks and leaving with him his letter of recommendation. Fully aware of how things work in Washington, Miles wrote to Rowan, "If you happen to know a senator or congressman it might be well for him to follow it up."[60] And so it came to pass that Rowan gained a new advocate in the U.S. Senate, Samuel M. Shortridge, a former lawyer in San Francisco. Shortridge was assured by Weeks that he would discuss with army officials the matter of awarding a distinguished service cross to Rowan for carrying a "message to Garcia."

On July 21, 1922, twenty-four years after the event, the War Department announced the award.[61] Furthermore, Rowan was also awarded a Silver Citation Star in recognition of having placed the field gun on Sudlon Mountain in January 1900 that so impressed Colonel Edward J. McClernand.[62] During a ceremony on August 28 at Fort Winfield Scott in the western portion of the Presidio, a battalion of coast artillerymen stood at attention as Brigadier General Chase W. Kennedy pinned the award on Rowan's chest.[63] His receiving the Distinguished Service Cross (DSC) qualified him for admittance into the Army and Navy Legion of Valor, an organization formed in 1890 by recipients of the Medal of Honor and later expanded to include winners of the DSC and the Navy Cross. In a press interview Rowan noted it was a good thing the medal was gold. "If the cross was iron it would have rusted away by now," he said. "Anyhow, what did I do to deserve it? 'Distinguished service' by a soldier or anyone else is to do well what he is ordered to do. In the old days we did not expect medals and stars and crosses. It was after our forces played a good part in the world war that we learned the graceful art of accepting decorations. However, I acknowledge that when every one else was being beribboned I felt a true part of it."[64] He was also not averse to blowing a few toots himself. In the months leading up to the award he spent a good deal of time rewriting his unpublished manuscript. The title was shortened to "How I Carried the Message to Garcia," and it lacked any attacks on Adjutant General Corbin. In the revised version, barely a third as long as the first draft and closer in tone to the *McClure's* article, one can detect the sure hand of a professional copy editor. Even lines borrowed from Hubbard are recast in standard English. For example, in response to McKinley's fictional question, "Where can I find a man who will carry a message to Garcia?" Major Wagner says, "There is a young officer here in Washington: a lieutenant named Rowan, who will carry it for you." The pamphlet was dedicated "to my wife, Josephine Morris Rowan."[65]

By this time Rowan had repeatedly denied carrying a physical message, but as an integral part of his life, the phrase could not be abandoned. In this new account of Rowan's receiving his instructions in the Army and Navy Club, Arthur L. Wagner, who had at the time recently turned forty-five, says to Rowan, who would soon turn forty, "Young man . . . you have been selected by the President to communicate with—or rather, to carry a message to—General Garcia, who will be found somewhere in the eastern part of Cuba." And, after a final handshake, "Get that message to Garcia!" The phrase continues popping up throughout the text until the final sentence, "I had carried my message to Garcia."

In this version of his journey Rowan added some exciting incidents that hadn't appeared in the *McClure's* article nor in any previously written descriptions of his trip. They weren't included in the highly detailed account written in 1917 or in a later official report written for the adjutant general. In the *McClure's* piece Gervasio Savio "had figured out the time-table" of the Spanish *lanches* along the Cuban coast and managed to avoid them. In the new version Rowan and his boatmates have an encounter with one:

A few miles away one of the dreaded lanches was bearing directly toward us.

A sharp command in Spanish and the crew dropped the sail. Another, and all save Gervacio, who was at the helm, were below the gunwale, and he was lounging over the tiller, keeping the boat's nose parallel with the Jamaican shore.

"He may think I am a 'lone fisherman' from Jamaica and go by us," said the cool-headed steersman.

So it proved. When within hailing distance the pert young commander of the lancha cried in Spanish: "Catching anything?" To which my guide responded, also in Spanish: "No, the miserable fish are not biting this morning!"

If only that midshipman, or whatever his rank, had been wise enough to lay alongside, he surely would have "caught something," and this story would never have been written.[66]

There was another close call while traveling to Bayamo when Rowan and his guides nearly collided with a detachment of Spanish soldiers: "I cocked my rifle and swung my Smith & Wesson into position for quick action and waited tensely for what was to follow." Fortunately, the Spaniards had not detected their presence, and a firefight was avoided. However, there was an even closer call later on. Some Spanish deserters had joined the Cubans, and Rowan was immediately suspicious of them:

Who could say that one or more of them might not leave camp at any time and warn the Spanish officials that an American was crossing Cuba, evidently bound for the camp of General Garcia? Would not the enemy make every effort to thwart him in his mission? So I said to Gervacio:

"Question these men closely and see that they do not leave camp during our stay!"

"Si, Senor!" was the reply.[67]

This more or less agrees with the account written in 1917, but the following near calamity appears in print for the first time in 1922:

I was awakened some time after midnight by the challenge of a sentinel, followed by a shot, and almost instantly a shadowy form appeared close by my hammock. I sprang up and out on the opposite side just as another form appeared and in less time than it takes to write it the first one had fallen as the result of a blow from a machete, which cut through the bones of his right shoulder to the lung. The wretch lived long enough to tell us that it was agreed if his comrade failed to get out of camp, he should kill me and prevent the carrying out of whatever project I was engaged in. The sentinel shot and killed the comrade.[68]

If Rowan had included these incidents in the *McClure's* article, he might have gotten his Medal of Honor, but they would have been at variance with what he'd told reporters in Tampa. To them he'd said that he'd seen no Spaniards. In mid-April 1922, in an account of his journey submitted to the office of the adjutant general, Rowan specifically mentioned, for the first time, meeting up with some Spanish deserters from whom he acquired information of "doubtful value," but not one word about an attack on his life—an unlikely omission.[69] It appears obvious these new adventures were inventions inserted over the years to add excitement to his story as he retold it to schoolchildren and fraternal organizations. Aníbal Escalante Beatón, who was present when Rowan arrived in Bayamo, recalled things differently; he claimed that any Spanish war vessels in the vicinity had completely abandoned their vigilance along the southwestern coast of Cuba for fear of meeting up with Admiral William Sampson's squadron. Furthermore, he said the mountainous area of Cuba they crossed was totally inaccessible to Spanish soldiers. The only attack Rowan endured, he reported, was from "*miradas de mosquitos y jenes* (black flies)." Escalante would surely have been told about any confrontations, had they occurred, and reported on them in detail.[70]

The thirty-two-page pamphlet was published by a friend of Rowan's in San Francisco, Walter D. Harney, and sold for twenty-five cents, or five for a dollar.[71] It would never rival Hubbard's piece in circulation, nor was it intended to. There was only one printing. Three years later the essay, with all references to alcohol and violence removed but with a few of Rowan's literary efforts added, appeared in an anthology published by Ginn and Company, coincidentally titled *America's Message*;[72] Rowan joined Calvin Coolidge, Walt Whitman, and a few dozen others in an effort by the editors to "reveal the significant ideals of American life" to high school students. A shorter version of the essay was printed in the *World* magazine on April 21, 1929, complete with a large cover drawing of a white-haired Wagner handing a youthful Rowan an envelope sealed with wax.

News accounts of Rowan's being awarded the DSC and silver Citation Star inspired Hollywood producers to consider making a second film based on his clandestine trip—or so Charles Phelps Cushing, a writer for the *American Legion Weekly*, claimed. According to Cushing, "rival scouts for motion picture corporations" were pursuing Rowan in and out of "Mill Valley, up hill and down dale and through the woodlands all around," their sworn purpose "to make him sign The Papers— contracts authorizing the corporations to film him as leading man in a six-reel thriller."[73] Rowan, perhaps remembering the previous bad experience, refused to sign.[74] But in early 1925 it looked as if Cushing had been correct. A classified ad began appearing in small-city newspapers under the "Female Help" heading: "Movie opportunity open to you. Expenses paid to Hollywood and guaranteed part in Metro-Goldwyn-Mayer's big motion picture, 'A Message to Garcia.' Write now for particulars. True Confessions Magazine, Robbinsdale, Minnesota." Other *True Confessions* advertising urged readers, "Get Into the Movies This New, Easy Way. This is your chance to break into the movies with a crash. Don't delay. You may be the very type we want." Successful applicants were promised $150 a week plus travel and hotel expenses. "Its only equal in cast and cost is BEN-HUR." A news release announced that Major and Mrs. Rowan would travel to Hollywood, where Rowan would be the film's technical director "so that it will be correct in all details."[75] MGM sent out a promotional piece to theater owners promising "one of the greatest audience ideas ever conceived for the box-office. . . . Telling the story of a man who carried a message through Hell because loyalty and love steeled his soul. Action! Love interest! Inspiration! It surges up into the heart with an appeal that cannot be denied."[76]

And then—nothing. No movie, no newly discovered starlets, no public explanation. The project quietly came to an end.

Newspapers and magazines kept Rowan's name and exploit alive, remembering in 1928 to note the thirtieth anniversary of the trip. Many of his various speaking engagements were also chronicled, whether at the national convention of the United Spanish War Veterans, a Lions Club luncheon, or a Boy Scout troop in a church basement.[77] Elsie Robinson, a writer for *McClure's*, frankly admitted that when she was assigned to interview Rowan in 1928, she had misgivings. "[O]bedience was not my favorite sport," she wrote. "I never could admire that boy who stood on the burning deck when all but him had fled.[78] In the eyes of history he might be a hero, but in my eyes he was—a sap. So, frankly, I've always wondered about heroes. . . . [W]ere they heroes because they were too dumb to be anything else?" But her meeting with Rowan changed her mind: "He's quite the last person you'd expect to find romping through jungles, risking fifty-seven varieties of most unpleasant death. He's powerful and determined enough, but he's as fastidiously modeled as a French dandy, in spite of his brawn. . . . No dumb yes-man this. Not at all the sort of a person who'd stand on a burning deck while the swimming was good. No sheepy obedience in those eyes, even at seventy." She went on to describe with soaring prose a romanticized version of Rowan's mission, closer to the truth than Hubbard's, but still far from what actually transpired.[79]

A year later, on the thirty-first anniversary of the mission, Rowan wrote a slightly revised version of his tale that appeared in the *Washington Post* and was subsequently reprinted in other newspapers. The encounter with the *lancha* and the attempted assassination were now a fixed part of the story, and Rowan told of leaping "from my hammock just in time to avoid a dagger meant for my heart."[80] From this point on, the incident was accepted as gospel truth and included in all longer biographical magazine articles, even being repeated in Rowan's obituary in the *New York Times*.

By the mid-1920s, as Rowan approached age seventy, he remained unsatisfied with his military status. He knew there was no possibility of being given even a "swivel-chair" assignment, nor did he want one. What he wanted was to be advanced in rank. Although popularly referred to as "Colonel Rowan," he had never permanently advanced beyond major, his rank at the time of retirement. A new lobbying effort was created to change that.

Julius Kahn was a popular congressman from San Francisco who died in office in 1924. He was replaced in a special election by his wife, Florence Prag Kahn, with whom Josephine Rowan was acquainted. Kahn was prevailed upon to introduce a bill in 1926 that would advance Rowan on the army's retired list so that he might receive the "pay and emoluments of a major general." The bill asserted that "Andrew Summers Rowan, at the risk of his life, and through the exercise of great resourcefulness of mind, precision of planning, boldness, and daring, delivered the message to General Garcia, thus accomplishing a deed which has become universally famous."[81] Rowan's friend Walter Harney, publisher of *How I Carried the Message to Garcia*, joined the lobbying effort, as did Bert Hubbard. They recruited a couple more members of Congress to assist in the passage of the bill.[82] Another fervent backer was Wells Goodykoontz, a congressman from West Virginia who in 1925 wrote a biographical article about Rowan that appeared in the *West Virginia Review* and the *Congressional Record*; the following year it was reprinted as a fourteen-page pamphlet by the Government Printing Office.[83] Goodykoontz, taking Rowan at his word, quite naturally included the *lancha* incident and Rowan's near assassination. None of this helped. Rowan wasn't high enough on anybody's to-do list on the Committee on Military Affairs for the bill to have a chance of being brought up before Congress. By 1928 it was a dead issue.

Throughout the 1920s Josephine continued her good works for the blind, and in 1925 she had the pleasure of meeting Helen Keller. San Francisco was one of the stops in 1925 made by Keller, her nurse Polly Thomson, and her ever-loyal teacher and companion, Annie Sullivan, as they "naively" barnstormed the country in the unsatisfied hope, as it turned out, of raising a $2 million endowment for the American Foundation for the Blind. Although there's no record of Josephine's donation among her papers, it must have been a sizable amount. She was one of a select group of "Bishops, Rabbis, and others who had rendered special service" to receive an expertly typewritten note from Keller before she left the city.[84] The letter is almost embarrassingly effusive, noting that "we three pilgrims of hope love you and bless you for all your kindness and sweet hospitality. We have been unspeakably touched and gladdened by your sympathy and co-operation in our endeavors for the blind of America.... I shall always associate you with the spirit-thrilling scent of red wood which clings about you, and seems a part of your personality." Keller's words regarding Rowan were equally overdone as she wrote of her "pride and joy" in having him as an ally in her "crusade against darkness." "I have a touch-image of the Man," she wrote, "surrounded by the splendor and devotion in which he is all radiantly wrapped and enshrined in the hearts of his countrymen. I am extraordinarily proud and very humble to be so intimately associated with his noble legend." This is the sort of language that can go to one's head, but it is typical of the praise that tumbled from Keller's nimble fingers. The woman knew how to extend a compliment.

In the summer of 1929, following a long period of drought and aided by strong winds, a fire ravaged its way from Mount Tamalpais into Blithedale Canyon. The Rowans' house was one of 130 homes destroyed. They chose not to rebuild. All their personal items in the house were lost, but fortunately the important articles collected during their life together remained in the Vallejo Street home, which a reporter described in the *San Francisco Daily News*: "In the treasure house of rare Filipino batiks, giant brass chow platters, woven baskets of Mindanao and Igaroo, Oriental figurines, teakwood tables, gongs, ebony chests, rugs, vases, pictures from a dozen different countries, the Rowans pursue a life of retirement and study, welcoming friends but shunning publicity."[85] One can envy their quiet and reposeful existence among a lifetime's accumulation of artifacts and acquaintances.

CHAPTER 12

The Myth Lives On

As with so many occurrences in American history after 1849, Andrew Summers Rowan's birth might be attributed to the discovery of gold at Sutter's Mill in Coloma, California. In the early 1840s young John M. Rowan, who was to be Andrew Rowan's father, went to work as a clerk for Andrew Summers Jr., owner of a number of businesses in Gap Mills, Virginia. In spite of many opportunities for advancement, John Rowan was stricken with gold fever in 1849 and left for California. Unlike so many other Forty-Niners, John hit pay dirt and returned home in 1855 with enough money to marry Virginia Summers, the boss's daughter, and settle down.[1] The couple moved into the Summerses' family home with Virginia's father, and it was there that Andrew Rowan was born on April 23, 1857.[2]

After Abraham Lincoln's election as president in 1860, a Virginia state convention adopted an ordinance of secession, 88 to 45. Thirty-two of the votes against secession were cast by delegates from the northwestern counties, including Monroe, in which Gap Mills was located. Monroe was among the counties that organized themselves as the independent state of West Virginia.[3]

Thus the citizens of both Virginia and West Virginia could claim Rowan as a native son, and on October 29, 1931, they jointly celebrated his fame at the dedication of a four-span truss bridge named in his honor over the New River that separates the two states. Both governors were scheduled to participate in the ceremony but sent surrogates in their stead. Rowan, now seventy-four, wasn't up to the long train ride from San Francisco. He sent a message of thanks, noting his dual citizenship. Ever the military mapmaker, he described the New River as being "a succession of pools, cauldrons and rapids which erodes its way through three states." A nephew, Louis Rowan, introduced a dozen near relatives who were present. Bert Hubbard also responded to his invitation with a letter in which he noted the appropriateness of naming a bridge in honor of the man who "bridged the gap between McKinley and Garcia." The event, which attracted thousands, went largely unnoticed outside the two states.[4]

Magazine and newspaper interviews grew infrequent, but they never disappeared completely. Many assignments for reporters seem to have been inspired by lists recalling "This Day in History," and nearly every year a reporter or two would visit Rowan on the anniversary of his exploit. Typical was an International News Service piece published April 30, 1932, that included some basic history of the Cuban situation in 1898, a repetition of Elbert Hubbard's fantasy account, and a quote or two from Rowan.

Through the years, friends, relatives, and complete strangers had sent Rowan news clippings that contained references to him. None of them would have realized that this modest, unassuming soldier had joined what *Time* magazine referred to as the "socialites, nouveaux riches, politicians, tycoons and stage folk" by subscribing to a clipping service, and that he had done so right from the beginning of his fame. For years he was "romeiked"; that was the popular term for scrapbooks compiled from press clippings, so named for Prussian-born Henry E. Romeike, who invented the clipping industry in 1881. In the 1930s Rowan would have paid a monthly fee of five dollars, plus seven and a half cents, for each clipping.[5]

His health had been declining for some years, and in early 1935 he received a blow from which he seems never to have recovered. His daughter Elizabeth had remarried at least once again, and on January 14 the *San Francisco News* carried a small item: "Funeral services for Mrs. Elizabeth Vaulte, daughter of Col. Andrew S. Rowan, who carried the famous message to Garcia, were held yesterday in New Rochelle, N.Y. Mrs. Vaulte died from an overdose of sleeping potion taken accidentally, according to the medical report. Colonel Rowan is a resident of San Francisco and has been ill for some time."[6]

That January a second incident caused the annual interviews to occur a couple months earlier than usual. Carlos García Velez, one of General Calixto García Íñiguez's thirteen or so offspring (born to at least seven women), had distinguished himself as an officer during the war with Spain and gone on to hold a number of important diplomatic posts.[7] In 1935, while serving as the Cuban ambassador to Mexico, García arrived in Washington, D.C., to search for the message that he, along with most others, believed Rowan had carried to his father. The difference between García and everybody else was that he was certain he'd seen the message; according to an Associated Press account, he recalled "that the message was a brief note from Secretary of War Alger to his father advising him of the United States' decision to land forces in Cuba, and inquiring as to ports of debarkation." García remembered— or thought he remembered—that it was he to whom Rowan had given the message and that he had passed it on to his father.[8] It is not surprising that his memory would have failed him more than thirty-five years later. At the time of his journey, Rowan had been referred to in the press as a "messenger"; and in an article in *Harper's Weekly*, it was stated that when Rowan met García "he delivered the dispatches that had been entrusted to him."[9] It is not surprising, then, that Elbert Hubbard would believe Rowan carried a written message—though the business about the "oil-skin pouch" strapped over Rowan's heart was Hubbard's inventive imagination at work. Nowhere in Rowan's *McClure's* article does he mention a message; and in his pamphlet, "How I Carried the Message to Garcia," written in 1922, he specifically stated the message was oral.[10] Despite this, García Velez spent two weeks in the basement of the Cuban embassy on Sixteenth Street digging through stored cases of old books and papers in a fruitless search for a piece of paper that never existed. Rowan, when asked, said, "The message is not lost because there was no message to lose; I carried it in my head." This is what he had been carefully saying for years. Somebody found Rowan's official report in the War Department's archives, in which he had written, "I at once delivered, orally, my message to Garcia," and that should have been the end of the matter.[11]

Hubbard's story had become such a part of America's cultural heritage that there were those who were disappointed to learn it wasn't entirely factual. A writer for the *Fresno Bee Republican* lamented, "It almost is too bad that Major Rowan felt called on to make notes. The Hubbard story was so much more exciting and dramatic. It is like the tale of George Washington and the cherry tree and others of that character, about which a lot of people feel if they are not true, they should have been."[12] In all those years the truth about the message had not even managed to penetrate Bert Hubbard's mind. He wrote Rowan, almost begging him to deny what he'd been reading in the newspapers: "Surely there was a written message from McKinley, wasn't there, which you actually delivered? Golly if there wasn't, then that's just too bad. It sort of punches a hole in Dad's little story about you." In a reply dictated to Josephine, Rowan referred Hubbard to his essay in the 1925 anthology in which he'd explicitly pointed out there was no written message. He also uncharacteristically complained about his health: "I have been suffering with arteriosclerosis which greatly and increasingly interferes with my activities."[13]

The flurry of news articles once again stirred up interest in Rowan, and as it turned out, Charles Cushing was correct when he predicted, somewhat prematurely, that Rowan's adventure would, for a second time, be made into a movie. In the summer of 1935 Luella Parsons, the Hollywood gossip columnist, announced that Wallace Beery was to star in a Darryl F. Zanuck production of *A Message to Garcia*.[14] This must have given some readers a start if they assumed the main character in the film would be based on Andrew Rowan. How could Beery, who was fifty-five at the time and whose screen persona film historian Leslie Halliwell described as "tough, ugly, slow-thinking and easy-going,"[15] possibly play the gallant army lieutenant? He couldn't, of course, but because he was a big draw in his day, a role was created for him and for which he was reportedly paid $75,000.[16] Beery was given top billing over Barbara Stanwyck, who was also playing a historically nonexistent role. Third in line came John Boles, a dashing singer and leading man of the period, and it was he who was to play the part of Lieutenant Rowan. Boles happened to be exactly Rowan's age at the time Rowan made his journey, though you wouldn't know it from his publicity photos, one of which he sent to Rowan with the inscription, "When you see Message to Garcia I hope you will okay my performance."

Figure 5. In the 1936 movie *A Message to Garcia*, President William McKinley (Del Henderson) shakes the hand of Lieutenant Andrew Rowan (John Boles) as Colonel Arthur Wagner (George Irving) looks on. Seconds later McKinley hands Rowan an envelope containing a message to be taken to General Calixto García. The scene is a total fabrication. Twentieth Century Fox.

Unlike the Edison production that was shot on location, the new version was filmed entirely on the Twentieth Century Fox lot in Movietone City, west of Beverly Hills. To add a little excitement to the jungle scenes, director George Marshall rented a half dozen live alligators, supplemented by stock footage of dozens of African crocodiles. There was a problem with the live alligators. During the winter months, when the movie was being shot, alligators spend most of their time sleeping, even in southern California. It would be necessary, the alligator farmer said, to heat the water up to seventy-five degrees—warm enough to wake them but still leave them sluggish enough to pose no danger; however, one of the alligators got too close to the steam line being used to heat the water and woke up completely. Had he been just a bit closer to John Boles, who at that moment was wading through the swamp in search of García, the story would have had a different ending.[17] That wouldn't have bothered the producers, since not a single scene in the film was historically accurate anyway.

At some point Rowan had written a film script himself, "My Mission and My Message to García: Rowan's Own Story of How He Found García in The Mountain Fastnesses of Cuba, 1898—Educational: Historical, Scientific, Dramatic." After some set-up scenes that demonstrate the need to gain information from General García in the "mountain fastnesses" of Cuba, the secretary of war says to President McKinley, "We have, sir, a fellow by the name of Rowan who can find García, if anyone can." So off Rowan goes, at first more or less following the broad outline of the actual journey. In his script he indicated a few interesting special effects such as a "double-exposure vision of Poe's 'Imp of the Perverse,'" who appears at Rowan's shoulder trying to cast doubts on the reliability of the Cubans and the safety of the mission. But Rowan says to himself, "Rowan, old boy, you have accepted this duty with all its risks. Your superiors rely on you; you must rely on your subordinates and mould them to your will. Go, and go at once!! This is your real mission to Garcia!!!" In another scene his guide Gervasio Savio dissolves into an image of Iago, who recites a few words from *Othello*. Throughout the script Rowan often has appropriate literary quotes at the ready, most often from Rudyard Kipling. Perhaps the most interesting special effect is a talking horse. Rowan, feeling sorry for his horse eating marsh grass, gives it a pat, and,

> The horse raises his head and turns it toward Rowan, abruptly but affectionately, kindly, [and says]:
> "Cut out the 'sob stuff'; I'm hungry, and this tough grass tastes good to me. I hope you will like your sea-horse."
> Turning to Collazo, Rowan says:

"A noble animal."

Collazo says:

"One of the most famous horses in Cuba. He was especially commandeered by General García for you."

After more detail than is usually given about the return trip, Rowan arrives in Tampa, Florida, to be greeted with cheers by military officers and news correspondents. Much as he enjoys the adulation, he declaims, "I must get on to Washington." The final scene (no. 113) takes place in the Cabinet Room, and the last words are those of President McKinley:

"You have done a very brave deed."

Rowan and the commanding General bow and withdraw.

(Iris out)[18]

There is no record of Rowan's having submitted the script to any movie producers, but it exists among his collected papers only as a carbon copy, which suggests the original was sent somewhere.

In February 1936 a seventy-eight-year-old Rowan gave a new twist to the story of his adventure during an interview with Lee Rashall, an International News Service correspondent. He surprised many people by adding a previously unknown character to the account of his trip to Cuba—a renegade Englishman named Fleming. "I've never spoken of this because I have regarded it as a contract of silence between two honorable men," said Rowan. "Fleming was a traitor to his country, England, but he was an honorable man to me." Fleming, he claimed, was a "white collar pirate" who had for years been carrying contraband and arms to the insurgent Cubans. In previous accounts, it was always the *mambises* (guerrillas) who, when they reached the Jamaican coast, provided the small boat in which they sailed to Cuba. But that was all to change. Rowan explained, "We gained the north coast of [Jamaica] at two A.M. one morning. Near the shore we saw lights and soon came upon a white man working beside a boathouse. The man lifted a torch to my face, and exclaimed, 'You are the first gentleman I have met on this coast in ten years! Who are you?' I explained my mission, and this man supplied me with the boat, asking no further questions.[19] If there were any follow-up questions from Rashall, their answers weren't reported.

In his unpublished "How I Carried President McKinley's Message to General Garcia," Rowan made a passing reference to a "very gentlemanly Englishman" among the assembled agents of the junta.[20] And in his movie script Rowan also included such a person, calling him Mr. Pray. The one problem with the story as told to Rashall is that it suggests the boat was acquired as the result of a chance meeting. In a letter to General Máximo Gómez, Tomás Estrada Palma, head of the New York junta, wrote that "Rowan went to Cuba in our boat, conducted by our people." There's absolutely no mention of a mysterious Brit. One is inclined, therefore, to believe such a man existed, but to question his importance to Rowan's sailing to Cuba. In none of his published accounts did Rowan mention the boat's name. According to Cuban cinematographer Max Tosquella, it was called either *El Mambi* or *La Patriota*. In his movie script, Rowan, on learning the boat has no name, says, "I shall christen it *Sin Nombre—the Nameless*."

On April 9, 1936, the movie *A Message to Garcia* premiered in New York at the Center Theatre in Rockefeller Center.[21] While it was generally well received, the *New York Times* film reviewer Frank S. Nugent panned the movie for its lack of historicity, noting that "it stands forth nakedly as an absurd and trivial melodrama which is made all the more annoying because Twentieth Century Fox would have you believe it was partly true. . . . It would be almost worth a trip to San Francisco to sit beside Lieutenant Rowan . . . and note his reactions to this melodramatization of his famous journey into the interior of Cuba."[22] American historian Stewart Holbrook claimed Rowan was so disgusted by the inclusion of a woman in the story that he refused to see it, but according to his sister, Virginia Caperton, he not only saw the movie in San Francisco but praised it highly. At an earlier time he would certainly have been outraged when his screen character—who was, after all, a married man with a young daughter—told Señorita Raphaelita, "No matter what happens, I love you . . . and always will."

But at age seventy-eight he may have enjoyed seeing himself portrayed as having had an affair with the alluring Barbara Stanwyck.

Aníbal Escalante Beatón, one of García's young adjutants at the time of Rowan's visit, saw the movie in Havana and was appalled by its deviation from the truth. He castigated the Cuban Film Review Commission, normally quick to use its censorious "scissors," for letting pass without a word a film filled with "fantasies and intolerable lies." Fortunately for his peace of mind, Escalante never saw an advertising piece that proclaimed "a scrap of paper that set a nation free!"

A Cuban reviewer acknowledged the movie's shortcomings, pointing out in particular that the supposed Cubans spoke with a Mexican accent that "wouldn't fool anybody" though, in fact, most Americans were fooled. He also mentioned the café scene in colonial Havana where Rowan first meets the fictional soldier of fortune played by Wallace Beery. During his first trip to the island, Rowan was never within four hundred miles of Havana, but the reviewer felt the inclusion of the scene was necessary to set the historical context. Overall, he thought the movie was well produced and depicted the Cuban patriots in a favorable light—especially García.[23]

For Rowan's seventy-ninth birthday that year, 350 young men of the Galileo High School ROTC, which included four rifle companies and a band, marched up Russian Hill—no small feat—to Rowan's house and serenaded him with a rendition of "There'll Be a Hot Time in the Old Town Tonight" as a celebration of his part in the Spanish-American War.[24]

In the December 5, 1936, *New Yorker* there appeared an article, one of a series under the general heading "Where Are They Now?" In this piece James Thurber, writing as Jared L. Manley, was concerned with the whereabouts of Andrew Summers Rowan. He retold the familiar story, pointing out some of Hubbard's distortions, but completely buying in to some of his more outrageous claims. It was, for the most part, a kindly look back at an old soldier. Surprisingly, the final paragraph repeated the worst of the libels against García, something that would have greatly upset Rowan had Josephine been insensitive enough to read it aloud.[25]

As the article made clear, Rowan was quite ill that winter. His doctors ordered him to remain at home in his sickroom, and as the Associated Press noted, he practiced the same obedience to those orders as he had thirty-nine years earlier when Wagner sent him off to Cuba. In spite of revelations concerning the lack of a written message and the noninvolvement of McKinley, the article's final paragraph repeated the old story: "Colonel Rowan delivered the message to General Garcia, a letter from President McKinley."[26] This was a myth that would never die.

By the time of his eighty-first birthday in 1938, Rowan was a full-time resident at the Letterman General Hospital in the Presidio. His most recent untoward episode involved a rib that was cracked during a fall. What would normally have been a minor accident was made worse by his increasingly frail health, yet doctors held out hope for a recovery.[27] He was still convalescing on July 27 as he sat in a wheelchair on the hospital's lawn, wrapped in blankets and wearing a wide-brimmed fedora. The occasion was the presentation of Cuba's highest honor, the Order of Carlos Manuel de Cespedes Award, pinned on him by the Cuban consul in San Francisco, José Joaquín Zarza.[28] This was no small thing. A few years earlier Cuban president (and later dictator) Gerardo Machado Morales said of the award, "We concede it only when a bit of our soul and all of our admiration goes with it."[29] In his speech Zarza said to Rowan,

Many years ago, with faith in God, and having for your only guide determination and courage, you performed a deed which has become a classic all over the earth. You have set up an everlasting lesson for the youth of your country. You have covered with prestige and glory the Army of this great nation. . . . Recognition usually comes late, the world forgets; but what a reward! Here, alongside with the Army, with your companions of yesterday, with your companions of today, dreaming of your dangerous excursions through the Cuban jungles, of the perils which you defied, feeling that you helped a small country to attain its Independence, you can rest, and go on dreaming all the beautiful

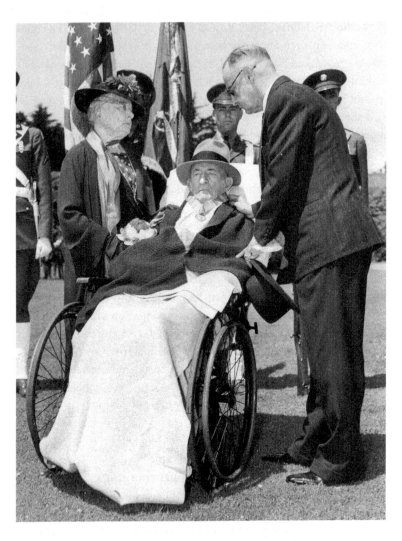

Figure 6. Major Andrew S. Rowan receiving Cuba's highest honor, the Order of Manuel de Céspedes Award, from Cuban Consul José Joaquín Zarza as Rowan's wife, Josephine, stands by. World Wide Photos.

things of the spirit, because looking up to you the younger generation, and the generations to come, will forever learn to love, to admire, and to emulate your example. The statue of deathless bronze which Elbert Hubbard wishes to set up in every school is already engraved in the hearts of every American.[30]

At the appropriate moment there was a seven-gun salute. Strictly speaking, officers beneath the rank of brigadier general are not eligible for a gun salute of any number. But Zarza, as a consul accredited to the United States, was eligible for a seven-gun salute. This may have been how army regulations were gotten around, and if people wanted to interpret the salute as being for Rowan, so be it. Throughout the entire ceremony the ailing Rowan said not a word. An editorial in the *Oakland Tribune* noted that General García and Elbert Hubbard were both gone, and "before long Colonel Rowan, ill at 81, will join them." "Maybe it is just as well. In this day, when much of the world's population is regimented under dictators, when the frontier has disappeared in our own country, and there are 13,000,000 unemployed to testify that individual self-reliance does not mean so much as it once did, there is much that the man who took the message to Garcia might not understand."[31]

There was one small problem with Rowan's receiving the Cuban medal—Article I, Section 9, of the U.S. Constitution expressly forbids such a thing. As an officer in the U.S. Army Rowan could not, "without the Consent of the Congress, accept of any present, Emolument, Office, or Title, of any kind whatever, from any King, Prince or foreign State." As always, Rowan had a friend in Congress, and in this case it was Representative Franck R. Havenner of California. On January 11, 1939, Havenner introduced a bill that would, after the fact, permit Rowan to accept the award.[32] In the meantime the medal had been sent to the State Department until Congress might act. Six months after its introduction, President Franklin Roosevelt signed the legislation, and the medal was mailed back to Rowan. This time there was no more ceremony than the opening of the package when it arrived, an act performed by Josephine, now the only person allowed to visit.[33]

Rowan's birthday that year was barely mentioned in the news-papers. No one interviewed him.[34]

Little by little, Rowan's name was forgotten even by people who should have remembered it. Norman Chandler, publisher of the *Los Angeles Times*, wrote in 1941, "In your history book, and mine, there was a story about 'carrying a message to Garcia.' I am somewhat vague, now, about who sent it—and who Garcia was."[35] And long gone were any notions about casting Rowan's image in bronze. In 1923 Rowan tried to remedy that situation himself. He had in the basement of the Vallejo Street house seven small, antique, bronze field pieces—two cannons and five mortars—that he'd "captured" in the Philippines. They were probably of Spanish manufacture, but such weapons had also been cast in the Philippines so it isn't certain. And it's never been clear on which tour of duty he acquired them, but it seems more likely to have occurred on Cebu.

West Virginia's capitol in Charleston burned down in 1921, and it took until 1923 to establish firm plans to build another, this one of stone. It was to be designed by Cass Gilbert, architect of the Supreme Court building in Washington. Rowan saw this as an opportunity to immortalize his mission, if not his visage, in bronze just as Hubbard had recommended. His brother John had at the time a law practice in Charleston, where he was politically well connected. In August 1923 Rowan sent a labored letter to John, telling him about the bronze pieces and explaining how he would like them used. "I see the possibility of connecting the history of our state (West Virginia) with that of the Spanish conquest of the Philippines and the American conquest 400 years later," he wrote, "and the part that our beloved state has taken in securing our country and advancing civilization—all of which ought to help to concentrate the attention of our youth on the fact that our state has played its part in the progress of the world."

And what might this overarching connection be? He continued, "It occurs to me that, as Elbert Hubbard's famous essay carries, at least, a suggestion of our state's part in our most successful and popular war which secured our sea lanes, that a bronze tablet displaying the part that a plain West Virginian took in securing those sea lanes, might, very properly, be a subject of decorative scheme in the new capitol building." What Rowan wanted was to have the antique bronze pieces melted down and recast in some sort of tablet on which a portion of the "A Message to Garcia" would be written "in the plainest lettering possible." And who knows? Maybe there'd be a bas-relief portrait of the man who carried the message. He even went so far as to suggest a sculptor: the Romanian-born artist George Julian Zolnay, who apparently was married to one of Rowan's distant cousins.

Dutiful brother that he was, John managed to get a bill introduced into the West Virginia legislature providing that such a tablet be erected. Nothing came of it, and the bronzes remained in the Vallejo Street basement until after Rowan died. At some later date Josephine made contact with Henry E. Caldabaugh, a Wheeling, West Virginia, resident who was associated with the United Spanish War Veterans, and she shipped the seven pieces to him. At a loss for what to do with them, Caldabaugh stored them in the basement of a Veterans of Foreign Wars hall, where they were rediscovered in 1958 and donated to the West Virginia Department of Archives and History and eventually made a part of the state museum's permanent collection.[36]

When it came to memorializing Rowan's trip in bronze, Cuba was far ahead of the United States. As early as 1929, a small monument—a circular bronze plate mounted on a free-standing marble tablet—had been erected in Mono Ciego, near Manatí Bay, to commemorate the departure of the boat that carried Rowan and his Cuban companions to Nassau.[37] Bigger things were in the works, including a number of bronze images of Rowan, but one suspects these had more to do with gaining favor with the United States than with honoring the message carrier.

When the American occupation of Cuba ended on May 20, 1902, there remained many effects of Spanish occupation and revolutionary devastation. Yet, by some measures, Cuba was in better condition than it had been since Christopher Columbus arrived 410 years earlier. General Leonard Wood, who has been described by an admirer as "one of the greatest colonial administrators in modern history," reformed every aspect of Cuban public life. But his two-and-a-half-year tenure wasn't long enough to refashion centuries-long cultural behavior, nor to properly train the Cuban people to manage the U.S.-style governmental and economic structures that had been imposed on them.[38] As a result of U.S. intervention and the subsequent occupation, postrevolutionary Cuba was not the republic the insurrectionists had in mind. Their new government was shaped by a constitution closely resembling that of the United States and not the framework they would have constructed themselves. Any movement toward land reform was thwarted, as hundreds of thousands of acres were acquired by North American individuals and corporations. With 60 percent of the rural land owned by foreigners, the profits thereby derived benefited few Cubans. Americans and other foreigners also controlled mining, manufacturing, banking, transportation, and power production. The corruption of the old days returned, its goal as always being short-term personal gain for those in power.[39]

The United States had been eager to end the expensive and burdensome military occupation of Cuba but not its control over what occurred there. The answer was an extraordinary appendix to the Cuban Constitution referred to as the Platt Amendment that pretty much guaranteed the hegemony of the United States over the island nation. When the United States pulled out, it left the door wide open so that it might come back at any time. Article III of the Platt Amendment stated, "That the Government of Cuba consents that the United States may exercise the right to intervene for the preservation of Cuban independence, the maintenance of a government adequate for the protection of life, property and individual liberty, and for discharging the obligations with respect to Cuba imposed by the Treaty of Paris on the United States, now to be assumed and undertaken by the Government of Cuba."[40] If read broadly enough, the amendment guaranteed the United States the right under the Cuban constitution to invade the island at its discretion. And so it did. U.S. troops occupied the country again from 1906 to 1909 (at the request of the Cuban government, believing itself unable to prevent a revolution), in 1912 (to protect U.S.-owned property during a revolt by Afro-Cubans), and from 1917 to 1922 (to intervene in yet another possible government overthrow). The country lurched from one corrupt government to another, always remaining, as one writer referred to it, America's "plantation." The succession of politicians at all levels of government was characterized by illegalities ranging from petty graft to embezzlement to murder, all of which eventually contributed to a wealthy retirement.[41]

At the start of the 1930s Cuba's economy, never too healthy to begin with, was in ruins as a result of the worldwide depression. Things got even worse when the United States, to protect its own sugar cane growers, increased the duty on Cuban sugar. It was a country in need of a strong hand.[42] In 1933 a strikingly handsome mulatto army sergeant, Fulgencio Batista y Zaldíva,[43] first brought wide attention to himself as a leader of the noncommissioned officers who protested policies regarding the treatment of enlisted men. Before the year was out, he had appointed himself colonel and was head of the army. Mob boss Meyer Lansky, who by this time had already recognized Cuba as an ideal site for mob expansion, saw Batista as the sort of leader he could do business with.[44]

In 1940, wanting to legitimize his dictatorial rule over Cuba, Batista shed his military uniform and ran for election as president under a new and—for Cuba—progressive constitution.[45] This was a period when Cuba and the United States needed one another more than ever. It was only a matter of time before the United States would enter the war against the Axis powers and would want naval and air bases in Cuba. The Cubans, for their part, would want a share of the millions of dollars to be spent on defense. As a display of its friendship with the United States, the Cuban government chose to have a number of ceremonies celebrating America's Independence Day on July 4, 1940, ten days before the election. One ceremony was held in the Acera de Louvre, the sidewalk café in front of the historic Hotel Inglaterra, where the elite and artistic elements of Havana had for decades met to discuss everything from the Paris art scene to football results.[46] Attended by government officials, members of patriotic societies, and representatives of the U.S. diplomatic corps, the ceremony was presided over by Comandante Luís Rodolfo Miranda y de la Rúa.

Miranda, as a twenty-year-old adjutant to General García, was one of the young officers present when Lieutenant Andrew Rowan had arrived in Bayamo forty-two years earlier. Throughout his career as soldier, government official, and diplomat, Miranda devoted himself to keeping the memory of the revolution alive and, not so incidentally, reminding people of his role in its execution. He had always been an irrepressible participant in the overthrow of the Spanish regime. Frederick Funston remembered him as a young lieutenant in the battle for Guaimaro in October 1896, climbing eighteen feet up a flagpole on a blockhouse to remove a Spanish flag that had been nailed there. As bullets whizzed past, and his fellow soldiers begged him to come down, he struggled up the four-inch-diameter pole, cut the flag loose with his pocketknife, and then dropped to the roof with his prize.[47]

The purpose of the ceremony in which Miranda participated on this particular July 4 was to dedicate—at long last—a bronze image of Rowan, forty-one years after it was first recommended. On a bas-relief plaque designed by the Cuban artist Juan Emilio Hernández Giró were images of both Rowan and García.[48] The plaque, surrounded on that day by a colorful display of flowers, was installed in the outside wall of the hotel.[49]

The following May, Comandante Miranda was in Bayamo to dedicate a second bronze plaque honoring Rowan's delivery of "EL MENSAJE A GARCÍA." The five-foot-high plaque, also designed by Hernández Giró, displayed Rowan's and García's likenesses imposed over billowing Cuban and American battle flags. The wording on the plaque, affixed to the plain block building in the center of town in which the two men met,[50] refers to Rowan as the "Portador del Famoso Mensaje Enviado por el Presidente de los eu de America William McKinley." In Cuba, as elsewhere, it was still believed that McKinley sent a physical message, just as Hubbard had described it. This was another grand celebration attended by government officials, local dignitaries, and a representative of the U.S. embassy, Colonel Albert L. Loustalot. Miranda, whose name was prominently displayed on the plaque just above the Cuban coat of arms, would have known there was no actual message from McKinley; he was, however, carefully ambiguous when he spoke to the sun-soaked crowd: "I was in Bayamo at the time. It was very early in the morning. There arrived a striking figure in civilian clothes, showing signs of great fatigue. The man was Rowan. He had arrived in a rowboat from Jamaica and then came by horseback to his rendezvous with General García. It was good to see him because his message was one from the United States pledging its full cooperation in Cuba's fight for liberty. And the United States kept its pledge."[51] Newspaper articles reporting the event noted that Rowan was too ill to attend the ceremony.

Eight months later, on January 10, 1943, Andrew Summers Rowan died in Letterman Hospital. That May, forty-five years after completing the mission to Cuba, his ashes were flown to Washington, D.C., for burial in the Arlington National Cemetery. Rowan died believing his ashes would be scattered over the Golden Gate from an army plane, a request the army said it would honor.[52] Perhaps it was Josephine who realized that would leave him without a proper monument. Whatever the reason, there was a change in plans, and his ashes were instead buried at Arlington with full military honors at 2:00 P.M. on May 14.[53] The military ceremony at his interment was not to be the last of the public honors he would receive.

On July 4 that same year, as part of Batista's continuing public relations campaign to impress Americans with his loyalty and friendship, Independence Day was celebrated to a greater degree in Havana than probably anywhere in the United States. A reported 80,000 Cubans of every class, some representing numerous professional and patriotic organizations, marched past the reviewing stand that Batista shared with his military chiefs and members of the foreign diplomatic corps. Special editions of the four major Havana dailies were devoted to honoring the United States, and the eight radio stations also had programming dedicated to the celebration.[54]

One of the major events of the day took place at the Plaza del Maine, the site of a monument built in memory of the sailors who died aboard the *Maine*. A crowd of white-sharkskin-suited officials headed by Batista gathered there on July 4, 1943. They were there at the behest of the Agrupación Pro-Enseñanza de Hechos Históricos and its president, Comandante Luís Rodolfo Miranda. That afternoon in the Plaza del Maine he presided at the dedication of a larger-than-life-size bronze bust of Lieutenant Andrew S. Rowan placed atop a marble pillar. Speaker after speaker extolled the virtues of "el estoico teniente" as each of them retold the mythic story that elevated Rowan to the level of the existing bronze pantheon in the Plaza that also included William McKinley, Theodore Roosevelt, and Leonard Wood.[55]

Ellis O. Briggs, the American chargé d'affaires in Cuba and one of the speakers at the ceremony, some years later recalled being concerned that a July noon in Havana, the time the unveiling was scheduled, "would be capable of giving sunstroke to a Galapagos turtle." Briggs claimed that it was he who was responsible for Batista's agreeing to white suits instead of the "morning coats and *pantalones de fantasia* that the Cuban State Department was demanding." Briggs remembered Miranda's "declaiming for an extra half-hour, with the Strait of Florida a molten mirror, searing my eyeballs. It was weeks before I could pass the Cuban memorial to the good Lieutenant Rowan, there on the Habana Malecon, without an inward shudder."[56]

By the time Josephine Rowan died at age ninety-five on January 15, 1949,[57] Andrew Summers Rowan was a name barely remembered by anyone. Hubbard's essay was still being published, but the public no longer associated the "fellow by the name of Rowan" with a real human being. The message to García—whoever García was—had long become separated from the man who carried it. That separation persists today. In a 2009 PBS production, *Elbert Hubbard: An American Original*, the importance of "A Message to Garcia" in establishing Hubbard and the Roycrofters as important cultural entities was readily admitted. But the name of Andrew Rowan was never mentioned. In a further irony, in 1930 there was unveiled on Main Street in East Aurora, New York (the Roycrofters' hometown), a huge bronze statue of—who else?—Elbert Hubbard.[58]

Rowan's name still lives on here and there: the 1931 bridge over the New River; the reading room for the blind in Salt Lake City; 650 acres owned by the West Virginia Department of Agriculture known as the Andrew S. Rowan Farm; a retirement home named for him in Sweet Springs, West Virginia; and Camp Rowan, a Civilian Conservation Corps camp erected during the Depression in Union County, West Virginia. Inspired by Hubbard's essay, an investment management group chose Rowan's name as being "symbolic of effort, intelligence and focus." Though not mentioning Rowan by name, in 2009 the rock group

Visqueen titled their album *Message to Garcia*. His name also survives on some public thoroughfares, including Rowan Road, in Guantánamo Bay, Cuba. In 2000 there was an effort to put Rowan's image on a U.S. postage stamp; the suggestion made it as far as the list for consideration in 2003, but nothing came of it.

In 1943, just three months after he died, and close to the anniversary of his meeting with García, a World War II liberty ship was named for him, one of 2,710 ships built to carry troops and supplies across the oceans. The Ship Naming Commission made the decision to name liberty ships after dead Americans who had contributed significantly to American life and history, the very first being christened the *Patrick Henry*.[59] The sponsor of the SS *Andrew Rowan*—which is to say the woman who swung the champagne bottle—was Mrs. Albert B. Chandler, wife of the governor of Kentucky. Unlike navy destroyers, also named for individuals, there were no biographical plates on liberty ships, so the merchant seamen aboard the *Andrew Rowan* probably had no idea who he was. In October of that same year the navy acquired the ship and renamed it USS *Rutilicus*. Following duty in the Asiatic-Pacific Theater the navy returned the ship to the Maritime Commission, and its name reverted to SS *Andrew Rowan*. After passage through the Panama Canal, it was berthed in the James River in Virginia where, it is certain, Rowan's name was not repainted on the ship's bow; nonetheless, his name would still have remained on the original brass identification plate mounted in the deckhouse. The ship was finally sold for scrap in 1971 to a company in Spain.[60]

May 1, 1961, was the sixty-third anniversary of Rowan's landing in Cuba. It was also twelve days after the defeat of the CIA-backed invasion force at Playa Girón, or as it is called in the United States, the Bay of Pigs.[61] An angry crowd gathered at the *Maine* monument to cheer as workers knocked the bronze eagle off the two pillars. At a later date the wording of the dedication was changed to read, "To the victims of the Maine, who were sacrificed to imperialist greed in its fervor to seize control of the island of Cuba."[62] Most of the eagle ended up in a museum in Havana, though the head was rescued by friends of the Americans, and it resides just down the road in the cafeteria of the

American Embassy, which was reestablished on July 20, 2015, when the two nations officially renewed diplomatic relations after more than fifty years of estrangement.[63] The bronze busts of McKinley, Roosevelt, Wood, and Rowan were also removed, and their whereabouts remain unknown, even to the government officials who supervise Havana's parks and monuments.[64] Similarly, the plaque on the Acera de Louvre has been either removed or covered over, and no one today remembers it ever existed. The plaque in Bayamo remains in place, as does one other bronze image of Rowan in Havana.

Along the Malecón not far from the Parque de Maine is the twice-life-size equestrian statue of Calixto García Íñiguez. Surrounding the statue are twenty-four bas-relief plaques illustrating significant moments in García's participation in the struggle for Cuban independence, one of these being his meeting with Andrew Rowan. The plaque shows the two men shaking hands.

In the United States there is only one known bronze image of Andrew Rowan, and it is located in the second-floor dining room of the Army and Navy Club in Washington, D.C. It was made from the same mold used for the Felix de Weldon bas-relief in Havana. Unlike that plaque, which has weathered to a blackish green, the Washington version is maintained in a rich gold tone that gleams under spotlights.

What is probably Rowan's most recent honor occurred in 1988 when his name was added to the Military Intelligence Corps Hall of Fame at Fort Huachuca, Arizona.[65]

So here and there one can find mementos of Andrew Summers Rowan, even though few people today know who he was. And those who recognize the name are more familiar with Hubbard's mythical hero than with the actual man. He left no direct descendants, only varying degrees of nephews, nieces, and cousins. While he was alive, people were proud to know him; and like any man worthy of the name, there were also some who disliked him.

Epilogue

In March 1906, on the thirtieth anniversary of its founding in Philadelphia, the John Wanamaker store distributed copies of "A Message to Garcia." A foreword inside the front cover noted,

> In France, the Bon March[é] of Paris distributed a million copies. Prince Hilakoff, Director of Railways in Russia, translated the essay into Russian and presented a copy to every officer in the Russian Army. The Mikado of Japan, not to be outdone, had the "Message" printed in Japanese, and a copy was placed in the hands of every Japanese soldier. In all, the "Message" has been translated into eleven languages, and reprinted more than twenty-five million times.
>
> The John Wanamaker Edition of the "Message to Garcia" is unique and peculiar,—different from anything else ever attempted. First, we give the "Message" as Elbert Hubbard wrote it. Second, we give the "Message" as it was translated back into English from Japanese by Professor Yone Kichikaschi, of the University of Tokio.[1]

This is one of the earliest references to Russian and Japanese editions. Author Elbert Hubbard expanded on the topic in a December 1, 1913, "Apologia" inserted into a later edition:

> At the time Mr. Daniels was distributing the "Message to Garcia," Prince Hilakoff, Director of Russian Railways, was in this country. He was the guest of the New York Central, and made a tour of the country under the personal direction of Mr. Daniels. The

Prince saw the little book and was interested in it, more because Mr. Daniels was putting it out in such big numbers, probably, than otherwise. In any event, when he got home he had the matter translated into Russian, and a copy of the booklet given to every railroad employee in Russia. Other countries then took it up, and from Russia it passed into Germany, France, Spain, Turkey, Hindustan, and China. During the war between Russia and Japan [1904–05], every Russian soldier who went to the front was given a copy of the "Message to Garcia." The Japanese, finding the booklets in possession of the Russian prisoners, concluded that it must be a good thing. And on order of the Mikado, a copy was given to every man in the employ of the Japanese government, soldier or civilian.[2]

All this has been repeated again and again, even in books and articles critical of Hubbard and his "preachment." The problem is that not much of it appears to be true.

The deviation from the truth starts with the insertion of a vagrant *a* in Prince Hilkoff's name. Khilkov, as it is spelled today and whose title is better translated as minister of ways and means of communications, spent three weeks touring American railroads, the purpose being to study methods and equipment for possible adoption in Russia. He landed in San Francisco by way of Vladivostok and worked his way east, where, on occasion, he was in the company of George Daniels, but this occurred in October 1896,[3] two and a half years before "Message" was written. In 1899, when the pamphlet was published, Khilkov had long since returned to Russia and never again visited the United States. He was fluent in English, having lived in this country for four years, and Daniels very probably mailed him a copy of the pamphlet, perhaps one of the first thousand. If so, Khilkov no doubt read it, but would he have been as enthusiastic as Daniels about the content? It's unlikely.

Khilkov, like his contemporary Leo Tolstoy, was progressive in his views. After serving as an officer in the Crimean War, he resigned his commission and eventually gave away most of his holdings. He traveled to the United States, becoming a dollar-a-day bolt cutter in

Philadelphia. This provided him an entry into railroading. According to one account it wasn't until he was transferred to Argentina, where he earned two dollars a day, that he could afford to bring over his wife and children. It was during this period that he learned to drive trains, working his way up to locomotive engineer and finally roundhouse superintendent. After a working stint in England, he returned to Russia and was appointed to successively higher railroading positions, becoming minister of ways and means of communications in January 1895.

Khilkov was once described by his immediate supervisor, Sergei Witte, as a "man of good character and of great experience in technical matters [but] not administrator enough to be equal to his ministerial tasks."[4] Willa Cather interviewed Khilkov during his visit in 1896 and she was impressed with his demeanor: "The Prince has very little in common with the dawdling noblemen of his country who ape French manners and French vices. He is more American than Russian in his manner."[5] There's evidence that he took a laid-back approach to his day-to-day responsibilities; an American visiting him in 1901 expected to find him dressed in similar dazzling garb as the officials waiting in his anteroom, but instead,

I was greeted by an elderly gentleman in a navy blue lounge suit, and with the easiest of manners. There was nothing Russian or official about him. He looked American, with his long, strong, bronzed face and a little tuft of beard that the Americans call a goatee. He spoke English like an American. . . . "I'm just a working man, you know—a sort of blacksmith. But I never worry. What is the good of worrying? When my work is done I like to shut it right away. Then I play tennis with my children, or I hunt and fish. That's what I like about English business men. When their work is finished it is really finished, and they go out of doors for exercise. Now, an American can't play golf without thinking about business. The Americans are a fine go-ahead people, the most go-ahead in the world, but if they would just think there was something else besides business, why I guess they'd get some real value out of life."[6]

This hardly sounds like Hubbard's long-suffering employer "striving with 'help' that does nothing but loaf when his back is turned." In spite of Witte's once referring to him as "naive,"[7] Khilkov would not have been so innocent as to print and distribute Hubbard's screed to hundreds of thousands of already angry rail workers, a third of which were employed by private companies.[8] And the ministry, not having the wealth of the New York Central Railroad, would have been hard-pressed to justify the expense—particularly so since a large percentage of the workers were unable to read.[9] The czar himself would have had better sense. The workers had genuine complaints, and railroad officials knew that if they were to have a stable, skilled labor force, they would have to improve the workers' lot.[10] In Russia in 1900, the railroad industry was the country's largest employer and was indeed the engine driving the industrial economy. Railroad workers were at the forefront of labor agitation, and in addition to higher pay they wanted to have shorter workdays and better working conditions and to be treated with respect and civility.[11] Hubbard's line about the "toe of a thick-soled No. 9 boot" would in itself have been enough to start a general strike. When the strike finally came in 1905, Khilkov spoke to striking train drivers from the cab of a locomotive, reminding them that he was one of them.[12] Had he previously passed out a pamphlet declaring that workers required a "first-mate with a knotted club" to keep them in line, he would never have dared stand up there in the first place. There's one further reason to believe Khilkov never embraced the message within the "Message": he is known to have strongly defended the Union of Railway Workers, the very group that initiated the strike.[13]

The conditions and complexities of czarist Russia at that time would have been beyond Hubbard's understanding. He would have known of the labor unrest, but he may very well have believed that distributing his "preachment" would have set things right. It would all seem so logical that he might have thought it happened, but there's no evidence it did.

If Khilkov didn't distribute the pamphlet to railway employees, it is still possible, however unlikely, that a high-ranking military officer might have ordered copies printed and handed out to all one million soldiers in the Russian army and to every sailor aboard the country's 272 ships—to say nothing of the 345,000 Cossacks plus the two million or so in the reserves and militia.[14] He might have, but does anyone really believe he did? At the time of this writing, no copy in Russian of this vintage has surfaced. And if members of the Russian military didn't carry copies, then Japanese soldiers couldn't have found them, and perhaps the Mikado didn't order copies given to all members of the Japanese government, civilian and military.

In March 1906, the same date as the Wanamaker edition of the "Message," a Roycrofter edition was published bound in limp suede with green silk doublures and gold stamping on the front cover. In addition to Hubbard's original "Message," it contained a partial copy of an edition translated into Japanese by Otsuka Nagataro, a student of a certain "Mr. Johnson" who, according to Otsuka, "ordered" him to do the work. It was printed at Kondo Shoten, Jiyoshi, Tokyo, a shop that specialized in foreign-language texts, an unlikely vendor for the production of a government publication that was to be distributed to the 850,000 members of the regular army and reserves plus thousands more civilian government employees[15]—especially so since there was a modern government printing office that would normally have been expected to do the work. This version is the only evidence Hubbard ever offered to demonstrate the existence of a Japanese government-issued pamphlet.

In this same edition and printed immediately following the Japanese version is a back-translation into English "by Yone Kichikaschi of the University of Tokio." To believe this is true, one would have to assume that Kichikaschi was unable to read his own language. In the Japanese version Otsuka translated "The President must secure his cooperation, and quickly," almost exactly as Hubbard wrote it. But according to the back-translation, he wrote, "The *Mikado* must secure his aid, and quite suddenly" (emphasis added). Why would Kichikaschi make that substitution? The Gilbert and Sullivan operetta *The Mikado* (1885) was a favorite around the world,[16] and Hubbard (for that's who surely wrote the back-translation) would have used the term to add (he thought) verisimilitude, and perhaps a little cuteness. What he wouldn't have known was that the Japanese of the Meiji Era

(1868–1912) did not use that term. Otsuka Nagataro didn't use the word in his translation, and a professor at the University of Tokyo certainly wouldn't have substituted "Mikado" for "President." Here's one more example out of many. Concerning a lazy and ignorant office clerk being sent to look up Correggio in an encyclopedia, Hubbard wrote, "He will look at you out of a fishy eye." Otsuka dropped the "fishy eye" metaphor in his translation, yet somehow Kichikaschi divined the original words and back-translated this as, "He will look at you out of a fishes eye." One can picture Hubbard, who was famous for his practical jokes,[17] chuckling to himself as he wrote it.

Bruce White has suggested that the name of the Japanese "translator" was inspired by two other names: Yone Noguchi, a Japanese writer of consciously awkward English verse, and Sadakichi Hartmann, a bohemian poet of German-Japanese ancestry who at one point lived at the Roycroft colony. White thought that readers would have been familiar with Noguchi's poetry and, therefore, been aware of the joke.[18] There may have been a few, but most readers of the "Message" weren't that well read, and they believed in and trusted Hubbard. John Wanamaker, an inexhaustibly energetic man with little formal education,[19] probably had no idea he was participating in a practical joke and wouldn't have appreciated being duped.

As with the Russian translation, no official Japanese copy of "A Message to Garcia" has been found,[20] and there seem to be no citations predating Hubbard's unverifiable assertion in 1906. This raises other questions: does Hubbard's claim that "from Russia it passed into Germany, France, Spain, Turkey, Hindustan, and China" have any validity? And did the Bon Marché really distribute a million copies?

Hubbard's estimates of the number of copies printed and the number of languages into which it was translated grew year by year.

Had he not gone down with the *Lusitania* in 1915, who can guess how many millions more copies he might have claimed? But even without his father's help, Elbert Hubbard II at one point claimed a circulation of eighty million.[21] In the 1926 bill to promote Andrew Summers Rowan to major general, retired, it was claimed that more than 225 million copies had been printed.[22]

Table 1.

Year	Number of Copies	Languages
1899 (Aug)	681,000	
1899 (Oct)	981,000	
1900 (Jan)[a]	1,021,000	
1900 (Jan)[b]	9 million	
1900	11 million	6
1901	15 million	9
1906	25 million	11
1913	40 million	All written languages

[a] R. W. G. Vail, "'A Message to Garcia': A Bibliographical Puzzle," *Bulletin of the New York Public Library* 34, no. 2 (1930): 76.

[b] Freeman Champney, *Art and Glory: The Story of Elbert Hubbard* (New York: Crown, 1968), 90.

In their 1977 survey of best sellers, Alice Hackett and James Burke estimated a circulation of four million, which at that time placed "A Message to Garcia" between Harold Robbins's *Where Love Has Gone* (3,976,000) and Bel Kaufman's *Up the Down Staircase* (4,046,319).[23] Interestingly enough, chapter 25 in Kaufman's novel is titled *A Message to Garcia*, a reference to a cliché-ridden speech to the school's honor students by one of the book's characters.[24] All three publications were the inspiration for movies, but only "Message" resulted in *two* productions: the silent version in 1916 from the Edison Company,[25] and the Twentieth Century Fox production of "agreeable embroidery"—or, if you prefer, "piece of historical claptrap"—in 1936.[26] In 1933 the story was dramatized on the NBC radio show *Great Moments in History*, accompanied by renditions of popular period music;[27] and the following year, the Nineteenth Infantry Regiment, while stationed at the Schofield Barracks in Hawaii, broadcast a staged interview with a stand-in for Rowan reciting his story. Four years later on the *Shell Chateau Hour*, George Raft re-created "the action and drama." And in 1953 Richard Widmark played Rowan on the weekly radio show

Suspense. Unlike the movie versions, in none of these did the hero require any female assistance to complete his mission.[28] In *The Single Star,* a 1949 novel about the war, Rowan gets passing mention as "a mysterious North American [who] had crossed the mountains from the southern coast and delivered a message to [García]." Later in the novel García mentions him by name, noting, "I cannot discuss what he told me."[29]

Making an accurate estimate of the essay's circulation would be impossible. It has been included in scores of anthologies and reprinted as a pamphlet an untold number of times. According to Stewart Holbrook, during World War I "millions more reprints were called for by Do-Good groups of various kinds, who inflicted them on soldiers, sailors, munitions workers, and school children."[30] It is still in print in many editions and of course available in electronic form. The official website of the Roycrofters tacitly acknowledges the preposterousness of Hubbard's 1913 claim of forty million by continuing to publish only that number, disregarding the probable hundreds of thousands of copies that have appeared in one form or another since then. With the advent of the Internet, many thousands more may have been added. Enter "Message to Garcia" in a search engine, and you'll get hundreds of hits. Most of these mention only the phrase, but many offer the essay reprinted in full. Does each reading of an electronic version add another number to the total circulation? In addition to physical reprints there are electronic and CD versions regularly offered for sale on eBay, and in 1971 there was an LP with Hubbard's son Bert reading the essay aloud. It should be noted that Elbert Hubbard II preferred to be called Bert, having once written, "There is no Second Elbert Hubbard."[31] Although Fra Elbertus had assembled much of his public display from the work of others, he was very much an original, as Bert learned when he tried to imitate his father and saw the Roycrofters dwindle into nostalgia.

Hubbard obviously exaggerated when he claimed that the "Message" was translated into "all written languages," but it can be found in many recent translations today: Czech, German, and Romanian, among others. In a letter to Rowan's father in 1899, George Daniels wrote that the New York Central would continue with the pamphlet's distribution "until the whole world reads of the noble work of your son and comprehends in some degree, at least, what it meant. I have today negotiated for the translation of 'A Message to Garcia' into Russian, Hungarian, German and French languages and am prepared for its distribution on the continent of Europe."[32] According to sales data compiled by the Beijing Open Book Market Consulting Center in 2005, Hubbard's preachment was among the top ten best sellers in China.[33] At least two companies, Enterprise Management Publishing House and Harbin Publishing House, have issued paperback versions. The Harbin edition also includes other inspirational essays and Rowan's essay, "How I Carried the Message to Garcia." It's unlikely that individuals were buying copies in these numbers for themselves; easier to believe is that as country folk streamed into the cities, they were being handed copies by their new employers.[34] This is still being done by the executives at some companies in the United States; however, much as they might appreciate Hubbard's exhortations to work hard, few if any CEOs follow his example when it comes to personal compensation: "All the money I make by my pen, all I get for lectures, all I make from my books, goes into the common fund of the Roycrofters—the benefit is for all. I want no better clothing, no better food, no more comforts and conveniences, than my helpers and fellow-workers have."[35] When Jeb Bush became governor of Florida in 1998, he gave a copy to his lieutenant governor, Frank Brogan, with the inscription, "You are a messenger." Eventually he gave copies to everyone on his staff and once referred to it as "awesome. It says it all."[36] So strongly did Bush feel about the "Message" that he had a copy included, along with his Black-Berry, in his formal gubernatorial portrait.[37] Bush, like the Chinese, was carrying on a tradition going back to George H. Daniels—using the essay to inspire loyalty and stick-to-itiveness and to combat, in Hubbard's words, "this incapacity for independent action, this moral stupidity, this infirmity of the will, this unwillingness to cheerfully catch hold and lift." It also has the side benefit of emphasizing who is to obey whom, as embodied in the biblical epigraph Hubbard later added:

As the cold of snow in the time of harvest, so is a faithful messenger to them that send for him: for he refresheth the soul of his masters. Proverbs 25:13.

There are servants who are sent for and there are masters who do the sending, and it's important to know to which group you belong. In everyday use the phrase "carry a message to Garcia" was understood to indicate a willingness to carry out a difficult assignment. In a conversation with Henry Kissinger, President Richard Nixon wondered aloud if Defense Secretary Melvin Laird "might be the guy we could send out there with a 'message to Garcia.'" And on another occasion concerning some straight talk with Attorney General John Mitchell, Nixon told John Ehrlichman that "the message to Garcia has got to be carried."[38] In this sense, the "Message" was tailor-made for the Boy Scouts of America. From the organization's inception in the United States in 1910, a scout was expected to perform such exercises as carrying a mock message "several miles through a forest to another camp of scouts [so that] his imagination [might] be stirred to an extent that will later enable him to carry a 'message to Garcia.'"[39] A passage in the 1917 *Boy Scouts Year Book* emphasizes the connection:

> When we say a Scout is trustworthy we first take it for granted that he is trustworthy in doing what is right. If he agrees to be at a certain place upon a certain day you can count upon him as you would upon George Washington; he will be there punctually on the minute. If he agrees to accomplish a certain task you can consider the task already performed. If he gives you certain information you can absolutely rely upon that information. If you give him a "Message to Garcia" you know that that message will be delivered, although the mountains, the wilderness, the desert, the torrents, the broad lagoons or the sea itself, separate him from "Garcia."[40]

These words would have had a strong effect on the sort of boy who would join the Scouts, then as now. Boy Scout officials, however, would

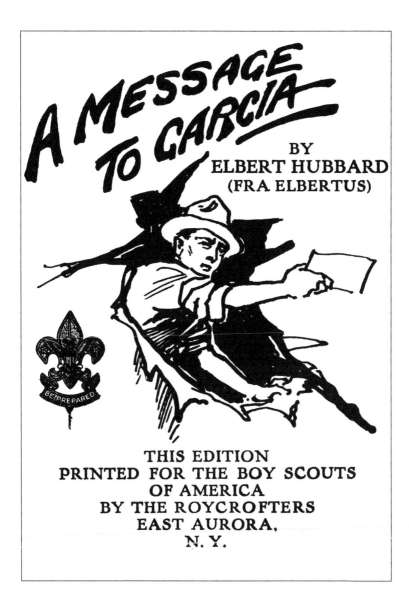

Figure 7. Just one of many editions of "A Message to Garcia" published for specific groups. Roycrofters.

have had to overlook the uncomfortable fact that Hubbard was an agnostic who once wrote, "The entire Christian doctrine of rewards and punishments, of a vicarious atonement, and the substitution of a pure and holy man for the culprit, is a vicious and misleading philosophy. That fear in some instances has deterred men from crimes, there is no doubt. But the error of religion as a police system lies in the fact that it makes superstition perpetual."[41] Robert Baden-Powell, founder of the Boy Scouts, once contributed an article to a San Francisco periodical for boys in which he outperformed Hubbard in a thoroughly inaccurate but inspiring retelling of Rowan's adventure.[42] He must have believed every word, it being unthinkable that Baden-Powell would bend the truth to make a point.

It wasn't only Boy Scout leaders who saw possibilities in the "Message" for inculcating values in young people. In 1931 it was recommended as the basis of a dramatization to improve the character of elementary students in Nebraska,[43] and it was the title of a boys' athletic activity in which every boy in a given class was able to participate and contribute his part to the class's overall achievement. To prepare for the activity, it was suggested that the teacher read the essay to the class and "have it intelligently discussed." Even in the twenty-first century it provides the theme for children's camp games.

The phrase became so common that it could be used metaphorically in newspaper columns with the assumption that its meaning would be understood by the average reader. But universal recognition faded over the years, and in the twenty-first century, in spite of many editions in print and easy electronic availability, few people have heard of "A Message to Garcia" and fewer still know what it implies. In 1978 a school board president read excerpts from the "Message" at his daughter's graduation. The reaction was overwhelmingly negative, and the speaker, a law enforcement officer named Alan Burton, was told that students should "learn to question authority" and not act "like sheep." Burton was thoroughly perplexed. Had Hubbard's "Message" become totally irrelevant? Some years later in an essay accompanying a new edition of the work, Burton reconsidered the matter and decided that in more recent times the message within the "Message" has been misunderstood: "What we are talking about is the simple concept of work ethic. We are *not* talking about religious dogma, or political pranks, or subservience, or taking advantage of another. We are *not* talking about questioning or not questioning authority. We are just talking about . . . well, doing the right thing." After sharing examples of employees who reported to him—men who showed initiative and loyalty, qualities that, among others, he felt would ultimately get them "ahead in life"— he admitted there are very few people who will profit from a reading of "A Message to Garcia": "Those who know how knew it from the start. They may have been born with the knowledge, they may have learned it from their mothers. God only knows where and how such people come by such traits. It may be that these people cannot help themselves. It is possible that they cannot do otherwise. And those who lack this ability cannot learn it, or so it seems."[44]

Burton is probably right about the lack of any real influence the essay might have had, but it doesn't seem to have occurred to him that Hubbard's poorly written bloviation was never designed to communicate values. It was composed, as Hubbard himself wrote, only as a "literary trifle" to fill out the pages of the *Philistine*.

NOTES

INTRODUCTION

1. Russell A. Alger, *The Spanish-American War* (New York: Harper, 1901), 9.

2. Murat Halstead, *The Story of Cuba: Her Struggles for Liberty . . . the Cause, Crisis and Destiny of the Pearl of the Antilles* (Chicago: Franklin Square Bible House, 1898), 644.

3. William T. Sampson, "Report of the Naval Court of Inquiry," in *Harper's Pictorial History of the War with Spain* (New York: Harper, 1899), 78. Three subsequent studies were conducted, the last of which, in 1998, concluded, "It is left to the independent reviewers of the data to evaluate the information and form an opinion" (Thomas B. Allen, ed., "What Really Sank the Maine?," *Naval History* 11 [1998]: 39). In other words, we still don't know.

4. John W. Lang, "The Message to Garcia," in *The American Historical Scene* (New York: Carlton House, 1937), 147; *Harper's Pictorial History*, 166.

5. Philip S. Foner, *A History of Cuba and Its Relations with the United States*, vol. 2, *1845–1895* (New York: International, 1963), 100.

6. Henry Cabot Lodge, *The War with Spain* (New York: Harper, 1899), 6–7.

7. Ivan Musicant, *Empire by Default: The Spanish American War and the Dawn of the American Century* (New York: Holt, 1998), 79.

8. Walter Millis, *The Martial Spirit: A Study of Our War with Spain* (Chicago: Dee, 1989), 10–13.

9. G. J. A. O'Toole, *The Spanish War: An American Epic, 1898* (New York: Norton, 1984), 38–44, 45, 58–59.

10. Ibid., 51.

11. Charles H. Brown, *The Correspondents' War: Journalists in the Spanish-American War* (New York: Scribner's, 1967), 8, 15, 25, 36.

12. Tristan Jones, *Incredible Voyage: A Personal Odyssey* (Kansas City, MO: Sheed Andrews and McMeel, 1977), 350.

13. Halstead, *Story of Cuba*, 55.

14. *Harper's Pictorial History*, 62.

15. Graham A. Cosmas, *An Army for Empire: The United States Army in the Spanish-American War* (Columbia: University of Missouri Press, 1971), 78–79.

16. Margaret Leech, *In the Days of McKinley* (New York: Harper, 1959), 150.

17. Dumas Malone, ed., *Dictionary of American Biography*, vol. 8 (New York: Scribner's, 1959), s.v. "Proctor, Redfield."

18. Chester Winston Bowie, "Redfield Proctor: A Biography" (PhD diss., University of Wisconsin, 1980), 353–63.

19. Redfield Proctor, "Conditions of Cuba under Spanish Rule," in *The American-Spanish War: A History by the War Leaders* (Norwich, CT: Haskell, 1899), 541–54.

20. O'Toole, *Spanish War*, 56.

21. Gerald F. Linderman, *The Mirror of War: American Society and the Spanish-American War* (Ann Arbor: University of Michigan Press, 1974), 37.

22. Leech, *In the Days of McKinley*, 172.

23. O'Toole, *Spanish War*, 82. The story of Hearst's telegram first appeared in a book of reminiscences by James Creelman, a reporter who covered the war. The problem is, he didn't happen to be in Cuba at the time of the supposed telegraphic exchange, and no one who was there, including Remington, ever referred to it. W. Joseph Campbell, "You Furnish the Legend, I'll Furnish the Quote," *American Journalism Review* 23 (2001): 16.

24. Thomas G. Paterson, "United States Intervention in Cuba, 1898: Interpretations of the Spanish-American-Cuban-Filipino War," *History Teacher* 29, no. 3 (1995): 267–69.

25. Michael Blow, *A Ship to Remember: The Maine and the Spanish-American War* (New York: Morrow, 1992), 32.

26. Bernard von Bülow, *Memoirs of Prince von Bülow: From Secretary of State to Imperial Chancellor, 1897–1903* (Boston: Little, Brown, 1931), 224.

27. Wolfgang Dreschler, "Germany and the Spanish-Cuban/American War," in *The War of 1898 and U.S. Interventions 1898–1934: An Encyclopedia*, ed. Benjamin R. Beede (New York: Garland, 1994), 202.

28. F. W. Hewes, "The Fighting Strength of the United States," *McClure's* 11, no. 3 (1898): 281.

29. David P. Trask, *The War with Spain in 1898* (New York: Macmillan, 1981), 46.

30. Wilson E. Strand, "Alfred Thayer Mahan," in Beede, ed., *War of 1898*, 2294–96.

31. Kaiser Wilhelm II, quoted in W. D. Puleston, *Mahan: The Life and Work of Alfred Thayer Mahan, U.S.N* (New Haven, CT: Yale University Press, 1939), 159.

32. Dreschler, "Germany and the Spanish-Cuban/American War," 202.

33. Philip S. Foner, *The Spanish-Cuban-American War and the Birth of American Imperialism*, vol. 1, *1895–1902* (New York: Monthly Review Press, 1972), 212–14.

34. "Cuba for American Negroes," *San Francisco Call*, May 7, 1898.

1. "IT IS MERITORIOUS TO BE A BOY AT WEST POINT"

1. *Annual Report of the Superintendent of the United States Military Academy* (Washington, DC: Government Printing Office, 1881), 32.

2. "Discipline at West Point," *New York Times*, June 15, 1893.

3. *Annual Report*, 10–11.

4. Williston Fish, *Short Rations* (New York: Harper, 1899), 28.

5. Williston Fish, *Memories of West Point, 1877–1881*, vol. 2, ed. and reproduced by Gertrude Fish Rumsey and Josephine Fish Peabody (Batavia, NY: Peabody, 1957), 639.

6. Ibid.

7. "The West Point Cadet," *Harper's Weekly*, July 1879, 526–27.

8. "Life at the Military Academy," *New York Times*, July 7, 1878.

9. *Annual Report*, 17.

10. Peter S. Michie, "Caste at West Point," *North American Review* 130, no. 283 (1880): 607.

11. *Official Register of the Officers and Cadets of the U.S. Military Academy, West Point* (June, 1881), 11.

12. Oath of Office, RG94, M-698, Roll 1002, National Archives and Records Administration.

13. Edward M. Coffman, *The Old Army: A Portrait of the American Army in Peacetime, 1874–1898* (New York: Oxford University Press, 1986), 218.

14. Bob Janiskee, "By the Numbers: Little Bighorn Battlefield National Monument," http://www.nationalparktraveler.com/2011/06/numbers-little-bighorn-battlefield-national-monument8258

15. Coffman, *Old Army*, 215.

16. Archibald Forbes, "The United States Army," *North American Review* 135, no. 309 (1882): 127, 132–33.

17. Jack D. Foner, *The United States Soldier between Wars: Army Life and Reforms, 1865–1898* (New York: Humanities, 1970), 82.

18. "Desertions in the Army," *New York Times*, December 21, 1884.

19. Foner, *The United States Soldier*, 18–24, 78, 86, 100–113.

20. "Desertions in the Army."

21. Robert McHenry, ed., *Webster's American Military Biographies* (New York: Dover, 1984), s.v. "Howard, Oliver Otis (1830–1909)."

22. "General Howard and Deserters," *New York Times*, December 16, 1883.

23. "The Army," *New York Times*, November 26, 1881.

24. Robert McHenry, *Webster's American Military Biographies* (New York: Dover, 1984), s.v. "Meigs, Montgomery Cunningham (1816–92)."

2. BECOMING AN INTELLIGENCE OFFICER

1. Edward M. Coffman, *The Old Army: A Portrait of the American Army in Peacetime, 1874–1898* (New York: Oxford University Press, 1986), 263.

2. George W. Cullum, *Biographical Register of the Officers and Graduates of the U.S. Military Academy at West Point, N.Y., since Its Establishment, in 1802*, supplement (Cambridge: Riverside Press, 1901), 4:353.

3.   Coffman, *Old Army*, 262.

4.   Warren A. Beck and Ynez D. Haase, *Historical Atlas of the American West* (Norman: University of Oklahoma Press, 1989), 36.

5.   Dan and Inez Morris, *Who Was Who in American Politics* (NY: Hawthorn, 1974), s.v. "Conrad, Charles Mynn."

6.   Paul F. Prucha, "The Settler and the Army in Frontier Minnesota," *Minnesota History* 29 (1948): 233.

7.   Michael L. Tate, *The Frontier Army in the Settlement of the West* (Norman: University of Oklahoma Press, 1999), 111–35.

8.   Ibid., 241.

9.   Gregory S. Camp, "Commerce and Conflict: A History of Pembina, 1797–1895," *North Dakota History* 60, no. 4 (1993): 22.

10.   William D. Thomson, "History of Fort Pembina: 1870–1895," *North Dakota History* 36, no. 1 (1969): 11, 19–24; Beck and Haase, *Historical Atlas of the American West*, 37.

11.   Williston Fish, *Memories of West Point, 1877–1881*, vol. 2, ed. and reproduced by Gertrude Fish Rumsey and Josephine Fish Peabody (Batavia, NY: Peabody, 1957), 641.

12.   Referring to the commanding officer as "the K.O." may have been a back-formation from KOW, considered to be the more discreet form of reference to the "commanding officer's wife" (as opposed to COW). John R. Elting, Dan Cragg, Ernest Deal, eds., *A Dictionary of Soldier Talk* (New York: Scribner's, 1984), s.v. "KOW."

13.   Fish, *Memories of West Point*, 641.

14.   "Post Returns, Fort Pembina, January 1882–July 1895," RG94, M-617, Roll 900, National Archives and Records Administration.

15.   Oliver Knight, *Life and Manners in the Frontier Army* (Norman: University of Oklahoma Press, 1978), 163–85; Thomson, "History of Fort Pembina," 32–33; Charles King, *Under Fire* (Philadelphia, PA: Lippincott, 1895), 459.

16.   Fish, *Memories of West Point*, 648.

17.   Thomson, "History of Fort Pembina," 34–35.

18.   Coffman, *Old Army*, 254–61.

19.   David Eggenberger, *A Dictionary of Battles* (New York: Crowell, 1967), s.v. "Wounded Knee."

20.   Thomson, "History of Fort Pembina," 32.

21.   Mary C. Gillett, *The Army Medical Department, 1865–1917* (Washington, DC: Center of Military History, 1995), 64.

22.   Thomson, "History of Fort Pembina," 36.

23.   Fish, *Memories of West Point*, 642–48.

24.   Nannie T. Alderson and Helena Huntington Smith, *A Bride Goes West* (Lincoln: University of Nebraska Press, 1969), 6.

25. Ibid., 8–16.

26. "Andrew B. Symns," http://skyways.lib.ks.us/genweb/atchison/ABSymnsbio .html.

27. "Post Returns, Fort Pembina, August 1886," RG94, M-617, Roll 900, National Archives and Records Administration.

28. "Personal," *Atchison Daily Champion*, April 7, 1887.

29. "The Local Record," *Atchison Daily Champion*, April 13, 1887.

30. "Personal," *Atchison Daily Globe*, November 14, 1988, January 10, 1988, February 24, 1888. For years in Atchison, anything connected with the Symns family or Andrew Rowan was considered a collectible artifact—even a cookbook. In 1957 it was reported in the *Atchison Daily Globe* that a Miss Mary Lukens owned a "treasured cookbook," over a hundred years old, that had belonged to Ida Rowan. This was not the cookbook she'd purchased in St. Paul, but was probably one of the items carried west by her mother. "Personal," *Atchison Daily Globe*, January 27, 1957.

31. D. C. Kingman, "Engineering Aspect of a Deep-Water Route from the Great Lakes to the Ocean," *Journal of the Military Service Institution of the United States* (March 1895): 276.

32. Shelby Foote, *The Civil War: A Narrative, Fort Sumter to Kernstown* (New York: Vintage, 1986), 794.

33. Robert G. Albion, *Five Centuries of Famous Ships: From the Santa Maria to the Glomar Explorer* (New York: McGraw-Hill, 1978), 238–44.

34. "The Treaty of Washington, May 8, 1871," in *Documents of American History*, vol. 1, *To 1898*, ed. Henry Steele Commager and Milton Cantor (Englewood Cliffs, NJ: Prentice Hall, 1988), 517–18.

35. Mark Mayo Boatner III, *The Civil War Dictionary* (New York: McKay, 1959), s.v. "Alabama Claims."

36. James Morton Callahan, *American Foreign Policy in Canadian Relations* (New York: Macmillan, 1937), 303–4.

37. George F. G. Stanley, *Louis Riel* (New York: McGraw-Hill, 1985), 1.

38. Callahan, *American Foreign Policy*, 338, 358, 359, 388, 394, 405, 415.

39. Marc B. Powe, *The Emergence of the War Department Intelligence Agency: 1885–1918* (Manhattan, KS: Military Affairs, 1975), 17.

40. Ibid., 18.

41. "Post Returns, Fort Pembina, September 1887," RG94, M-617, Roll 900, National Archives and Records Administration.

42. Andrew S. Rowan, "Battle-fields of the Canadian North-West Territories," *Journal of the Military Service Institution of the United States* 8, no. 31 (1887): 223–46.

43. Robert G. Angevine, "Mapping the Northern Frontier: Canada and the Origins of the US Army's Military Information Division, 1885–1898," *Intelligence and National Security* 16, no.3 (2002): 122–23, 131.

44.   "Post Returns, Fort Pembina, July and August 1889," RG94, M-617, Roll 900, National Archives and Records Administration.

45.   Angevine, "Mapping the Northern Frontier," 131–33.

46.   "An album containing photographic prints and maps showing harbors, railroads, and bridges in Canada," RG165, File No. AWC, 3071-D, National Archives and Records Administration.

47.   "Personal," *Atchison Daily Globe*, October 7, 1889, October 22, 1889, November 18, 1889, December 9, 1889.

48.   D. M. Taylor to Andrew Rowan, RG165, File No. AWC, 3071-D, National Archives and Records Administration.

49.   Cullum, *Biographical Register*, vol. 4, 353; vol. 4, supplement, 349.

50.   Graham A. Cosmas, *An Army for Empire: The United States Army in the Spanish-American War* (Columbia: University of Missouri Press, 1971), 6.

51.   "Personal," *Atchison Daily Globe*, January 14, 1891, March 30, 1891, April 7, 1891.

52.   Intercontinental Railway Commission, *Intercontinental Railway Commission*, vol. 1, pt. 1 (Washington, DC: Intercontinental Railway Commission, 1898), 10–22.

53.   Montgomery M. Macomb, *Report of Surveys and Explorations Made by Corps No. 1 in Guatemala, El Salvador, Honduras, Nicaragua and Costa Rica, 1891–1893* (Washington, DC: Intercontinental Railway Commission, 1898), 11–12.

54.   Ibid.

55.   David McCullough, *The Path between the Seas: The Creation of the Panama Canal 1870–1914* (New York: Simon and Schuster, 1977), 104, 106, 118–119, 203, 231.

56.   Macomb, *Report of Surveys and Explorations*, 27–50; Montgomery M. Macomb to Andrew Summers Rowan, May 13, 1892.

57.   "Personal," *Atchison Daily Globe*, June 9, 1892, and June 20, 1892.

58.   "New York to Patagonia," *New York Times*, 18 July 1920.

59.   Elizabeth Bethel, "The Military Information Division: Origin of the Intelligence Division," *Military Affairs* 11, no. 1 (1947): 20.

60.   "General Orders No. 23," *Journal of the Military Service Institution of the United States* 32 (1903): 325.

61.   Angevine, "Mapping the Northern Frontier," 134, 135.

62.   "Papers and Recommendations Filed in Connection with the Application," RG94, 1264, ACP 367 85, National Archives and Records Administration.

63.   Cullum, *Biographical Register*, vol. 4, supplement, 2920.

64.   Cosmas, *Army for Empire*, 31.

65.   *Official Register of the Officers and Cadets of the U.S. Military Academy, West Point* (June, 1881), 11.

66.   Andrew Rowan and M. M. Ramsey, *The Island of Cuba* (New York: Holt, 1896), iii–x.

67. "Memoirs, History, Biography," *New York Times*, June 5, 1897, 11.

68. "Minor Notices," *American Historical Review* 2, no. 3 (1897): 576.

69. Cullum, *Biographical Register*, vol. 4, supplement, 2601.

70. T. R. Brereton, *Educating the U.S. Army: Arthur L. Wagner and Reform, 1875–1905* (Lincoln: University of Nebraska Press, 2000), xi.

71. George W. Cullum, *Official Register of the Graduates of the U.S. Military Academy, 1875* (New York: Cambridge Riverside Press, 1875), 10–11.

72. Powe, *Emergence*, 28.

73. Arthur L. Wagner, *The Service of Security and Information* (Kansas City, MO: Hudson-Kimberly, 1903), 15–16.

74. Bethel, "Military Information Division," 22.

75. Cosmas, *Army for Empire*, 75.

76. Wagner, *Service of Security and Information*, 48.

77. Arthur L. Wagner, "Memorandum," December 28, 1897, RG165, File AWC 6831-1, National Archives and Records Administration.

78. Joan M. Jenson, *Army Surveillance in America, 1775–1980* (New Haven, CT: Yale University Press, 1991), 59.

79. Wagner, "Memorandum."

80. David P. Trask, *The War with Spain in 1898* (New York: Macmillan, 1981), 27–28.

81. Paul F. Boler, *Presidential Anecdotes* (New York: Oxford University Press, 1981), 191, 197.

82. Henry Cabot Lodge, *The War with Spain* (New York: Harper, 1899), 28.

83. Trask, *War with Spain*, 34.

84. Cosmas, *Army for Empire*, 73.

85. Russell A. Alger, *Report of the Secretary of War, Message from the President of the United States to the Two Houses of Congress*, v.1 (Washington, DC, 1899), 247.

86. Russell A. Alger, *The Spanish-American War* (New York: Harper, 1901), 7; Cosmas, *Army for Empire*, 89–97.

87. Alger, *Spanish-American War*, 9.

88. Trask, *War with Spain*, 39.

89. G. J. A. O'Toole, *The Spanish War: An American Epic, 1898* (New York: Norton, 1984), 97.

90. Trask, *War with Spain*, 174.

91. Joan M. Jensen, *Army Surveillance in America, 1775–1980* (New Haven, CT: Yale University Press, 1991), 61.

92. Wells Goodykoontz, *Major Andrew S. Rowan, a West Virginian: The Man Who Carried the Message to Garcia* (Washington, DC: Government Printing Office, 1926).

93. Andrew Summers Rowan, *How I Carried the Message to Garcia* (San Francisco: William D. Harney, 1922), 6.

94. "The Man Who Delivered That 'Message to Garcia,'" *Literary Digest* 74, no. 10 (1922): 50.

95. Rowan, *How I Carried the Message*, 8.

96. E. C. Wescott to Andrew Summers Rowan, September 26, 1913, Box 3, Andrew Summers Rowan Papers, Hoover Institution Archives, Stanford University.

97. Lodge, *War with Spain*, 35.

98. Louis A. Dent to William R. Day, April 20, 1898, RG59, T31, Roll 35, National Archives and Records Administration.

99. Jensen, *Army Surveillance in America*, 61.

100. "The Man Who Delivered That 'Message to Garcia,'" 50.

101. Goodykoontz, *Major Andrew S. Rowan*, 362.

102. Max Tosquella, *The Truth about the Message to Garcia*, translated by I. F. Berndes and Charles Dujol (Havana: n.p., 1955), chap. 1.

103. Trask, *War with Spain*, 2. Dent made the common mistake of assuming that Tomás Estrada Palma could be referred to by his final surname. Cubans followed the Spanish custom of the period and bestowed two surnames on children, the first being the name of the father and the second that of the mother. As in many cultures it is the father's name that becomes the family name; thus, Dent should have referred to him as Estrada or Estrada Palma. The mistake can be made both ways. In *Reminiscencias Cubanas de la Guerra y de la Paz*, by Luís Rodolfo Miranda, Andrew Summers Rowan is listed in the index as "Summers Rowan, Andrew."

104. Charles V. Kirchman, "The Message to Garcia: The Anatomy of a Famous Mission," *Mankind: The Magazine of Popular History* 4, no. 9 (1974): 46–53; Louis A. Dent, Despatch No. 91, RG59, T31, Roll 35, National Archives and Records Administration.

105. Andrew S. Rowan to Arthur Wagner, April 20, 1898, RG59, T31, Roll 35, National Archives and Records Administration.

106. Andrew Rowan, deposition before E. O. Whitodes, May 17, 1898, RG94, 367, ACP 85, 85731, National Archives and Records Administration.

107. Andrew S. Rowan, "My Ride across Cuba," *McClure's* 11, no. 4 (1898): 373; "The Man Who Delivered That 'Message to Garcia,'" 50.

108. Dent, Despatch No. 65, RG59, T31, Roll 35, National Archives and Records Administration.

109. Tosquella, *Truth about the Message*, chap. 1.

110. Ibid.; Philip S. Foner, *A History of Cuba and Its Relations with the United States*, vol. 2, *1845–1895* (New York: International, 1963), 340.

111. Dent, Despatch No. 84, RG59, T31, Roll 35, National Archives and Records Administration.

112. Dent, Despatch No. 91, RG59, T31, Roll 35, National Archives and Records Administration.

113. Ibid., 5–6.

114. Rowan to Wagner, April 23, 1898, Charles V. Kirchman Papers, 8.

115. Dent, Despatch 91, RG59, T31, Roll 35, National Archives and Records Administration.

116. Rowan, "My Ride across Cuba," 373.

117. Marrion Wilcox, *A Short History of the War with Spain* (New York: Stokes, 1898), 95.

118. Tosquella, *Truth about the Message*, chap. 6.

119. Rowan, "My Ride across Cuba," 374.

120. "The Man Who Delivered That 'Message to Garcia,'" 50.

121. Wilcox, *Short History*, 96.

122. Theodore Roosevelt, "Review of Alfred Thayer Mahan's *The Influence of Sea Power upon History*," *Atlantic Monthly* 66 (1890): 567.

123. Warren Zimmerman, *First Great Triumph: How Five Americans Made Their Country a World Power* (New York: Farrar, Straus and Giroux, 2002), 175–76, 241–42.

124. Nathan Sargent, *Admiral Dewey and the Manila Campaign* (Washington, DC: Naval Historical Foundation, 1947), 10, 22.

125. Louis A. Peake, "Andrew Summers Rowan and the Message from Garcia," *West Virginia History* 44, no. 3 (1983): 234.

126. "The Man Who Delivered That 'Message to Garcia,'" 50.

127. Andrew Summers Rowan, "How I Carried President McKinley's Message to General García," unpublished manuscript, December 11, 1917, 17; John W. Lang, "The Message to Garcia," in *The American Historical Scene* (New York: Carlton House, 1937), 147.

128. Tosquella, *Truth about the Message*, chap. 1.

129. Rowan, "My Ride across Cuba," 375.

130. Cullum, *Biographical Register*, vol. 4, supplement, 353.

131. "Lieut. Rowan's Mission," *New York Times*, May 16, 1898.

132. Rowan, "My Ride across Cuba," 375–6.

133. Elting E. Morison, ed., *The Letters of Theodore Roosevelt* (Cambridge, MA: Harvard University Press, 1951), 821.

134. Rowan, "How I Carried President McKinley's Message," 24.

135. Rowan, "My Ride across Cuba," 377.

136. "The Battle of Manila Bay, Order of Battle," http://www.spanamwar.com/mbay.htm#ORDER.

137. Alan Johnson and Dumas Malone, eds., *Dictionary of American Biography*, vol. 3 (New York: Scribner's, 1959), s.v., "Dewey, George."

138. Trask, *War with Spain*, 100–105.

139. "Baby Names and the Spanish-American War," http://http://www.nancy.cc /2011/07/10/baby-names-the-spanish-american-war/.

3. "A MOST PERILOUS UNDERTAKING"

1. Therese L. Kraus, "García, Calixto," in *The War of 1898 and U.S. Interventions 1898–1934: An Encyclopedia*, ed. Benjamin R. Beede (New York: Garland, 1994), 195.

2. Juan J. E. Casasús, *Calixto García: El Estratega* (Miami, FL: La Moderna Poesia, 1981), 21.

3. Larry Daley, "A Biography of Major General Calixto Ramón García Iñiguez," http://www.spanamwar.com/Garciabio.htm.

4. Kraus, "García," 195.

5. Philip S. Foner, *The Spanish-Cuban-American War and the Birth of American Imperialism* (New York: Monthly Review Press, 1972), 1:107, 149, 151–52, 162–63, 164, 167–68.

6. Luís Martínez-Fernández, ed., *Encyclopedia of Cuba: People, History, Culture* (Westport, CT: Greenwood Press, 2003), s.v. "García Íñiguez, Calixto."

7. Foner, *Spanish-Cuban-American War*, 1:186.

8. "Cuban Affairs," *New York Times*, September 17, 1874.

9. "Cuban Affairs," *New York Times*, September 19, 1874.

10. Casasús, *Calixto García*, 108.

11. Ulises Estrada Lescaille, "Allende's Death in Combat," http://www.walter lippmann.com/docs049.html.

12. Casasús, *Calixto García*, 119–20.

13. Ibid., 23, 120–31.

14. "General Calixto Garcia. Born 1840. Died December 11, 1898," *Harper's Weekly*, December 24, 1898, 1263.

15. Ada Ferrer, *Insurgent Cuba: Race, Nation, and Revolution: 1868–1898* (Chapel Hill: University of North Carolina Press, 1999), 82.

16. Martínez-Fernández, *Encyclopedia of Cuba*, s.v. "Grajales, Mariana," and "Maceo Graljales, Antonio."

17. Ferrer, *Insurgent Cuba*, 70–83.

18. Casasús, *Calixto García*, 132.

19. Ferrer, *Insurgent Cuba*, 78–79.

20. Larry Daley, "A Biography of Brigadier General Calixto (Garcia-Iñiguez) Enamorado," http://www.spanamwar.com/calixtoenamorado.

21. Casasús, *Calixto García*, 138–39; Charles Petrie, "From the Death of Philip II to 1945," in *The History of Spain* (London: Eyre and Spottiswoode, 1952), 343.

22. Foner, *Spanish-Cuban-American War*, 1:xx.

23. Martínez-Fernández, *Encyclopedia of Cuba*, s.v. "Martí, José (as Political Leader)."

24. Philip S. Foner, *A History of Cuba and Its Relations with the United States, 1845–1895* (New York: International, 1963), 2:355–57.

25. "Disaster for Insurgents," *New York Times*, February 2, 1896.

26. "Indignant Cubans Meet," *New York Times*, January 30, 1896.

27. "The Garcia Expedition," *New York Times*, January 31, 1896.

28. "The Spanish Counsel Will Not Talk," *New York Times*, January 29, 1896.

29. "Indignant Cubans Meet."

30. "Captured in the Bay," *New York Times*, February 26, 1896.

31. "Collazo Safely Landed," *New York Times*, March 19, 1896.

32. Years later he commented that "being of Irish parentage, I was favorably disposed toward dynamite on general principles." "Dynamite Johnny" O'Brien, quoted in Horace Smith, *A Captain Unafraid: The Strange Adventures of Dynamite Johnny O'Brien* (New York: Harper, 1912), 48.

33. Smith, *Captain Unafraid*, 85–92.

34. Louis A. Pérez Jr., *Cuba: Between Empires* (Pittsburgh, PA: Pittsburgh University Press, 1883), 165–68.

35. Foner, *Spanish-Cuban-American War*, 1: 76–78.

36. Graham A. Cosmas, *An Army for Empire: The United States Army in the Spanish-American War* (Columbia: University of Missouri Press, 1971), 76–77.

37. Of sixty-four filibustering ventures from the United States, only thirty-seven successfully landed. John Lawrence Tone, *War and Genocide in Cuba, 1895–1898* (Chapel Hill: University of North Carolina Press, 2008), 87.

38. Foner, *Spanish-Cuban-American War*, 1:14–36.

39. David P. Trask, *The War with Spain in 1898* (New York: Macmillan, 1981), 208.

40. Cosmas, *Army for Empire*, 76.

41. "A Spanish Soldier's Views on Cuba," *Saturday Review*, May 7, 1898.

42. Cosmas, *Army for Empire*, 81.

43. Andrew Summers Rowan, "How I Carried President McKinley's Message to General García," unpublished manuscript, December 11, 1917, 26; "Lieut. Col. Andrew S. Rowan, U. S. A.," *New York Times Sunday Magazine*, July 3, 1898.

44. Enrique Collazo, *Los Americanos en Cuba* (Havana: Instituto Cubano del Libro, 1972), 99–100.

45. Little had ever been publicly discussed regarding Rowan's success or failure in his mission until an analysis by Charles V. Kirchman, a retired intelligence officer,

appeared in 1974 in an issue of *Mankind: The Magazine of Popular History.* The magazine folded a few years later and disappeared from view. I managed to obtain a copy of the article only through the kindness of Kirchman's son Mark, who also provided me with copies of his father's transcriptions of documents. Charles Kirchman was also responsible for getting many of the documents associated with Rowan's mission declassified.

46. Arthur L. Wagner, "Memorandum," February 26, 1898, RG165, File AWC 6831-1, National Archives and Records Administration.

47. Louis A. Dent, Despatch No. 91, RG59, T31, Roll 35, National Archives and Records Administration.

48. Casasús, *Calixto García*, 275.

49. Foner, *Spanish-Cuban-American War*, 2:341.

50. Rowan, "How I Carried President McKinley's Message," 27–28.

51. Andrew S. Rowan, "My Ride across Cuba," *McClure's* 11, no. 4 (1898): 378.

52. Marrion Wilcox, *A Short History of the War with Spain* (New York: Stokes, 1898), 97–98.

53. Rowan, "How I Carried President McKinley's Message," 27.

54. Ibid., 27, 30; Rowan, "My Ride across Cuba," 378–79.

55. Trask, *War with Spain*, 111–12.

56. Rowan, "How I Carried President McKinley's Message," 31.

57. Collazo, *Los Americanos en Cuba*, 102.

58. Andrew Summers Rowan, Deposition before E. O. Whitodes, RG94, ACP 85, 85731, National Archives and Records Administration.

59. "Dangerous Mission of Lieutenant Rowan," *Columbus Dispatch*, April 27, 1898, 1.

60. Cable from Louis Dent to William Day, RG59, T31, Roll 35, National Archives and Records Administration.

61. "Warning to Newspapers," *New York Times*, April 26, 1898.

62. Louis Dent to William R. Day, April 28, 1898, Charles V. Kirchman Papers, 21.

63. "Reporters Must Be Careful," *New York Times*, April 29, 1898.

64. Charles H. Brown, *The Correspondents' War: Journalists in the Spanish-American War* (New York: Scribner's, 1967), vii.

65. Arthur Wagner to Henry Corbin, April 28, 1898, Charles V. Kirchman Papers (Mark Kirchman, Silver Spring, Maryland), 23.

66. Correspondence between Louis Dent and William Day, April, 1898, RG59, T31, Roll 35, National Archives and Records Administration.

67. Telegram from Andrew Rowan to Arthur Wagner, May 9, 1898, Charles V. Kirchman Papers, 42.

68. Ibid., 39.

69. "Rowan's Mission Fulfilled," *New York Times*, May 10, 1898, 2.

70. Arthur L. Wagner to Andrew S. Rowan, May 16, 1898, Box 3, Ideal Scrapbook 100, Andrew Summers Rowan Papers, Hoover Institution Archives, Stanford University.

71. T. R. Brereton, *Educating the U.S. Army: Arthur L. Wagner and Reform, 1875–1905* (Lincoln: University of Nebraska Press, 2000), 3.

72. Letter from Louis Dent to John B. Moore, May 10, 1898, RG59, T31, Roll 35, National Archives and Records Administration.

73. *Correspondence Relating to the War with Spain: Including the Insurrection in the Philippine Islands and the China Relief Expedition, April 15, 1898, to July 30, 1902* (Washington, DC: Center of Military History, 1993), 1:14.

74. Russell A. Alger, *The Spanish-American War* (New York: Harper, 1901), 70.

75. Arthur L. Wagner, *Report on the Santiago Campaign, 1898* (Kansas City, MO: Franklin Hudson, 1908), 21.

76. *Message from the President of the United States to the Two Houses of Congress*, vol. 1 (Washington, DC: Government Printing Office [GPO], 1899), 471, 491.

77. Ibid., 529.

78. Wagner, *Report*, 20, 25.

79. Alfred Thayer Mahan, *Lessons of the War with Spain and Other Articles* (Boston, MA: Little, Brown, 1899), 76, described a "fleet in being," a phrase that originated in 1690, as being "one, the existence and maintenance of which, although inferior, on or near the scene of operations, is a perpetual menace to the various more or less exposed interests of the enemy, who cannot tell when a blow may fall, and who is therefore compelled to restrict his operations."

80. Poultney Bigelow, "In Camp at Tampa," *Harper's Weekly*, June 6, 1898, 550.

81. Gone are the "Hydriotic Esplanade," the casino, servants' housing, conservatory, power plant, boathouse, kennels, racetrack, golf course, sanitarium, and other outbuildings. But, amazingly, the main hotel building still exists, appearing little different (at least outwardly) than it did in 1898. Such extravagance couldn't survive the passing of the Gilded Age as a commercial enterprise. It was purchased by the City of Tampa in 1904 and since 1933 has been leased to the University of Tampa for one dollar per year. The southern wing of the first floor is now the Henry B. Plant Museum, which includes one room devoted to the Spanish-American War.

82. Maria White, *Through the Keyhole: A Young Person's Guide to the Henry B. Plant Museum* (Tampa, FL: Henry B. Plant Museum, 2000), 11–12; Michael Blow, *A Ship to Remember: The Maine and the Spanish-American War* (New York: Morrow, 1992), 285.

83. Alger, *Spanish-American War*, 65.

84. Theodore Roosevelt, *Theodore Roosevelt: An Autobiography* (New York: Scribner's, 1925), 221.

85. Richard Harding Davis, *The Cuban and Porto Rican Campaigns* (New York: Scribner's, 1898), 46–49, 53.

86. "Lieut. Rowan's Mission," *New York Times*, May 16, 1898.

87. Telegram from Henry Corbin to Andrew Rowan, May 16, 1898, Box 3, Scrapbook 100, Rowan Papers.

88. Wells Goodykoontz, *Major Andrew S. Rowan, a West Virginian: The Man Who Carried the Message to Garcia* (Washington, DC: GPO, 1926), 1235.

89. *Historical Statistics of the United States: Colonial Times to 1970*, part 1 (Washington, DC: U.S. Department of Commerce, 1975), 26.

90. Louis A. Peake, "Andrew Summers Rowan and the Message from Garcia," *West Virginia History* 44, no. 3 (1983): 227–28.

91. *Annual Report of the Board of Visitors to the United States Military Academy* (Washington, DC: GPO, 1880), 6–7.

92. Rowan, Deposition before Whitodes.

93. Department of State, letter to General H. C. Corbin, May 28, 1898, RG94, 367, ACP 85 85731, National Archives and Records Administration.

94. As a result of the circumstances surrounding his return, Rowan may have lost some standing among his superiors in the War Department. Alger, *Spanish-American War*, 42, devoted a page to secret missions to Cuba and Puerto Rico, never once mentioning Rowan by name but lauding Whitney at length. And in the revised edition of *The Service of Security and Information* (Kansas City, MO: Hudson-Kimberly, 1903), 180, Arthur L. Wagner chose Whitney and not Rowan to exemplify the modern military spy. These two instances may mean nothing, but they are suggestive.

95. "Lieut. Rowan's Promotion," *Kansas Semi-Weekly Capital*, May 22, 1898.

96. Letter from Nelson Miles to Henry Corbin, RG94, E.25, A127268, National Archives and Records Administration; "Lieut. Rowan's Mission," *New York Times*, May 16, 1898.

97. Rowan, "My Ride across Cuba," 379.

98. George W. Cullum, *Biographical Register of the Officers and Graduates of the U.S. Military Academy at West Point, N.Y., since Its Establishment, in 1802*, supplement (Cambridge: Riverside Press, 1901), 4:350.

99. Letter from Nelson Miles to Henry Corbin, RG94, E.25, A127268, National Archives and Records Administration.

100. Vincent J. Cirillo, *Bullets and Bacilli: The Spanish-American War and Military Medicines* (New Brunswick, NJ: Rutgers University Press, 2004), 33–35.

101. "Praise for Lieut. Rowan," *New York Times*, May 26, 1898.

102. Rowan, "My Ride across Cuba," 379.

4. AMERICA TAKES A STEP TOWARD EMPIRE

1. Russell A. Alger, *The Spanish-American War* (New York: Harper, 1901), 15–16; Graham A. Cosmas, *An Army for Empire: The United States Army in the Spanish-American War* (Columbia: University of Missouri Press, 1971), 98–99.

2. Theodore Roosevelt, *The Rough Riders* (New York: New American Library, 1961), 14.

3. Paul H. Jeffers, *Colonel Roosevelt: Theodore Roosevelt Goes to War, 1897–1898* (New York: John Wiley, 1996), fourth unnumbered page following 148.

4. Dale L. Walker, *The Boys of '98: Theodore Roosevelt and the Rough Riders* (New York: Doherty, 1998), 118.

5. Roosevelt, *Rough Riders*, 29.

6. Alger, *Spanish-American War*, 412.

7. Mary C. Gillett, *The Army Medical Department, 1865–1917* (Washington, DC: Center of Military History, 1995), 173.

8. George Edward Graham, *Schley and Santiago: An Historical Account of the Blockade and Final Destruction of the Spanish Fleet under Command of Admiral Pasquale Cervera, July 3, 1898* (Chicago: Conkey, 1902), 146.

9. David P. Trask, *The War with Spain in 1898* (New York: Macmillan, 1981), 119–23, 125–36.

10. G. J. A. O'Toole, *The Spanish War: An American Epic, 1898* (New York: Norton, 1984), 237.

11. Cosmas, *Army for Empire*, 193–94.

12. Paul H. Carlson, *"Pecos Bill": A Military Biography of William R. Shafter* (College Station: Texas A&M University Press), 1896, 163.

13. Cosmas, *Army for Empire*, 194.

14. Herman Hagedorn, *Leonard Wood: A Biography* (New York, 1931) 1:155.

15. Trask, *War with Spain*, 175, 185.

16. Teresa Dean, "A Woman's View of Tampa," *Leslie's Weekly*, July 14, 1898.

17. O'Toole, *Spanish War*, 244.

18. Cuba may be "ninety miles from home," if one counts the southernmost point on the Florida Keys as home, but the distance by ship from Tampa Bay to Santiago on Cuba's southeastern shore is a thousand miles.

19. Richard Harding Davis, *The Cuban and Porto Rican Campaigns* (New York: Scribner's, 1898), 86–89.

20. W. T. Sampson to the Secretary of the Navy, June 22, 1898, *Annual Report of the Navy Department* (Washington, DC: Government Printing Office [GPO], 1898), 500.

21. The drink named for this site, composed of rum, lime, sugar, and shaved ice, was discovered here in 1909 by Lucius W. Johnson, a medical officer on the USS *Minnesota*, and it was he who introduced it to the United States. Robert D. Hershey Jr., "Amid Many Daiquiris, a Club Closes," *New York Times*, January 2, 1984.

22.   Alger, *Spanish-American War*, 79.

23.   Richard Titherington, "Our War with Spain," *Munsey's* 20, no. 6 (1899): 915.

24.   Henry Cabot Lodge, *The War with Spain* (New York: Harper, 1899), 112.

25.   Michael Blow, *A Ship to Remember: The Maine and the Spanish-American War* (New York: Morrow, 1992), 297–98; Albert E. Smith, *Two Reels and a Crank* (New York: Garland, 1985), 59.

26.   R. W. Stallman and E. R. Hagerman, *The War Dispatches of Stephen Crane* (New York: New York University Press, 1964), 137–38; Arthur L. Wagner, *Report on the Santiago Campaign, 1898* (Kansas City, MO: Franklin Hudson, 1908), 60, 127.

27.   Wagner, *Report*, 129–30.

28.   Cosmas, *Army for Empire*, 157, 211; *Message from the President of the United States to the Two Houses of Congress*, vol. 1 (Washington, DC: GPO, 1899), 306.

29.   Wagner, *Report*, 55; Blow, *Ship to Remember*, 300–306; O'Toole, *Spanish War*, 278.

30.   Alger, *Spanish-American War*, 136, 144, 146.

31.   Aníbel Escalante Beatón, *Calixto García: Su Campaña en el 95* (Havana: Editorial de Ciencias Sociales, 1973), 547.

32.   Trask, *War with Spain*, 230.

33.   Ibid., 230, 235–37; Alger, *Spanish-American War*, 146.

34.   Charles Johnson Post, *The Little War of Private Post: The Spanish-American War Seen up Close* (Boston, MA: Little, Brown, 1960), 162.

35.   Charles H. Brown, *The Correspondents' War: Journalists in the Spanish-American War* (New York: Scribner's, 1967), 330.

36.   Roosevelt, *Rough Riders*, 92.

37.   Peter Collier, *The Roosevelts: An American Saga* (New York: Simon and Schuster, 1994), 99.

38.   Theodore Roosevelt to Henry Cabot Lodge, July 19, 1898, in *The Letters of Theodore Roosevelt*, ed. Elting E. Morison (Cambridge, MA: Harvard University Press, 1951), 853.

39.   The pistol, which eventually became one of the artifacts on display at Sagamore Hill, was stolen twice. The first time it was found in some nearby woods; in 1990 it was stolen again and voluntarily returned by the thief sixteen years later. Benjamin Gibberd, "So History Can Live On, a Pistol Is Returned," *New York Times*, June 18, 2006.

40.   Edmond Morris, "Charge!," *New York Times Book Review*, November 7, 1999, 47; Walker, *Boys of '98*, 270–71; "Medal of Honor Ceremony," EFE News Service, January 16, 2001.

41.   Trask, *War with Spain*, 243, 245, 248–50.

42.   Wagner, *Report*, 50.

43. Trask, *War with Spain*, 265–66.

44. Blow, *Ship to Remember*, 329–30; O'Toole, *Spanish War*, 236–38; Edgar Stanton Maclay, *Life and Adventures of "Jack" Philip: Rear Admiral United States Navy* (New York: Baker and Taylor, 1903), 6.

45. "Captain Evans's Account," in "The Naval Battle of Santiago," in *Harper's Pictorial History of the War with Spain* (New York: Harper, 1899), 365.

46. Blow, *Ship to Remember*, 358.

47. "Account by Lieutenant Hazeltine, Commanding the *Hist* during the Events Narrated," in "The Naval Battle of Santiago," in *Harper's Pictorial History*, 370–71.

48. *Correspondence Relating to the War with Spain* (Washington, DC: Center of Military History, 1993), 1:79.

49. Joseph Wheeler, *The Santiago Campaign 1898* (Port Washington, NY: Kennikat, 1971), 111–13, 119.

50. Blow, *Ship to Remember*, 370–71.

51. *Correspondence Relating to the War*, 1:626.

52. Assistant Attorney General to L. D. Tyson, telegram, RG94, 367, ACP 85, National Archives and Records Administration.

53. George W. Cullum, *Biographical Register of the Officers and Graduates of the U.S. Military Academy at West Point, N.Y., since Its Establishment, in 1802*, supplement (Cambridge: Riverside Press, 1901), 4:350.

54. E. J. McClernand, "The Santiago Campaign," in *The Santiago Campaign: Reminiscences of the Operations for the Capture of Santiago de Cuba in the Spanish-American War, June and July, 1898* (Richmond, VA: Society of the Army of Santiago de Cuba), 1927, 38–39.

55. *Message from the President of the United States to the Two Houses of Congress*, vol. 1 (Washington, DC: GPO, 1899), 351.

56. Wheeler, *Santiago Campaign*, 122–3.

57. Escalante Beatón, *Calixto García*, 616–17.

58. Carlson, *"Pecos Bill,"* 181–82.

59. "Hail, Columbia" is today the prescribed honors music of the vice president.

60. Wheeler, *Santiago Campaign*, 182.

61. Trask, *War with Spain*, 209–10.

62. McClernand, "Santiago Campaign," 8.

63. R. A. Alger to William R. Shafter, telegram, July 7, 1898, Shafter Correspondence, Reel 4, Document 761, William Rufus Shafter Papers, 1862–1938, Stanford University Libraries, Stanford, CA.

64. *Racine Journal*, July 21, 1898.

65. *Reno Evening Gazette*, July 19, 1898.

66. "Pretensions of Cuban Soldiers," *New York Times*, July 20, 1898.

67. Calixto García to William Shafter, letter, July 19, 1898. Redwood City, 1975, Reel 3, Documents 306–7, Shafter Papers.

68. William Shafter to Calixto García, July 20, 1898, Reel 4, Document 413, Shafter Papers.

69. Trask, *War with Spain*, 323. It should be noted that no American naval officers were invited to be present at the surrender, a fact that irked Sampson greatly. In his official report he wrote, "I do not think the commanding general quite appreciates how necessary a part our forces were to the reduction of Santiago and the surrender of its garrison, independently of the effect of our shell, which latter was undoubtedly one of the principal causes of the surrender at this time." Alger, *Spanish-American War*, 243.

70. "The Independence of Cuba" in *Documents of American History*, vol. 2, *Since 1898*, ed. Henry Steele Commager and Milton Cantor (Englewood Cliffs, NJ: Prentice Hall, 1988), 5.

71. Philip S. Foner, *The Spanish-Cuban-American War and the Birth of American Imperialism* (New York: Monthly Review Press: 1972), 2:392.

72. Henry Huntington Powers, "The War as a Suggestion of Manifest Destiny," *Annals of the American Academy of Political and Social Science* 12 (1898): 173–75.

5. THE CREATION OF AN AMERICAN MYTH

1. Henry Cabot Lodge, *The War with Spain* (New York: Harper, 1899), 173.

2. Milagros Flores Román, "A Spy Named Whitney," *CRM: The Journal of Heritage Stewardship* 11 (1998): 34–35; David P. Trask, *The War with Spain in 1898* (New York: Macmillan, 1981), 114–15, 118, 340–41; Russell A. Alger, *The Spanish-American War* (New York: Harper, 1901), 42.

3. Nelson A. Miles, "The War with Spain—IIII," *North American Review* 169 (1899): 125.

4. Walter Millis, *The Martial Spirit* (Chicago: Dee, 1989), 338.

5. Finley Peter Dunne, *Mr. Dooley in Peace and in War* (Boston: Small, Maynard, 1898), 34.

6. Richard Harding Davis, *The Cuban and Porto Rican Campaigns* (New York: Scribner's, 1898), 347; Linda H. Davis, *Badge of Courage: The Life of Stephen Crane* (Boston: Houghton Mifflin, 1998), 276–77.

7. W. Nephew King, *The Story of the Spanish-American War and the Revolt in the Philippines* (New York: Collier, 1900), 209–10.

8. Dard Hunter, "Elbert Hubbard and 'A Message to Garcia,'" *New Colophon* 1, no. 1 (1948): 33.

9. August F. Jaccaci to Lieutenant Rowan, June 8, 1898, Box 6, Andrew Summers Rowan Papers, Hoover Institution Archives, Stanford University.

10. Andrew S. Rowan, "My Ride across Cuba," *McClure's* 11, no. 4 (1898): 372–73.

11. Davis, *Cuban and Porto Rican Campaigns*, 303.

12. Vincent J. Cirillo, *Bullets and Bacilli: The Spanish-American War and Military Medicines* (New Brunswick, NJ: Rutgers University Press, 2004), 32–33.

13. J. G. Gilmore to Andrew Rowan, letter, August 22, 1898, RG94, E949767, National Archives and Records Administration.

14. Andrew Summers Rowan, quoted in Trumbull White, *Our New Possessions* (Chicago: National Education Union, 1898), 607–8.

15. Hugh Thomas, *Cuba: The Pursuit of Freedom* (New York: Harper and Row, 1971), 897, 905.

16. Rowan, quoted in White, *Our New Possessions*, 607–9.

17. Ray Stannard Baker, "General Leonard Wood," *McClure's* 14, no. 4 (1900): 371–74.

18. Leonard Wood, "Santiago since the Surrender," *Scribner's* 25, no. 5 (1899): 515–27.

19. Juan J. E. Casasús, *Calixto García* (Miami, FL: La Moderna Poesia, 1981), 331–32.

20. "Gen. Garcia Heard From," *New York Times*, April 14, 1896.

21. Editorial, *New York Times*, April 15, 1896.

22. L. D. Tyson to Henry Corbin, telegram, September 29, 1898; Assistant Adjutant General to L. D. Tyson, telegram, October 6, 1898, RG94, 367, ACP 85, National Archives and Records Administration.

23. "A Terrific Gale," *Dallas Morning News*, October 20, 1898.

24. "Lieut. Rowan in Town," *New York Times*, October 20, 1898.

25. August F. Jaccaci to Colonel Rowan, October 20, 1898, Box 6, Rowan Papers.

26. Report to J. C. Gilmore from Andrew Rowan and Charles Parker, November 3, 1898, RG94, E949767, National Archives and Records Administration.

27. Nelson A. Miles, *Annual Report of the Major General Commanding the Army to the Secretary of the War 1898* (Washington, DC: Government Printing Office [GPO], 1898), 37.

28. "Cuban Army Disbanding," *New York Times*, September 14, 1898; *New York Times*, October 20, 1898, 5.

29. "Cuban Delegates Coming," *New York Times*, November 18, 1898.

30. "Cuban Commission Here," *New York Times*, November 22, 1898.

31. "Cubans to See President McKinley," *New York Times*, December 1, 1898; "Cuban Delegates Meet the President," *New York Times*, December 3, 1898; "Cubans Meet in Washington," *New York Times*, December 4, 1898.

32. "Gen. Garcia Seriously Ill," *New York Times*, December 9, 1898; "Gen. Garcia's Condition Alarming," *New York Times*, December 10, 1898.

33. "General Calixto Garcia," *New York Times*, December 12, 1898.

34. "Gen. Garcia's Daughter Dead," *New York Times*, December 28, 1898.

35. "Riot over Garcia's Death," *New York Times*, December 13, 1898; "The Funeral of Gen. Garcia," *New York Times*, December 14, 1898.

36. "Gen. Garcia's Body Removed," *New York Times*, February 5, 1899; "Havana is Disappointed," *New York Times*, February 9, 1899; "Gen Garcia Laid to Rest," *New York Times*, February 12, 1899.

37. "Personal," *Atchison Daily Globe*, July 5, 1898.

38. "Almost Everything You Ever Wanted to Know about the Roycrofters," http://www.roycrofter.com/faq.htm.

39. Jean-François Vilain, "The Roycroft Printing Shop: Books, Magazines and Ephemera," in *Head, Heart, and Hand: Elbert Hubbard and the Roycrofters*, ed. Marie Via and Marjorie Searl (Rochester, NY: University of Rochester Press, 1994), 24–25, 49.

40. Robert L. Beisner, "'Commune' in East Aurora," *American Heritage* 22, no. 2 (1971): 74. There is little doubt that Hubbard visited the Kelmscott Press, but other than his saying so, there is no proof of his meeting Morris, and at least one writer, Jean-François Vilain, has suggested it never happened. Vilain, "Roycroft Printing Shop," 24, 49.

41. Charles F. Hamilton, *Roycroft Collectibles* (New York: Barnes, 1980), 24.

42. Alan Burton, *A Message to Garcia . . . Revisited* (n.p.: Silver Lake, 1986), 21.

43. Elbert Hubbard, "An Interesting Personality," *Cosmopolitan* 32 (1902): 316. Had Lieutenant Henry H. Whitney received a similar amount of newspaper coverage, Bert might easily have argued that it was he who was the true hero of the war, and the catchphrase would have been "a message to Gómez."

44. Elbert Hubbard, *A Message to Garcia* (East Aurora, NY: Roycrofters, 1899), 5–6.

45. Ibid., 3–4. At age thirty-nine Hubbard decided to enter Harvard University and earn a degree. He was abashed to discover his early education, enhanced by his extensive reading, qualified him for enrollment only as a special student in a limited number of classes. He lasted only three months and forever bore a grudge against higher education in general and Harvard in particular. David Arnold Balch, *Elbert Hubbard: Genius of Roycroft* (New York: Stokes, 1940), 108–10.

46. Hubbard, *Message to Garcia*, 7–8.

47. Ibid., 10–11.

48. Bert Hubbard, *Impressions* (East Aurora, NY: Roycrofters, 1921), 128–29.

49. Stewart H. Holbrook, *Lost Men of American History* (New York: Macmillan, 1946), 297.

50. Elbert Hubbard, "An Interesting Personality," *Cosmopolitan* 32 (1899): 316.

51. Chester Winston Bowie, "Redfield Proctor: A Biography" (PhD diss., University of Wisconsin, 1980), 385, 391.

52. "Atchison Affairs," *Atchison Daily News*, January 26, 1899; "Personal," *Atchison Daily News*, February 14, 1899.

53. "Mrs. A. S. Rowan," *Atchison Daily Globe*, February 17, 1899.

54. *Correspondence Relating to the War with Spain: Including the Insurrection in the Philippine Islands and the China Relief Expedition, April 15, 1898, to July 30, 1902* (Washington, DC: Center of Military History, 1993), 1:627.

55. Ibid., 1:329.

56. "Message to Garcia," *Daily Gazette*, June 6, 1899, Box 9 Scrapbook 3, Rowan Papers.

57. George H. Daniels, "From Remarks Made by George H. Daniels, General Passenger Agent, New York Central Railroad, at the 115th Meeting of the New York Universalist Club at the St. Denis Hotel, New York, Monday Evening, May 22, 1899," in Elbert Hubbard, *A Message to Garcia*, Four Track Series No. 25, second half million ed. (New York: New York Central and Hudson River Railroad, 1899), 17.

58. Hubbard used handmade paper for his printed products, but none was manufactured by the Roycrofters; it was made to order and watermarked with the Roycrofter devices in England, Holland, or Italy. Hunter, "Elbert Hubbard and 'A Message to Garcia,'" 29.

59. J. R. Pond, *Eccentricities of Genius: Memories of Famous Men and Women of the Platform and State* (New York: Dillingham, 1900), 355–56.

60. Newspaper clipping, June 21, 1900, Box 2, Scrapbook 7, Rowan Papers.

61. Hubbard presented his personal copy of the first edition to the New York Public Library; on January 5, 1900, he gave the twenty-page, pencil-written copy of the original manuscript to the Buffalo Public Library. R. W. G. Vail, "'A Message to Garcia': A Bibliographical Puzzle," *Bulletin of the New York Public Library*, 34, no. 2 (1930): 72.

62. James Moran, *Printing Presses: History and Development from the Fifteenth Century to Modern Times* (Berkeley: University of California Press, 1978), 148–49.

63. Vail, "'Message to Garcia,'" 71–76.

64. Hubbard, *Message to Garcia*, Four Track Series No. 25, 19, 22, 25–26.

65. Letter, *New York Times*, August 12, 1899.

66. Freeman Champney, *Art and Glory: The Story of Elbert Hubbard* (New York: Crown, 1968), 89.

67. Jules Zanger, "'A Message to Garcia': The Subsidized Hero," *American Studies* 20, no. 1 (1979): 102.

68. "Universalists at Dinner," *Brooklyn Daily Eagle*, May 23, 1899.

69. Elbert Hubbard to Captain Rowan, May 8, 1899, Box 9, Scrapbook 3, Rowan Papers.

70. "Capt. A. S. Rowan," *Atchison Daily Globe*, June 2, 1899.

71. Ibid.

72. "They gave a reception . . . ," *Emporia Weekly Gazette*, June 8, 1899.

73. "How to Treat a Hero: A Tribute to Atchison by Edward F. Trefz in the St. Joe Herald," *Atchison Daily Globe*, June 3, 1899.

74. "Multiple News Items," *Atchison Daily Globe*, August 5, 1989.

75. "The Death of Mrs. Symns," *Atchison Daily Globe*, September 14, 1900.

76. Hunter, "Elbert Hubbard and 'A Message to Garcia,'" 32–33.

77. Lodge, *War with Spain*, 268–69; "Treaty of Peace with Spain," in *Documents of American History*, vol. 2, *Since 1898*, ed. Henry Steele Commager and Milton Cantor (Englewood Cliffs, NJ: Prentice Hall, 1988), 7.

78. Michael Blow, *A Ship to Remember: The Maine and the Spanish-American War* (New York: Morrow, 1992), 389.

79. Rudyard Kipling, "The White Man's Burden," *McClure's* 12, no. 4 (1899): 202–3.

80. George W. Cullum, *Biographical Register of the Officers and Graduates of the U.S. Military Academy at West Point, N.Y., since Its Establishment, in 1802* (Cambridge: Riverside Press, 1910), 5:324; *Correspondence Relating to the War with Spain*, 2:1039.

6. EXACTLY WHERE ARE THE PHILIPPINES?

1. Cesar Adib Majul, *Mabini and the Philippine Revolution* (Quezon City: University of the Philippines Press, 1960), 62–63.

2. Reynaldo Clemeña Ileto, *Pasyon and Revolution: Popular Movements in the Philippines, 1840–1910* (Quezon City: Ateneo de Manila University Press, 1979), 4.

3. Teodoro M. Kalaw, *The Philippine Revolution* (Kawilihan, Philippines: Jorge B. Vargas Filipiniana Foundation, 1969), 1.

4. Eufronio M. Alip, *In the Days of General Emilio Aguinaldo: A Study of the Life and Times of a Great Military Leader, Statesman, and Patriot Who Founded the First Republic in Asia* (Manila: Alip, 1969), 9.

5. Majul, *Mabini and the Philippine Revolution*, 66–67.

6. Pedro S. de Auchútegui and Miguel A. Bernard, *Aguinaldo and the Revolution of 1896: A Documentary History* (Quezon City: Ateneo de Manila University Press, 1972), 5–8.

7. David P. Trask, *The War with Spain in 1898* (New York: Macmillan, 1981), 394.

8. Auchútegui and Bernard, *Aguinaldo and the Revolution*, 28–40; Gregorio F. Zaide, *The Philippine Revolution*, rev. ed. (Manila: Modern Book, 1968), 141.

9. Auchútegui and Bernard, *Aguinaldo and the Revolution*, 41–43.

10. For centuries the Mexican dollar was the most common currency in use throughout the Americas, the Caribbean, and much of Asia. It was particularly

popular in the Philippines, which had no coinage of its own until the middle of the nineteenth century. A. Piatt Andrew, "The End of the Mexican Dollar," *Quarterly Journal of Economics* 18, no. 3 (1904): 321.

11.   Emilio Aguinaldo y Famy, *My Memoirs*, vol. 1 (Manila: n.p., 1967), 186–87.

12.   Auchútegui and Bernard, *Aguinaldo and the Revolution*, 550.

13.   "Philippine Insurgents Sail," *New York Times*, December 28, 1897; Auchútegui and Bernard, *Aguinaldo and the Revolution*, 558.

14.   George Dewey, *Autobiography of George Dewey: Admiral of the Navy* (Annapolis, MD: Naval Institute Press, 1987), 50.

15.   Margaret Leech, *In the Days of McKinley* (New York: Harper, 1959), 160–61.

16.   Theodore Roosevelt, *Theodore Roosevelt: An Autobiography* (New York: Scribner's, 1925), 211.

17.   Trask, *War with Spain*, 80–81.

18.   Leon Wolff, *Little Brown Brother: How the United States Purchased and Pacified the Philippines* (London: Longman's, 1961), 46; Ivan Musicant, *Empire by Default: The Spanish American War and the Dawn of the American Century* (New York: Holt, 1998), 200.

19.   Wolff, *Little Brown Brother*, 55.

20.   Stanley Karnow, *In Our Image: America's Empire in the Philippines* (New York: Random House, 1989), 103–4.

21.   Ibid., 104.

22.   George Dewey, "Commander Dewey's Account," in *Harper's Pictorial History of the War with Spain* (New York: Harper, 1899), 234–35.

23.   Trask, *War with Spain*, 104.

24.   Brian McAllister Linn, *The Philippine War, 1899–1902* (Lawrence: University Press of Kansas, 2000), 8; Wolff, *Little Brown Brother*, 57.

25.   Emilio Aguinaldo y Famy, *True Version of the Philippine Revolution* (n.p.: Dodo Press, n.d.), 10.

26.   Charles H. Brown, *The Correspondents' War: Journalists in the Spanish-American War* (New York: Scribner's, 1967), 196–98.

27.   Advertisement, *Harper's New Monthly* 583 (1898): 90; Adelbert M. Dewey, *The Life and Letters of Admiral Dewey: From Montpelier to Manila* (Akron, OH: Werner, 1899), 411.

28.   At a banquet in Dewey's honor before he left for the Asiatic Station, a specially written song prophesized his victory. After the Battle of Manila Bay a stanza was added:

> Along the far Philippine coast,
> Where flew the flag of Spain,
> Our Admiral to-day can boast,
> " 'Twill never fly again."

29. "Dewey's Invincible Squadron," *Munsey's* 19, no. 3 (1898): 401.

30. *Annual Reports of the Navy for the Year 1898* (Washington, DC: Government Printing Office [GPO], 1898), 104.

31. Wolff, *Little Brown Brother*, 70–73.

32. Zaide, *Philippine Revolution*, 181–83.

33. It took a while, but they achieved self-rule on January 28, 1909. Geoff Simons, *Cuba: From Conquistador to Castro* (New York: St. Martin's, 1996), 217.

34. Leech, *In the Days of McKinley*, 323–27.

35. Dewey, *Life and Letters*, 211.

36. *Correspondence Relating to the War with Spain: Including the Insurrection in the Philippine Islands and the China Relief Expedition, April 15, 1898, to July 30, 1902* (Washington, DC: Center of Military History, 1993), 2:648–49.

37. Musicant, *Empire by Default*, 542, 546.

38. Linn, *Philippine War*, 3, 7.

39. *Correspondence Relating to the War with Spain*, 2:648–49, 690.

40. Leech, *In the Days of McKinley*, 326.

41. Adjutant General's Office, Military Information Division, *Military Notes on the Philippines* (Washington, DC: GPO, 1898), 24–25.

42. "The Religious Press and the Philippines," *Literary Digest* 17 (1898): 290.

43. Leech, *In the Days of McKinley*, 323–24.

44. "A Newspaper Plebiscite on the Philippines," *Literary Digest* 17 (1898): 307–8.

45. Foster Rhea Dulles, *The Imperial Years* (New York: Crowell, 1966), 154.

46. Finley Peter Dunne, *Mr. Dooley in Peace and in War* (Boston, MA: Small, Maynard, 1898), 43. Many Americans might have blushed at reading this exchange. When it came to the Philippines, few people were any more knowledgeable than Mr. Hennessy; and even if they went looking for information, they would have had a hard time finding it. The most comprehensive collection of Philippiniana at the time was in Barcelona, owned by the Compañía General De Tabacos De Filipinas. Eventually these books and papers, along with thousands of other items scattered around the world, were purchased by the bibliophilic business magnate Edward E. Ayer. In 1911 Ayer donated his collection to the Newberry Library of Chicago, where it still resides. Frank C. Lockwood, *The Life of Edward Ayer* (Chicago, IL: McClure's, 1929), 83–87.

47. Linn, *Philippine War*, 3, 5.

48. Dumas Malone, ed., *Dictionary of American Biography*, vol. 6 (New York: Scribner's, 1959), s.v. "Merritt, Wesley."

49. Stephen D. Coats, *Gathering at the Golden Gate: Mobilizing for War in the Philippines, 1898* (Ft. Leavenworth, KS: Combat Studies Institute Press, 2006), 86.

50. Adjutant General's Office, Military Information Division, *Military Notes on the Philippines*, title page, table of contents.

51. *Arthur L. Wagner: The Man Who Wrote the Book on Intelligence,* http://huachuca .army.mil/files/History_MWAGNER.PDF, 6.

52. Ibid., 9.

53. *Correspondence Relating to the War with Spain,* 2:637, 643–48, 676.

54. Wesley Merritt and Henry Corbin, telegraphic communications, RG94, 367, ACP 85, National Archives and Records Administration.

7. A GLORIOUS UNDERTAKING

1. Stephen D. Coats, *Gathering at the Golden Gate: Mobilizing for War in the Philippines, 1898* (Ft. Leavenworth, KS: Combat Studies Institute Press, 2006), 30–31, 279.

2. Russell A. Alger, *The Spanish-American War* (New York: Harper, 1901), 21; Graham A. Cosmas, *An Army for Empire: The United States Army in the Spanish-American War* (Columbia: University of Missouri Press, 1971), 167–71; "The Manila Expedition," *New York Times,* May 22, 1898; Fred Greguras, comp., "Spanish-American War Camps 1898–99," http://www.usgennet.org/usa/ne/topic/military /SpanishAmericanWar/span_am_camps/pg1.htm, 2–3.

3. *Correspondence Relating to the War with Spain: Including the Insurrection in the Philippine Islands and the China Relief Expedition, April 15, 1898, to July 30, 1902* (Washington, DC: Center of Military History, 1993), 2:707–8.

4. "Manila Expedition Delayed," *New York Times,* May 16, 1898.

5. Coats, *Gathering at the Golden Gate,* 279.

6. William F. Strobridge, "Now Here I Am in the Army," *Nebraska History* 53, no. 3 (1972): 332.

7. Coats, *Gathering at the Golden Gate,* 63.

8. Strobridge, "Now Here I Am," 331.

9. Greguras, "Spanish-American War Camps," 3.

10. Mary C. Gillett, *The Army Medical Department, 1865–1917* (Washington, DC: U.S. Army Center of Military History, 1995), 133.

11. Brian McAllister Linn, *The Philippine War, 1899–1902* (Lawrence: University Press of Kansas, 2000), 12.

12. "Gossip in San Francisco," *New York Times,* May 15, 1898.

13. William Allen White, "When Johnny Went Marching Out," *McClure's* 11, no. 2 (1898): 198–205.

14. Coats, *Gathering at the Golden Gate,* 96.

15. Earle Ashley Walcott, "The War between Spain and the United States—II," *Overland Monthly and Out West Magazine* 32, no. 187 (1898): 83; Oscar King Davis, "Off for Manila," in *Harper's Pictorial History of the War with Spain* (New York: Harper, 1899), 265.

16. Ibid., 83.

17. "Troops off for Manila," *New York Times*, May 24, 1898.

18. "Troops Sail for Manila," *New York Times*, May 26, 1898.

19. See various reports of the voyage of the transports in *Correspondence Relating to the War with Spain* 2:767–79; Oscar King Davis, "At Honolulu," in Wilcox, *Harper's Pictorial History*, 266.

20. David P. Trask, *The War with Spain in 1898* (New York: Macmillan, 1981), 385.

21. Davis, "At Honolulu," 266.

22. Thomas A. Bailey, "The United States and Hawaii during the Spanish-American War," *American Historical Review* 36, no. 3 (1931): 556.

23. Pauline N. King, "Introduction," in William Adam Russ Jr., *The Hawaiian Republic (1894–98) and Its Struggle to Win Annexation* (Selinsgrove, PA: Susquehanna University Press, 1992), ix.

24. Thomas M. Anderson, "Our Rule in the Philippines," *North American Review* 170 (1900): 277.

25. Gregorio F. Zaide, *The Philippine Revolution*, rev. ed. (Manila: Modern Book, 1968), 215.

26. Ibid., 209.

27. Anderson, "Our Rule in the Philippines," 78.

28. Zaide, *Philippine Revolution*, 212; Linn, *Philippine War*, 24.

29. Zaide, *Philippine Revolution*, 211.

30. *Correspondence Relating to the War with Spain*, 2:754.

31. Wesley Merritt, "The Manila Campaign," in *The American-Spanish War: A History by the War Leaders* (Norwich, CT: Haskell, 1899), 279.

32. Anderson, "Our Rule in the Philippines," 282.

33. *Correspondence Relating to the War with Spain*, 2:765.

34. Jennie L. Hobart, *Memories* (privately printed, 1930), 66.

35. Alan Johnson and Dumas Malone, eds., *Dictionary of American Biography*, vol. 7, pt. 2 (New York: Scribner's, 1959), s.v. "Otis, Elwell Stephen."

36. Frederick Funston, *Memories of Two Wars: Cuban and Philippine Experiences* (Lincoln: University of Nebraska Press, 2009), 159.

37. Linn, *Philippine War*, 27–29.

38. Stuart Creighton Miller, *Benevolent Assimilation: The American Conquest of the Philippines, 1899–1903* (New Haven, CT: Yale University Press, 1982), 47.

39. "Introductory Note," in Adjutant General's Office, Military Information Division, *Military Notes on the Philippines* (Washington, DC: Government Printing Office, 1898), iii.

40. William J. Pomeroy, *American Neo-Colonialism: Its Emergence in the Philippines and Asia* (New York: International, 1970), 51.

41. James Rusling, "Interview with President McKinley," *Christian Advocate* 78 (1903): 137–38, reprinted in Ray Ginger, ed., *The Nationalization of American Life, 1877–1900* (New York: Free Press, 1965), 281–82. This is a more or less believable summary of what McKinley might have said to a group of visiting Methodists, but as Lewis Gould has pointed out, James F. Rusling, the retired Civil War officer who recounted this conversation three years after the event (when McKinley was dead), once wrote that he'd heard similar words from President Abraham Lincoln. Rusling was present as Lincoln spoke to General Daniel Sickles after the Battle of Gettysburg:

> I don't want you and Colonel Rusling here to say anything about this—at least not now. People might laugh if it got out. . . . I went to my room one day and got down on my knees, and prayed Almighty God for victory at Gettysburg. . . . And then and there I made a solemn vow with my Maker, that if He would stand by you boys at Gettysburg, I would stand by Him. And after thus wrestling with the Almighty in prayer, I don't know how it was, and it is not for me to explain, but, somehow or other, a sweet comfort crept into my soul that God Almighty had taken the whole business there into His own hands.

Lewis L. Gould, *The Spanish-American War and President McKinley* (Lawrence: University Press of Kansas, 1982), 109; Abraham Lincoln, quoted in James F. Rusling, *Men and Things I Saw in Civil War Days* (New York: Eaton and Mains, 1899), 15.

42. Gould, *Spanish-American War*, 109; Margaret Leech, *In the Days of McKinley* (New York: Harper, 1959), 339–40.

43. "Treaty of Peace with Spain," in *Documents of American History*, vol. 2, *Since 1898*, ed. Henry Steele Commager and Milton Cantor (Englewood Cliffs, NJ: Prentice Hall, 1988), 7.

44. Miller, *Benevolent Assimilation*, 112.

45. *Correspondence Relating to the War with Spain*, 2:858–59.

46. William Thaddeus Sexton, *Soldiers in the Sun: An Adventure in Imperialism* (North Stratford, NH: Ayer, 2000), 91; Donald Chaput, "Private William W. Grayson's War in the Philippines, 1899," *Nebraska History* 61, no. 3 (1980): 355, 361.

47. Linn, *Philippine War*, 42.

48. Marrion Wilcox, ed., *Harper's History of the War In the Philippines* (New York: Harper, 1900), 109; Benito J. Legarda Jr., *The Hills of Sampaloc: The Opening Action of the Philippine-American War, February 4–5, 1899* (Makati City, Philippines: Bookmark, 2001).

49. Linn, *Philippine War*, 44.

50. "Fired the First Gun," *Daily Iowa State Press*, September 2, 1899.

51. Thomas D. Thiessen, "The Fighting First Nebraska: Nebraska's Imperial Adventure in the Philippines, 1898–1899," *Nebraska History* 70, no. 3 (1989): 235.

52. Legarda, *Hills of Sampaloc*, 47.

53.　Charles Edward Russell, *The Outlook for the Philippines* (New York: Century, 1922), 93n.

8. CAPTAIN ROWAN IN COMMAND

1.　Shafter to Adjutant General, July 25, 1899, and Otis to AGWAR, August 22, 1899, in *Correspondence Relating to the War with Spain: Including the Insurrection in the Philippine Islands and the China Relief Expedition, April 15, 1898, to July 30, 1902* (Washington, DC: Center of Military History, 1993), 2:1038, 1059.

2.　George H. Daniels to Captain A. S. Rowan, July 5, 1899, Box 9, Scrapbook 3, Andrew Summers Rowan Papers, Hoover Institution Archives, Stanford University.

3.　Marrion Wilcox, ed., *Harper's History of the War in the Philippines* (New York: Harper, 1900), 210.

4.　Brian McAllister Linn, *The Philippine War 1899–1902* (Lawrence: University Press of Kansas, 2000), 32–33.

5.　Wilcox, *Harper's History*, 129–31; Linn, *Philippine War*, 67–68.

6.　Efficiency Report in Case of Andrew Summers Rowan, Succinct Account of Services, June 30, 1900, 367 ACP 85, National Archives and Records Administration; Resil B. Mojares, *The War against the Americans: Resistance and Collaboration in Cebu: 1899–1906* (Quezon City: Ateneo de Manila University Press, 1999), 38.

7.　Arthur Stevenson, ed., *Webster's New Geographical Dictionary* (Springfield, MA: G. and C. Merriam, 1980), s.v. "Philippines."

8.　U.S. Department of the Treasury, U.S. Coast and Geodetic Survey, *Atlas de Filipinas* (Washington, DC: Government Printing Office [GPO], 1900), 5.

9.　Adjutant General's Office, Military Information Division, *Military Notes on the Philippines* (Washington, DC: GPO, 1898), 243.

10.　"Our New Possessions—The Philippines," *Harper's Weekly*, March 18, 1899, 269.

11.　Sidney Lens, *The Forging of the American Empire* (New York: Apollo, 1974), 188.

12.　William Thaddeus Sexton, *Soldiers in the Sun: An Adventure in Imperialism* (North Stratford, NH: Ayer, 2000), 87–88.

13.　Stuart Creighton Miller, *Benevolent Assimilation: The American Conquest of the Philippines, 1899–1903* (New Haven, CT: Yale University Press, 1982), 67.

14.　*Correspondence Relating to the War with Spain*, 2:1075–76; Mojares, *War against the Americans*, 48–50.

15.　Andrew S. Rowan, "Operations in Bocaue Mountains," October 1–3, 1899, in *Annual Reports of the War Department for the Fiscal Year Ended June 30, 1900*, pt. 5 (Washington, DC: GPO, 1900), 164–66.

16.　Ibid.

17.   Mojares, *War against the Americans*, 51.

18.   George W. Cullum, *Biographical Register of the Officers and Graduates of the U.S. Military Academy at West Point, N.Y., since Its Establishment, in 1802*, pt. 2 (Cambridge: Riverside Press, 1901), 4:200.

19.   Wilcox, *Harper's History*, 349.

20.   Ibid.

21.   All correspondence and documents relating to this affair are found in RG395, 2607, Box 3, transmittal folder containing true copies of all relevant documents, National Archives and Records Administration.

22.   Andrew S. Rowan, "Report to Adjutant General, Military Sub-District of Cebu," February 18, 1900, RG395, 2007, National Archives and Records Administration.

23.   Henry H. Rutherford, "Report to Capt. Andrew S. Rowan," March 28, 1900, and 2nd and 3rd Endorsements, May 15 and May 27, 1900, RG395, 2007, Box 1, National Archives and Records Administration.

24.   Andrew S. Rowan, "Report to Adjutant General, Sub-District of Cebu," April 16, 1900, RG395, 2007, Box 1, National Archives and Records Administration.

25.   Andrew S. Rowan, Report to Adjutant General, RG395, 2607, Box 2, National Archives and Records Administration.

26.   Letter from Hughes to Snyder, March 19, 1900, RG395, 2607, Box 2, National Archives and Records Administration.

27.   Thrice-Monthly Report, June 30, 1900, RG395, 2607, Box 2, National Archives and Records Administration.

28.   Mojares, *War against the Americans*, 5–16.

29.   George H. Daniels to Andrew S. Rowan, December 8, 1899, Box 2, Scrapbook 7, Rowan Papers.

30.   Mojares, *War against the Americans*, 42.

31.   Cullum, *Biographical Register*, vol. 5, pt. 1 (1910), 2347.

32.   Rowan to McClerndon, July 7, 1900, RG395, 2607, Box 2.

33.   Rowan to McClerndon, September 18, 1900, RG395, 2607, Box 2.

34.   Mojares, *War against the Americans*, 68.

35.   Ibid., 66.

36.   Canute Vandermeer, "Population Patterns on the Island of Cebu: 1500 to 1900," *Annals of the Association of American Geographers* 57, no. 2 (1967): 326–27; Rowan to McClerndon, September 12, 1900, RG395, 2607, Box 2, National Archives and Records Administration; Mojares, *War against the Americans*, 118.

37.   Rowan to McClerndon, December 12, 1900, RG395, 2607, Box 3, National Archives and Records Administration.

38.   David P. Barrows, "Education and Social Progress in the Philippines," *Annals of the American Academy of Political and Social Science* 30 (1907): 71.

39. "Captain A. S. Rowan," *Daily Picayune,* December 23, 1900.

40. All correspondence related to the affair of the missing rations and other medical issues involving Major W. F. Lippitt can be found in RG395 2607, Box 3, National Archives and Records Administration.

41. Mary C. Gillett, *The Army Medical Department, 1865–1917* (Washington, DC: U.S. Army Center of Military History, 1995), 213–20.

42. Ibid., 301–2.

43. Ibid., 301.

44. All correspondence related to the charge of disobedience against Lieutenant Little can be found in RG395, 2607, Box 3, National Archives and Records Administration.

45. C. G. Harger Jr., *A Message from Garcia Answering "A Message to Garcia" by Elbert Hubbard* (Rochester, NY: Yawman and Stupp, 1900).

46. "New Books," *Washington Post,* January 14, 1901.

47. Bert Leston Taylor, "A Line-o-Type or Two," *Chicago Daily Tribune,* April 12, 1901; *The Bilioustine* 1–2 (1901); Advertisement, *Chicago Daily Tribune,* June 15, 1901.

9. AN IDYLLIC SPOT TO SPEND THE WAR

1. *Correspondence Relating to the War with Spain: Including the Insurrection in the Philippine Islands and the China Relief Expedition, April 15, 1898, to July 30, 1902* (Washington, DC: Center of Military History, 1993), 2:1027.

2. *Annual Reports of the War Department for the Fiscal Year Ended June 30, 1900,* pt. 7 (Washington, DC: Government Printing Office [GPO], 1900), 235.

3. George P. Scriven, "An American in Bohol, The Philippines, 1899–1900," Special Collections Library, Duke University, http://scriptorium.lib.duke.edu/scriven /bohol-history.html, 3, 13, 15, 17.

4. "The Natives of Bohol," *Massillon Independent,* July 7, 1900.

5. Ramon Villegas, *Tubod: The Heart of Bohol* (Manila: NCAA, 2003), 36.

6. *Annual Reports of the War Department,* 235.

7. Andrew Rowan, Report to Adjutant General, December 18, 1900, RG395, 2607, Box 3, National Archives and Records Administration.

8. Andrew S. Rowan, Report to Adjutant General, January 17, 1901, RG395, 2607, Box 3, National Archives and Records Administration.

9. Andrew S. Rowan, Report to Adjutant General, January 21, 1901, RG395, 2607, Box 4, National Archives and Records Administration.

10. "Funston Describes Torture," *Washington Post,* February 22, 1902.

11. "Two Tell of Water Cure," *Chicago Daily Tribune,* April 15, 1902; "Water Cure Common in Isles," *Chicago Daily Tribune,* May 11, 1902; "Torture of Priest," *Washington*

Post, April 24, 1902; "The Water Cure Described," *New York Times,* May 4, 1902; "Officer Who Took Water Cure," *Washington Post,* April 24, 1902.

12. "Joint Resolution Honoring Andrew S. Rowan," Acts of the Legislature of West Virginia, Twenty-Fifth Regular Session, 1901, 463–64.

13. Alan Johnson and Dumas Malone, eds., *Dictionary of American Biography,* vol. 5 (New York: Scribner's, 1959), s.v. "Hobart, Garrett Augustus."

14. Jennie L. Hobart, *Memories* (privately printed, 1930), 28–31. The president's young and beautiful wife was severely affected by her mother's death, a hard labor during the birth of a second child who also died within months, and a number of ailments, all of which left her at times mentally and physically incapacitated. Margaret Leech, *In the Days of McKinley* (New York: Harper, 1959), 16–17.

15. Theodore Roosevelt, *Theodore Roosevelt: An Autobiography* (New York: Scribner's, 1925), 308–9.

16. "Gov. Roosevelt's Position," *New York Times,* February 13, 1900.

17. "Delegates Cheer Roosevelt," *New York Times,* June 20, 1900.

18. Leech, *In the Days of McKinley,* 559.

19. Johnson and Malone, *Dictionary of American Biography,* vol. 6, s.v. "McKinley, William."

20. Adjutant General's Office, Military Information Division, *Military Notes on the Philippines* (Washington, DC: GPO, 1898), 242.

21. U.S. Department of the Treasury, U.S. Coast and Geodetic Survey, *Atlas de Filipinas* (Washington, DC: GPO, 1900), 5, map 23; Arthur J. Stevenson, ed., *Webster's New Geographical Dictionary* (Springfield, MA: G. and C. Merriam, 1980), 156.

22. Information regarding Rowan's arrival with Company I on the island of Bohol, including the murder of Sergeant Daly and subsequent events, will be found in RG395, 4912, Box 5, National Archives and Records Administration: Andrew S. Rowan, *Memorandum,* 1, undated; Thomas Woodbury, Report to Adjutant General, May 15, 1901; Edwin Glenn, Report to the Adjutant General, June 22, 1901, Interviews conducted with soldiers of Company I, 19th Infantry Division.

23. Rowan, *Memorandum,* 1.

24. James L. Anderson to Adjutant General, March 25, 1901, RG395, 2607, Item 4, National Archives and Records Administration.

25. Glenn, Report to the Adjutant General, 9.

26. Glenn interview with S. A. McMahan in ibid., 20.

27. Glenn interview with Carl Peters in ibid., 58.

28. Glenn interview with Andrew Rowan in ibid., 2. No one else reported hearing anything other than "Don't shoot that man." Rowan might have said the other words; he might only have thought them. It's seldom possible to accurately reconstruct what has happened in the excitement of a moment.

29. A soldier not with Company I who happened to be watching the scene, Private Joseph Linsey of the Signal Corps, later swore under oath that the prisoner was standing still while he was shot from behind by a single individual.

30. Glenn interview with Charles Hamilton in Glenn, Report to the Adjutant General, 33.

31. Glenn interview with John Watson in ibid., 36.

32. Telegraphic exchange between Andrew Rowan and Thomas Woodbury, April 30, 1901, RG 395, 4912, Box 5, National Archives and Records Administration.

33. Ibid.

34. Rowan, *Memorandum*, 15.

35. Thomas Woodbury to Andrew Rowan, May 4, 1901, RG 395, 4912, Box 5, National Archives and Records Administration.

36. Woodbury, Report to Adjutant General, 2.

37. Ibid., 4.

38. During the Philippine War the term *hike* was used to describe forays into the countryside; thus the title *The Hiker* for many of the bronze statues memorializing soldiers of the period. The most frequently reproduced was sculpted by Theo Alice Ruggles Kitson and cast by the Gorham Company of Providence, Rhode Island. More than fifty-two replicas of this six-foot statue were made between 1921 and 1956, most of them situated in the Northeast. Another popular statue was sculpted by Allen George Newman in 1904; it was produced in nine-foot and seven-foot versions and can be found in many cities throughout the country. Typically these were purchased by veterans' organizations.

39. Woodbury, Report to Adjutant General, 5.

40. In a letter to his parents, Private Watson later wrote, "The men caught the spy who murdered Daly. They would have tortured him to death, but some man with a cooler head shot the wretch in the head." ("Filipino's Treacherous Act," *New York Times*, July 8, 1901.

41. There's been a persistent story that the murder of Corporal Daly was a revenge killing, resulting from his having raped the murderer's fiancée. This story appears in no contemporary accounts, and no credible source can be found to verify it. The rumor that Casabas repeated—that the murderer was mentally unstable—may be as close to the truth as any. Many historical records stored in Philippine government archives were destroyed during World War II. In the 1950s, the Bureau of Public Schools commissioned a nationwide research and compilation of data gleaned from meager municipal and church records, and especially from the memories of living people. An older man in Jagna was recorded as saying, "During the American occupation there was no trouble until the time when a certain fool from Duero killed an American sentry." Philippines Bureau of Public Schools, Division of Bohol, *History and Cultural Life of the Town of Jagna and Its Barrios* (Philippines Bureau of Public Schools, 1953), 8.

42. Glenn, Report to the Adjutant General, 5.

43. Ibid., 5.

44. Ibid., 7.

45. Ibid., 8.

46. Ibid., 11.

47. Marrion Wilcox, *Harper's History of the War In the Philippines* (New York: Harper, 1900), 205.

48. "Destroyed A Town, Renewed Insurrection," *Oakland Tribune*, June 18, 1901.

49. "Filipino Town Put to Torch," *Washington Post*, June 19, 1901.

50. "Captain Rowan's Act Caused Insurrection to Be Renewed," *Atlanta Constitution*, June 19, 1901; "Renew Hostilities in Bohol Because Capt. Rowan Burned a Town," *New York Times*, June 19, 1901.

51. "A Murderous Gang in Cebu," *Manila Times*, June 27, 1901.

52. "Filipinos Seek Revenge," *New York Times*, July 18, 1901.

53. "Capt. Rowan Acquitted," *Monroe Watchman*, July 25, 1901.

54. "Burning Filipino Towns," *United States Army and Navy Journal and Gazette of the Regular and Volunteer Forces*, July 27, 1901, 1164.

55. "Burning Filipino Towns," *Manila Times*, September 12, 1901.

56. Rowan, *Memorandum*, 15.

57. Leech, *In the Days of McKinley*, 584, 592–96.

58. "Confession of the Assassin," *Chicago Daily Tribune*, September 8, 1901.

59. "Drag Net Out for Anarchists," *Chicago Daily Tribune*, September 16, 1901.

60. Two days earlier Roosevelt visited Proctor's Vermont Marble Company, then the largest producer of marble in the world, which, as Senator Reed implied in 1898, was profiting nicely by providing raw material for memorials to the dead. The memorial to McKinley in Buffalo—a twenty-four-foot shaft guarded by four recumbent lions—is entirely of Vermont marble. "Roosevelt at Rutland Fair," *Washington Post*, September 6, 1901; E. H. Brush, "McKinley Memorials in Sculpture," *American Monthly Review of Reviews* 36 (1907): 467–69.

61. "Roosevelt at Rutland Fair"; "Mr. Roosevelt on Route," *New York Times*, September 7, 1901; "Roosevelt Goes to the Bedside," *Chicago Daily Tribune*, September 7, 1901.

62. "Mr. Roosevelt Gets Reassuring News," *New York Times*, September 8, 1901.

63. "Mr. Roosevelt Goes Home," *Washington Post*, September 11, 1901.

64. Doris Ursitti, "Trail to the Presidency," *Columns*, Fall 1991.

65. Roosevelt, *Theodore Roosevelt*, 349.

66. "Judge John R. Hazel," *Chicago Daily Tribune*, September 15, 1901.

67. "Mr. Roosevelt Is Now the President," *New York Times*, September 15, 1901.

68. Theodore Roosevelt to Henry Cabot Lodge, Sept. 13, 1901, in *Theodore Roosevelt: Letters and Speeches*, ed. Louis Auchincloss (New York: Library Classics of the United States, 2004), 243.

69. Norman Cameron, "The U.S. Military Occupation of Bohol: 1900–1902," http://library.duke.edu/rubenstein/scriptorium/scriven/bohol-history.html.

70. "Provincia de Bohol, Cuadro de los jefes y oficiales de las Tropas Nacionalistas de dicha provincia," Box 6, Rowan Papers.

71. *Correspondence Relating to the War with Spain*, 2:1800.

72. "Longs for End of War," *Davenport Daily Republican*, November 7, 1901.

73. "Christmas Base Ball," *Massillon Independent*, January 16, 1902.

74. *Correspondence Relating to the War with Spain*, 2:1811.

75. "Bright Future Ahead of Isles," *Chicago Daily Tribune*, February 2, 1902.

76. Malone, *Dictionary of American Biography*, vol. 4, s.v. "Funston, Frederick."

77. Frederick Funston, *Memories of Two Wars: Cuban and Philippine Experiences* (Lincoln: University of Nebraska Press, 2009), 384–426.

78. *Correspondence Relating to the War with Spain*, 2:1262–63.

79. William John Bridges, "Dauntless: The Life and Times of Frederick Funston" (PhD diss., University of Nebraska, 2002), 230–31.

80. *Correspondence Relating to the War with Spain*, 2:1885.

81. George W. Cullum, *Biographical Register of the Officers and Graduates of the U.S. Military Academy at West Point, N.Y., since Its Establishment, in 1802* (Cambridge: Riverside Press, 1910), 5:324.

10. MAJOR ROWAN IN LOVE AND WAR

1. Angel Island Conservancy, "Ft. McDowell (aka East Garrison)," http://angelisland.org/history/ft-mcdowell-aka-east-garrison/.

2. "President Theodore Roosevelt's Proclamation Formally Ending the Philippine 'Insurrection' and Granting of Pardon and Amnesty, July 4, 1902," http://www.msc.edu.ph/centennial/tr020704.html.

3. Michael Blow, *A Ship to Remember: The Maine and the Spanish-American War* (New York: Morrow, 1992), 416.

4. Efficiency Report of Captain A. S. Rowan, 19th Infantry, for the Fiscal Year ending June 30, 1903, RG94, 367, ACP 85, National Archives and Records Administration.

5. Individual Service Report of Captain A. S. Rowan, 19th Infty. for the Period from June 30, 1902 to June 30, 1903, Form A, RG94, 367, ACP 85, National Archives and Records Administration.

6. Adjutant General to Andrew Rowan, letter, RG94, 487045, National Archives and Records Administration.

7. Mary A. Browne to Theodore Roosevelt, RG95, RCP, National Archives and Records Administration.

8. In May 1904, Roosevelt would make a fifteen-minute whistle-stop speech at the railroad depot in Manhattan at which the grateful ladies of the Temperance Union

would no doubt have been in attendance. Manhattan/Riley County Preservation Alliance, "A History of Manhattan's Union Pacific Depot," http://www.preserve-manhattan.org/projects.html.

9.   Shaffer went on to command the 347th Infantry Regiment in World War I.

10.   Andrew Rowan to Adjutant General, September 10, 1903, RG94, 367, ACP 85, National Archives and Records Administration.

11.   Stephen P. Glick and L. Ian Charters, "War Games and Military History," *Journal of Contemporary Army History* 18, no. 4 (1983): 577.

12.   John K. Mahon, *History of the Militia and the National Guard* (New York: Macmillan, 1985), 138.

13.   Daniel M. Sebby, "The 1904 Joint Encampment for Field Instruction of United States Troops and the Organized Militia of California," http://www.militarymuseum.org/CpAtacadero.html.

14.   W. F. Pride, *The History of Fort Riley* (privately printed, 1926), 235.

15.   "The Death of Mrs. Symns," *Atchison Daily Globe*, September 14, 1900.

16.   "Personals," *Atchison Daily Globe*, October 10, 1899.

17.   Special Orders No. 10, WD, August 26, 1903, RG94, 367, ACP 85, National Archives and Records Administration.

18.   "The Death of Mrs. Symns."

19.   Service Report, June 30, 1903, RG94, 367, ACP 85, National Archives and Records Administration.

20.   "Map of the Maneuver District near American Lake, Wash.," 1904, Box 8, Andrew Summers Rowan Papers, Hoover Institution Archives, Stanford University; Donna L. Sinclair, *The Making of a Military Town: Vancouver, Washington and the Vancouver National Historic Reserve, 1898–1920* (Vancouver, WA: Center for Columbia River History, 2005), 49; "Army and national guard troops hold American Lake Maneuvers beginning on July 1, 1904," *Online Encyclopedia of Washington History*, http://www.historylink.org/index.cfm?DisplayPage=output.cfm&file_id=7069.

21.   It might have occurred to an acute observer of the day that the maneuvers marked a signal moment in the passing of the military horse. In a small article in the *Washington Post* it was reported that an "automobile constructed for military purposes, and the first of its kind, will be put to an exhaustive test during the maneuvers." "California Maneuvers," *Washington Post*, August 7, 1904.

22.   "Signal Corps Maneuvers," *Washington Post*, December 31, 1904.

23.   Sebby, "The 1904 Joint Encampment."

24.   "Troops Are Reviewed by General," *Oakland Tribune*, August 22, 1904.

25.   "Rowan to Marry Again?," *Topeka State Journal*, July 28, 1904.

26.   "An Interesting Engagement," *Oakland Tribune*, August 8, 1904. Ida Conquest was a popular leading lady of the late nineteenth and early twentieth centuries.

27.   "An Interesting Engagement."

28. "Gen. MacArthur Goes to Camp," *Oakland Tribune*, August 9, 1904.

29. "Hotel El Paso de Robles," http://freepages.genealogy.rootsweb.com/~npmelton /elpaso99.htm.

30. This arts and crafts chapel, only nine years old when the Rowans were married there, is still located at 2107 Lyon Street near the Presidio and has been designated a national historic landmark. Today, as then, it offers its services as a nondenominational wedding chapel; Swedenborgian Church of San Francisco, http://www .sfwedding.org/.

31. "Captain Rowan Weds His Love Very Quietly," *San Francisco Call*, August 8, 1904.

32. "A Luncheon," *Oakland Tribune*, September 27, 1904.

33. News Brief, *San Francisco Call*, October 2, 1904.

34. "How Society Woman Fosters Meritorious Philanthropy," *San Francisco Call*, June 30, 1902.

35. "Public Library for the Blind," *San Francisco Call*, August 19, 1902.

36. "Breakfast to Miss Conquest," *Oakland Tribune*, March 21, 1903.

37. News Brief, *New York Herald Tribune*, August 14, 1904.

38. Rowan was a great correspondent, and evidence of their courtship could surely be found in the letters that passed between them—if there were any extant letters. Among the seventeen books and boxes of his papers in the Hoover Archives at Stanford University and the three boxes of material in the Josephine Rowan collection in the archives of the San Francisco Historical Society, there is not a single letter, note, or other bit of correspondence between the two. Nor is there any correspondence with other close friends or relatives. It would have been Josephine who donated the papers, and it had to have been she who chose to keep their personal lives hidden.

39. Sinclair, *Making of a Military Town*, 3.

40. "A Brilliant Mardi Gras," *Oakland Tribune*, March 1, 1905.

41. "President Theodore Roosevelt's Proclamation."

42. Peter Gordon Gowing, *Mandate in Moroland: The American Government of Muslim Filipinos 1899–1920* (Quezon City: Philippine Center for Advanced Studies, 1977), 12.

43. Moshe Yeger, *Between Integration and Secession: The Muslim Communities of the Southern Philippines, Southern Thailand, and Western Burma/Myanmar* (Lanham, MD: Lexington, 2002), 214–15.

44. James R. Arnold, *The Moro War: How America Battled a Muslim Insurgency in the Philippine Jungle, 1902–1913* (New York: Bloomsbury, 2011), 98.

45. Jack C. Lane, *Armed Progressive: General Leonard Wood* (San Rafael, CA: Presidio Press, 1978), 14–16.

46. Hermann Hagedorn, *Leonard Wood: A Biography*, vol. 2 (New York: Harper, 1931), 4–5.

47.   Leonard Wood to William H. Taft, December 16, 1903, in *Report of the Philippine Commission* (Washington, DC: Government Printing Office, 1903), 490. Roosevelt, who appointed Taft to the position, wrote in 1901, when he was still vice president, that someone suggested as the right person for the job of governor of the Philippines "ought to combine the qualities which would make a first-class President of the United States with the qualities which would make a first-class Chief Justice of the United States, and that the only man he knew who possessed all these qualities was Judge William Howard Taft, of Ohio. The statement was entirely correct." It was more correct than even Roosevelt could have known. Taft was president 1909–1913 and chief justice 1921–1930, though some might argue with the adjective "first-class." (Theodore Roosevelt, "Governor William H. Taft," *Outlook* 66 [1901]: 166.)

48.   Arnold, *Moro War*, 96–98. There's little doubt that Wood saw himself as ultimately becoming, as had his friend Theodore Roosevelt, the commander in chief. And, in fact, he came to the 1920 Republican National Convention with a sizable number of votes in his pocket. Adept at military maneuvering, he was easily outgunned by professional politicians.

49.   Gowing, *Mandate in Moroland*, 150.

50.   Arnold, *Moro War*, 101–2.

51.   Ibid., 110.

52.   *San Francisco Call*, May 15, 1905.

53.   Albert W. C. T. Herre, "Lanao—Lovely Land of Romance," *Scientific Monthly* 38, no. 6 (1934): 536.

54.   *San Francisco Call*, November 8, 1905.

55.   Herre, "Lanao," 535. The tall, hardwood dipterocarp trees that once comprised 80 percent of commercially viable timber in the Philippines have been nearly depleted.

56.   Edward M. Coffman, *The Old Army: A Portrait of the American Army in Peacetime, 1874–1898* (New York: Oxford University Press, 1986), 76.

57.   "Major Rowan's Report," March 2, 1906, RG395, Camp Keithley, Box 11, National Archives and Records Administration.

58.   Efficiency Report, February 12, 1906–June 30, 1906, RG94, 367, ACP 85, National Archives and Records Administration.

59.   Camp Keithley, 1906, RG395, Box 11, National Archives and Records Administration.

60.   Ibid.

61.   The army at that time was a small place. Ainsworth lost his job in 1912 in a dispute with Leonard Wood, who by then had been appointed chief of staff.

62.   Coffman, *Old Army*, 62.

63.   "Fifteenth Infantry Regiment," http://www.15thinfantry.org/1953yearbookpdf/history.pdf.

64. Efficiency Report of Major Andrew S. Rowan, 15th Infantry, Col. Walter S. Scott, June 30, 1909, RG94, 367, ACP 85, National Archives and Records Administration.

65. Still in existence, it was renamed the Colonel Andrew S. Rowan Reading Room for the Blind in 1943.

66. Camp Keithley, 1906.

67. Henry Mills Alden to Major A. S. Rowan, August 1, 1906, Scrapbook 10, Rowan Papers.

68. Josephine Morris Rowan Papers, 1894–1949, California Historical Society.

69. The Fifteenth began moving to Asia in November 1911 and, as a unit, wouldn't return to the United States for thirty-seven years.

70. Efficiency Report of Major Andrew S. Rowan.

71. Andrew S. Rowan, "How I Carried President McKinley's Message to General García," Box 6, n.d., 64, Rowan Papers.

11. THE COMPLEXITIES OF RETIREMENT

1. The house, as a part of the Vallejo Street Crest Historic District, is now included in the National Register of Historic Places and renowned for its architectural significance. It, along with 1032 (now gone) and 1034, marked the beginning of the end of the Victorian gewgaws that had characterized San Francisco's architecture up to that point. Although hardly appearing daring today, these simple shingled houses were a startling departure in the 1880s. Perhaps by coincidence, perhaps not, they were designed by the amateur architect Joseph Worcester, who also happened to be the minister of the Swedenborgian Church in which the Rowans had been married five years earlier. Worcester, a transplanted New Englander, was an intellectual and cultural leader during Josephine's heyday, and they almost certainly would have been acquainted. "Joseph Worcester," http://geocitiessites.com/SiliconValley /Orchard/8642/worcester.html; Catherine Bigelow, "The Selling of San Francisco: How Much Does a Piece of History Cost in This Town?," http://www.sfgate.com/cgi -bin/article.cgi?file=/c/a/2003/08/03/CM18934.DTL&type=printable.

2. "Wedding Mystery Stirs the Gossips," *San Francisco Call*, August 25, 1910; Society Page, *San Francisco Call*, August 25, 1910.

3. "Woman Gets $100,000 Legacy," *Chicago Daily Tribune*, May 25, 1911; "Andrew B. Symns," http://www.ksgenweb.org/atchison/ABSymnsbio.html. Ida was, in fact, one of ten offspring, six of them having died in infancy. "The Death of Mrs. Symns," *Atchison Daily Globe*, September 14, 1900.

4. Freeman Champney, *Art and Glory: The Story of Elbert Hubbard* (New York: Crown, 1968), 93.

5. Felix Shay, *Elbert Hubbard of East Aurora* (New York: Wise, 1926), 247, 255, 257.

6. Robert L. Beisner, "'Commune' in East Aurora," *American Heritage* 22, no. 2 (1971): 106.

7. Morris Bishop, "Roycroft Revisited," *New Yorker*, October 8, 1938, 40.

8. Champney, *Art and Glory*, 92.

9. Shay, *Elbert Hubbard*, 246.

10. Bruce A. White, *Elbert Hubbard's The Philistine: A Periodical of Protest (1895–1915)* (Lanham, MD: University Press of America, 1989), 125.

11. L. Ron Hubbard, the founder of Scientology, claimed, as the son of Harry Ross Hubbard, to be Elbert's nephew. Elbert had no brothers named Harry, but it's *possible* that Harry's father, James Hubbard of Fayette, Iowa, was one of Silas's brothers. This would make L. Ron at best Elbert's second cousin—at least legally. L. Ron's father was an orphan who had been adopted by Mr. and Mrs. James Hubbard, so there is no genetic connection. In 1956, L. Ron Hubbard dedicated the ninth edition of *Dianetics* to his "uncle" Elbert. Roycroft Campus Corporation, "Elbert Hubbard and L. Ron Hubbard," http://roycroftcampuscorporation.typepad.com/roycroftcampuscorporation/2008/04/elbert-hubbard.html; Russell Miller, *Bare-Faced Messiah: The True Story of L. Ron Hubbard* (New York: Holt, 1987), 11.

12. Elbert Hubbard, "An Interesting Personality," *Cosmopolitan* 32, no. 3 (1902): 317. As Champney, *Art and Glory*, 31, notes, "The reliability of Hubbard's autobiographical remarks is a question that pops up every time we touch a Hubbard statement about himself. Two somewhat opposing compulsions are noticeable: to display himself, to boast and confess; and to befog the record with inaccuracy, fantasy and invention."

13. Beisner, "'Commune' in East Aurora," 105–6.

14. Champney, *Art and Glory*, 33, 37, 50.

15. Charles F. Hamilton, *As Bees in Honey Drown: Elbert Hubbard and the Roycrofters* (New York: Barnes, 1973), 97.

16. "Elbert Hubbard," *Marshall Expounder*, April 25, 1902; "Mrs. Elbert Hubbard Sues," *Washington Post*, December 10, 1902; "Elbert Hubbard Marries," *New York Times*, January 21, 1904.

17. The college, founded in 1901 by Secretary of War Elihu Root, is now located in Carlisle, Pennsylvania.

18. The statue of Frederick the Great, a bronze duplicate of a marble statue in Berlin, was a personal gift from Kaiser Wilhelm to Theodore Roosevelt and was installed with great hoopla on November 19, 1904. In 1918, as a result of congressional and public protest, it was put in storage. Nine years later, it was placed again on its pedestal, only to disappear at the start of World War II. In 1954 it followed the War College to Carlisle, Pennsylvania, where it will remain on view until the next war with Germany. No other statues of great military figures were ever erected on the site. Sean Sims, "Ever Wonder What Frederick the Great is Doing in Carlisle?" http://www.pennlive.com/editorials/index.ssf/2010/08/ever_wonder_what_frederick_the.html.

19. S. 2854, 62d Congress, 1st Session (June 22, 1911); C. W. Watson to the Adjutant General, June 26, 1911; Fred C. Ainsworth to C. W. Watson, June 28, 1911;

George P. Wetmore to W. L. Stimson, August 4, 1911; W. L. Stimson to George P. Wetmore, October 30, 1911. (Letters found at AG 1843358, National Archives and Records Administration).

20. William Whitney, ed., *The Century Dictionary and Cyclopedia* (New York: Century, 1899), s.v. "pragmatic."

21. A. S. Rowan to Roland Holt, February 12, 1913, Henry Holt Archives, Princeton University Library; A. S. Rowan to Messrs. Henry Holt & Co., February 16, 1913, Henry Holt Archives, Princeton University Library; "Taft Orders More Ships to Mexico," *Chicago Daily Tribune*, February 12, 1913.

22. S. 8441, 63d Congress (February 10, 1913).

23. Memorandum for the Secretary of War, Office of the Chief of Staff, February 14, 1913, National Archives and Records Administration.

24. Two letters from the corresponding secretary of the Richmond County chapter of the Daughters of the American Revolution to the secretary of war, December 11, 1913, and January 15, 1914, National Archives and Records Administration.

25. "Roosevelt Eager to Fight in Mexico," *New York Times*, April 23, 1914.

26. "Mrs. de Bolt Is Witness in Lawsuit," *Oakland Tribune*, June 2, 1914; "'Billie' de Bolt Seeking Divorce," *Oakland Tribune*, January 14, 1915; "Court May Not Grant Petition for Freedom," *Oakland Tribune*, January 20, 1915; "Mrs. 'Billie' DeBolt Asks Divorce; Army Belle Gives Society a Shock," *Washington Post*, January 24, 1915; "'Rah! Rah!' Boy Loses Bride," *Oakland Tribune*, May 18, 1915.

27. Frank Morton Todd, *The Story of the Exhibition*, vol. 5 (New York: Putnam's, 1921), 256–68; "Cuba Takes Title to Site for Pavilion," *Oakland Tribune*, September 25, 1913.

28. Carlton J. H. Hayes, *A Political and Cultural History of Modern Europe*, vol. 2 (New York: Macmillan, 1916), 572–78.

29. Page Smith, *America Enters the World: A People's History of the Progressive Era and World War I* (New York: McGraw-Hill, 1985), 468.

30. Champney, *Art and Glory*, 33.

31. Marie Via and Marjorie Searl, *Head, Heart, and Hand: Elbert Hubbard and the Roycrofters* (Rochester, NY: University of Rochester Press, 1994), 48.

32. "The Indictment of Fra Elbertus," *Oakland Tribune*, January 18, 1913.

33. If this seems unlikely, it should be remembered that sixty years later Ralph Ginzburg, publisher of *Eros*, served eight months of a three-year sentence before being paroled, after having been found guilty of violating the same law. "Ginzburg Paroled," *New York Times*, July 28, 1972.

34. Smith, *America Enters the World*, 308.

35. "Jail Nearly Gets 'Fra Elbertus,'" *Chicago Daily Tribune*, January 12, 1913.

36. Beisner, "'Commune' in East Aurora," 108.

37. Upton Sinclair, *The Brass Check* (New York: Boni, 1936), 37, 314.

38. "Elbert Hubbard's Price," *Harper's Weekly*, January 30, 1915, 112.

39. Advertisement, *New York Times*, May 1, 1915.

40. "Sails, Undisturbed by German Warning," *New York Times*, May 2, 1915.

41. Diana Preston, *Lusitania: An Epic Tragedy* (New York: Walker, 2002), 45, 244, 401–2.

42. "The Last Word: Letter to Elbert Hubbard II from Ernest C. Cowper, A Surviving Passenger of the Lusitania," March 12, 1916, https://sites.google.com/site/2000ceatthefourcorners/Home/table-of-contents-1/classic-texts-arcane-spiritual-traditions/last-words-elbert-hubbard-on-the-lusitania.

43. "United States Must Act at Once on Lusitania, Says Colonel Roosevelt," *New York Times*, May 10, 1915.

44. "Lieut. Deem Takes Bride," *Washington Post*, October 22, 1915; "Former Mrs. de Bolt Weds Navy Officer," *Oakland Tribune*, November 5, 1915; "From: Dictionary of American Naval Fighting Ships, Vol. III, p.1," http://www.hazegray.org/danfs/submar/ss19a.txt; "Mrs. de Bolt Will Go Back to Paris," *Oakland Tribune*, January 15, 1915.

45. Smith, *America Enters the World*, 487.

46. P. C. March to Andrew Rowan, RG94, 367, APC 85, National Archives and Records Administration.

47. "Movies," *Reno Evening Gazette*, February 3, 1917.

48. Smith, *America Enters the World*, 489, 499.

49. "Must Exert All Our Power," *New York Times*, April 3, 1917.

50. Andrew Rowan to William Ingraham, RG94, 367, APC 85, National Archives and Records Administration.

51. Peter Collier, *The Roosevelts: An American Saga* (New York: Simon and Schuster, 1994), 187–88.

52. Arthur Wagner died in Asheville, North Carolina, on June 17, 1905. It was the same day on which his promotion to brigadier general was signed. Robert McHenry, ed., *Webster's American Military Biographies* (New York: Dover, 1894), s.v. "Wagner, Arthur Lockwood."

53. H. C. Corbin to A. S. Rowan, telegram, May 16, 1898, Box 3, Ideal Scrapbook 100, Andrew Summers Rowan Papers, Hoover Institution Archives, Stanford University.

54. George W. Cullum, *Biographical Register of the Officers and Graduates of the U.S. Military Academy at West Point, N.Y., since Its Establishment, in 1802*, 6B (Saginaw, MI: Seemann and Peters, 1920), 3:2502.

55. Andrew Rowan, "How I Carried President McKinley's Message to General García," n.d., title page, 1–10, 15, 16, 17, 64, 73–5, Box 6, Rowan Papers.

56. Andrew Rowan, "Pacifism and Its Cure—Universal Training," Box 6, Rowan Papers.

57. "Death Takes Col. Andrew S. Rowan Former Local Resident," *Mill Valley Record*, January 12, 1943.

58. Photo File R, Mill Valley Historical Society.

59. "Col. Rowan at Old Mill School," *Mill Valley Record*, September 30, 1922.

60. Lt. Gen. Nelson A. Miles to Andrew Rowan, June 26, 1922, Box 3, Rowan Papers.

61. Rowan's Military Information Division colleague, Henry H. Whitney, received the same award during this period for his secret mission to Puerto Rico. "Henry Howard Whitney," http://www.arlingtoncemetery.net/hhwhitney.htm.

62. "Was Messenger to Garcia," *Washington Post*, May 31, 1922; "Award Hero's Cross to Bearer of Famed Message to Garcia," *Washington Post*, July 22, 1922.

63. "Col. A. S. Rowan Decorated," *Mill Valley Record*, September 2, 1922.

64. "Garcia Messenger Glad Cross Is Gold," *Danville Bee*, July 25, 1922.

65. Andrew Summers Rowan, *How I Carried the Message to Garcia* (San Francisco, CA: Harney, 1922).

66. Ibid., 14.

67. Ibid., 20.

68. Ibid, 20–21.

69. Andrew Rowan to the Adjutant General, April 14, 1922, Box 9, Envelope 6, Rowan Papers.

70. Aníbel Escalante Beatón, *Calixto García: Su Campaña en el 95* (Havana: Editorial de Ciencias Sociales, 1973), 443–55.

71. Rowan, *How I Carried the Message*.

72. Will C. Wood, Alice Cecilia Cooper, and Frederick A. Rice, *America's Message* (New York: Ginn, 1925), 165–95.

73. A reel in those days generally held one thousand feet of film, which took about ten minutes to run. Readers at the time would have understood that six reels referred to a major movie lasting about an hour. Leslie Halliwell, *The Filmgoer's Companion*, 6th ed. (New York: Hill and Wang, 1977), s.v. "Reel."

74. Charles Phelps Cushing, "The Man Who Found Garcia," *American Legion Weekly*, September 8, 1922, 9.

75. "How You Can Get into the Movies," "A Picture for Showmen!," and "To Direct Film," Box 11, Rowan Papers; Classified ad, *Ogden Standard-Examiner*, January 4, 1925.

76. "A Picture for Showmen!," Box 11, Rowan Papers.

77. "Spanish War's Vets to Meet," *Reno Evening Gazette*, July 12, 1923; "Boy Scouts to Hear Garcia Messenger," *Oakland Tribune*, August 19, 1925; "Army Men to Be Guests of Lions," *Oakland Tribune*, November 15, 1925.

78. This is a reference to Felicia Hernan's often anthologized—and much-parodied—1826 poem "Casabianca," based on a supposed real incident in which a boy remains aboard a burning ship in battle because he hadn't been ordered off by his father, the commander, who lies unconscious down below.

79. Elsie Robinson, "At Last—The Inside Story of How He Became a Hero," *New McClure's* 61, no. 1 (1928): 66.

80. Andrew Summers Rowan, "How I Got the Message to Garcia," *Washington Post*, April 28, 1929.

81. H.R. 12435, 69th Congress, 1st Session (May 25, 1926).

82. Various letters, Box 13, Rowan Papers.

83. Wells Goodykoontz, *Major Andrew S. Rowan, a West Virginian: The Man Who Carried the Message to Garcia* (Washington, DC: Government Printing Office, 1926), 361–63, 383.

84. Anne Sullivan Macy to M. C. Migel, New York City, June 25, 1925, http://www.afb.org/AnneSullivan/lettertoMigel.asp.

85. "How To Be Happy Though Married," *San Francisco Daily News*, January 13, 1931.

12. THE MYTH LIVES ON

1. Oren F. Morton, *A History of Monroe County, West Virginia* (Baltimore, MD: Regional Publishing, 1980), 261, 397–98.

2. M. R. Shirey, "Andrew S. Rowan and the Message to Garcia," *West Virginia Review* 15, no. 2 (1937): 38.

3. Charles Henry Ambler, *West Virginia: The Mountain State* (New York: Prentice Hall, 1940), 305–21; Morton, *History of Monroe County*, 151.

4. "Conley to Speak," *Charleston Gazette*, October 24, 1931; "Col. Rowan Unable to Attend Event," "Author's Son Unable to Attend Bridge Opening," "The Inspiration for Today's Celebration . . . ," "Citizens of Two States Gather at Span Celebration," Scrapbook 11, Andrew Summers Rowan Papers, Hoover Institution Archives, Stanford University.

5. "Clipping Business," *Time*, May 30, 1932; "Death of Henry Romeike," *New York Times*, June 4, 1903.

6. "Funeral Conducted for Rowan Daughter," *San Francisco News*, January 14, 1935.

7. "Garcia's Service to Cuba," *New York Times*, April 20, 1924.

8. Letter from Claxton Garcia to Secretary of War Alger, May 1, 1898, Box 9, Envelope 4, Rowan Papers.

9. "A Messenger to Garcia," *New York Times*, April 27, 1898; "Lieut. Col. Andrew S. Rowan," *New York Times*, July 3, 1898; "Lieutenant-Colonel Rowan's Exploit," *Harper's Weekly*, July 2, 1898, 643.

10. Andrew Summers Rowan, *How I Carried the Message to Garcia* (San Francisco: Harney, 1922), 6.

11. "Real Message to Garcia Lost; Garcia's Son Hunts It in D.C.," *Washington Post*, June 14, 1935; "Message to Garcia Oral, Files Reveal," *Oakland Tribune*, January 17, 1935; "Message to Garcia Sought by His Son," *Washington Post*, January 27, 1935; *Time*, January 28, 1935.

12. "Story Deflated," *Fresno Bee Republican*, February 3, 1935.

13. Bert Hubbard to Colonel Andrew S. Rowan, January 28, 1935, and Andrew S. Rowan to Bert Hubbard, n.d, Box 7, Rowan Papers.

14. Parsons was apparently unaware of the Edison film that appeared when she was in her midthirties or, as she notoriously pretended, in her early twenties.

15. Leslie Halliwell, *The Filmgoer's Companion*, 6th ed. (New York: Hill and Wang, 1977), s.v. "Beery, Wallace."

16. "Film Shorts," *New York Times*, March 29, 1936.

17. "So Mr. Marshall Wanted a Jungle," *New York Times*, April 5, 1936.

18. Andrew S. Rowan, "My Mission and My Message to García," n.d., Box 6, Rowan Papers.

19. Lee Rashall, "Carrier Reveals Untold Chapter," *Woodland Daily Democrat*, February 6, 1936.

20. Andrew Summers Rowan, "How I Carried President McKinley's Message to General García," unpublished manuscript, December 11, 1917, 20.

21. "A Message to Garcia (1936)," http://www.tcm.com/tcmdb/title/83360/A -Message-to-Garcia/; Center Theatre program, Box 9, Folder 6, Rowan Papers.

22. Frank S. Nugent, "Gene Fowler and W. P. Lipscomb Rewrite History in 'A Message to Garcia,' at the Center," *New York Times*, April 15, 1936.

23. Aníbel Escalante Beatón, *Calixto García: Su Campaña en el 95* (Havana: Editorial de Ciencias Sociales, 1978), 432–36.

24. "Colonel Rowan Has Birthday Serenade," *San Francisco News Junior*, May 1936.

25. Jared L. Manley [James Thurber], "Where Are They Now?," *New Yorker*, December 5, 1936, 41–45.

26. "'Message to Garcia' Hero Marks His 80th Birthday," *New York Times*, August 24, 1937.

27. "Noted 'Messenger' Reported Better," *Oakland Tribune*, April 12, 1938.

28. "Col. Rowan Decorated by Cuba," *New York Times*, July 28, 1938; "Medal from Garcia," *Time*, August 8, 1938, 8–9.

29. "Cuba, Central Hershey, 1916–46," http://www.hersheyarchives.org/essay /details.aspx?EssayId=16&Rurl=%2fresources%2fsearch-results.aspx%3fType%3dS earch%26Text%3dwe%2bconcede%2bit%26StartMonth%3d%26EndMonth%3d%2 6StartDay%3d%26EndDay%3d%26StartYear%3d%26EndYear%3d; Geoff Simons, *Cuba: From Conquistador to Castro* (New York: St. Martin's, 1996), 233–37.

30. José Joaquín Zarza to Colonel Andrew Summers Rowan, July 27, 1938, Theodore Wores Papers, Box 1, Folder 4, Department of Special Collections, Stanford University Library.

31. "That Message to Garcia," *Oakland Tribune*, August 8, 1938.

32. "On Capitol Hill," *Washington Post*, January 12, 1939.

33.   "'Message to Garcia' Bearer Gets Congress O.K. on Medal," *Oakland Tribune*, July 17, 1939.

34.   "'Message to Garcia' Hero is 82, Still Sick," *Fresno Bee Republican*, April 24, 1939.

35.   "Message to Garcia," *Modesto Bee*, January 7, 1941.

36.   West Virginia Industrial and Publicity Commission, "News Release," December 17, 1958, and Henry E. Caldabaugh to Kyle McCormick, December 1, 1958, West Virginia Archives and History Library; Shirley Donnelly, "Rowan Gave Cannon to West Virginia," *Beckley Post Herald*, November 13, 1968.

37.   Max Tosquella, *The Truth about the Message to Garcia*, translated by I. F. Berndes and Charles Dujol (Havana: self-published, 1955), chap. 4.

38.   Herbert L. Matthews, *Cuba* (New York: Macmillan, 1964), 2, 85.

39.   Louis A. Pérez, *Cuba: Between Reform and Revolution*, 2nd ed. (New York: Oxford University Press, 1995), 191–99.

40.   "The Platt Amendment," in *Documents of American History*, vol. 2, *Since 1898*, ed. Henry Steele Commager and Milton Cantor (Englewood Cliffs, NJ: Prentice Hall, 1988), 28.

41.   Pérez, *Cuba*, 217, 223, 416.

42.   Ibid., 252.

43.   As a young worker on the United Fruit Railroad he was known as El Mulato Lindo (The Pretty Mulatto). T. J. English, *Havana Nocturne: How the Mob Owned Cuba—And Then Lost It to the Revolution* (New York: Morrow, 2007), 61.

44.   English, *Havana Nocturne*, 15.

45.   Simons, *Cuba*, 250–54; Clifford L. Staten, *The History of Cuba* (Westport, CT: Greenwood, 2003), 62; Irwin F. Gellman, *Roosevelt and Batista: Good Neighbor Diplomacy in Cuba, 1933–1945* (Albuquerque: University of New Mexico Press, 1973), 180–83, 224.

46.   "La Habana: La Ciudad que todo el tiempo reflexionar," *Diarios de Viaje*, July 27, 2007.

47.   Frederick Funston, *Memories of Two Wars: Cuban and Philippine Experiences* (Lincoln: University of Nebraska Press, 2009), 74.

48.   Luís Rodolfo Miranda, *Reminiscencias Cubanas de la Guerra y de la Paz* (Havana: Fernandez y Cia, 1941), 114.

49.   H. Kenneth Dirlam, *Bits of History: From Talks Here and There* (Mansfield, OH: Richland County Historical Society, 1962), photo caption: "Ceremony dedicating the bronze plaque at the Acera del Louvre in Havana"; "Cubans to Honor Rowan," *New York Times*, July 3, 1940; "Cuba Celebrates the 4th," *New York Times*, July 5, 1940; "Comandante Miranda y de la Rúa," http://guije.com/public/carteles/3319/miranda/index.html. The plaque has since disappeared, and its whereabouts are unknown.

50.   The building, to which the plaque is still attached, now serves as a municipally owned art gallery and cultural center.

51. "Famous Native Son Is Honored," *Beckley Sunday Register*, May 31, 1942.

52. "Rowan Dies; Took Message to Garcia," *New York Times*, January 12, 1943.

53. "Major Rowan Rites Friday at Arlington," *Washington Post*, May 11, 1943.

54. "80,000 Parade in Havana," *New York Times*, July 5, 1943.

55. *Rowan: Protagonista del "Mensaje a Garcia"* (Havana: Agrupación Pro-Enseñanza de Hechos Históricos, 1943).

56. Ellis O. Briggs, "No Charge for the Extra Buttons," *Foreign Service Journal*, December 1961, 23–24.

57. "Rowan's Widow, 95, Dies," *New York Times*, January 16, 1949.

58. "Elbert Hubbard: An American Original—Preview," http://www.pbs.org/video /2171500018/; Charles F. Hamilton, *As Bees in Honey Drown: Elbert Hubbard and the Roycrofters* (New York: Barnes, 1973), 125.

59. Peter Elphick, *Liberty: The Ships That Won the War* (Annapolis: Naval Institute Press, 2001), 102.

60. "Liberty Freighter Is to Be Launched Monday," *Modesto Bee*, April 24, 1943; John Gorley Bunker, *Liberty Ships: The Ugly Ducklings of World War II* (Annapolis: Naval Institute Press, 1972), 40–41, 48–49; "Shipyards and Suppliers for U.S. Maritime Commission During World War II," http://www.usmm.org/shipbuild.html; "USS Rutilicus (AK-113)," https://commons.wikimedia.org/wiki/File:Rutilicus_(AK-113) .jpg; "Rutilicus AK-113," http://historycentral.com/navy/AK/rutilicus.html.

61. Simons, *Cuba*, 296–97.

62. Louis A. Pérez, "Incurring a Debt of Gratitude: 1898 and the Moral Sources of United States Hegemony in Cuba," *American Historical Review* 104, no. 2 (1999): 395–96.

63. Embassy of the United States, Havana, Cuba, "About the U.S. Embassy: History," http://havana.usembassy.gov/about_the_usint.html.

64. "Monument to the victims of [the] Maine," http://www.webhavana.com/en /monument_to_the_victims_of_maine.html.

65. "The National Cryptologic Museum and the Military Intelligence Corps Hall of Fame," http://asachitose.com/page7.htm.

EPILOGUE

1. Elbert Hubbard, "A Message to Garcia" (East Aurora, NY: John Wanamaker Stores, 1906).

2. R. W. G. Vail, "'A Message to Garcia': A Bibliographical Puzzle," *Bulletin of the New York Public Library* 34, no. 2 (1930): 75–76.

3. "Prince Hilkoff's Adieu," *New York Times*, October 21, 1896.

4. Sergei Witte, *The Memoirs of Count Witte*, trans. and ed. Abraham Yarmolinsky (New York: Fertig, 1967), 325.

5.   Willa Cather, *The World and the Parish: Willa Cather's Articles and Reviews 1893-1902* (Lincoln: University of Nebraska Press, 1970), 837.

6.   John Foster Fraser, *The Real Siberia* (New York: Appleton, 1902), 6-7.

7.   Henry Reichman, "Tsarist Labor Policy and the Railroads, 1885-1914," *Russian Review* 42 (1983): 57.

8.   Ibid., 51.

9.   B. N. Mironov, "Literacy in Russia, 1797-1917," *Soviet Studies in History* 25, no. 3 (1986-87): 100.

10.   Reichman, "Tsarist Labor Policy," 56-57.

11.   Jonathon Sanders, "Lessons from the Periphery: Saratov, January 1905," *Slavic Review* 46, no. 2 (1987): 341.

12.   "By Sledge and Rail Across Siberia," *Harper's Weekly* 41, no. 2121 (1897): 806-10.

13.   Witte, *Memoirs*, 256.

14.   T. V. Paul, *Asymmetric Conflicts: War Initiation by Weaker Powers* (New York: Cambridge University Press, 1994), 42.

15.   Ibid.

16.   Richard Trauber, *Operetta: A Theatrical History* (New York: Oxford University Press, 1983), 69, 176.

17.   David Arnold Balch, *Elbert Hubbard: Genius of Roycroft* (New York: Stokes, 1940), 188.

18.   Bruce White, *Elbert Hubbard's The Philistine: A Periodical of Protest (1895-1915)* (Lanham, MD: University Press of America, 1989), 126-27.

19.   Alan Johnson and Dumas Malone, eds., *Dictionary of American Biography*, vol. 10 (New York: Scribner's, 1959), s.v. "Wanamaker, John."

20.   Maureen Donovan, Japanese studies librarian and associate professor at Ohio State University, conducted an electronic search for both Russian and Japanese editions in August 2007. She cautions that items published in the thousands and even millions disappear all the time, and that early twentieth-century libraries were not in the habit of gathering and storing ephemera. Furthermore, the Russian State Library in Moscow (formerly the Lenin Library) had, at the time of the search, probably not completed transferring information regarding its holdings from cards to its electronic catalog. Taking these facts into consideration, not finding references to government-issued Russian and Japanese versions of the "Message" is far from proving that they never existed.

21.   Robert L. Beisner, "'Commune' in East Aurora," *American Heritage* 22, no. 2 (1971): 109.

22.   H.R. 12435, 69th Congress, 1st Session, 2.

23.   Alice Payne Hackett and James Henry Burke, *80 Years of Best Sellers 1895-1975* (New York: Bowker, 1977), 12.

24. Bel Kaufman, *Up the Down Staircase* (Edgewood Cliffs, NJ: Prentice Hall, 1965), 161.

25. "A Message to Garcia," http://www.tcm.com/this-month/article/518057%7C0/A-Message-to-Garcia.html. Edison himself has been quoted as saying about Hubbard, "He was of big service to me in telling me the things I knew, but which I did not know I knew, until he told me." This sounds more Hubbardian than Edisonian, and there's never been a citation indicating the original source, but who knows?

26. John Walker, ed., *Halliwell's Film Guide* (New York: HarperCollins, 1995), 755.

27. "The Microphone Presents," *New York Times*, April 16, 1933.

28. "Suspense: 1942–1962," http://www.escape-suspense.com/2008/03/richard-widmark.html; Nineteenth Infantry Radio Broadcast, July 18, 1934, typescript, Box 3, Andrew Summers Rowan Papers, Hoover Institution Archives, Stanford University; "Motion Picture Star Is Cast in Chateau Program," *Fresno Bee Republican*, March 6, 1937.

29. W. Adolphe Roberts, *The Single Star: A Novel of Cuba in the '90s* (Indianapolis, IN: Bobbs-Merrill, 1949), 295, 297.

30. Stewart H. Holbrook, *Lost Men of American History* (New York: Macmillan, 1946), 297.

31. Bert Hubbard, *Impressions* (East Aurora, NY: Roycrofters, 1921), 13.

32. George H. Daniels to John M. Rowan, June 20, 1899, Box 9, Scrapbook 3, Rowan Papers.

33. Sean Creehan, "China," *Atlantic Monthly*, May 2005, 131.

34. Rowan's name is rendered in Chinese by two common family names transliterated in pinyin as *luowen*.

35. Elbert Hubbard, "An Interesting Personality," *Cosmopolitan* 32 (1902): 319.

36. William Yardley, "Jeb Bush to Staff: Just Read it," *St. Petersburg Times*, June 21, 2000.

37. Joni James, "Jeb Bush Pictured with Blackberry in Official Portrait," *St. Petersburg Times*, December 22, 2006.

38. "Richard M. Nixon Presidential Recordings: Nixon Conversation 033-101," http://millercenter.org/presidentialrecordings/rmn-033-101; "President Richard M. Nixon Watergate tapes press coverage and campaign funding (Part 2 of 3)," https://www.wyzant.com/resources/lessons/history/hpol/nixon/watergate/press-coverage-2.

39. "Baden Powell's Boy Scout Plan Invades America," *New York Times*, May 24, 1910.

40. Franklin K. Mathiews, ed., *The Boy Scouts Yearbook* (New York: Appleton, 1917), 36.

41. Elbert Hubbard, *The Philosophy of Elbert Hubbard* (Aurora, NY: Roycrofters, 1916), 91.

42. "Lord Baden-Powell, Founder of Scouts, Sends Message," *San Francisco News Junior,* n.d., Box 9, Folder 6, Rowan Papers.

43. F. M. Gregg, "Character Education in Practice," *Nebraska Educational Journal* 11, no. 9 (1931): 560–2.

44. Alan Burton, *A Message to Garcia . . . Revisited* (n.p.: Silver Lake, 1986), 21–29.

SELECTED BIBLIOGRAPHY

ARCHIVAL COLLECTIONS

Henry Holt Company Archives, Princeton University.
Charles V. Kirchman Papers, privately held.
Mill Valley Historical Society, Mill Valley, CA.
National Archives and Records Administration, Washington, DC, and College Park, MD.
National Library of the Philippines, Manila.
Ohio Historical Society, Columbus.
William Rufus Shafter Papers, 1862–1938, Stanford University Libraries.
Andrew Summers Rowan Papers, Hoover Institution Archives, Stanford University.
Josephine Morris Rowan Papers, 1894–1949, California Historical Society, San Francisco.
Stanford University Library, Department of Special Collections.
West Virginia Archives Library, Charleston.

GOVERNMENT PUBLICATIONS AND DOCUMENTS

Acts of the Legislature of West Virginia, Twenty-Fifth Regular Session, 1901.
Adjutant General's Office, Military Information Division. *Military Notes on the Philippines*. Washington, DC: Government Printing Office (GPO), 1898.
Alger, Russell A. *Report of the Secretary of War*, vol. 1. Washington, DC, 1899.
Annual Report of the Board of Visitors to the United States Military Academy. Washington, DC: GPO, 1880.
Annual Report of the Major General Commanding the Army to the Secretary of the War. Washington, DC: GPO, 1898.
Annual Report of the Navy Department. Washington, DC: GPO, 1898.
Annual Report of the United States Military Academy, 1881.
Annual Reports of the Navy for the Year 1898. Washington, DC: GPO, 1898.
Annual Reports of the War Department. Washington, DC: GPO, 1900.
Annual Reports of the War Department for the Fiscal Year Ended June 30, 1900. Part 5. Washington, DC: GPO, 1900.
Correspondence Relating to the War with Spain: Including the Insurrection in the Philippine Islands and the China Relief Expedition, April 15, 1898, to July 30, 1902. 2 vols. Washington, DC: Center of Military History, 1993.
Edwin Glenn, Report to the Adjutant General, June 22, 1901.
Gillett, Mary C. *The Army Medical Department, 1865–1917*. Washington, DC: Center of Military History, 1995.

Historical Statistics of the United States: Colonial Times to 1970. Part 1. Washington, DC: U.S. Department of Commerce, 1975.

Intercontinental Railway Commission. *Intercontinental Railway Commission,* vol. 1, pt. 1. Washington, DC: Intercontinental Railway Commission, 1898.

"Joint Resolution Honoring Andrew S. Rowan." Acts of the Legislature of West Virginia, Twenty-Fifth Regular Session, 1901.

Journal of the Military Service Institution of the United States 32, 1903.

Memorandum for the Secretary of War, Office of the Chief of Staff, February 14, 1913.

Message from the President of the United States to the Two Houses of Congress. Vol. 1. Washington, DC: Government Printing Office, 1899.

Official Register of the Officers and Cadets of the U.S. Military Academy, West Point. June, 1881.

U.S. Department of the Treasury, U.S. Coast and Geodetic Survey. *Atlas de Filipinas,* 1900.

NEWSPAPERS

Army and Navy Journal and Gazette of the Regular and Volunteer Forces
Atchison (KS) Daily Champion
Atchison (KS) Daily Globe
Atchison (KS) Daily News
Beckley (WV) Post Herald
Beckley (WV) Sunday Register
Bilioustine
Charleston (WV) Gazette
Chicago Daily Tribune
Fresno Bee (CA) Republican
Harper's Weekly
Leslie's Weekly
Manila Times
Mill Valley (CA) Record
Modesto (CA) Bee
Monroe (WV) Watchman
New York Herald
New York Times
Oakland Tribune
Reno Evening Gazette
San Francisco Call
San Francisco Daily News
San Francisco News Junior
Washington Post
Woodland (CA) Daily Democrat

ARTICLES AND BOOK CHAPTERS

Anderson, Thomas M. "Our Rule in the Philippines." *North American Review* 170 (1900).

Angevine, Robert G. "Mapping the Northern Frontier: Canada and the Origins of the US Army's Military Information Division, 1885–1898." *Intelligence and National Security* 16, no. 3 (2002).

"The Battle of Manila Bay (Cavite): Order of Battle." http://www.spanamwar.com/mbay.htm#ORDER.

Beisner, Robert L. "'Commune' in East Aurora." *American Heritage* 22, no. 2 (1971).

Bethel, Elizabeth. "The Military Information Division: Origin of the Intelligence Division." *Military Affairs* 11, no. 1 (1947).

Bigelow, Poultney. "In Camp at Tampa." *Harper's Weekly* 42 (1898).

Bishop, Morris. "Roycroft Revisited." *New Yorker*, October 2, 1938.

Briggs, Ellis O. "No Charge for the Extra Buttons." *Foreign Service Journal*, December 1961.

Cameron, Norman. "The U.S. Military Occupation of Bohol, 1900–1902." http://library.duke.edu/digitalcollections/.

Camp, Gregory S. "Commerce and Conflict: A History of Pembina, 1797–1895." *North Dakota History* 60, no. 4 (1993).

Chaput, Donald. "Private William W. Grayson's War in the Philippines, 1899." *Nebraska History* 61, no. 3 (1980).

Daley, Larry. "A Biography of Brigadier General Calixto (Garcia-Iñiguez) Enamorado," http://www.spanamwar.com/calixtoenamorado.htm.

Daniels, George H. "From Remarks Made by George H. Daniels, General Passenger Agent, New York Central Railroad, at the 115th Meeting of the New York Universalist Club at the St. Denis Hotel, New York, Monday evening, May 22, 1899." In Elbert Hubbard, *A Message to Garcia*, Four Track Series No. 25, second half million ed. New York: New York Central and Hudson River Railroad, 1899.

Davis, Oscar King. "At Honolulu." In *Harper's Pictorial History of the War with Spain*. New York: Harper, 1899.

———. "Off for Manila." In *Harper's Pictorial History of the War with Spain*. New York: Harper, 1899.

Dean, Teresa. "A Woman's View of Tampa." *Leslie's Weekly*, July 14, 1898.

Dewey, George. "Commander Dewey's Account." In *Harper's Pictorial History of the War with Spain*. New York: Harper, 1899.

Dreschler, Wolfgang. "Germany and the Spanish-Cuban/American War." In *The War of 1898 and U.S. Interventions 1898–1934: An Encyclopedia*, edited by Benjamin R. Beede. New York: Garland, 1994.

Forbes, Archibald. "The United States Army." *North American Review* 135, no. 309 (1882).

"Frederick N. Funston's Service Record Compiled in 1903 by the Adjutant General's Office." http://www.sfmuseum.net/1906/funston.html.

Goodykoontz, Wells. *Major Andrew S. Rowan, a West Virginian: The Man Who Carried the Message to Garcia*. Washington, DC: Government Printing Office, 1926.

Herre, Albert W. C. T. "Lanao—Lovely Land of Romance." *Scientific Monthly* 38, no. 6 (1934).

Hewes, F. W. "The Fighting Strength of the United States." *McClure's* 11, no. 3 (1898).

Hubbard, Elbert. "An Interesting Personality." *Cosmopolitan* 32 (1902).
———, ed. *Philistine: A Periodical of Protest* 8, no. 4 (1899).
Hunter, Dard. "Elbert Hubbard and 'A Message to Garcia.'" *New Colophon* 1, no. 1 (1948).
King, Pauline N. "Introduction." In William Adam Russ Jr., *The Hawaiian Republic (1894–98) and Its Struggle to Win Annexation*. Selinsgrove, PA: Susquehanna University Press, 1992.
Kipling, Rudyard. "The White Man's Burden." *McClure's* 12, no. 4 (1899).
Kirchman, Charles V. "The Message to Garcia: The Anatomy of a Famous Mission." *Mankind: The Magazine of Popular History* 4, no. 9 (1974).
Kraus, Theresa L. "García, Calixto." In *The War of 1898 and U.S. Interventions 1898–1934: An Encyclopedia*, edited by Benjamin R. Beede. New York: Garland, 1994.
Lang, John W. "The Message to Garcia." In *The American Historical Scene*. New York: Carleton House, 1937.
Manley, Jared L. [James Thurber]. "Where Are They Now?" *New Yorker*, December 5, 1936.
Merritt, Wesley. "The Manila Campaign." In *The American-Spanish War: A History by the War Leaders*. Norwich, CT: Haskell, 1899.
Michie, Peter S. "Caste at West Point." *North American Review* 130, no. 283 (1880).
Mironov, B. N. "Literacy in Russia, 1797–1917." *Soviet Studies in History* 25, no. 3 (1986).
"The Naval Battle of Santiago." In *Harper's Pictorial History of the War with Spain*. New York: Harper, 1899.
Nugent, Frank S. "Gene Fowler and W. P. Lipscomb Rewrite History in 'A Message to Garcia,' at the Center." *New York Times*, April 15, 1936.
Peake, Louis A. "Andrew Summers Rowan and the Message from Garcia." *West Virginia History* 44, no. 3 (1983).
Peréz, Louis A., Jr. "Incurring a Debt of Gratitude: 1898 and the Moral Sources of United States Hegemony in Cuba." *American Historical Review* 104, no. 2 (1999).
Petrie, Charles. "From the Death of Philip II to 1945." In *The History of Spain*. London: Eyre and Spottiswoode, 1952.
Powers, Henry Huntington. "The War as a Suggestion of Manifest Destiny." *Annals of the American Academy of Political and Social Science* 12 (1898).
"President Theodore Roosevelt's Proclamation Formally Ending the Philippine 'Insurrection' and Granting of Pardon and Amnesty, July 4, 1902," http://filipino.biz.ph/history/tr020704.html.
Proctor, Redfield. "Conditions of Cuba under Spanish Rule." In *The American-Spanish War: A History by the War Leaders*. Norwich, CT: Haskell, 1899.
Prucha, F. Paul. "The Settler and the Army in Frontier Minnesota." *Minnesota History* 29 (1948).
"Richard M. Nixon Presidential Recordings: Nixon Conversation 033-101," http://millercenter.org/presidentialrecordings/rmn-033-101.
Robinson, Elsie. "At Last—The Inside Story of How He Became a Hero." *New McClure's* 61, no. 1 (1928).

Román, Milagros Flores. "A Spy Named Whitney." *CRM* 11 (1998).

Roosevelt, Theodore. "Review of Alfred Thayer Mahan's *The Influence of Sea Power upon History.*" *Atlantic Monthly* 66 (1890).

Rowan, Andrew S. "Battle-Fields of the Canadian North-West Territories." *Journal of the Military Service Institution of the United States* 8, no. 31 (1887).

———. "How I Carried President McKinley's Message to General García." Unpublished manuscript, December 11, 1917.

———. "How I Got the Message to Garcia." *Washington Post*, April 28, 1929.

———. "My Mission and My Message to García." N.d., Box 6, Andrew Summers Rowan Papers, Hoover Institution Archives, Stanford University.

———. "My Ride across Cuba." *McClure's* 11, no. 4 (1898).

———. "Operations in Bocaue Mountains." In *Annual Reports of the War Department for the Fiscal Year Ended June 30, 1900.* Part 5. Washington, DC: GPO, 1900.

———. "Pacifism and Its Cure—Universal Training." Box 6, Andrew Summers Rowan Papers, Hoover Institution Archives, Stanford University.

Rusling, James. "Interview with President McKinley." *Christian Advocate* 78 (1903). Reprinted in *The Nationalization of American Life, 1877–1900*, edited by Ray Ginger. New York: Free Press, 1965.

Sampson, William T. "Report of the Naval Court of Inquiry." In *Harper's Pictorial History of the War with Spain.* New York: Harper, 1899.

Sebby, Daniel M. "The 1904 Joint Encampment for Field Instruction of United States Troops and the Organized Militia of California." http://www.military museum.org/CpAtacadero.html.

Shirey, M. R. "Andrew S. Rowan and the Message to Garcia." *West Virginia Review* 15, no. 2 (1937).

Strand, Wilson E. "Alfred Thayer Mahan." In *The War of 1898 and U.S. Interventions 1898–1934: An Encyclopedia*, edited by Benjamin R. Beede. New York: Garland, 1994.

Strobridge, William F. "Now Here I Am in the Army." *Nebraska History* 53, no. 3 (1972).

Swift, Eben. "An American Pioneer in the Cause of Military Education." *Journal of the Military Institution of the United States* 44 (1909).

Taylor, Bert Leston. "A Line-o-Type or Two." *Chicago Daily Tribune*, April 12, 1901.

Thiessen, Thomas D. "The Fighting First Nebraska: Nebraska's Imperial Adventure in the Philippines, 1898–1899." *Nebraska History* 70, no. 3 (1989).

Thomson, William D. "History of Fort Pembina: 1870–1895, *North Dakota History* 36, no. 1 (1969).

Vail, R. W. G. "'A Message to Garcia': A Bibliographical Puzzle." *Bulletin of the New York Public Library* 34, no. 2 (1930).

Vandermeer, Canute. "Population Patterns on the Island of Cebu: 1500 to 1900." *Annals of the Association of American Geographers* 57, no. 2 (1967).

Vilain, Jean-François. "The Roycroft Printing Shop: Books, Magazines and Ephemera." In Marie Via and Marjorie Searl, *Head, Heart, and Hand: Elbert Hubbard and the Roycrofters.* Rochester, NY: University of Rochester Press, 1994.

Walcott, Earle Ashley. "The War between Spain and the United States—II." *Overland Monthly and Out West Magazine* 32, no. 187 (1898).

White, William Allen. "When Johnny Went Marching Out." *McClure's* 11, no. 2 (1898).

Wood, Leonard. "Santiago Since the Surrender." *Scribner's* 25, no. 5 (1899).

Yardley, William. "Jeb Bush to Staff: Just Read It." *St. Petersburg Times*, June 21, 2000.

Zanger, Jules. "'A Message to Garcia': The Subsidized Hero." *American Studies* 20, no. 1 (1979).

BOOKS, PAMPHLETS, AND REPORTS

Aguinaldo y Famy, Emilio. *My Memoirs*, vol. 1. Manila: n.p., 1967.

———. *True Version of the Philippine Revolution*. N.p.: Dodo Press, n.d.

Albion, Robert G. *Five Centuries of Famous Ships: From the Santa Maria to the Glomar Explorer*. New York: McGraw-Hill, 1978.

Alderson, Nannie T., and Helena Huntington Smith. *A Bride Goes West*. Lincoln: University of Nebraska Press, 1969.

Alger, Russell A. *The Spanish-American War*. New York: Harper, 1901.

Alip, Eufronio M. *In the Days of General Emilio Aguinaldo: A Study of the Life and Times of a Great Military Leader, Statesman, and Patriot Who Founded the First Republic in Asia*. Manila: Alip, 1969.

Ambler, Charles Henry. *West Virginia: The Mountain State*. New York: Prentice Hall, 1940.

The American-Spanish War: A History by the War Leaders. Norwich, CT: Haskell, 1899.

Arnold, James R. *The Moro War: How America Battled a Muslim Insurgency in the Philippine Jungle, 1902–1913*. New York: Bloomsbury, 2011.

Arthur L. Wagner: The Man Who Wrote the Book on Intelligence, http://huachuca .army.mil/files/History_MWAGNER.PDF.

Auchinclose, Louis, ed. *Theodore Roosevelt: Letters and Speeches*. New York: Library Classics of the United States, 2004.

Auchútegui, Pedro S. de, and Miguel A. Bernard. *Aguinaldo and the Revolution of 1896: A Documentary History*. Quezon City: Ateneo de Manila University Press, 1972.

Balch, David Arnold. *Elbert Hubbard: Genius of Roycroft*. New York: Stokes, 1940.

Beck, Warren A., and Ynez D. Haase. *Historical Atlas of the American West*. Norman: University of Oklahoma Press, 1989.

Beede, Benjamin R., ed. *The War of 1898 and U.S. Interventions, 1898–1934: An Encyclopedia*. New York: Garland, 1994.

Blow, Michael. *A Ship to Remember: The Maine and the Spanish-American War*. New York: Morrow, 1992.

Boatner, Mark Mayo, III. *The Civil War Dictionary*. New York: McKay, 1959.

Boler, Paul F., Jr. *Presidential Anecdotes*. New York: Oxford University Press, 1981.

Brereton, T. R. *Educating the U.S. Army: Arthur L. Wagner and Reform, 1875–1905*. Lincoln: University of Nebraska Press, 2000.

Brown, Charles H. *The Correspondents' War: Journalists in the Spanish-American War*. New York: Scribner's, 1967.

Bunker, John Gorley. *Liberty Ships: The Ugly Ducklings of World War II*. Annapolis, MD: Naval Institute Press, 1972.

Burton, Alan. *A Message to Garcia . . . Revisited*. N.p.: Silver Lake, 1986.

Callahan, James Morton. *American Foreign Policy in Canadian Relations*. New York: Macmillan, 1937.

Carlson, Paul H. *"Pecos Bill": A Military Biography of William R. Shafter*. College Station: Texas A&M University Press, 1896.

Casasús, Juan J. E. *Calixto García: El Estratega*. Miami: La Moderna Poesia, 1981.

Cather, Willa. *The World and the Parish: Willa Cather's Articles and Reviews 1893–1902*. Lincoln: University of Nebraska Press, 1970.

Champney, Freeman. *Art and Glory: The Story of Elbert Hubbard*. New York: Crown, 1968.

Cirillo, Vincent J. *Bullets and Bacilli: The Spanish-American War and Military Medicine*. New Brunswick, NJ: Rutgers University Press, 2004.

Coats, Stephen D. *Gathering at the Golden Gate: Mobilizing for War in the Philippines, 1898*. Ft. Leavenworth, KS: Combat Studies Institute Press, 2006.

Coffman, Edward M. *The Old Army: A Portrait of the American Army in Peacetime, 1874–1898*. New York: Oxford University Press, 1986.

Collazo, Enrique. *Los Americanos in Cuba*. Havana: Instituto Cubano del Libro, 1972.

Collier, Peter. *The Roosevelts: An American Saga*. New York: Simon and Schuster, 1994.

Commager, Henry Steele, and Milton Cantor, eds. *Documents of American History*. Vol. 1, *To 1898*. Englewood Cliffs, NJ: Prentice Hall, 1988.

———, eds. *Documents of American History*. Vol. 2, *Since 1898*. Englewood Cliffs, NJ: Prentice Hall, 1988.

Cosmas, Graham A. *An Army for Empire: The United States Army in the Spanish-American War*. Columbia: University of Missouri Press, 1971.

Cullum, George W. *Biographical Register of the Officers and Graduates of the U.S. Military Academy at West Point, N.Y., since Its Establishment, in 1802*. 6 vols. Cambridge: Riverside Press, 1901–50.

———. *Official Register of the Graduates of the U.S. Military Academy, 1875*. New York: Cambridge Riverside Press, 1875.

Davis, Linda H. *Badge of Courage: The Life of Stephen Crane*. Boston: Houghton Mifflin, 1998.

Davis, Richard Harding. *The Cuban and Porto Rican Campaigns*. New York: Scribner's, 1898.

Dewey, Adelbert. *The Life and Letters of Admiral Dewey*. Akron, OH: Werner, 1899.

Dewey, George. *Autobiography of George Dewey: Admiral of the Navy*. Annapolis: Naval Institute Press, 1987.

Dirlam, H. Kenneth. *Bits of History*. Mansfield, OH: Richland Country Historical Society, 1962.

Dulles, Foster Rhea. *The Imperial Years*. New York: Crowell, 1966.

Dunne, Finley Peter. *Mr. Dooley in Peace and in War*. Boston: Small, Maynard, 1898.

English, T. J. *Havana Nocturne: How the Mob Owned Cuba—And Then Lost It to the Revolution*. New York: Morrow, 2007.

Escalante Beatón, Aníbel. *Calixto García: Su Campaña el 95*. Havana: Editorial de Ciencias Sociales, 1978.

Ferrer, Ada. *Insurgent Cuba: Race, Nation, and Revolution: 1868–1898*. Chapel Hill: University of North Carolina Press, 1999,

Fish, Williston. *Memories of West Point, 1877–1881*. Vol. 2, edited by Gertrude Fish Rumsey and Josephine Fish Peabody. Batavia, NY: Peabody, 1957.

———. *Short Rations*. New York: Harper, 1899.

Foner, Jack D. *The United States Soldier between Wars: Army Life and Reforms, 1865–1898*. New York: Humanities, 1970.

Foner, Philip S. *A History of Cuba and Its Relations with the United States*. Vol. 2, *1845–1895*. New York: International, 1963.

———. *The Spanish-Cuban-American War and the Birth of American Imperialism*. Vol. 1, *1895–1898*. New York: Monthly Review Press, 1971.

———. *The Spanish-Cuban-American War and the Birth of American Imperialism*. Vol. 2, *1898–1902*. New York: Monthly Review Press, 1972.

Foote, Shelby. *The Civil War: A Narrative, Fort Sumter to Kernstown*. New York: Vintage, 1986.

Funston, Frederick. *Memories of Two Wars: Cuban and Philippine Experiences*. Lincoln: University of Nebraska Press, 2009.

Gould, Lewis L. *The Spanish-American War and President McKinley*. Lawrence: University Press of Kansas, 1982.

Gowing, Peter Gordon. *Mandate in Moroland: The American Government of Muslim Filipinos 1899–1920*. Quezon City: Philippine Center for Advanced Studies, 1977.

Graham, George Edward. *Schley and Santiago: An Historical Account of the Blockade and Final Destruction of the Spanish Fleet under Command of Admiral Pasquale Cervera, July 3, 1898*. Chicago: Conkey, 1902.

Hackett, Alice Payne, and James Henry Burke. *80 Years of Best Sellers 1895–1975*. New York: Bowker, 1977.

Hagedorn, Hermann. *Leonard Wood: A Biography*. Vol. 1. New York: Kraus Reprint, 1969.

———. *Leonard Wood: A Biography*. Vol. 2. New York: Harper, 1931.

Halliwell, Leslie. *The Filmgoer's Companion*. 6th ed. New York: Hill and Wang, 1977.

Halstead, Murat. *The Story of Cuba: Her Struggles for Liberty . . . the Cause, Crisis and Destiny of the Pearl of the Antilles*. Chicago: Franklin Square Bible House, 1898.

Hamilton, Charles F. *As Bees in Honey Drown: Elbert Hubbard and the Roycrofters*. New York: Barnes, 1973.

———. *Roycroft Collectibles*. New York: Barnes, 1980.

Harger, C. G., Jr. *A Message from Garcia Answering "A Message to Garcia" by Elbert Hubbard*. Rochester, NY: Yawman and Stupp, 1900.

Harper's Pictorial History of the War with Spain. New York: Harper, 1899.

Hobart, Jennie L. *Memories*. Privately printed, 1930.

Holbrook, Stewart H. *Lost Men of American History*. New York: Macmillan, 1946.

Hubbard, Bert. *Impressions*. East Aurora, NY: Roycrofters, 1921.

Hubbard, Elbert. *A Message to Garcia*. East Aurora, NY: Roycrofters, 1899.

———. *A Message to Garcia*. East Aurora, NY: John Wanamaker Stores, 1906.

———. *The Philosophy of Elbert Hubbard*. East Aurora, NY: Roycrofters, 1916.

Ileto, Reynaldo Clemeña. *Pasyon and Revolution: Popular Movements in the Philippines, 1840–1910*. Quezon City: Ateneo de Manila University Press, 1979.

Jeffers, Paul H. *Colonel Roosevelt: Theodore Roosevelt Goes to War, 1897–1898*. New York: John Wiley, 1996.

Jenson, Joan M. *Army Surveillance in America, 1775–1980*. New Haven, CT: Yale University Press, 1991.

Johnson, Alan, and Dumas Malone, eds. *Dictionary of American Biography*. Vol. 3. New York: Scribner's, 1959.

Kalaw, Teodoro M. *The Philippine Revolution*. Kawilihan, Philippines: Jorge B. Vargas Filipiniana Foundation, 1969.

Karnow, Stanley. *In Our Image: America's Empire in the Philippines*. New York: Random House, 1989.

Kaufman, Bel. *Up the Down Staircase*. Edgewood Cliffs, NJ: Prentice Hall, 1965.

King, Charles. *Under Fire*. Philadelphia: Lippincott, 1895.

King, W. Nephew. *The Story of the Spanish-American War and the Revolt in the Philippines*. New York: Collier, 1900.

Knight, Oliver. *Life and Manners in the Frontier Army*. Norman: University of Oklahoma Press, 1978.

Lane, Jack C. *Armed Progressive: General Leonard Wood*. San Rafael, CA: Presidio Press, 1978.

Leech, Margaret. *In the Days of McKinley*. New York: Harper, 1959.

Legarda, Benito J., Jr. *The Hills of Sampaloc: The Opening Action of the Philippine-American War, February 4–5, 1899*. Makati City, Philippines: Bookmark, 2001.

Linderman, Gerald F. *The Mirror of War: American Society and the Spanish-American War*. Ann Arbor: University of Michigan Press, 1974.

Linn, Brian McAllister. *The Philippine War, 1899–1902*. Lawrence: University Press of Kansas, 2000.

Lodge, Henry Cabot. *The War with Spain*. New York: Harper, 1899.

Macomb, Montgomery M. *Report of Surveys and Explorations Made by Corps No. 1 in Guatemala, El Salvador, Honduras, Nicaragua and Costa Rica*. Washington, DC: Intercontinental Railway Commission, 1898.

Mahon, John K. *History of the Militia and the National Guard*. New York: Macmillan, 1985.

Majul, Cesar Adib. *Mabini and the Philippine Revolution*. Quezon City: University of the Philippines Press, 1960.

Martínez-Fernández, Luís, ed. *Encyclopedia of Cuba: People, History, Culture*. Westport, CT: Greenwood Press, 2003.

Mathiews, Franklin K., ed. *The Boy Scouts Yearbook*. New York: Appleton, 1917.

Matthews, Herbert L. *Cuba*. New York: Macmillan, 1964.

McClernand, E. J. "The Santiago Campaign." In Society of the Army of Santiago de Cuba, *The Santiago Campaign*. Richmond, VA: Society of the Army of Santiago de Cuba, 1927.

McCullough, David. *The Path between the Seas: The Creation of the Panama Canal 1870–1914*. New York: Simon and Schuster, 1977.

McHenry, Robert, ed. *Webster's American Military Biographies*. New York: Dover, 1984.

Miller, Stuart Creighton. *Benevolent Assimilation: The American Conquest of the Philippines, 1899–1903*. New Haven, CT: Yale University Press, 1982.

Millis, Walter. *The Martial Spirit: A Study of Our War with Spain*. Chicago: Dee, 1989.

Miranda, Luís Rodolfo. *Reminiscencias Cubanas de la Guerra y de la Paz*. Havana: Fernandez y Cia, 1941.

Mojares, Resil B. *The War against the Americans: Resistance and Collaboration in Cebu: 1899–1906*. Quezon City: Ateneo de Manila University Press, 1999.

Morison, Elting E., ed. *The Letters of Theodore Roosevelt*. Cambridge, MA: Harvard University Press, 1951.

Morris, Dan, and Inez Morris. *Who Was Who in American Politics*. New York: Hawthorn, 1974.

Morton, Oren F. *A History of Monroe County, West Virginia*. Baltimore: Regional Publishing, 1980.

Musicant, Ivan. *Empire by Default: The Spanish-American War and the Dawn of the American Century*. New York: Holt, 1998.

O'Toole, G. J. A. *The Spanish War: An American Epic, 1898*. New York: Norton, 1984.

Paul, T. V. *Asymmetric Conflicts: War Initiation by Weaker Powers*. New York: Cambridge University Press, 1994.

Pérez, Louis A. *Cuba between Empires: 1878–1902*. Pittsburgh: University of Pittsburgh Press, 1983.

———. *Cuba between Reform and Revolution*. New York: Oxford University Press, 1995.

Philippines Bureau of Public Schools, Division of Bohol. *History and Cultural Life of the Town of Jagna and Its Barrios*. N.p.: Philippines Bureau of Public Schools, 1953.

Pomeroy, William J. *American Neo-Colonialism: Its Emergence in the Philippines and Asia*. New York: International, 1970.

Post, Charles Johnson. *The Little War of Private Post: The Spanish-American War Seen up Close*. Boston: Little, Brown, 1960.

Powe, Marc B. *The Emergence of the War Department Intelligence Agency: 1885–1918*. Manhattan, KS: Military Affairs, 1975.

Preston, Diana. *Lusitania: An Epic Tragedy*. New York: Walker, 2002.

Pride, W. F. *The History of Fort Riley*. Privately printed, 1926.

Puleston, W. D. *Mahan: The Life and Work of Alfred Thayer Mahan, U.S.N.* New Haven, CT: Yale University Press, 1939.

Roberts, W. Adolphe. *The Single Star: A Novel of Cuba in the '90s*. Indianapolis: Bobbs-Merrill, 1949.

Roosevelt, Theodore. *The Rough Riders*. New York: New American Library, 1961.

———. *Theodore Roosevelt: An Autobiography*. New York: Scribner's, 1925.

Rowan, Andrew Summers. *How I Carried the Message to Garcia*. San Francisco: William D. Harney, 1922.

Rowan, Andrew Summers and M. M. Ramsey. *The Island of Cuba*. New York: Holt, 1896.

Rowan: Protagonista del "Mensaje A Garcia." Havana: Agrupación Pro Enseñanza de Hechos Historicos, 1943.

Sargent, Nathan. *Admiral Dewey and the Manila Campaign*. Washington, DC: Naval Historical Foundation, 1947.

Sexton, William Thaddeus. *Soldiers in the Sun: An Adventure in Imperialism*. North Stratford, NH: Ayer, 2000.

Shay, Felix. *Elbert Hubbard of East Aurora*. New York: Wise, 1926.

Simons, Geoff. *Cuba: From Conquistador to Castro*. New York: St. Martin's, 1996.

Sinclair, Donna L. *The Waking of a Military Town: Vancouver, Washington and the Vancouver National Historic Reserve, 1898–1920*. Vancouver, WA: Center for Columbia River History, 2005.

Smith, Albert E. *Two Reels and a Crank*. New York: Garland, 1985.

Smith, Horace. *A Captain Unafraid: The Strange Adventures of Dynamite Johnny O'Brien*. New York: Harper, 1912.

Smith, Page. *America Enters the World: A People's History of the Progressive Era and World War I*. New York: McGraw-Hill, 1985.

———. *The Nation Comes of Age: A People's History of the Ante-Bellum Years*. New York: McGraw-Hill, 1981.

Stallman, R. W., and E. R. Hagerman. *The War Dispatches of Stephen Crane*. New York: New York University Press, 1964.

Stanley, George F. G. *Louis Riel*. New York: McGraw-Hill, 1985.

Staten, Clifford L. *The History of Cuba*. Westport, CT: Greenwood, 2003.

Tate, Michael L. *The Frontier Army in the Settlement of the West*. Norman: University of Oklahoma Press, 1999.

Thomas, Hugh. *Cuba: The Pursuit of Freedom*. New York: Harper and Row, 1971.

Tosquella, Max. *The Truth about the Message to García*, trans. I. F. Berndes and Charles Duhol. Havana: Self-published, 1955.

Trask, David F. *The War with Spain in 1898*. New York: Macmillan, 1981.

Via, Marie, and Marjorie Searl. *Head, Heart, and Hand: Elbert Hubbard and the Roycrofters*. Rochester, NY: University of Rochester Press, 1994.

Villegas, Ramon. *Tubod: The Heart of Bohol*. Manila: NCAA, 2003.

Von Bülow, Bernard. *Memoirs of Prince von Bülow: From Secretary of State to Imperial Chancellor, 1897–1903*. Boston: Little, Brown, 1931.

Wagner, Arthur L. *Report of the Santiago Campaign, 1898*. Kansas City, MO: Franklin Hudson, 1908.

———. *The Service of Security and Information*. Kansas City, MO: Hudson-Kimberly, 1903.

Walker, Dale L. *The Boys of '98: Theodore Roosevelt and the Rough Riders*. New York: Doherty, 1998.

Walker, John, ed. *Halliwell's Film Guide*. New York: HarperCollins, 1995.

Wheeler, Joseph. *The Santiago Campaign 1898*. Port Washington, NY: Kennikat, 1971.

White, Bruce A. *Elbert Hubbard's The Philistine: A Periodical of Protest (1895–1915)*. Lanham, MD: University Press of America, 1989.

White, Maria. *Through the Keyhole: A Young Person's Guide to the Henry B. Plant Museum*. Tampa, FL: Henry B. Plant Museum, 2000.

White, Trumbull. *Our New Possessions*. Chicago: National Education Union, 1898.

Wilcox, Marrion, ed. *Harper's History of the War in the Philippines*. New York: Harper, 1900.

——. *A Short History of the War with Spain*. New York: Frederick Stokes, 1898.

Witte, Sergei. *The Memoirs of Count Witte*. Translated and edited by Abraham Yarmolinsky. New York: Fertig, 1967.

Wolff, Leon. *Little Brown Brother: How the United States Purchased and Pacified the Philippines*. London: Longman's, 1961.

Wood, Will C., Alice Cecilia Cooper, and Frederick A. Rice. *America's Message*. New York: Ginn, 1925.

Yeger, Moshe. *Between Integration and Secession: The Muslim Communities of the Southern Philippines, Southern Thailand, and Western Burma/Myanmar*. Lanham, MD: Lexington, 2002.

Zaide, Gregorio F. *The Philippine Revolution*. Rev. Ed. Manila: Modern Book, 1968.

Zimmerman, Warren. *First Great Triumph: How Five Americans Made Their Country a World Power*. New York: Farrar, Strauss and Giroux, 2002.

DISSERTATIONS

Bowie, Chester Winston. "Redfield Proctor: A Biography." PhD diss., University of Wisconsin, 1980.

Bridges, William John. "Dauntless: The Life and Times of Frederick Funston." PhD diss., University of Nebraska, 2002.

INDEX

CPSIA information can be obtained
at www.ICGtesting.com
Printed in the USA
LVOW01s0535231016
509786LV00005B/7/P